Suffrage

Suffrage

The Epic Struggle for Women's Right to Vote

Susan L. Poulson

 PRAEGER®

An Imprint of ABC-CLIO, LLC

Santa Barbara, California • Denver, Colorado

Library of Congress Control Number: 2019020663

ISBN: 978-1-4408-6788-0 (print)
      978-1-4408-6789-7 (ebook)

23 22 21 20 19   2 3 4 5

This book is also available as an eBook.

Praeger
An Imprint of ABC-CLIO, LLC

ABC-CLIO, LLC
147 Castilian Drive
Santa Barbara, California 93117
www.abc-clio.com

This book is printed on acid-free paper ∞

Manufactured in the United States of America

For Bobby, Laura & Julia

Once upon a time there was a great movement
for liberty of the subject class and it was won.[1]

—Carrie Chapman Catt

---

1. Carrie Chapman Catt to Alice Stone Blackwell, September 13, 1943, Catt Papers, Library of Congress, 4, in Robert Booth Fowler, *Carrie Catt: Feminist Politician* (Boston: Northeastern, 1988), 155.

Contents

Abbreviations

People

AB	Alva Belmont
ABB	Antoinette Brown Blackwell
AHS	Anna Howard Shaw
AP	Alice Paul
ASB	Alice Stone Blackwell
CCC	Carrie Chapman Catt
HBB	Henry Browne Blackwell
HBS	Henry Brewster Stanton
IBH	Isabella Beecher Hooker
LS	Lucy Stone
SBA	Susan B. Anthony
ST	Sojourner Truth
WLG	William Lloyd Garrison

Organizations

AERA	American Equal Rights Association
AWSA	American Woman Suffrage Association
ICW	International Council of Women
IWSA	International Woman Suffrage Alliance
NAOWS	National Association Opposed to Woman Suffrage

NAWSA   National American Woman Suffrage Association
NWP   National Woman's Party
NWSA   National Woman Suffrage Association
WESA   Washington Equal Suffrage Association
WPU   Women's Political Union
WSP   Woman Suffrage Party
WTUL   Women's Trade Union League

Libraries and Archives

LC   Library of Congress
SCA   Smith College Archives
SL   Schlesinger Archives
TUL   Tulane University Library
UKSC   University of Kentucky Special Collections
VCA   Vassar College Archives

Others

BSC   Belmont Suffrage Clippings
HWS   *History of Woman Suffrage*
SBA   *Life and Work of Susan B. Anthony*
SBASB   *Susan B. Anthony Scrapbooks*
SP   *Selected Papers of Elizabeth Cady Stanton & Susan B. Anthony*

CHAPTER ONE

Awakening

On a summerlike day in May 1840, a young couple climbed aboard the *Montreal* in New York Harbor for their honeymoon voyage to the United Kingdom. The *Montreal* was a packet ship, a 542-ton workhorse that plied the Atlantic six times a year between the busy ports of England and New York. Its three masts, each bearing triplets of giant sails and miles of line rigged along the crossbars, towered above the deck as the crew loaded the hold below. Captain Seth Griffing and his first mate made their final preparations as passengers bade farewell to family and friends. The bride raced her brother-in-law around the ship in a last-minute game of tag, her wavy chestnut hair bouncing as she ran. "I had a desperate chase after him all over the vessel, but in vain," she later recalled.[1] The game made them laugh and eased the pain of separation. The bride and groom would be gone for seven months.

Travel to Europe would become a well-worn path for many American newlyweds eager to see the cultural tapestry of the Old World, but this couple was different. Henry and Elizabeth Cady Stanton were embarking on a mission to confront the greatest moral evil of the age—slavery. Over the next several years, as Elizabeth would observe the struggle to liberate slaves, and awaken to her own subordination, slowly, tentatively, and with a good dose of self-doubt, she would join others to confront the laws and traditions that restricted women—norms embedded so deeply in American life that they seemed like "common sense." But first she had to imagine a different world.

The Stantons had married after a whirlwind courtship. Elizabeth was a Cady—the most prominent family in Johnstown, New York, a prosperous town a day's ride northwest of Albany. Her mother Margaret was an American aristocrat, the tall, refined daughter of Colonel James Livingston, a Revolutionary War hero who had thwarted Benedict Arnold's attempt to deliver West Point to the British. Elizabeth admired her mother, who rode horses with command and was "courageous, self-reliant, and at her ease under all circumstances and in all places."[2] Her father Daniel had risen from humble beginnings to become a well-respected judge who dabbled in politics, serving for years in the New York State Legislature and a single term in the U.S. House of Representatives.

The Cadys lived in a stately home at the edge of the main square, a short walk from the Fulton County Courthouse where Judge Cady presided. It was a bustling household, with eleven children, several servants, and a slave, Peter Teabout, before New York ended slavery in the late 1820s. Elizabeth liked to play outdoors with her younger sister Margaret in the stream that ran through the center of town and to build snow forts in winter. She delighted in small acts of defiance, sneaking into the garret with her sister to nibble on stores of hickory nuts and maple sugar cakes. Her parents, she later recalled, "were as kind, indulgent, and considerate as the Puritan ideas of those days permitted," but there was more fear than love, and she had "a confused memory of being often under punishment."[3] The Cady children were well educated, first in Johnstown schools, then college for the boys, and for Elizabeth, the Troy Female Seminary, which was an early higher education institution for women founded in 1814 by Emma Willard. There, Elizabeth received the message often delivered in women's higher education in the mid-nineteenth century—that women could be educated in traditionally male subjects such as logic, mathematics, and criticism, along with subjects like domestic science, sketching, and singing, all to become respectable wives and mothers. Elizabeth would learn to view her world critically and see the man-made roots of accepted institutions, but would have few outlets for action.

After graduating at seventeen, Elizabeth enjoyed the next six years in the suspended existence of a well-educated young woman. She read widely on the new trends of phrenology and homeopathic medicine as well as the romantic poems and novels of Lord Byron, Samuel Taylor Coleridge, and Sir Walter Scott. She discussed legal matters with her father and brother-in-law and traveled the state of New York to visit family and friends. She was slender and pretty, and took pride in dressing well. She sang while playing piano and guitar and enjoyed balls, dances, and hayrides. She was witty and irreverent with a penchant for practical jokes. When a suitor once challenged her to remain silent during an entire carriage ride, she fashioned a dummy out of straw, wrapped it in her coat and hat, placed it in the carriage, and sent him off. By twenty-three, most women her age had married and produced children, but Elizabeth enjoyed her independence and was in no rush to wed.

At the age of twenty-four, Elizabeth would follow a trajectory set by her new husband's political ambitions. Henry bore the moral fervor of his Puritan ancestors. His mother Susan Brewster descended from William Brewster, leader of the Mayflower Pilgrims, and several of Henry's family had served as officers in the Revolutionary War and as members of Congress. His father, a Connecticut wool merchant, provided the family with a comfortable existence, including the services of a slave whose melancholy songs, Henry said, made him determined to "become the champion of the oppressed colored races of my country."[4] Swept up by a charismatic religious revival as a teenager, he decided to study at the Lane Theological Seminary in Cincinnati under Lyman Beecher, the prominent Presbyterian theologian who cofounded the American Temperance Society. There, however, just across the river from slave-holding Kentucky, his abolitionist sentiments ruined his prospects for success. When he and his professor Theodore Weld called for immediate emancipation and tried to mix students with blacks from the local community, the Lane Trustees barred abolitionist activity on campus, fearing social unrest and damage to the seminary's reputation. Rather than yield, Henry, Weld, and more than forty other "Lane Rebels" left. Many went to join Oberlin College in northern Ohio, which, when it opened in 1837, was the first college in the United States to admit blacks and adopt coeducation.

Henry became a full-time abolitionist, speaking in towns across the North as an agent for the American Anti-Slavery Society. Tall, handsome, and a stirring speaker, he could sway people to support the unpopular reform. In Rhode Island, a local constable tasked with serving a warrant for vagrancy to prevent Henry from speaking was so moved by his speech that he became the first to sign the anti-slavery petition. Henry met mobs in every state east of Indiana—with the exception of Vermont—more than two hundred during his abolitionist career. In Providence, Rhode Island, opponents shook their fists and shouted as they charged to the front of the hall where he was speaking, forcing him to stop. In Portland, Maine, the local sponsors of his lecture had to escort him to safety through a hostile crowd. And in Upstate New York, after he spoke at a local church, a mob burned it down.

While lecturing in Central New York, Henry stayed at the home of Gerrit and Ann Smith. Gerrit Smith was one of the wealthiest men in America, whose father, a business partner of John Astor, was the largest landowner in New York. Gerrit was also Elizabeth Cady's cousin, the son of her mother's eldest sister, and a generation older. Though more than six feet tall and large-framed, Gerrit was a gentle host who would greet an acquaintance as "My dear friend."[5] The Smiths lived in the town of

Peterboro on an impressive thirty-acre estate with rolling lawns, well-tended gardens, rows of fruit and ornamental trees, a grain mill and "a fine artificial fountain of living water."[6] In the middle of the grounds, atop a gently sloping hill, stood the Smith's white Greek revival mansion with a grand hallway, a library, a heated conservatory, extensive living quarters, and enough servants to keep everything in good order. It was an island of luxury among spare homes of hard-working farmers and artisans. There was no spot on earth that seemed so like paradise, an elderly guest once remarked with tears in his eyes as Gerrit's wife Ann inquired of his night's sleep and pinned roses to his lapel. The Smiths welcomed a range of visitors with a bountiful table and rooms ready for their stay. There were Oneida people who came unannounced, runaway slaves who hid in the attic, and itinerant reformers who exposed Elizabeth to ideas that her conservative parents avoided.

Elizabeth visited the Smiths at least once a year where she found "an atmosphere of love and peace, of freedom and good cheer," and it was there that she first met Henry in the fall of 1839.[7] Each day she joined other guests who filled two carriages that traveled through flaxen fields and regal forests to attend reform meetings, sometimes as far as ten miles away, often returning by moonlight. Elizabeth saw Henry speak on abolition and was "deeply impressed by his power."[8] At night, at the Smiths' fireside, guests debated with lofty sentiments how to improve society, something Elizabeth later reminisced as "among the great blessings of my life."[9] One morning Henry invited Elizabeth for a horseback ride among the undulating hills around Peterboro, stopping along the way to admire the fall colors and each other. Henry suddenly proposed. Elizabeth was surprised, but smitten with the handsome and charismatic man, a decade older, who had spent years working for a noble cause. She agreed to marry him.

Judge Cady, everyone knew, was unlikely to approve. Her cousin Gerrit advised Elizabeth to write her father about the engagement before she left Peterboro to "draw the hottest fire while still in safe harbor."[10] Stanton had two strikes against him: he was poor, and he was an abolitionist. Cady expected his daughters to marry men who could provide a comfortable living. His two elder daughters, Tryphena and Harriet, had married lawyers who were Judge Cady's former law students, but Henry was barely able to survive on his salary, which often went unpaid. Even more troubling was Henry's work for abolition.

When Elizabeth returned to Johnstown, two men she most admired and depended upon—Judge Cady and her brother-in-law Edward Bayard—lectured her on the difficulties of marriage and finance. Stanton's proposal was imprudent, her father believed, because he had never held regular employment and "has no trade or profession."[11] Elizabeth was shocked. Her friends and family had previously painted "the marriage relation in the most dazzling colors," she said, but after she and Henry became engaged, they warned that marriage was "beset with dangers and disappointments" and that men were "depraved and unreliable."[12] After four months of constant pressure, Elizabeth broke the engagement. She hadn't yet learned to trust her own judgment.

Henry did what he could to allay Judge Cady's concerns. He did not hide his controversial politics, but he did defend his ability to support Elizabeth. Henry wrote to Elizabeth—really to her father—to deflect any suspicion that he was marrying her for money. He had been financially independent since the age of thirteen, he pointed out, and put himself and two brothers through school. "I have never received a dollar's gratuitous aid from anyone, though it has been frequently pressed upon me," Henry wrote. "I always declined it, because I knew it would relax my perseverance and detract from my self-reliance, and because I was aware that if I would be a man, I must build my own foundation with my own hands."[13] Henry filled his letters to Elizabeth with praise and poetry—she was "cheerful and brilliant," he told her, "the loveliest correspondent I ever had."[14] He refused to acknowledge a broken engagement and paraphrased Thomas More in a call for fidelity. "The heart that loves truly, love, never forgets, But as truly loves on to the close."[15]

Time was running out. The American Anti-Slavery Society had appointed Henry as a delegate to the World Anti-Slavery Convention in London, the first international gathering dedicated to abolition, and his lengthy trip would begin soon. Faced with the prospect of not seeing Henry for nearly a year, Elizabeth finally agreed to marry. She "wishes to go with me that the storm may blow over while she is absent," Henry wrote a friend.[16] With little time to plan and little desire to aggravate the Cady family, Henry and Elizabeth wed in Johnstown on the 1st of May, 1840. Like many brides, Elizabeth wore a white gown and received "shining silver presents."[17] But the couple made a telling alteration to their wedding vows: Elizabeth omitted—over the objection of the minister—the bride's traditional promise to obey her husband. "I obstinately refused to obey one with whom I was supposed I was entering into an equal relation," Elizabeth later wrote.[18]

After eight months of fluctuating romance and a hasty wedding, the Stantons set off on the *Montreal*. The sails clapped as they caught the wind and the ship began its slow, rhythmic roll over the water. Sailors in worn shirts and loose trousers climbed the masts and flitted about the deck, giving "the impression of specters rather than of men," a passenger wrote, while Captain Griffing issued commands in "deep, sepulcher tones" and sailors sang "Yo-o-o-ho-ho-o" as they tugged at the ropes and sails.[19] The *Montreal* was a solid ship built to withstand the winter gales of the North Atlantic. Live oak from Southern forests formed the hull, and masts hewn from giant white pine trunks from the coast of Maine held firm even in the worst of storms. On a transatlantic voyage of more than three thousand miles, a sturdy ship and an able crew could make the difference between life and death.

So could luck. The day before the Stantons boarded the *Montreal*, the packet ship *Poland* left New York for France with an experienced crew of thirty-one sailors, three officers, and an able captain. Five days into the voyage, lightning struck the foremast and ignited bales of cotton stowed below, causing the most dreaded of all catastrophes—fire at sea. The crew battened down the hatches to smother the flames as the captain put his twenty-four passengers in small boats they towed behind, sending along hot coffee and roasted chickens to sustain their spirits. Just before the *Poland* sank, a passing ship rescued the passengers and crew.

For those who paid full fare, accommodations on the *Montreal* were comfortable, even lavish, with carpeting, and a carved maple and mahogany interior, accented in gold leaf. But the cheaper cabins, with only a small chest of drawers and a bed or hammock, were cramped and stifling. Many passengers sought refuge on the deck, enchanted by the changing moods of the ocean. There were "all the colors which poetry has given to the sea, black, white, myrtle green, emerald blue, dark, bright, silver, and flame-color," a passenger reflected, while by moonlight the ocean shimmered "like a field of snow-crust in a dark January night in New England."[20] Meals in the common room were ample and provided often—breakfast at nine, lunch at noon, dinner at four and tea at night. Passengers on packet ships often gathered in the evening to play whist and chess, to read and gossip. "Some of us felt it rather annoying to be so long at table," a passenger wrote, "but it is a custom established on board these packets, for the sake, I believe, of those who happen to find the day too long."[21] The best captains—Seth Griffing among them—could command a ship *and* tell a good story, and though only thirty, he had many colorful tales of life at sea.

Elizabeth passed time studying slavery, anxious as the wife of a delegate to the Convention to know enough to answer questions others may ask. James G. Birney, a fellow passenger and delegate, offered his assistance and they spent hours together, pacing the deck as he shared the ideas that inspired and often divided abolitionists. Birney was born on a Kentucky plantation and received his first slave at the age of six, as a birthday gift from his father. But he saw the inhumanity of slavery, as did several of his teachers, a local Baptist preacher, and his Irish aunt who insisted on paying slaves for their work. When his open dislike of slavery spoiled both his political aspirations in Kentucky and a brief legal career in Alabama, Birney moved to Cincinnati and became an abolitionist. Even there, however, he faced opposition. In the summer of 1836, a mob ransacked the office of his abolitionist newspaper, threw his furniture out the second story window and dragged his printing press through the streets, past the mayor—who did nothing—and tossed it into the Ohio River as onlookers cheered. Next, the mob ran to a public lodging house looking for Birney. There, a burly young man braced his six-foot-two frame across the entrance to stop them. It was twenty-eight-year-old Salmon Chase, devoted abolitionist and future governor of Ohio and Chief Justice of the U.S. Supreme Court.

"You will pay for your actions," someone in the mob yelled.

"I [can] be found at any time," Chase replied.[22]

Birney was proper and particular, Elizabeth noted, "a polished gentleman of the old school."[23] She soon realized that his criticisms of others were often veiled disapproval of her. One day she gleefully told him that he need not be so indirect and "might take me squarely in hand and polish me up as speedily as possible."[24] So he did. It was impolite for her to call her husband "Henry" in public, Birney told her. She should call him "Mr. Stanton." And when sailors hoisted Elizabeth to the masthead in a chair to give her a bird's-eye view of the ocean, as they did with some of the male passengers, Birney told her she was "unladylike."[25]

"Bless me!" Elizabeth exclaimed after Birney voiced a whole list of complaints. "What a catalog in one day! I fear my Mentor will despair of my ultimate perfection." Birney scoffed at her cavalier retort. "I should have more hope if you seemed to feel my rebukes more deeply," he said, "but you evidently think them of too little consequence to be much disturbed by them."[26] Captain Griffing tried to rescue Elizabeth from her regimen of instruction by inviting her to explore the ship and to sit with him while he regaled her with stories.

After eighteen days at sea without incident, the *Montreal* docked at Torquay, 180 miles west of London. The Stantons made their way east on a stagecoach driven by a large, white-gloved coachman and a red-suited postman who blew his horn as they passed through villages. The English countryside was charming, "like a miniature landscape which you see reflected in your watch crystal, an inverted telescope, or the eye of a horse as you hold him by the mouth," another *Montreal* passenger wrote.[27] Elizabeth found the trip like "a journey in fairyland" filled with roses, daffodils, and blooming trees. "We had heard that England was like a garden of flowers," she wrote, "but we were wholly unprepared for such wealth of beauty."[28]

When the Stantons finally arrived, London seemed like the center of the world. Nearly two million people lived there, six times the population of New York, and more than in any other city on earth. Its commerce stretched to the corners of the globe, supported by a large merchant fleet and the most powerful navy on the seas. Railroads brought visitors and goods to the city while omnibuses—enclosed wagons drawn by horses— transported nearly a million people each day along thoroughfares paved with granite. A small army of lamplighters tended the network of gas-lights that illuminated the city at night. Ruling over the empire that gave rise to this mighty metropolis was Queen Victoria, nearly the same age as Elizabeth and like her, newly married.

But there was also a dark side of London. Class distinctions were sharp. A small aristocracy wielded disproportionate wealth and influence while masses of the poor crowded into London neighborhoods plagued by crime and disease. Much of the city reeked of human and animal waste and a gray-brown pungent fog descended on the city for days at a time. London was "miles of close walls and pits of houses, where the inhabit-ants gasped for air, stretched far away towards every point of the com-pass," Charles Dickens wrote in his social satire *Little Dorrit*. When the Stantons finally reached their lodgings on Queen Street, Elizabeth found it "the gloomiest abode I have ever seen."[29] But the next day her mood lightened as other American anti-slavery delegates began to arrive. Among them was a woman who would transform her life.

Notes

1. A. J. Delatour, *Daily Record of the Thermometer for Ten Years, from 1840 to 1850, as Kept at Delatour's, Formerly Lynch and Clark's* (New York City: R. Craighead Printer, 1850), 14; Elisabeth Griffith, *In Her Own Right: The Life of Elizabeth Cady Stanton*, First Edition (New York; Oxford: Oxford University Press, 1984), 35; Robert Greenhalgh Albion, *Square Riggers on Schedule: The New York Sailing Packets to England, France, and the Cotton Ports*, First Edition (Princeton, NJ: Princeton University Press, 1938), 280; Clara Jeanette Stone, *Genealogy of the Descendants of*

Jasper Griffing (New York: De Baun & Morgenthaler, printers, 1881), 103; Elizabeth Cady Stanton, *Eighty Years and More: Reminiscences, 1815–1897* (Boston: Northeastern University Press, 1993), 72–73.

2. Stanton, *Eighty Years,* 3.

3. Ibid., 4, 12.

4. Henry Brewster Stanton, *Random Recollections* (Johnstown, PA: Blunck & Leaning, 1885), 8.

5. Lawrence J. Friedman, *Gregarious Saints: Self and Community in Antebellum American Abolitionism, 1830–1870* (Cambridge, Cambridgeshire; New York: Cambridge University Press, 1982), 101.

6. George Thomas, Esq., *Personal Recollections of Gerrit Smith* (Utica, NY: Author, 1875), Onondaga County Public Library, www.nyhistory.com/gerritsmith/descript.htm.

7. Stanton, *Eighty Years,* 52–53.

8. Ibid., 58–59.

9. Ibid.

10. Ibid., 61.

11. Daniel Cady to Gerrit Smith, December 14, 1839, Smith Papers, Syracuse U.; William Lloyd Garrison to Helen Garrison, June 29, 1840, Garrison Papers, Boston Public Library, in Judith Wellman, *The Road to Seneca Falls: Elizabeth Cady Stanton and the First Woman's Rights Convention,* First Edition (Urbana: University of Illinois Press, 2004), 43.

12. Stanton, *Eighty Years,* 71.

13. HBS to ECS, January 4, 1840, *Letters,* 4–5, in Griffith, *Stanton,* 33.

14. HBS to ECS, January 1, 1840, HBS to ECS, January 2, 1840, in Ann D. Gordon, ed., *The Selected Papers of Elizabeth Cady Stanton and Susan B. Anthony* (New Brunswick, NJ; London: Rutgers University Press, 2001), 1:1–2 (hereafter cited as *SP*).

15. HBS to ECS, ibid. Stanton quotes the poem by Thomas Moore in modified form in *SP,* 1:1. (See note 1 in *SP,* 1:3.)

16. HBS to Amos Phelps, April 17, 1840, BPL, in Griffith, *Stanton,* 32.

17. ECS to her granddaughter and namesake, Elizabeth Cady Stanton, June 16, 1882, Stanton Papers, [Vassar], in Wellman, *Seneca Falls,* 44.

18. Stanton, *Eighty Years,* 72.

19. The descriptions of the ship and crew are from passengers who described their travel from New York to the United Kingdom on board the *Montreal*: Samuel Horatio Stearns, *Life and Select Discourses* (Boston: Josiah A. Stearns and Whipple A. Damrell, 1838), 75; Letter written by Jonathan Blanchard on board the ship *Montréal* on May 23, 1843, reprinted in *The Philanthropist,* Special Collections, Buswell Library, Wheaton College, https://wheaton.box.com/s/he700vioxey6hl223yiwn8xue18ggpqb.

20. Blanchard, *The Philanthropist,* May 23, 1843.

21. Harriet Martineau, *Retrospect of Western Travel v. 1* (London: Saunders and Otley, 1838), 21.

22. Salmon P. Chase, in Niven, *Salmon P. Chase,* 48, in Doris Kearns Goodwin, *Team of Rivals: The Political Genius of Abraham Lincoln* (New York: Simon & Schuster, 2006), 108–9.

23. Stanton, *Eighty Years,* 73.

24. Ibid.

25. Ibid., 74.

26. Ibid.

27. Blanchard, *Philanthropist,* June 12, 1843, Special Collections, Buswell Library, Wheaton College, https://wheaton.box.com/s/he700vioxey6hl223yiwn 8xue18ggpqb.

28. Stanton, *Eighty Years,* 77.

29. Ibid., 78.

CHAPTER TWO

The Quaker

As the Stantons set sail on the *Montreal*, a second boat of abolitionists was already headed for London. The voyage of the packet ship *Roscoe* had begun smoothly as a steamer towed the ship from the congested New York Harbor five miles out to sea, where the crew unfurled its sails. Passengers settled into the routine of gathering for meals during the day and enjoying each other's company in the evening. But south of Nantucket, the *Roscoe* ran into heavy storms. A week later in the mid-Atlantic, another storm was so violent that it snapped one of the yards on the mizzenmast. Waves pummeled the ship as it launched "towards the heavens, and plunged down again to the depths to meet the cold embrace of the foaming waters," one passenger wrote, as billows of frothy sea cascaded onto the deck and splayed into rainbows of spray.[1] Even Captain Henry Huttleston said it was worse than the January crossings known for their turbulence.[2]

But the ocean storms were temporary and dissipated well before the *Roscoe* docked in Liverpool. The turmoil inside the ship, which had been brewing for years, did not. Onboard were several delegates to the World Anti-Slavery Convention who were deeply divided over the role of women at the Convention. Some, like Henry Grew, a Baptist minister from Philadelphia, believed that only men should participate. Others, including his daughter Mary, and George Bradburn, a Unitarian minister and member of the Massachusetts legislature, were determined to have women accepted as delegates. At the center of this conflict was another passenger, Lucretia Mott, a forty-seven-year-old Quaker and mother of six who was a leader among women abolitionists.

Lucretia was a diminutive woman who often made a large impression on those she met. A scant five feet tall, with neatly parted brown hair tucked under a cap and modest clothes, she was spirited and principled. When Philadelphia prisons confined inmates in isolation, she pressed for education and rehabilitation. When slavery seemed part of the natural order of things, she shunned cotton, sugar, and other commodities produced by those in bondage and joined organizations to end it. And when women's subordination was seen as essential to a good society, she put forth a vision of equality. "Mrs. Mott," Elizabeth wrote after meeting her in London, "was to me an entire new revelation of womanhood."[3]

Lucretia Coffin Mott was born on Nantucket Island, an eleven-mile rock protrusion a few hours' sail from Cape Cod, where five thousand inhabitants culled a living from the sea. Her father, Thomas Coffin, Jr., was a ship captain who hunted sperm whales for their oil and baleen, a flexible bony product used in women's corsets. With his early success, he bought a large, handsome house just above the marshland near the harbor. He was kindly, but often absent for months, sometimes years. When Lucretia was seven, her father sailed for South America to capture seals and trade them in East Asia. Near Chile, however, the Spanish Navy forced him into port and confiscated his ship. He battled in court to regain his vessel, even teaching himself Spanish to plead his case, but lost hope after several months and headed home, alone, walking north across the Andes to Brazil and then sailing to Nantucket where he appeared, to the surprise of his family, on their doorstep. Lucretia had not seen her father for three years.

With sea-faring men often away, women were the mainstays of daily life. Lucretia's mother, Anna Folger Coffin, raised seven children and managed a large, orderly home almost single-handedly. Before daybreak, Lucretia dressed by candlelight to lay the table and fetch water from the neighborhood pump. After school, she cared for her younger brothers and sisters. By the age of eleven, she could knit, sew, and

Abolitionist and women's rights activist Lucretia Mott, ca. 1858. (Courtesy Friends Historical Library)

prepare cod, stewed cranberries, Indian dumplings, and other traditional Nantucket dishes passed on from mother to daughter. Anna ran a "Shop of Goods" from her front parlor to sell wares she purchased on occasional visits to Boston. The women knitted a social fabric to sustain island life and ease their burdens. When the ships were in port, the men often joined in daily routines set by women, and when they left, life went on.

The cultural center of the island was the Quaker Meeting, where the Coffins worshipped twice a week. The formal name for Quakers, the Society of Friends, reflected their radical vision of equality. Adherents were to live in simple homes and don clothes that ranged from humble gray to somber blue. The Quakers' most distinctive repute came from a social conscience cultivated in worship and in a network of schools. They were the first to condemn slavery and joined abolition groups in such numbers that many Americans saw the movement as a Quaker undertaking. The Nantucket Meeting rejected slavery in 1716, the first in the nation to do so. "Humanity," Lucretia often tearfully recited from a Quaker reader on slavery, "shudders at your account."[4] Some Quaker women became renowned speakers as they traveled to other Meetings. Lydia Maria Child, an abolitionist who lived and worked among Quaker women, thought them "superior to women in general in habits of reflection and independent modes of thinking." Their activism "elevates in them a sense of their own dignity and importance," Thomas Clarkson, the well-known British abolitionist agreed. It "produces in them thought, and foresight, and judgment."[5]

Even on an island peopled with strong women, Lucretia stood out as a child for her willfulness. Her schoolmates called her "spitfire" and her mother, who scolded her for "liking to give as good as she got," called her "long tongue."[6] In her middle teens, she taught at the Nine Partner School, a coeducational Quaker boarding school north of New York City, and met her partner in reform and in life—James Mott, a handsome, lanky young teacher from Long Island. She was energetic and engaging, while he, a friend noted, had a "quiet power, exerting constant influences for good, while attracting comparatively little of public notice and making little noise in the world."[7] After marrying in 1811, the Motts lived in Philadelphia, where James sold wool and cotton. Lucretia bore six children and took pride in frugal homemaking, baking a dozen pies before others awoke, knitting as she talked to visitors, and gathering guests around the kitchen table while she washed dishes.

The Motts opened their large, red-brick house to visiting reformers. Former president John Quincy Adams stayed there on his way to Washington, D.C., where he led anti-slavery efforts in the House of Representatives. Charles Dickens called on them when he visited Philadelphia to inspect the Eastern State Penitentiary and expose the brutality of solitary confinement, which he later described in his American travelogue as "a man buried alive."[8] William Lloyd Garrison, a tall, thin twenty-four-year-old abolitionist with a prominent nose and an intensity in his eyes that his small, oval glasses could not conceal, first visited in 1830 after serving seven weeks in a Baltimore jail for libeling a slave trader. Garrison's insistence upon immediate rather than gradual emancipation intensified the Motts' abolitionist views. At considerable financial risk, James dropped cotton from his business, and Lucretia gave up her beloved ice cream and other products made with sugar harvested by slaves and instead bought candy made with "free sugar" that carried the motto: "Take this, my friend, you must not fear to eat. No slave hath toiled to cultivate this sweet."[9]

When Garrison returned to Philadelphia three years later for the first national convention of abolitionists, the Motts once again made their home a center of welcome. While sixty-four male delegates attended the convention, the women prepared oysters, pickled herring, spiced tongue, fruit, breads, and cakes for an afternoon tea catering to upwards of fifty guests. Lucretia placed anti-slavery propaganda on a table in her front parlor, including a seal carved not with the standard depiction of a male slave, asking "Am I not a Man and a Brother?" but with a woman slave, asking "Am I not a Woman and a Sister?"[10] One morning a delegate invited the women to the proceedings. Lucretia, her mother, and her daughter Anna "clapped on their bonnets" and hurried several blocks south to the convention, where they slipped into the back to watch and knit as the men debated.[11] Lucretia rose to ask the chair—tentatively—if she could make grammatical suggestions for the abolitionist declaration. He agreed willingly, and her comments were well received. The convention secretary, the poet John Greenleaf Whittier, thought her "a beautiful and graceful woman, with a clear, sweet voice."[12] Lucretia said the experience "inspired me with a little more boldness to speak on other subjects."[13]

The next day, Lucretia was shocked to find some delegates afraid to sign the abolition declaration. "If our principles are right, why should we be cowards?" she asked, standing in a room full of men. "Why should we wait for those who never had the courage to maintain the inalienable rights of the slave?" A delegate explained their hesitation—that signing an abolitionist document could damage one's business and social standing. After a long pause, Lucretia's voice rang clear. "James, put down thy name!"[14]

As the convention culminated with the formation of the American Anti-Slavery Society, the men thanked the women for their support and advised them to form their own abolitionist organization. That week more than two dozen women formed the Philadelphia Female Anti-Slavery Society and having "no idea of the meaning of preambles, and resolutions and votings," asked James McCrummel, an influential black Philadelphia dentist, to head their meeting.[15] Many of the members were Quakers, and more than a third were black, including Sarah McCrummel; Charlotte, Harriet, Margaretta, and Sarah Forten, from a wealthy family that made its fortune from sail making; and Grace Bustill Douglass, a milliner, and her daughter Sarah Douglass, who ran an academy for black girls. For the next two years, Society members held an annual fair to support a school for black children and gathered thousands of signatures on anti-slavery petitions to present to Congress. They made small contributions in a formidable struggle, but by leaving their homes and pleading with the public for support on a political and humanitarian issue, the women gradually entered the political arena.

In 1835, two years after its formation, the Philadelphia Female Anti-Slavery Society gained two members who nudged women abolitionists toward pursuing rights for women. Sarah and Angelina Grimké were sisters from a wealthy South Carolina family so repulsed by slavery that they moved to Philadelphia, became Quakers, and joined the abolitionist movement. "Above all, try to persuade your husband, father, brothers and sons that *slavery is a crime against God and man*," Angelina wrote in *An Appeal to the Christian Women of the South*.[16] The Grimké sisters toured Northern states to share their first-hand experiences of slavery, addressing only women at first, mostly in homes or small groups—since a mixed-sex audience was considered promiscuous. But in February 1837, at an abolitionist event in New York, one man refused to leave and Angelina continued to speak. For the next six months, in more than sixty-seven towns all across the North, the Grimkés spoke to over forty thousand people in mixed audiences. They addressed the sexual exploitation of slave women in oblique references, coded words, and half-spoken descriptions that everyone nevertheless understood. Their success emboldened abolitionist women. The troubled world "demands of woman the awakening and vigorous exercise of powers which womanhood has allowed to slumber for ages," a leader of Boston women abolitionists said.[17] The Grimké sisters, Lucretia observed, were freeing women's minds and raising "the low estimate of woman's labors."[18]

The Grimkés offended traditionalists. The General Assembly of the Congregational Church, the most powerful church in Massachusetts, warned of the "dangers which at present seem to threaten the female character, with wide spread and permanent injury."[19] They approved of gentle reasoning with men at home, but when a woman "assumes the place and tone of man as a public reformer," she loses her feminine capacity for subtle influence, and "her character becomes unnatural."[20] The Grimké sisters' talk of sexual relations between white men and women slaves opens the way to "degeneracy and ruin."[21] Sarah was determined. Would it not be more noble to raise women up than to keep them under foot? she asked in a published letter. "I ask no favors for my sex," she wrote. "All I ask of our brethren is that they will take their feet from off our necks, and permit us to stand upright on the ground which God has designed us to occupy."[22]

Angelina Grimké took women's rights into her marriage when she wed a fellow abolitionist in May 1838. Theodore Weld was a thirty-five-year-old bachelor who had vowed to remain single until slavery ended and campaigned against it so vigorously that he acquired the label the "most-mobbed man in America." Nor did his worn coat, unkempt hair, and temperament of "deep, wild gloom" recommend him to marriageable women. "Mercy, I hope that young man never gets married," one woman thought as she observed his dour visage.[23] She would pity his wife, she said. But over the course of several months, Weld and Angelina fell in love and planned a wedding to exemplify their ideals. The invitations featured a slave in chains, and their eighty guests included William Lloyd Garrison, Gerrit Smith, Henry Stanton, Lewis Tappan, and several free black people, including Betsy Dawson and her daughter, two former slaves from the Grimké plantation. In their marriage vows exchanged at the Philadelphia home of Angelina's sister, Theodore claimed "only that authority which love would give," and Angelina omitted the traditional promise to obey her husband.[24]

Later that day, abolitionists from around the country gathered to dedicate the new Pennsylvania Hall, one of the largest buildings in Philadelphia. Abolitionists constructed it after public venue owners refused them. "There is probably no city in the known world, where dislike, amounting to hatred of the coloured population, prevails more than in the city of brotherly love," British abolitionist Joseph Sturge concluded after his American tour.[25] The Hall's soaring neoclassical gallery could hold more than three thousand people. The ancient world, John Greenleaf Whittier noted in a poem he composed for the dedication, had accepted slavery. Here, in "A free arena for the strife of mind, To caste, or sect, or color unconfined," they gathered to fight it.[26]

But many Philadelphians saw Pennsylvania Hall as a provocation. Crowds gathered outside, and on the third night, as women abolitionists from across the North entered the Hall, thousands turned their fury on the building. "What is a mob?" Angelina asked, as stones smashed the windowpanes, the shards of glass kept at bay by internal shutters. "What would the breaking of every window be? Any evidence that we are wrong, or that slavery is a good and wholesome institution?" If the mob were to attack, "would this be any thing compared with what the slave endured?"[27] The crowd outside suddenly burst through the doors while the police stood by. The abolitionists kept on. The next day, the mob grew. Be "steadfast," Lucretia told the abolitionist women. Do not "be alarmed by a little *appearance* of danger."[28] At the end of the meeting, black and white women joined in pairs to exit through the hostile crowd. Later that night, after the mayor sent the police home, the mob burst into the Hall, piled books and furniture onto the stage, broke the gas pipes, and set a fire. A smaller group charged three blocks west toward the Mott home where eleven delegates were staying. Lucretia sent her mother, two young daughters, and some of their furniture and possessions to a neighbor's house for safety. William Lloyd Garrison, Maria Chapman, and several others fled. Others, mostly local abolitionists who refused to be intimidated, stayed. At the last moment, one of them went into the street as the mob approached. "On to the Motts," he shouted, slyly misdirecting them.[29] The mob pivoted south and turned its fury on a black church and orphanage. Back at Pennsylvania Hall, the fire department sprayed water on the surrounding buildings. When one company tried to save the Hall itself, other firefighters turned their hoses to drench them. Pennsylvania Hall burned to the ground. It had been open for four days.

While abolitionists presented a unified front in the face of opposition, they divided over tactics. Should they seek abolition through the political process with all its messy schemes and compromises? Or should they abstain from politics and attempt to sway opinion through reason and morality, leaving the tactical struggles to others? Garrison and his followers insisted on moral suasion alone and welcomed women to the movement as a potent moral force. Another group favored political pressure. Altering consciences would take too long or might never happen at all, they believed, and women were ill-suited for the tumult of politics, their presence a distraction. In 1839, this faction formed the Liberty Party, which discouraged women's participation in the abolition movement.

Abby Kelley, a Quaker abolitionist and one of eight daughters of a central Massachusetts farm family, became a lightning rod for these divisions. She rejected the notion that men were natural leaders and women were natural followers. "The human mind in its natural structure, in its constitution, is the same, wherever found—whether enveloped in a black or white, a male or a female exterior."[30] Her lectures attracted large crowds, including some who were just curious to see a woman speak in public. Conservative abolitionists worried about "Abby Kelleyism." "No woman shall speak or vote where I am moderator," the lead minister at the 1840 Connecticut Anti-Slavery Society meeting thundered. "I will not countenance such an outrage on decency. I will not consent to have women lord it over men in public assemblies. It is enough for women to rule at home."[31] Another minister complained that Kelley traveled widely "with she knows not whom, but always with *men*, husbands leaving their wives to become her knights errant, calling all men brothers," he exclaimed. "I blush for the sex!"[32] The Society voted to silence her. These divisions tore apart the American Anti-Slavery Society at its annual meeting in May 1840. When Garrison nominated Kelley for the business committee, the conservative faction objected, and when she was elected, nearly three hundred delegates left to form a rival organization, the American and Foreign Anti-Slavery Society, not out of spite or expediency, they said, but in accordance with Scripture and the will of God.

In the midst of this controversy, an invitation to the World Anti-Slavery Convention arrived at anti-slavery organizations across the North. British abolitionists who had recently ended slavery in the British Empire sought to end it worldwide, inviting "friends of the slave in every nation and of every clime."[33] After conservative American abolitionists wrote the British that some Americans would interpret this to include women, the British sent a revised invitation asking organizations to forward names of the "gentleman who are to represent them."[34] But it was too late— Garrison's followers had already selected women as delegates, including Lucretia Mott, who in May 1840 was on the *Roscoe* heading to the United Kingdom. During the three weeks at sea, passengers gathered to debate temperance, women's rights, materialism, and other subjects to "exercise our combativeness, veneration, consciousness, or self-esteem, as the case may be," one passenger wrote.[35] At the end of the voyage, several British men asked if they could offer a toast "in honor of the ladies of America." No, the women replied, American women "did not deputize gentlemen to do their business, but did it themselves."[36] The men laughed and cheered for the women.

Before the Motts arrived in London, Elizabeth Cady Stanton had worried that her husband Henry's affiliation with conservative abolitionists might offend Lucretia. But when Lucretia finally arrived at the lodgings for the American delegates, she greeted Elizabeth with gentility and grace. The boarding house on Queens Street soon became a battleground as conservatives argued that women should not attend the Convention.

Joseph Sturge, the principal organizer of the Convention and an English Quaker noted for his support of radical egalitarianism, pleaded with the women to stay away. Their presence contradicted English practice and would agitate the Convention. Reverend Nathaniel Colver stormed out of the room when Lucretia replied that the "colored man too was said to be *constitutionally* unfit to mingle with the white man."[37] Samuel Jackman Prescod, a black man from Barbados, warned the women that their admission would invite scorn and ridicule to the abolition cause. Abolitionists had received similar arguments for the exclusion of colored people from their own meetings, Lucretia replied, but they had never yielded to "such flimsy arguments."[38] American women had worked in the abolitionist cause for more than a decade, developing their skills and confidence. Whether he liked it or not, they were determined to attend. Elizabeth watched Lucretia rebut arguments with reason, humor, and dignity. "How beautiful she looked to me that day," Elizabeth later wrote.[39]

Notes

1. Mary Grew, *Mary Grew's Diary*, May 12, 1840. Alma Lutz Collection, SL, 1–2.

2. George Bradburn and Frances H. Bradburn, *A Memorial of George Bradburn* (Boston: Cuples, Upham and Co., 1883), 43.

3. Elizabeth Cady Stanton, Susan B. Anthony, and Matilda Joslyn Gage, *History of Woman Suffrage*, Vol. 1 (Salem, MA: Ayer Company, 1985), 420 (hereafter cited as *HWS*).

4. Margaret Hope Bacon, *Valiant Friend: The Life of Lucretia Mott* (New York: Walker & Co., 1980), 13.

5. Christopher Densmore, "The Quaker Tradition: Sustaining Women's Rights" (originally prepared for the National Women's Studies Association Annual Meeting, Oswego, NY, 1998), 2, http://ubib.buffalo.edu/libraries/units/archives/urr/NWSA.html; Bacon, *Valiant Friend*, 16–17.

6. "Nantucket's Daring Daughters: A Brief Look at the Quaker 'Spitfire,' Lucretia Coffin Mott," *Nantucket Chronicle*, 1, https://www.nantucketchronicle.com/nation-nantucket/2014/nantuckets-daring-daughters-a-brief-look-quaker-spitfire-lucretia-coffin-mott, accessed October 19, 2018.

7. Mary Grew, *James Mott: A Biographical Sketch* (Ithaca, NY: Cornell University Library, 1868), 5.

8. Charles Dickens, *American Notes* (Gloucester: Peter Smith, 1968), 122.

9. Dorothy Sterling, *Lucretia Mott: Gentle Warrior* (Garden City, NY: Doubleday, 1964), 77.

10. Bacon, *Valiant Friend*, 55.

11. Sterling, *Lucretia Mott*, 83.

12. Ibid.

13. Anna Davis Hallowell, *James and Lucretia Mott: Life and Letters* (Boston: Houghton Mifflin, 1884), 115.

14. Bacon, *Valiant Friend*, 57.

15. Hallowell, *James and Lucretia Mott*, 121.

16. Angelina Grimké, "Appeal to the Christian Women of the South," 1836, in Kathryn Kish Sklar, ed., *Women's Rights Emerges within the Anti-Slavery Movement, 1830–1870: A Brief History with Documents*, First Edition (Boston: Bedford/St. Martin's, 2000), 87.

17. Maria Weston Chapman, *Proceedings of the Anti-Slavery Convention of American Women* (New York, 1837), 3, in Ira V. Brown, "Cradle of Feminism: The Philadelphia Female Anti-Slavery Society, 1883–1840," *Pennsylvania Magazine of History & Biography* 102, no. 2 (April 1978): 156.

18. Bacon, *Valiant Friend*, 75.

19. "Pastoral Letter: The General Association of Massachusetts to Churches under Their Care" 1837, in Sklar, *Women's Rights*, 120–21.

20. Ibid.

21. Ibid., 121.

22. Sarah Grimke to Mary S. Parker, July 17, 1837, https://arquivo.pt/wayback/20090724001330/ http://www.pinn.net/~sunshine/book-sum/grimke3.html, accessed October 23, 2017.

23. Gerda Lerner, *The Grimke Sisters of South Carolina, Pioneers for Women's Rights and Abolition* (New York: Schocken, 1971), 205–6.

24. Ibid., 242.

25. Joseph Sturge, "The Metropolis of Prejudice," in Philip Stevick, *Imagining Philadelphia: Travelers' Views of the City from 1800 to the Present* (Philadelphia: University of Pennsylvania Press, 1996), 160.

26. John Greenleaf Whittier, "Address on the Opening of Pennsylvania Hall—Antislavery Literature Project," http://antislavery.eserver.org/tracts/poetry/whittierpennsylvaniahall, accessed February 14, 2015.

27. Angelina Grimke Weld's Speech at Pennsylvania Hall, cited at http://www.pbs.org/wgbh/aia/part4/4h2939t.html, accessed June 18, 2008.

28. Lucretia Mott, "Report of a Delegate to the Anti-Slavery Convention of American Women," *Liberator*, September 28, 1838, in Carol Faulkner, *Lucretia Mott's Heresy: Abolition and Women's Rights in Nineteenth-Century America* (Philadelphia: University of Pennsylvania Press, 2011), 78.

29. Bacon, *Valiant Friend*, 78.

30. Abby Kelley, "The Woman Question," in *The Hartford Connecticut Observer* and *New York Congregationalist*, March 7, 1840, 38, in Keith Melder, "Abby Kelley and the Process of Liberation," in Jean Fagan Yellin and John C. Van Horne, eds., *The Abolitionist Sisterhood: Women's Popular Culture in Antebellum America* (Ithaca, NY: Cornell University Press, 1994), 242.

31. *Liberator*, May 29, 1840, 86, in Melder, "Abby Kelley," 242.

32. *National Anti-Slavery Standard*, October 8, 1840, 71, in Melder, "Abby Kelley," 243.

33. Hallowell, *James and Lucretia Mott*, 138, in Kathryn Kish Sklar, "'Women Who Speak for an Entire Nation': American and British Women Compared at the World Anti-Slavery Convention, London 1840," *Pacific Historical Review* 59, no. 4 (November 1990): 461.

34. Letter from the Committee of the British and Foreign Anti-Slavery Society, February 15, 1840. Papers of Henry Stanton, File 2 of 3, National Women's Rights Historic Park, Seneca Falls, New York.

35. Grew Diary, May 15, 1840, 5.

36. Ibid., May 26, 1840, 8.

37. Mott Diary, June 11, 1840, in Frederick B. Tolles, *Slavery and the Woman Question: Lucretia Mott's Diary of Her Visit to Great Britain to Attend the World Anti-Slavery Convention of 1840* (Haverford, PA: Friends Historical Association, 1952), 29.

38. Ibid.

39. ECS Eulogy at Lucretia Mott Memorial Service, January 19, 1881, in *HWS*, 1:420.

CHAPTER THREE

The World Anti-Slavery Convention

June 12–23, 1840

On June 12, 1840, the World Anti-Slavery Convention opened in one of London's largest public meeting places, Freemasons' Hall on Great Queen Street. With a lofty interior more than sixty feet high and forty feet wide and walls studded with stately pilasters, it was a venue to inspire bold action. Over four hundred delegates claimed their seats in the central hall and hundreds more crowded into the gallery to observe. Most delegates were from the United Kingdom and the West Indies, veterans of the British abolition movement. Others came from countries where slavery or some form of human bondage still existed. Forty were American. By eleven in the morning, as sunlight filtered in through semi-circular windows, the hall had filled.

Delegates looked on as a string of dignitaries arrived. They cheered as Thomas O'Connell, the champion of Irish nationalism, took his seat. Henry Beckford, a former Jamaican slave, told the gathering to "look at me and work on."[1] The highlight was the entrance of Thomas Clarkson, the eighty-one-year-old scion of the British abolition struggle. For nearly a half-century, he and William Wilberforce had worked to end slavery throughout the British Empire. They succeeded when Parliament passed the Slavery Abolition Act in 1833. Wilberforce died just three days after the act passed, but here, nearly seven years later, the elderly and feeble Clarkson slowly made his way to the front of the hall, his young grandson by his side. The audience stood quietly, some with tears in their eyes. Only a deep-toned "Amen," twice repeated, broke the silence. It was the sounding, one delegate later said, of "the death warrant of slavery all over the earth."[2] Clarkson told the Convention he had worked for abolition since he was twenty-four, but would gladly do it again. "Take courage," he said, "be not dismayed, go on, persevere to the last."[3]

After the introductions finished, the veneer of moral unity splintered over the issue festering just below the surface—whether to accept the eight women delegates from the United States. Mott and Elizabeth, seated next to each other, watched as the male delegates began to debate. "The excitement and vehemence of protest and denunciation could not have been greater, if the news had come that the French were about to invade England," Elizabeth later wrote.[4]

Wendell Phillips, the talented orator from Boston known as "abolition's golden trumpet," spoke first.[5] "There are several of my co-delegates, who though in this Hall, have not received an entrance as members of the Convention," he said, and "some of us feeling ourselves, shall I use too harsh a term when I say, aggrieved!" The invitation had asked for "friends of the slave," and Americans had elected to send several women, including Phillips's wife Ann, who looked on from the side. He motioned that the Convention as a whole decide the issue. Professor William Adam, also of Boston, concurred. "Female exertion is the very life of us, and of all that we have done, and all we hope to do," he proclaimed. "To exclude females, would be to affix a stigma upon them."[6]

A member of the organizing committee explained that the invitation was intended only for men, and while they appreciated women's efforts, their inclusion was not customary in Britain. British Member of Parliament John Bowring disagreed. A queen ruled them, after all. "I look upon this delegation from America as one of the most interesting, the most encouraging, and the most delightful symptoms of the times," he said.[7]

Several clergymen from both sides of the Atlantic condemned the inclusion of women. It violated "the ordinance of Almighty God," the Reverend Grew said, as his daughter Mary watched from the side. Few Americans even wanted women delegates, the Reverend Colver from Boston stated. Had they known that women were to be accepted, many of the male delegates would not have come. A British minister noted that while Queen Victoria ruled Britain, she had appointed her husband Prince Albert to represent her at the Convention. "I have no objection to woman's being the neck to turn the head aright," he offered, "but do not wish to see her assume the place of the head."[8]

The Reverend J. Burnet, a minister from South London, insisted on following British norms. "As we are in England let us act as England does; and when English abolitionists come to America, we shall expect the same ready conformity."[9] Better to cancel the Convention than admit women, he said.

George Bradburn, a Unitarian minister who served in the Massachusetts legislature, told delegates that women had been the principal supporters behind all his success in abolition. Do not take "the English
yardstick to measure the American mind," he said in a booming voice.[10]
When a mob confronted the great British abolitionist George Thompson
during his visit to the United States, it was women who formed a protec-
tive ring around him.

Thompson himself replied. Women were indeed integral to abolition,
he said, but the delegates were straying from the topic at hand—slavery.
He asked the Americans, "With all the respect I can express, to withdraw
their motion."[11]

Wendell Phillips and his allies refused. It was "a matter of conscience,"
Phillips said. Massachusetts elected the women and "we have not changed
by crossing the water." If the men abandoned women, how could they ask
for their help?[12]

Tensions grew as a vote neared. The Reverend J. A. James hoped that a
vote to exclude women would not offend the Americans, and that the
quarrel "will be only like the notes of discord sometimes introduced in
the best concerted music, to make the harmony the sweeter."

The British Reverend C. Stovel was less charitable. "If it tears your
Societies to pieces in the United States, why would you tear in pieces our
Convention?" he asked, shaking his Bible overhead. Should the "paltry
question" of women's inclusion delay the great humanitarian issue before
them, he asked?[13]

"No!" Stovel shouted, answering his own question.[14]

It was time to vote. The more than four hundred male delegates were
among the most astute reformers of the era, able to perceive racial injustice when most of their peers could not. But faced with the question of
whether to admit women as equals, nine in ten voted against. Women's
equality, in intellect and agency, was beyond the pale even for them. The
Convention did permit women—and this was a concession—to sit to the
side behind a waist-high rail and observe in silence.

Phillips tried to put the best face on the resounding defeat. There was
"no unpleasant feeling in our minds," he reassured the delegates. Americans would now "act with the utmost cordiality," and American women
would sit behind the barrier with as much interest as if they had been
accepted. But Elizabeth felt that Phillips had "far mistaken their real feelings and been insensible to the insults offered them."[15] She seethed with
indignation as she listened to "narrow-minded bigots, pretending to be
teachers and leaders of men."[16] Several notables visited Mott and asked
that she stay at the Convention as an inspiration to British women. An

Irish journalist proclaimed her "the lioness of the convention," though Mott later quipped that she felt more like "sheep for the slaughter."[17]

William Lloyd Garrison arrived at the Convention six days late, delayed by a pressing abolitionist meeting at home. He was shocked to find the women sitting to the side in silence and joined them there in protest. Delegates pleaded with America's most prominent abolitionist—even Mott urged him to participate—but Garrison steadfastly refused.

Later, back at the boarding house, the American women waged a battle with several male compatriots. The corpulent Reverend Colver withstood the barrage, fortified, he said, by his "weapon of defence"—his Bible.[18] James G. Birney, who had schooled Elizabeth on abolition as they paced the deck of the *Montreal*, became so agitated that he left to room elsewhere. Outside the Convention, the American women became a popular spectacle. "Our delegation is regarded as quite a phenomenon, which everyone is anxious to see," Mary Grew wrote in her diary.[19] A steady stream of visitors "look upon us with countenances of mingled astonishment and respect."[20] As Mott addressed small groups in and around London, she spread her ideas like seeds cast in the soil for the future. Joanna Bonham-Carter, the daughter of an abolitionist Member of Parliament, heard Mott and enthusiastically shared the notion of expanding roles for women with her twenty-year-old niece, Florence Nightingale. Fourteen years later, Nightingale, the founder of modern nursing, would become an icon of independent womanhood as she nursed soldiers during the Crimean War.

Mott and Elizabeth bonded as they walked arm in arm to the Convention, huddled for hours on a bench at the British Museum while others viewed exhibits, and conferred at night in front of the fireplace in their lodgings on Queen Street. The young bride listened eagerly to the mother of six as she talked of Mary Wollstonecraft, Frances Wright, the Grimké sisters, and others who protested women's subordination. Elizabeth had never heard a woman talk so openly. "It seemed to me like meeting a being from some larger planet, to find a woman who dared to question the opinions of Popes, Kings, Synods, Parliaments, with the same freedom that she would criticize an editorial in the *London Times*, recognizing no higher authority than the judgment of a pure-minded, educated woman."[21] When Mott urged her to think for herself and live by her own convictions, Elizabeth felt a new sense of liberation, "like suddenly coming in to the rays of the noon-day sun, after wandering with a rushlight in the caves of the earth."[22] Garrison noted Elizabeth's ardor. "Mrs. Stanton is a fearless woman, and goes for woman's rights with all her soul," he wrote to his wife.[23] Mott found Elizabeth spritely and engaging, "gaining daily in our affections."[24]

After eleven days, with the delegates publicly dedicated to abolishing slavery around the world, the Convention ended, and the Americans returned home in staggered voyages. No one was certain what would come of the Convention—"we trust that a great good will result to the cause of freedom, though it had not been as democratic as Americans wanted," Mary Grew ruminated in her diary. "The future must reveal what it has done."[25]

It would take years for resentment over the treatment of women to congeal into a movement. But the irony of excluding one part of humanity at a convention dedicated to liberating another stirred a deep discontent. "How does this principle apply to *my* condition?" an elected woman delegate to the Convention began to ask herself. "Do laws and customs leave *me* the free exercise of all my powers?"[26]

Notes

1. Mott Diary, June 12, 1840, 31.

2. Benjamin R. Hayden, the official painter for the Convention, in Stephen H. Hobhouse, *Joseph Sturge: His Life and Work* (London: J.M. Dent & Sons, 1919), 93; Douglas H. Maynard, "The World's Anti-Slavery Convention of 1840," *The Mississippi Valley Historical Review* 47, no. 3 (December 1960): 459.

3. *Proceedings of the General Anti-Slavery Convention, Called by the Committee of the British and Foreign Anti-Slavery Society, and Held in London, from Friday, June 12th to Tuesday, June 23rd, 1840* (London: British and Foreign Anti-slavery Society, 1841), 3. (hereafter cited as *London Proceedings*).

4. *HWS*, 1:54.

5. Sklar, "Women Who Speak," 467–68.

6. *London Proceedings*, 24.

7. Ibid., 25.

8. Ibid., 28.

9. Ibid., 27.

10. Ibid., 30.

11. Ibid., 35.

12. Ibid., 36.

13. Ibid.

14. Ibid., 43.

15. *HWS*, 1:60.

16. Stanton, *Eighty Years*, 81.

17. LM to Elizabeth Pease, April 28, 1846, in Hallowell, *James and Lucretia Mott*, 280.

18. *HWS*, 1:62.

19. Grew Diary, June 17, 1840, 33–34.

20. Ibid.

21. *HWS*, 1:422.

22. Ibid.

23. WLG to Helen Garrison, June 29, 1840, in Clare Taylor, *British and American Abolitionists* (Edinburgh, Chicago: Edinburgh University Press, 1975), 93.

24. Mott Diary, June 21, 1840, 41.

25. Grew Diary, June 23, 1840, 38.

26. Lydia Maria Child, "To Abolitionists," *Standard*, May 20, 1841, in Carolyn L. Karcher, ed., *The First Woman in the Republic: A Cultural Biography of Lydia Maria Child* (Durham, NC: Duke University Press Books, 1998), 615. Child was an elected delegate to the London Convention but did not attend.

CHAPTER FOUR

Home

After seven months in the British Isles, the Stantons sailed home on one of the first ocean-faring steamships, joining a steady stream of eighteen hundred vessels that entered New York Harbor that year. Elizabeth was eager to return. "I never loved my country, my home, my friends, as I do now," she wrote before they left England.[1] They settled into her parents' comfortable home in Johnstown. Henry studied law with Judge Cady, while Elizabeth devoured books on history and politics, taught Sunday school, and took long walks and horse rides with her sisters.

In March 1842, Elizabeth gave birth to a boy, Daniel Cady, and struggled to find her footing as a mother. Daniel was born with a bent collarbone, which the doctor bandaged, reassuring her that it would heal. But when Daniel wailed and his fingers turned purple, Stanton undid the doctor's work, fashioned a less severe bandage, and proudly announced her success when he returned. Still, Elizabeth felt adrift and uncertain as Daniel fussed. She read about early childhood and began a running battle with her child's nurse, an older woman with years of experience, over how best to tend to an infant. When the nurse advised her to feed the baby constantly—Elizabeth breast-fed Daniel every two hours and let him rest. When the nurse kept the windows shut, even in pleasant weather—Elizabeth opened them. When the nurse swaddled Daniel so tightly that he could barely move his arms and legs—Elizabeth undid it. She also refused to give Daniel the nurse's opioid concoctions. She even locked herself and the baby in the bedroom to prevent her father and husband from rousing the sleeping Daniel from his crib. At six months old, Daniel was a happy, healthy little boy. Elizabeth learned to trust her own judgment, relying on "neither men nor books absolutely."[2] Motherhood was the greatest of all professions, she wrote years later, "requiring more knowledge than any other department in human affairs."[3]

Later that year, the Stantons moved to Boston to foster Henry's political career while he worked as a patent attorney. Boston in the 1840s was thick with reformers trying to alter inherited norms. A new generation of theologians were reinterpreting the tenets of Calvinism, educators were reworking traditional teaching methods, and visionaries were seeking a more just society—a collective agitation that made Boston a kind of "moral museum," Stanton wrote.[4] Horace Mann, head of the new Massachusetts Board of Education, proposed a statewide network of publicly financed common schools staffed by trained teachers. It would foster upward mobility and a shared culture, inculcating the habits and virtues he believed were necessary in a modern republic. Bronson Alcott opened a private school near Boston Common to encourage children's natural spontaneity and rejected the rote memorization and strict discipline of traditional schooling. Surrounded by busts of Plato, William Shakespeare, and Sir Walter Scott, Alcott taught by the Socratic method and let children themselves decide matters of discipline. In South Boston, Samuel Gridley Howe opened the Perkins Institution, the nation's first school for the deaf and blind. The handsome Harvard-trained surgeon had returned from Europe a hero after fighting for Greek independence and assisting a Polish insurrection against czarist Russia. Yet rather than pursuing a lucrative private surgical practice, Howe devoted his life to helping his marginalized students function in everyday life by teaching them to read and communicate. Charles Dickens was so impressed with Howe's work that he dedicated a chapter of his American travelogue to a description of Laura Bridgman, a Perkins student left deaf and blind from scarlet fever at the age of two. If one were to meet a man in downtown Boston "with a decent coat and a clean shirt," a British journalist told his readers, he was likely "either a lecturer, a Unitarian minister, or a poet; possibly the man might be all three at once."[5]

Elizabeth Cady Stanton and her daughter, Harriot, in 1856. (Library of Congress)

Transcendentalists in and around Boston challenged the Calvinist belief in the depravity of man and the Unitarian emphasis on calm rationalism. People are innately good, they asserted, and truth may be discerned through one's own intuition and reflection, "to believe your own thought, to believe that what is true for you in your private heart is true for all men," Ralph Waldo Emerson said.[6] But those who pursued truth in such a manner would face resistance, he warned. "To be great," Emerson famously wrote, "is to be misunderstood."[7] Transcendentalists established Brook Farm, a 170-acre community ten miles outside of Boston, to promote equality and creativity through shared labor. At Fruitlands, another planned community thirty miles northwest of Boston, residents shunned leather, ate a vegan diet of mostly uncooked vegetables, and avoided cotton and other products linked to slavery.

Elizabeth welcomed these challenges to accepted norms. "All sorts of new ideas are seething," she wrote her mother, "but I haven't either time or place even to enumerate them, and if I did you and my good father would probably balk at most of them."[8] She visited Brook Farm; conversed with Bronson Alcott; had tea with William Lloyd Garrison in his home; and met Frederick Douglass, the abolitionist who escaped slavery in Maryland and became a renowned speaker against it. Douglass seemed like "an African Prince," she said after their first meeting, "conscious of his dignity and power, grand in his physical proportions, majestic in his wrath, as with keen wit, satire, and indignation he portrayed the bitterness of slavery."[9] Stanton especially revered Theodore Parker, a popular Unitarian minister who preached that Christ's message of love, compassion, and benevolence should be lived as a social principle. He denounced slavery, the Northern businessmen who profited from it, and Christian preachers who tolerated it. Still chilled by her "dark Scotch Presbyterian days," Stanton found his message liberating and walked for miles in Boston winters to hear him preach.[10]

Elizabeth also met women who broke boundaries. Lydia Maria Child, who Garrison hailed as "the first woman in the Republic," had penned the nation's first anti-slavery book and chafed at the subordination of women.[11] Maria Weston Chapman and her sisters founded the Boston Female Anti-Slavery Society, which held petition drives for abolition and ran large annual bazaars to fund black institutions. She met Margaret Fuller, an extraordinary intellectual from a learned and principled family. Fuller's grandfather had refused to support the Constitution because it accommodated slavery; her father, a member of Congress, taught her Latin, French, Greek, logic, and rhetoric as a young girl; and her mother had "that spontaneous love of every living thing, for man, and beast, and tree, which restores the golden age," Fuller wrote.[12] Ralph Waldo Emerson considered Fuller the best-educated person he knew. Talking with her, he told his brother, was "like being set in a large place. You stretch your limbs and dilate to your utmost size."[13] Yet as a woman, Fuller had few means to earn a living through her intellect, "nothing to do," a friend observed in his diary, "no place in the world & fears she never shall have."[14] After the early death of her father, Fuller began weekly two-hour "Conversations," where women paid a small sum to hear Fuller talk and to share their hopes and grievances. Citing the heroic, vain, and sexually robust deities of Greek mythology, Fuller explored the great questions of human existence. What was the purpose of life? What was distinctly feminine or masculine? At first, only half of the more than two dozen regular participants spoke, but Fuller encouraged others to join the conversations. "Nothing I hate to hear of so much as *woman's lot*," she said.[15] Women were as intellectually capable as men, she believed, and it was their duty to speak up. More than two hundred women, including Elizabeth, participated in at least one of Fuller's gatherings.

Elizabeth bore two more sons in 1844 and 1845 and relished homemaking for her growing family. Prosperous enough to afford household help, she took pride in her clean, white laundry, paid extra to have firewood neatly stacked, and pickled and preserved produce for the winter months. A beautiful home with healthy children and a contented mother was better than a picture of family happiness on a wall, she said. The Stantons often entertained on their upper piazza overlooking Boston Harbor. Elizabeth particularly enjoyed the sunset as it highlighted the ships below, observing that "the most reserved people are apt to grow confidential at such an hour."[16] Her years in Boston were "some of the happiest days of my life, enjoying, in turn, the beautiful outlook, my children, and my books,"[17] she later recalled. It "was all I could desire."[18]

During extended visits to the new townhouse in Albany that Judge Cady purchased as he served on the New York Supreme Court, Elizabeth made her first attempts to shape public policy as the New York legislature considered the rights of married women. Marriage was the defining institution in a woman's life, even if she never acquired a husband. Girls were raised for it, young women were measured by it, and it legally defined a woman's existence long after her husband died. It was also a contract that stripped away most of her power. The single woman, a feme sole under English common law, enjoyed an independent legal existence with limited rights. She could choose her domicile, sign contracts, inherit property, and dispose of her wealth as she saw fit. But when a woman married—and nine in ten did in the mid-1800s—she became a feme covert and lost many of her rights. In marriage, "the very being or legal existence of the woman is suspended," Lord William Blackstone wrote in *Commentaries on the Laws of England*.[19] In everyday life, this meant that a married woman could not control her wages or inheritance and could not sign a contract or initiate a legal action. A husband was sanctioned to punish his wife—with physical force if necessary—and had full control of children as well as the right to sexual access to his wife's body, whether she willed it or not. As a girl in her father's study, Elizabeth saw women plead their cases against unjust laws and abusive husbands. His law students sometimes teased Elizabeth by paging through law books to find and recite the most egregious statutes that subordinated women, leaving her in tears of frustration. Decades later, with no surviving son, Judge Cady faced the reality of property laws that favored men over married women. After he and his wife died, his estate would pass to his sons-in-law.

With the support of her extended family and hired household help to watch her young children, Elizabeth was able to spend time lobbying for legal change and partnered with Ernestine Potowski Rose, the immigrant daughter of a Polish rabbi. Rose had found women hesitant to challenge their own subordination as she lectured in favor of women's property rights across New York. Women still had no concept of having rights, Rose said, like a hopelessly sick patient who was "unconscious of his pain and suffering."[20] When the New York legislature finally passed the Married Women's Property Act in 1848 to give wives control over their own wages and inheritance, both Rose and Elizabeth found that it raised women's expectations. "The right to property," Elizabeth said, "is the dawning of a civil existence for woman."[21]

Seneca Falls

Elizabeth thrived in Boston, but Henry did not. He failed to win a congressional seat in a district north of Boston as the Liberty Party candidate, and the nightly campaigning exhausted him. He suffered chronic headaches and bundled himself in layers of clothing to fend off the Massachusetts winds he believed had killed his mother. He was unhappy and wanted to move.

In 1847, after five years in Boston, the Stantons moved to Seneca Falls, New York, a bustling town on a spur of the Erie Canal. Seneca Falls was closer to family and friends and would be a good base to support Henry's political aspirations. Judge Cady had purchased a rundown Greek revival house at the edge of town as a stopping point on his circuit rides for the

New York Supreme Court. "You believe in woman's capacity to do and dare," Cady said as he handed his daughter a check for repairs, "now go ahead and put your place in order."[22] Elizabeth deposited her children with her parents in Johnstown and began to refurbish her new home. She bought bedspreads, blue and white dishes, and put up blue and green wallpaper while carpenters added a front porch, a storage shed, and a new kitchen. After a month, the Stantons moved in. Summer breezes carried the cacophonous thumping of sawmills, gristmills, and pump factories to their door. The Stantons could hear music from canal boats filled with people heading west and sounds from barges piled high with lumber, wheat, and corn heading east as the boats floated around a curve near the Stanton home. Coachmen on large red stagecoaches blew horns to announce their arrival in town as they traveled the Seneca Turnpike at the north end of the Stanton property. Trains paralleling the canal whistled as they entered Seneca Falls.

Elizabeth worried that Henry would find Seneca Falls too small for his ambitions. But it was Elizabeth herself who found the change from Boston "somewhat depressing."[23] Henry was often away in Washington or stumping through New York on behalf of the Liberty Party, while she struggled at home with their three young boys. Elizabeth disciplined lightly—perhaps a reaction to her own childhood—and her boys were high-spirited and mischievous, sometimes drawing complaints from neighbors. The boys also struggled with illnesses, contracting malaria and suffering from fevers and lethargy that lasted for months. When Henry's sister and brother-in-law made an extended visit to the Stanton home, their baby succumbed to whooping cough, the fifth child they lost to illness. Elizabeth's joy and pride in making a beautiful and orderly home "all faded away in the struggle to accomplish what was absolutely necessary from hour to hour."[24]

In the midst of her discontent, Elizabeth received a letter from her friend Jane Hunt, who lived in nearby Waterloo. Lucretia and James Mott were staying in Waterloo with Lucretia's sister Martha Coffin Wright, Hunt told her. Hunt invited Elizabeth to join them all for a visit. On Sunday, July 9, Elizabeth took the train to the Hunts' stately brick house at the edge of town, where she met the Hunts' Waterloo neighbor Mary Ann M'Clintock, Martha Wright, and Lucretia Mott, whom she had not seen for several years. There, in the comfortable parlor with a red velvet sofa and a square marble-topped table, Stanton unleashed her frustrations "with such vehemence and indignation that I stirred myself, as well as the rest of the party, to do and dare anything," she later recalled.[25] It was a receptive group. As Quakers, the Hunts, Motts, and M'Clintocks were active in several reform efforts that involved women. They decided to hold a convention for women's rights—not in the future, but in the next week, before Mott left town. They quickly planned for a public meeting and, as dark settled in, wrote an announcement for the local newspapers. Two days later, the *Seneca County Courier* printed their notice:

WOMAN'S RIGHTS CONVENTION.—A Convention to discuss the social, civil, and religious condition and rights of woman, will be held in the Wesleyan Chapel, in Seneca Falls, N.Y., on Wednesday and Thursday, the 19th and 20th of July, current; commencing at 10 o'clock A.M. During the first day the meeting will be exclusively for women, who are earnestly invited to attend. The public generally are invited to be present on the second day, when Lucretia Mott, of Philadelphia, and other ladies and gentlemen, will address the convention.[26]

Women's rights were already under discussion in some circles. Abolitionists debated them for more than a decade and, just a month earlier, Stanton's cousin Gerrit Smith, the Liberty Party's presidential candidate, had demanded "universal suffrage in its broadest sense, females as well as males being entitled to vote."[27] But this would be the first convention dedicated solely to women's rights. The women arranged to use the Wesleyan Methodist Church, which could accommodate a few hundred people. They wrote to friends and fellow reformers for support and to request letters that could be read at the convention if the authors could not attend themselves. Stanton spread the word in Seneca Falls and wrote to Lydia Maria Child and Maria Weston Chapman in Boston. M'Clintock solicited local Quakers, and Mott appealed to Frederick Douglass in Rochester. No one knew how many would come. Mott was a well-known speaker, the *Seneca Falls Courier* editor wrote. "We expect to derive much pleasure and profit from her remarks."[28] Nineteen-year-old Charlotte Woodward, who lived with her family in Waterloo making gloves for low wages, read the notice with excitement and went from house to house, finding other women reading it—some in disbelief, others curious.

At home the next week, Elizabeth outlined a speech and a Declaration to serve as a document of protest. The following Sunday, she took the morning train to the M'Clintock house in Waterloo, a solid two-story brick home with a modest portico and several fireplaces to keep the family warm during New York winters. Stanton, Mary Ann M'Clintock, and her two adult daughters spent the afternoon revising Elizabeth's Declaration around a graceful mahogany tea table. They read speeches and resolutions from other protests and searched for the right tone to match "the inauguration of a rebellion such as the world had never before seen."[29] Other reform documents were too tame, they thought, and they felt "helpless and hopeless as if they had been suddenly asked to construct a steam engine," Stanton later recalled.[30] Then, when one of them read the Declaration of Independence with great spirit, they decided to use it as a model for their own demands. They scoured laws, customs, constitutions, religious practices, and came up with sixteen grievances, "as good a bill of impeachment against our sires and sons as they had against old King George," Elizabeth said.[31] They called their new document the Declaration of Sentiments.

Elizabeth took the five o'clock train home to Seneca Falls, documents in hand. The Convention would begin in three days. On her own, Stanton added another demand—a resolution calling for the vote. "Resolved, that it is the duty of women of this country to secure to themselves their sacred right to the elective franchise."[32] It was a radical sentiment, beyond what many reformers thought proper. Even Mott thought it would bring ridicule. Henry was "thunderstruck" and warned Elizabeth that the demand for the vote would turn the first women's rights convention "into a farce."[33]

Notes

1. ECS to Daniel C. Eaton, August 18, 1840, in Theodore Stanton and Harriot Stanton Blatch, eds., *Elizabeth Cady Stanton: As Revealed in Her Letters Diary and Reminiscences*, 2 vols. (New York and London: Harper & Brothers Publishers, 1922), (reprint edition: Forgotten Books, 2012), 2:6.

2. Stanton, *Eighty Years*, 120.

3. Ibid., 112.

4. ECS to Elizabeth Neall, February 3, 1843, Gay Papers, Columbia, in Wellman, *Seneca Falls*, 160.

5. Thomas O'Connor, *The Athens of America: Boston, 1825–1845* (Amherst: University of Massachusetts Press, 2006), 110.

6. Ralph Waldo Emerson, "Self-Reliance," in Ralph Waldo Emerson and Phillip Lopate, *The Annotated Emerson*, ed. David Mikics, Annotated Edition (Cambridge, MA: Belknap Press, 2012), 160–61.

7. Ibid., 168.

8. ECS to Margaret Livingston Cady, July 17, 1845, in Stanton and Blatch, *Letters*, 2:13.

9. ECS, *Washington Evening Star*, February 2, 1895, 2, in Rayford W. Logan, Introduction, in Douglas, *Life and Times*, 19, in Wellman, *Seneca Falls*, 161.

10. ECS to J. G. Whittier, November 28, 1843, in Stanton and Blatch, *Letters*, 2:11.

11. William Lloyd Garrison, "Mrs. Child," *Genius of Universal Emancipation*, November 20, 1829, 85, in Karcher, *Lydia Maria Child*, xi.

12. R. W. Emerson, W. H. Channing, and J. F. Clarke, *Memoirs of Margaret Fuller Ossoli*, (Boston: Phillips, Sampson, 1852), 1:12–13, in Joan M. Von Mehren, *Minerva and the Muse: A Life of Margaret* Fuller (Amherst: University of Massachusetts Press, 1994), 12.

13. *ELII*, 32, in Megan Marshall, *The Peabody Sisters: Three Women Who Ignited American Romanticism*, Reprint Edition (Boston: Mariner Books, 2006), 98.

14. Quoted in Charles Capper, *Margaret Fuller: An American Romantic Life, v. 1, The Private Years* (New York: Oxford University Press, 1992), 117, in Megan Marshall, *Margaret Fuller: A New American Life* (Boston, New York: Houghton Mifflin Harcourt, 2013), 63.

15. "Margaret Fuller's Boston Conversations," 215–16, in Marshall, *Margaret Fuller*, 140.

16. Stanton, *Eighty Years*, 141.

17. Ibid., 138.

18. Ibid., 136.

19. Lord William Blackstone, *Commentaries on the Laws of England*, 1765, in Stephanie Coontz, *Marriage, a History: From Obedience to Intimacy or How Love Conquered Marriage* (New York: Viking, 2005), 186.

20. *HWS*, 1:693.

21. ECS Address to New York Legislature, February 14, 1854, in Gordon, *SP*, 1:248.

22. Stanton, *Eighty Years*, 144.

23. Ibid., 145.

24. Ibid., 147.

25. Ibid., 148.

26. *Seneca County Courier*, July 11, 1848, in *HWS*, 1:67.

27. Proceedings of National Liberty Convention Held at Buffalo, NY, June 14 and 15, 1848, (Utica: S.W. Green, 1848) 14, in Wellman, *Seneca Falls*, 176.

28. *Seneca Falls Courier*, July 18, 1848, in Wellman, *Seneca Falls*, 194.

29. "Seneca Falls Convention," in *HWS*, 1:68.

30. Ibid.

31. ECS, *Revolution*, September 17, 1868, 161–62, in Wellman, *Seneca Falls*, 192.

32. *Report of the Women's Rights Convention*, 5, in Wellman, *Seneca Falls*, 193.

33. Laura Curtis Bullard, "Elizabeth Cady Stanton," *Our Famous Women* (Hartford, 1888), 613–14 in Wellman, *Seneca Falls*, 193.

CHAPTER FIVE

The Seneca Falls Convention

On the morning of Wednesday, July 19, 1848, as the cooler temperatures of the night yielded to the rising sun, nineteen-year-old Charlotte Woodward climbed aboard her family's wagon with a half dozen of her friends and headed four miles east to Seneca Falls. Lucretia Mott and her sister Martha Coffin Wright boarded a train in Auburn for the fifteen-mile trip west. Wright was normally witty and vivacious, but at six months pregnant with her seventh child, she felt "very stupid & dispirited" at "the prospect of having more Wrights than I wanted."[1] James Mott stayed behind, feeling unwell. So did their daughter Martha, who "thinks she is not quite enough of a reformer to attend such a Convention," Mott wrote in a note to Stanton, although Mott really suspected that Martha simply wanted to spend the day with her cousins.[2]

In an age of reform, when extraordinary individuals and small groups were attempting to alter fundamental social practices, this was the first convention to address women's rights. By the summer of 1848, temperance groups were revealing the dangers of liquor and would ultimately bring about a dramatic decline in per capita consumption, abolitionists had for years exposed the cruelty of slavery and would soon see its end, and education reformers were convincing governments to develop public school systems that would one day become standard across the nation. But the organized effort to alter the position of women in society, which would require change so deep, so unsettling to religion, to the economy, to the fundamental rhythms of everyday life, was just beginning.

Stanton, nervous about the day ahead, gathered her papers and walked to the center of Seneca Falls, accompanied by her sister Harriet and eleven-year-old nephew Daniel. Along the way, they passed a half-dozen mills lining the riverbank, a string of solid, brick shops, and a hotel that once hosted the Revolutionary War hero General Lafayette. From a distance, they saw a small crowd gathered in front of the Wesleyan

Methodist Church, locked out of the building. Stanton sent Daniel through an open window to unlock the door. Once inside, Stanton spread her papers and law books on a table at the front of the church, while Mott quietly watched people enter and settle into the wooden pews. The advertisement for the Convention had invited only women to the first day, but when over three dozen men arrived unexpectedly, the leaders conferred and agreed to let them stay. Mary Ann M'Clintock and her four daughters joined Mott and Stanton at the front. The sanctuary was already beginning to warm.

At 11 A.M., an hour after the appointed commencement, Stanton called the Convention to order. The time had come for women to discuss their rights, she said. Mott urged the women to "throw aside the trammels of education" and engage in debate. Stanton then read aloud the Declaration of Sentiments. "We hold these truths to be self-evident; that all men and women are created equal," Stanton began. Women had suffered patiently under an unjust government, and it was time to demand equality. Stanton read the list of "repeated injuries and usurpations on the part of man toward woman, having in direct object the establishment of an absolute tyranny over her." Man has made a married woman "civilly dead," giving himself rights to her property and wages, and framing divorce laws to his advantage. He has monopolized nearly all profitable jobs and left her to underpaid occupations. He has created a double standard "by which moral delinquencies which exclude women from society, are not only tolerated, but deemed of little account in man." He claims all religious authority and subordinates women in the churches. He has used all means to undermine her confidence, "to lessen her self-respect," and make her a willing dependent.[3] When Stanton finished reading, one woman in the audience asked her to read the entire Declaration again, one paragraph at a time. Stanton did so, pausing for discussion and revision. After two and a half hours, the temperature nearing ninety degrees, the Convention took a break. People milled around their horses and carriages, eating packed lunches in the shade.

In the afternoon, the women discussed the resolutions—eleven claims to greater social, religious, and economic power. Laws that subordinate women are "of no force or authority"; those contrary to the happiness of women are invalid; a single moral standard should apply to both men and women.[4] The most audacious resolution—calling for the "sacred right to the elective franchise"—met no reported opposition. At the end, volunteers moved about the sanctuary gathering signatures. That evening, under the gentle illumination of candlelight, Mott reviewed developments in the abolition, temperance, and peace movements in a sanctuary mostly filled with local people. Progress was gradual, Mott said, but she welcomed this new movement and hoped it "would soon assume a grandeur and dignity worthy of its importance."[5]

At home that night, Stanton reflected on the first day of the Convention, elated and somewhat surprised that she could ably present her views. The lively debate had been civil, the Declaration was well received, and Mott's speech had been "one of the most eloquent, logical and philosophical discourses we ever listened to," the editor of a local paper wrote.[6]

On the second day, when men were invited to attend, nearly three hundred people filled the main floor and spread into the upper gallery. Frederick Douglass arrived from Rochester, though still recovering from having his tonsils removed. When he first met Stanton in Boston, she had convinced him of "the wisdom & truth of the new gospel of woman's rights," Douglass later recalled.[7] Three husbands of organizers were there: Thomas M'Clintock, Richard Hunt, and James Mott—but not Henry Stanton, who was several hours away giving a speech on abolition. Ansel Bascom, a wealthy Seneca Falls resident who owned a woolen mill and a block of commercial buildings in the center of town, sat with his daughter Mary. He was known for embracing nascent reform movements, including temperance, homeopathic medicine, and abolition, and once lent his orchard for a talk by abolitionist Abby Kelley after local pastors barred her from their churches. Bascom was a "fine leader" and "a good talker," some in town said, but others thought him "anxious to dig up the hatchet" or just plain "obnoxious."[8]

Unsettled by the larger mixed audience of men and women, Stanton and Mott asked James Mott to preside over the second day of the Convention. His earnest demeanor added a palpable dignity to the proceedings. Stanton read aloud the Declaration of Sentiments as revised the day before. Several men and women spoke in support and, after a few alterations, the Convention adopted it without dissent. About a third of those present added their signatures—sixty-eight women signed the Declaration itself and thirty-two men signed a supporting document "in favor of the movement."[9] Most of the signatories were from Seneca Falls or nearby Waterloo and were already active in other reform movements. Eighty-one-year-old Catherine Shaw was the eldest and fourteen-year-old Susan Quinn, the daughter of an illiterate Irish immigrant, was the youngest. Charlotte Woodward signed and was the only one there known to live long enough to see women get the right to vote. In the afternoon, the reading of the resolutions stirred "spirited and spicy" debate, but Stanton stood her ground, arguing that to seek equality women must be able to shape legislation, and Douglass strongly defended her.[10] In the end, a majority of those present voted to support the resolutions, including the demand for suffrage.

That evening, with the sanctuary still warm from the summer heat, Mott offered a final resolution calling on men and women to join in "zealous and untiring effort" to end the male monopoly of religious authority and to open all facets of commerce to women.[11] All agreed to the resolution. With the business portion of the Convention behind them and the many battles for women's rights ahead, Mott ended the gathering with a well-received speech on the nature of reform.

Back home in Rochester, Douglass lauded the Convention's "brilliant talents and excellent dispositions" in his *North Star* anti-slavery newspaper. But prejudice was deep, he warned. "A discussion of the rights of animals would be regarded with far more complacency by many of what are called the *wise* and *good* of our land, than would be a discussion of the rights of woman."[12] Nathan Milliken, editor of the local *Seneca County Courier*, who had signed in support of the Declaration of Sentiments, predicted "disapprobation and contempt." The resolutions were "startling to those who are wedded to the present usages and laws of society," he told his readers.[13] Horace Greeley, editor of the *New York Tribune*, the most influential newspaper in the country, gave a tepid endorsement. Women's rights reformers made "novel" assumptions when they opposed deeply held habits, he wrote. They might have been "unwise and mistaken," and it was "easy to be smart, to be droll, to be facetious in opposition," but they made an "assertion of a natural right and as much must be conceded."[14]

Nearly half of the newspapers that reported on the Convention were critical. The *Syracuse Recorder* declared it foolish, while the *New York Herald* mocked the notion that women think themselves qualified for public office. "A pretty girl is equal to ten thousand men, and the mother is, next to God, all-powerful," a Philadelphia paper asserted. "The ladies of Philadelphia, therefore, under the influence of the most serious, 'sober second thoughts,' are resolved to maintain their rights as Wives, Belles, Virgins and Mothers, and not as Women."[15] Other papers grappled with the profound implications of women's equality. The Albany *Mechanic's Advocate* accused women at the Convention of neglecting their homes while seeking "fundamental changes in the public and private, civil and religious, moral and social relations of the sexes, of life, and of the Government." All true women "will instantly feel that this is unwomanly."[16] Several pastors had attended the Convention in silence and later denounced it from their pulpits. One friend of Lucretia Mott told her that a minister in his Massachusetts town called Mott "the worst of women."[17] As public backlash intensified, several women withdrew their signatures from the Declaration, including Harriet Eaton, Stanton's sister, under pressure from her husband and father.

Stanton wrote letters to several newspapers to defend the Convention. They had not met "to discuss fashions, customs, or dress, the rights of man or the propriety of the sexes changing positions," she wrote, "but simply our own inalienable rights, our duties, our true sphere."[18] Nor did they attack religion. The Bible would be a "great Charter of Human Rights" except that it was "too often perverted by narrow, bigoted, sectarian teachers as to favor all kinds of oppression, and to degrade and crush humanity itself."[19] In private, Stanton welcomed the newspaper coverage, even if negative. "It will start women thinking, and men too," she wrote Mott. Progress begins when people first think of an issue. "The great fault of mankind is that it will not think."[20]

Two weeks later, many of the western New Yorkers who had attended the Convention at Seneca Falls arranged a second women's rights convention in Rochester. Mott, Stanton, the M'Clintocks, and Douglass were there. This time, the Convention named a woman president—Abigail Bush, an abolitionist mother of four. Bush was nervous, and some feared that an inexperienced woman would confirm prejudice against women leaders. But Bush ably guided the Convention. When shouts of "louder, louder" came from some who struggled to hear several nervous women speak, Bush gently reminded them that "we present ourselves here before you, as an oppressed class, with trembling frames and faltering tongues." She asked them to "bear with our weakness now in the infancy of the movement."[21]

As she had done at Seneca Falls, Stanton read aloud the Declaration of Sentiments and asked anyone with objections to speak up and not hold their criticisms until after the Convention. When a woman wondered whether a husband and wife with differing political opinions might damage their marriage, Mott replied that Quakers had long considered women equal and "none of the results so much dreaded have occurred."[22] When a man spoke of women as "the better half," Mott warned of flattery.[23] Douglass, too, answered mild criticisms. When some complained of women barely being able to survive on their earnings, Stanton offered a resolution to condemn low wages for women and spoke of "the necessity of reforms commencing at home."[24] Yet momentum for women's rights stalled after Rochester. Mott could not secure a Philadelphia venue willing to house a women's rights meeting and found most women too timid to speak in public. Paulina Wright, a New York reformer, blamed women, who "hug their chains because they hate responsibility."[25]

Susan B. Anthony, a respected teacher in Canajoharie, New York, a small town 150 miles east of Rochester, heard about the Convention in letters from her parents who attended and from her friend, Abigail Bush, who had presided at the meeting. Bush described her anxiety leading the Convention and the kindness of Mott, who afterward gently held her and thanked her. "I cried like a baby" when it was over, she wrote to Anthony.[26] Anthony was sympathetic to the new movement, but too absorbed by her teaching to get involved.

Notes

1. Martha Coffin Wright to LM, October 1, 1848, Garrison Family Papers, SCA in Sherry H. Penney and James D. Livingston, *A Very Dangerous Woman: Martha Wright and Women's Rights* (Amherst: University of Massachusetts Press, 2004), 2.

2. LM to ECS, July 16, 1848, in *SP*, 1:163.

3. "Women's Rights Convention Held at Seneca Falls," July 19–20, 1848, in *SP*, 1:75–82.

4. Ibid., 77.

5. *Seneca County Courier*, July 21, 1848, in Wellman, *Seneca Falls*, 196–97.

6. *Auburn National Reformer*, August 3, 1848, in ECS Papers, LC, in *SP*, 1:84.

7. Frederick Douglass to ECS, October 22, 1885, in Philip S. Foner, ed., *Frederick Douglass on Women's Rights* (Westport, CT: Greenwood Press, 1976), 163, in Wellman, *Seneca Falls*, 161.

8. Lum, typescript, SFHS, 11, in Wellman, *Seneca Falls*, 121.

9. *SP*, 1:82.

10. *Seneca County Courier*, July 21, 1848, in Wellman, *Seneca Falls*, 202.

11. *Seneca Falls Report* in *SP*, 1:83.

12. *The North Star*, July 28, 1840, in *HWS*, 1:74.

13. Nathan Millikan, *Seneca County Courier*, July 21, 1848, in Wellman, *Seneca Falls*, 208.

14. Geoffrey C. Ward and Kenneth Burns, *Not for Ourselves Alone: The Story of Elizabeth Cady Stanton and Susan B. Anthony* (New York: Knopf, 1999), 41.

15. *Public Ledger and Daily Transcript*, n.d., in *HWS*, 1:804.

16. *Mechanic's Advocate*, n.d., in *HWS*, 1:804.

17. LM to ECS, October 3, 1848, in Beverly Wilson Palmer, ed., *Selected Letters of Lucretia Coffin Mott* (Urbana; Chicago: University of Illinois Press, 2002), 173.

18. ECS to George G. Cooper, Editor of *The National Reformer*, September 14, 1848, in Stanton and Blatch, *Letters*, 2:19.

19. Ward and Burns, *Ourselves*, 42.

20. ECS to LM, September 30, 1848, in Stanton and Blatch, *Letters*, 2:21.

21. The Rochester Convention, August 2, 1848, in *HWS*, 1:76.

22. Ibid., 1:79.

23. "Proceedings of the Women's Rights Convention Held at the Unitarian Church, Rochester, NY, August 2, 1848," Revised by Mrs. Amy Post, 4, in Susan B. Anthony Scrapbook, Rare Books Room, LC (hereafter noted as *SBASB*), 1:1–2.

24. *The National Reporter*, August 17, 1848, in *SBASB*, 1:1.

25. Paulina Wright to ECS, September 19, 1848, in Sally McMillen, *Seneca Falls and the Origins of the Women's Rights Movement* (New York: Oxford University Press, 2009), 102.

26. Abigail Bush to SBA, April 14, 1848, Gannett Papers, URL, in Kathleen L. Barry, ed., *Susan B. Anthony: A Biography* (New York: New York University Press, 1988), 62.

CHAPTER SIX

Lucy Stone

In the summer of 1848, the same summer as the Seneca Falls Convention, twenty-nine-year-old Lucy Stone visited Horticultural Hall at the north end of Boston Common to view one of the most popular works of art ever exhibited in the United States—*The Greek Slave* by Hiram Powers. It was a life-size marble statue depicting a Greek woman sold into slavery during the Greek War of Independence from the Ottoman Turks. The slave's hands were bound by chains, her face turned to the side with a sad, pensive expression—and she was naked. Powers grew up in New England and knew American squeamishness with nudity, but he believed his statue would not offend. He fashioned the statue's hands to obscure the lower torso, left the pubic area undefined, and chiseled it from pristine white Seravezza marble. The exhibit's pamphlet contained an endorsement from a minister who said the demure pose and pained expression protected the slave from sexual ogling. "Surely, there is no indecency in the attitude and expressions of my Slave," Powers told his agent.[1]

Still, *The Greek Slave* ignited moral panic as it was displayed across the nation. "Our eastern cities are growing in impurity, and so is the great west," a prominent group of Ohio ministers warned as the statue headed their way. "Would Christ or his apostles have patronized such an exhibition?"[2] Some demanded separate viewing hours for men and women, and the *Christian Advocate and Journal* advised that the statue be exhibited in a hall with no doors or windows.[3] The crowds came anyway—more than a hundred thousand Americans in over a dozen cities paid the sizable admission fee of twenty-five cents to view it. In New York City, it was the highest-grossing art exhibit in its history. Its implicit critique of slavery in the American South stirred controversy.

But Stone saw something different as she circled the statue in quiet contemplation. For her, the suffering slave "with fettered hands and half averted face" represented "millions of women who must be freed."[4] That same night, when she met with leaders of the American Anti-Slavery Society who employed her as an abolition lecturer, Stone shed "hot tears" as she told them that she wanted to work for women's rights.[5] Her supervisor Rev. Samuel May listened with sympathy but reminded her that the Society paid her six dollars a week to speak for abolition. "I was a woman before I was an abolitionist," Stone replied, "I must speak for the women."[6] Reluctant to lose a talented speaker, May offered a compromise—to pay Stone four dollars to lecture on abolition on the weekends and let her speak for women during the rest of the week. Stone agreed and became the first paid lecturer for women's rights, joining Mott and Stanton as a major force in the new movement.

Stone came from a long line of rebellious, patriotic fighters proudly remembered in family lore. Her grandfather died fighting the French in the Battle of Quebec, and her father was a captain during the American Revolution and a leader of Shay's Rebellion against high taxes in the 1780s. Her parents, Francis and Hannah Stone, raised their nine children with ceaseless hard work on their 145-acre farm seventy miles west of Boston. Her father was stern and stingy; Hannah pilfered from his wallet and sold homemade cheese in secret to pay for household goods. "There was only one will in our home," Stone later reflected, "and that was my father's."[7] When Stone was born, her mother was sorry to have given birth to a girl. "A woman's life is so hard," she said.[8]

Stone resented women's subordination even as a girl. After she and her sisters learned to read and write—enough to perform the tasks of a farm wife—her father refused to pay for more schooling. Stone, however, was determined to go to college like her brothers. She gathered berries and nuts from local woods to pay for schoolbooks and, at sixteen, taught school in a nearby town for a dollar a week and room and board with a family—half the pay of a male teacher. Two epiphanies during her youth quickened her resentment. Stone belonged to a sewing circle that made clothes for male missionaries. But while sewing and listening to Mary Lyon appeal for funds to establish a school for women, she put down the shirt she was sewing, and vowed that, from then on, she would sew only for women. A few years later, while sitting in the balcony of her church, listening to the reading of a pastoral letter that reprimanded the Grimké sisters for their public speaking, Stone bristled with resentment, poking her cousin's ribs until they were black and blue. The letter intended to silence women made Stone more determined to speak.

After saving her teaching salary for several years, Stone set off for Oberlin College in August 1843. She traveled alone—by train to Buffalo, across

Lake Erie on a schooner, sleeping with other women at one end of the deck while an elderly woman kept an eye on her luggage, and by stagecoach from Cleveland to Oberlin—all at the cost of more than a month's salary. The Oberlin campus was a half-dozen buildings connected by a boardwalk, all situated on a fenced, twelve-acre green, and a lone church. Campus life was pious and austere, designed to elevate students' sensibilities. Students were to avoid tea, coffee, alcohol, and spicy foods; to abstain from playing cards, gambling, and arguing; and to perform two hours of manual labor per day to reduce costs.

Oberlin's admission of black students and women was progressive for the age, but Stone thought the college had not gone far enough. She challenged administrators and faculty members almost as soon as she arrived. After confronting the faculty board for paying women student teachers less than men in its Preparatory School, the board changed its policy. When the ladies board called her to account for removing her bonnet during a sermon, Stone claimed she suffered from severe headaches. The board permitted her to be bareheaded in church so long as she sat in the last row. Stone supported William Lloyd Garrison's demand for immediate emancipation and encouraged "Come-outers"—parishioners who left church in the middle of a sermon, slamming the door as they exited to protest their church's tolerance of slavery. Some quietly admired Stone's independence; others saw her as a troublemaker. "They hate Garrison and women's rights," Stone wrote. "I love both, and often find myself at swords' points with them."[9]

In Stone's third year at Oberlin, a new student who later became a pioneer in the women's rights movement and a lifelong friend arrived: Antoinette Brown. Brown had wanted to study theology since childhood after hearing a sermon by Oberlin president Charles Grandison Finney. Like Stone, Brown taught school for years to pay for college and arrived in Oberlin in 1846 at the age of twenty-one. Brown first heard about Stone in the stagecoach on her way to college, when an Oberlin trustee advised her to avoid Lucy Stone. She was a "very bright girl," he said, "but eccentric, a Garrisonian, and much too talkative on the subject of woman's rights."[10] Brown first noticed Stone in the dining hall, debating three men sitting across the table "with much earnestness and with very positive convictions." She was surprised that Stone looked so young, about sixteen, "a small round-faced girl in a neat calico frock, her hair cut round at the neck and hanging just above the neatest, whitest, turned-down collar—which by the way she always washed and ironed herself."[11]

Stone and Brown soon formed a protest partnership. They challenged a school policy that permitted only men to debate in public. When a sympathetic professor permitted them to debate each other, a novelty that drew a large crowd, Oberlin leaders forbade any further public debates by women. They then met in nearby woods to debate in secret, arriving by separate routes to avoid suspicion and posting a guard on the perimeter. Their most formidable challenge was convincing Oberlin to grant Brown a degree in theology. Oberlin professors opposed women in the ministry, and the college would not give a theology degree to a woman. "You can never do it," Stone told Brown one evening. "I am going to do it," Brown replied.[12] When Brown's professor assigned her a paper on scriptural passages that silenced women in the church, she wrote a defiant essay. Stone's protests continued until her final moments on campus. By tradition, each graduating class selected a few students to read their own essays at graduation. But to preserve women's modesty, men were required to read women's essays. When Stone's fellow students selected her to speak at their graduation in 1847, she declined to participate unless she could read her own essay. The faculty refused. With the exception of one woman and two men, other students selected to speak at graduation supported Stone by also refusing to write essays. Stone sat in silent protest at the graduation ceremony.

After college, Stone became an itinerant speaker for the Massachusetts Anti-Slavery Society. She was harassed and hampered as she traveled from town to town. Many handbills she posted to advertise abolition talks were pulled down. Some who promised her help never showed for fear of ostracism. One listener sprayed her with a hose in midwinter. Another hit her in the head with a Bible. When someone threw an egg at her through an open window as she

Lucy Stone, a well-known orator, suffragist, and abolitionist from Massachusetts. In 1847, Stone became the first woman from her state to graduate with a college degree. (Library of Congress)

was speaking, she wiped it off her dress without missing a beat. "If you could as easily remove from your minds the seeds of truth which I have sown in them tonight as I can this stain from my garment," she told the audience, "I should feel that my work here had been in vain. You cannot."[13] Stone's parents admonished that her job as a speaker "would disgrace the whole family," and her mother urged her to marry, have children, and confine her abolitionist proselytizing to her neighborhood. "No, Mother," Stone replied, "if in this hour of the world's need I should refuse to lend my aid, however small it may be, I should have no rights to think of myself a Christian, and I should forever despise Lucy Stone."[14] Despite her view that she was doing her Christian duty, leaders of her own church expelled her without warning, wounding her deeply, and ignoring her pleas for an opportunity to explain her actions.

After viewing *The Greek Slave* statue in the summer of 1848, Stone lectured on women's rights for two years. She often drew large audiences and learned that a small fee "kept out the stampers and the hoodlums, and in no wise prevented those who were interested from attending."[15] Many did not know what to expect from a woman speaker, and unfavorable rumors abounded. An Indiana newspaper reported that Stone was seen "in the back room smoking a cigar and swearing like a trooper!"[16] "You she-hyena," another paper screamed, "don't you come here."[17] The inhabitants of one town expected a big, manly woman wearing heavy boots and were surprised to see a small, refined woman in a black satin dress with a touch of white lace at the neck. Through her talks, Stone hoped to raise expectations, to create a tension between how women see their lives and how they should be. After lectures, women often approached Stone to share their struggles in private.

In the spring of 1850, Stone and ten other delegates to the American Anti-Slavery Society Convention thought it was time to hold a national meeting for women's rights, one that would attract high-profile reformers. They decided to hold it in Worcester, a city forty miles west of Boston that was a transportation hub for railroads and stagecoaches. Stone and Paulina Wright Davis, a wealthy Rhode Island reformer, were tasked with organizing the convention.

Davis issued the call for the Worcester Convention. "Come, then, to this Convention. It is your duty, if you are worthy of your age and country," it said.[18] Make women's rights one of the "hundred forms of effort for the world's redemption from the sins and sufferings which oppress it."[19] Davis appealed for conciliatory relations between men and women. The last two regional women's rights conventions had exhibited some bitterness toward men, she thought. "The sexes should not, for any reason or by any chance, take hostile attitudes towards each other," she wrote.[20] Eighty-nine people, including dozens of men and dignitaries from a variety of reform movements, signed the call: William Lloyd Garrison, Wendell Phillips, William Henry Channing, Bronson Alcott, Lucretia Mott, and many more. But would people come? Ralph Waldo Emerson, the grand intellectual of the age who championed a variety of reforms, declined. "A public convention called by women is not very agreeable to me," he wrote Davis in his reply. He did not want women to enter politics and hoped that women themselves would not want to do so either. The best women "would decline such privileges if offered," he added.[21]

Davis wanted Margaret Fuller to head the women's rights movement and wrote to Fuller in Europe, inviting her to return home for the Convention.[22] Forty-year-old Fuller had become, in absentia, a leading intellect on women's rights. In her book *Woman in the Nineteenth Century*, Fuller encouraged women to "search their own experience and intuitions" and to develop their capacity for leadership to breach boundaries that restrain women.[23] Fuller drew upon mythical and historical women to inspire female autonomy: Isis, the ancient Egyptian Goddess of wisdom, marriage, and health; Minerva, the Roman Goddess of wisdom; the Muse, a Goddess of inspiration for the arts and literature with the power of intuition. Women and men vary more as individuals than by sex, she believed. "There is no wholly masculine man, no purely feminine woman." Courage and determination are no more manly than womanly. Men support the subordination of women because they want "to be lord in a little world, to be superior at least over one," and cling to their advantage "under the slavery of habit."[24] Fuller's audacity shocked readers. "It is a *bold* book," wrote Lydia Maria Child, Fuller's childhood friend and a noted author. "I should not have dared to have written some things in it, though it would have been safer for me, being married."[25] Edgar Allan Poe said it was a book only a "few women in the country could have written, and no woman in the country would have published."[26] But Fuller erred, he wrote, in thinking that she represented her sex.

In July 1850, after four years in Europe, Fuller sailed home to the United States. She had become the *New York Tribune*'s first female foreign reporter, interviewing the likes of George Sand, William Wordsworth, and Thomas Carlyle for the handsome salary of $500 a year. In Rome, she fell in love and bore a son with Giovanni Angelo Ossoli, an Italian marquis. She joined Ossoli in a rebellion to create an Italian Republic, reporting on it for the *Tribune* as she volunteered in a hospital. Fuller sailed home with Ossoli and her son on the *Elizabeth,* a stout wood-hulled merchant ship carrying 150 tons of Carrara marble and a statue of John C. Calhoun. On their last evening on board, anchored a quarter-mile off the coast of Fire Island, New York, the first winds of a hurricane arrived just as passengers settled in for the night. At 2:30 in the morning, the ship's hull slammed into a sand bar. Loose slabs of marble in the hold punctured the hull, and the ship flooded. Passengers took refuge on the forecastle to await the dawn. As the sun rose, people on the beach saw passengers and crew jump overboard, some lashing themselves to planks. Several made it to shore, badly bruised, at least one barely conscious. The ship's contents were strewn in a long trail along the shore—luggage, almonds, juniper berries, oil—along with the body of Fuller's son, Nino. A sailor tenderly laid him out on the beach and covered him with a neckerchief. More flotsam tumbled in—the Ossoli trunk and carpetbag, bolts of silk, oil paintings, woody spines from the ship—but the bodies of Fuller and Count Ossoli were never found. Ralph Waldo Emerson urged Henry David Thoreau to travel to the scene of the disaster to see what he could find. Thoreau combed five miles of shoreline, scanning the beach for any signs, and interviewing those who had witnessed the debacle.[27] "I found the young men playing at dominoes with their hats decked out with the spoils of the drowned," he said, and someone had recovered Count Ossoli's coat.[28] Thoreau tore off a button and returned with it to Massachusetts.

On the same day Margaret Fuller succumbed to the wrath of the hurricane, Lucy Stone stood at her brother Luther's deathbed in Illinois as he suffered his final hours. She had planned to prepare for the Worcester Convention at Davis's comfortable home in Providence. Instead, she cared for her brother, who was dying of typhoid fever, and whose pregnant wife Phebe stayed away for fear of falling ill herself. Stone's brother died shortly after she arrived, and she spent weeks arranging the funeral and settling the estate before heading east in late August with seven-months' pregnant Phebe, making frequent stops for her to rest. In eastern Illinois, less than a hundred miles into the trip, Phebe went into labor and gave birth to a stillborn boy. Stone arranged yet another funeral, comforting her sister-in-law, who had hoped the baby would "renew the sundered tie" to her late husband.[29] In eastern Indiana, Stone herself fell ill with typhoid. For eighteen days, alone in a shabby hotel with broken windows and drafty winds, she drifted in and out of consciousness with "no one to give me a drop of water."[30] Stone and Phebe finally made it back to Stone's home in early October. Weak and exhausted, Stone did not think she would make the

Worcester Convention. "It is a grievous disappointment to me, but can't be helped," she wrote a friend.[31]

Notes

1. Rev. Orville Dewey, "Powers' Statues," *The Union Magazine of Literature and Art* (October 1847): 236.

2. *Western Christian Advocate*, November 29, 1848, in Richard P. Wunder, *Hiram Powers: Vermont Sculptor, 1805–1873*, v. 1 (New York: University of Delaware Press 1991), 233.

3. Ibid., 226.

4. Alice Stone Blackwell, *Lucy Stone: Pioneer of Woman's Rights*, Second Edition (Norwood, MA: Plimpton, 1930), 89.

5. Ibid., 90.

6. Biographical Notes of LS Compiled by Henry Blackwell in BLC, Ctr. 86, in Andrea Moore Kerr, *Lucy Stone: Speaking Out for Equality* (New Brunswick, NJ: Rutgers University Press, 1992), 51–52.

7. Elinor Rice Hays, *Morning Star: A Biography of Lucy Stone*, 1818–1893 (New York: Harcourt, Brace & World, Inc., 1961), 14.

8. Ibid.

9. Ibid., 52.

10. Antoinette Blackwell, "Aunt Nettie's Reminiscences," and Lasser and Merrill, *Friends and Sisters*, 5, in Sally G. McMillen, *Lucy Stone: An Unapologetic Life* (New York: Oxford University Press), 53.

11. Hays, *Morning Star*, 49.

12. Gilson Manuscript, 59, "Antoinette Brown Blackwell, The First Woman Minister," Blackwell Family Papers, SL, Folders 3–14 in Beverly Ann Zink-Sawyer, *From Preachers to Suffragists: Woman's Rights and Religious Conviction in the Lives of Three Nineteenth-Century American Clergywomen* (Louisville, KY: Westminster John Knox Press, 2003), 32.

13. Hays, *Morning Star*, 83.

14. Ibid., 64–65.

15. Ibid., 83.

16. Ibid.

17. Ibid., 93.

18. The "Call" to the Worcester Convention, John F. McClymer, *This High and Holy Moment: The First National Women's Rights Convention, Worcester, 1850*, First Edition (San Diego; London: Cengage Learning, 1999), 68.

19. Ibid., 67.

20. Ibid.

21. Ralph Rusk and Eleanor Tilton, *The Letters of Ralph Waldo Emerson*, 10 vols. (New York: Columbia University Press, 1939–95), 4:229–30, in

L. Gougeon, "Emerson and the Woman Question: The Evolution of His Thought," *New England Quarterly* 71, no. 4 (1998): 575.

22. Stanton, Anthony, and Gage later claim that Davis had asked Fuller to head the Convention, but Von Mehren reports that Davis had only wished her to attend the Convention. There is no evidence of her reply. *HWS*, 1:217; Joan Von Mehren, *Minerva and the Muse: A Life of Margaret Fuller* (Amherst: University of Massachusetts Press, 1994), 339.

23. *Woman in the Nineteenth Century,* v.–vi. in Von Mehren, *Minerva*, 193.

24. *Woman in the Nineteenth Century* (New York: np, 1845) in Eve Kornfeld, *Margaret Fuller: A Brief Biography with Documents*, First Edition (Boston: Bedford/St. Martin's, 1996), 177, 179.

25. Lydia Maria Child to Louisa Loring, February 8, 1845, SL, 219, in Karcher, *Lydia Maria Child*, 226.

26. Edgar Allen Poe, "Sarah Margaret Fuller," in Kornfeld, ed., *Margaret Fuller*, 233.

27. Bayard Taylor, "The Wreck on Fire Island," NYDT, July 23, 1850, 4, in Von Mehren, *Minerva*, 334–36.

28. Colleen Walsh, Harvard Staff Writer, "Uncovering What Thoreau Uncovered: Report on Margaret Fuller's Death Is Acquired by Houghton," July 31, 2015, https://news.harvard.edu/gazette/story/2015/07/uncovering-what-thoreau-uncovered/.

29. LS to Samuel May, July 25, 1850, BLC, in Kerr, *Stone*, 59.

30. Ibid.

31. LS to Samuel May, October 13, 1850, BLC, in Kerr, *Stone*, 59.

CHAPTER SEVEN

Worcester

For Boston physician Harriot Hunt, the first National Women's Rights Convention in Worcester was "a fulfillment of unuttered hopes, of half-formed desires."[1] She knew it would draw non-conformists and dissenters. Several friends warned her not to associate with the "motley crew."[2] But after fifteen years of practicing medicine, she believed women's ailments stemmed largely from their inferior social status. For their own health, and for the good of society, the lot of women must improve.

Non-conformists did come to Worcester. The strident Abby Kelley Foster came with her husband, Stephen Foster, an abolitionist who shared her zeal for reform. They lived near Worcester on a farm where they hosted a steady stream of reformers and people escaping slavery on the Underground Railroad. Abby Price came from Hopedale, a Christian pacifist community twenty miles from Worcester. Antoinette Brown came, three years after completing the requirements for a theology degree at Oberlin—though she and Lucy Stone lost their struggle to get the college to grant her the degree. Brown feared that her religious views would make her "a stranger in a strange land and it would be hard for the people to understand me," she wrote in her acceptance to Paulina Wright Davis's call to attend.[3] But she came anyway, ready to promote religion as an ally to the movement. More people tried to attend the Convention than the third floor of Brinley Hall could hold—over a thousand at one point, most of them men—so many had to be turned away. As the planners had hoped, many there were reformers with national reputations, including Garrison, Phillips, Douglass, Alcott, Mott, Channing, and Rose. Major newspapers from Boston and New York City sent reporters to cover the Convention. Stanton was noticeably absent, deciding to sit out the Convention at home, six months pregnant with her fourth child. Yet she sent a letter of support and a speech to be read in her name.

The audience hushed when Antoinette Brown opened the Convention with a moment of silence to honor the memory of Margaret Fuller. Fuller saw through "the sham and pretenses of society," Brown said, and recognized the "crushed hope, the stifled aspiration which makes so many women's lives sad."[4] Fuller's view of womanhood transcended the false restraints society imposed on women's lives, "something more than the wifely loyalty, the motherly devotion of which every little hamlet furnishes notable examples."[5] Fuller claimed human rights for all, and promoted a prophetic vision of a society in which men and women would be equal in the eyes of the law and in religion.

For two days, the Convention debated the scope of women's rights. What was the true nature of woman, of man, and what was shaped by society? What caused the oppression of women, and what would end it? Paulina Wright Davis said that male dominance was only a phase in historical development, the legacy of a time when men's physical strength provided them an advantage in the struggle to survive in nature. Women's subordination may have been a "temporary necessity," Davis said, but the rough world of the past was giving way, an age of peace emerging, and "the uprising of womanhood is its prophecy and foreshadow."[6] This "radical and universal revolution" would be a long struggle. Old habits die slowly, and traditional attitudes persist just "as the shadows of night stretch far into the morning, sheltered in nooks and valleys from the rising light."[7] Reformers should proceed cautiously. Moving too fast could pervert the cause or provoke a counteraction. History is but "a monument of buried hopes" as revolutions often devolve into insurrections, she said, and religious reformations often substitute "a new error for an old one." Davis appealed for conciliation between men and women. "Harsh judgment and harsh words will neither weaken opposition nor strengthen our hands."[8]

Lucretia Mott was not looking for conciliation. Women must speak the truth, however unpleasant, "with an earnestness and a severity that should make the ears of man tingle for the degraded position in which he has kept woman during so many ages," she said.[9]

Some blamed women's subordination on religion. They claimed it taught a woman to elevate a man's desires and ambitions above her own and compelled her to obey him. Antoinette Brown responded with a learned and earnest scriptural defense that impressed many. When St. Paul said, "Wives submit yourselves to your husbands," he was not condoning patriarchal rule but instead was stating a parable about submitting to a necessary evil, she said. "Thy desire shall be to thy husband and he shall rule over thee" was not a heavenly "endorsement of patriarchal rule, but rather a warning of the sinful state of all humanity."[10]

Many speakers called for better education for women. Broader training would elevate women's wages by removing artificial restrictions that limited them to a few occupations. It would also go a long way to end prostitution, Abby Kelley Foster argued, in a speech that shocked many for its reference to an unspeakable subject. Abby Price called for equal compensation for similar labor. "The washer-woman works as hard in proportion as the wood-sawer, yet she makes not more than half as much by a day's work," she said,

Abby Kelley Foster, a social activist and vocal abolitionist during the 1830s–1870s. Foster worked closely with the American Anti-Slavery Society. (Library of Congress)

adding that the Hopedale Community where she lived made no distinction between the work of men and women.[11] Bronson Alcott challenged the prevailing belief that exercise damaged a woman's health and beauty. A "higher development of physical power," he observed, was fully compatible "with high intellectual and moral power," and the beauty ideal of "white, transparent skin" was an indication of disease more than health.[12]

Everyone at the Worcester Convention agreed that women were artificially restricted, but they differed on the nature of womanhood. Many believed women possessed a distinctive nature, what some called "true womanhood," and that the sexes were different, but equal. "Nature does not teach that men and women are unequal, but only that they are unlike," Davis said.[13] Abby Price called it "co-equality."[14] Some there claimed that women were more ethical than men—more compassionate, more refined. Elevate woman in society and "charity, morality, and every other humanizing sympathy in principle would flow from her into its essence and purity," Ernestine Potowski Rose asserted to loud applause.[15] Rev. William Henry Channing was so confident in women's moral superiority that he

proposed an annual Congress of Women to "make their highest sentiments bear on the evils of war, of slavery, and on the interests of power
and freedom."[16]

Abby Kelley Foster flatly rejected the concept of separate spheres for
the sexes. Boys and girls should be educated together, and social distinctions between men and women should be eliminated. When she suggested that a woman was as qualified as a man to be president, the
audience applauded, but her belief that all gender distinctions should be
abolished was too controversial even for this group.

Some worried about the social costs of women's equality. Would
women abandon the home and become too "mannish"?[17] Abby Price recommended that only mature women who had been good homemakers
should be active in worldly affairs. Even with political rights we "will
attend to our previous home duties faithfully, cheerfully, but we must do
it voluntarily."[18] Stanton, speaking outside the Convention, said neither
parent should seek political office while children are in the home. "Children need the watchful care and wise teachings of fathers as well as of
mothers," she said. In an appeal that echoed her own life experience with
an absent husband, Stanton advised that "no man should give up his profitable business, leave his wife and children month after month, and year
after year, and make his home less for any false ideas of patriotism, for
any vain love of display or ambition for fame and distinction."[19]

Wendell Phillips partially blamed women for their subordination, since
they helped shape public morals but did little to alter them. Men are not
natural tyrants, he said, but simply perpetuate inherited injustice. "Very
few men get beyond the smoke of their father's cabins."[20] Ernestine
Potowski Rose agreed, claiming the greatest hurdle she encountered was
from women who believed they *were* inferior to men.

"It strikes me, Madam President, that Rose has made a better apology
for man than he could make for himself," Mott said, prompting laughter
from the audience. "Woman is crushed, but nobody is to blame; it is circumstance that have crushed her. So the poor slave. He is crushed, but
nobody crushed him. It just happened so," she mocked. "It is an abstract
evil, that's all." Women do not promise to "love, honor and obey," Mott
said, but only assent when the priest asks her.[21] The audience laughed
again. Submission should not be mistaken for consent, Abby Kelley
agreed. A slave standing next to his master will attest to his happy and
contented state for fear of the whip. So it is with a woman, who shrinks
from displeasing "her lord and master."[22]

Frederick Douglass urged women not to wait for their rights but to
seize them, just as he had done as a black man, though it meant he had

been forcibly ejected from train cars and boat cabins, and had been physically attacked. Claiming wears down the opposition. He also warned against "the greatest weapon that will be used against us,"—ridicule. Because arguments for women's rights are "invulnerable," opponents would use mockery, just as they had after the Seneca Falls Convention two years prior.[23]

More than a thousand people packed Brinley Hall for the final meeting, some leaning in the doors to hear speakers exhort women to action. To better society, Channing encouraged women to use their "pure and elevating influence."[24] Sarah Tyndale, a successful merchant of fine china, encouraged women to pursue business. Mountains of opposition lay ahead, Mott said, and they should prepare. "Mighty powers are at work," she said, "and who shall stay them?"[25] Lucy Stone, still weak from her illness, attended the Convention but was quiet until the end. She rose and spoke with her trademark simplicity. Before the Convention, she had worried that only a few would attend, mostly the familiar faces seeking women's rights. Now, she rejoiced at its wider appeal. Reformers should petition legislatures for suffrage and property rights to make woman "the coequal and helpmate of Man in all the interests, and perils and enjoyments of human life," she said. A woman's gravestone, she ended to thunderous applause, should indicate more than "she was the 'relict' of somebody."[26]

The Worcester Convention raised the call for women's rights to a higher level. The tentative tone of Seneca Falls was gone. Abby Kelley Foster declared that she had come not to ask for rights, "but to demand them; not to get down on my knees and beg for them, but to claim them."[27] The Convention attracted a prominent and diverse audience that treated the subject with seriousness and set the parameters of debate for the coming decades. The audience left with a heightened awareness and determination to act as they "seemed to have caught the spirit of the speakers," the *New York Tribune* reported.[28] Harriot Hunt, the Boston physician who had held such high hopes for the Worcester Convention, went home elated. It was "the first national historic act of woman to ask the why and wherefore of her political nonentity in this glorious republic," she wrote. "It was the voice of liberty struggling for utterance."[29]

National newspapers magnified the Convention's influence. Some reporting was critical. "The Worcester Fanatics—Progress of Socialism, Abolition, and Infidelity," the *New York Herald* wrote.[30] But the *New York Tribune*'s lengthy, positive reports on the debates reached more than fifty thousand subscribers across the nation. Antoinette Brown, the *Tribune* reported, was "an ingenious theologian, a good scholar, an easy speaker, and her spirit was truly religious and modest."[31]

Eight hundred miles west on the Michigan frontier, fifteen-year-old Olympia Brown listened as her parents read aloud the *Tribune* account of the Convention. "The speeches stirred my soul; the names of the participants loomed up before me as the names of great heroes often inspire young boys," she later wrote. "They seemed to me like prophets of a better time."[32] Across the Atlantic, Harriet Taylor, a British thinker and wife of prominent Member of Parliament John Stuart Mill, read the *Tribune's* reports and hoped that Great Britain would follow the American lead. She predicted that the "organized agitation on a new question" at Worcester would become one of the most important movements of the future.[33]

Notes

1. Harriot K. Hunt, *Glances and Glimpses; Or Fifty Years Social, Including Twenty Years Professional Life*, Reprint of the 1856 Edition by John P. Jewett and Co. Cleveland, OH 1856 (Cambridge: Source Book Press, n.d.), 250.

2. Ibid.

3. HB to LS, August 13, 1850, Blackwell Family Papers, Schlesinger Church Library, folder 26, in Zink-Sawyer, *From Preachers to Suffragists*, 27.

4. Olympia Brown, "On Margaret Fuller," in Dana Greene, ed., *Suffrage and Religious Principle: Speeches and Writings of Olympia Brown* (Metuchen, London: Scarecrow Press, 1986), 57.

5. Ibid., 55.

6. *The Proceedings of the Woman's Convention, Held at Worcester, 1850*, October 23–24, 1850, in McClymer, *This High and Holy Moment*, 76 (hereafter cited as *Worcester Proceedings*).

7. Ibid., 79.

8. Ibid., 78.

9. "Women's Rights Convention at Worcester, Mass," *New York Tribune*, October 24, 1850, in McClymer, *This High and Holy Moment*, 84.

10. *New York Tribune*, October 24, 1850, in McClymer, *This High and Holy Moment*, 134.

11. *Worcester Proceedings*, 92.

12. *New York Tribune*, October 26, 1850, in McClymer, *This High and Holy Moment*, 140.

13. *Worcester Proceedings*, 78.

14. Ibid., 89.

15. *Boston Daily Mail*, October 24, 1850, in McClymer, *This High and Holy Moment*, 107.

16. *New York Tribune*, October 25, 1850, in McClymer, *This High and Holy Moment*, 112.

17. Ibid.

18. *Worcester Proceedings*, 99.

19. ECS to Worcester Convention, October 20, 1850, in McClymer, *This High and Holy Moment*, 107, 125.

20. *Worcester Proceedings*, 124.

21. *New York Tribune*, October 25, 1850, in McClymer, *This High and Holy Moment*, 114.

22. *New York Herald*, October 25, 1850, in McClymer, *This High and Holy Moment*, 116.

23. *New York Tribune*, October 26, 1850, in McClymer, *This High and Holy Moment*, 140.

24. Ibid., 148.

25. Ibid.,149.

26. Ibid.

27. *New York Herald*, October 25, 1850, in McClymer, *This High and Holy Moment*, 104.

28. *New York Tribune*, October 24, 1850, in McClymer, *This High and Holy Moment*, 103.

29. Hunt, *Glances*, 254.

30. *New York Herald*, October 29, 1850, 4, in McClymer, *This High and Holy Moment*, 154–55.

31. *New York Tribune*, October 24, 1850, in McClymer, *This High and Holy Moment*, 154–55, 134.

32. Olympia Brown, *Acquaintances*, 9, in Zink-Sawyer, *From Preachers to Suffragists*, 44–45.

33. "Enfranchisement of Women," reprinted from the *Westminster and Foreign Quarterly Review* for July 1851, in McClymer, *This High and Holy Moment*, 180.

CHAPTER EIGHT

Sojourner Truth

In May 1851, in a small stone church in Akron, Ohio, with a crowd so large that latecomers had to sit on the steps of the pulpit, a vibrant voice for women's rights came forth. She possessed neither the family heritage of Elizabeth Cady Stanton nor the college education of Lucy Stone. She was, in fact, illiterate. But when forty-four-year-old Sojourner Truth walked to the front of the gathering, she claimed a dignity her society did not readily grant. She was tall—six feet by most estimates, with broad shoulders and arms made strong by decades of toil. And, as she spoke in her deep, resonant voice about women's subordination, she projected an authenticity of experience that no other women's right speaker conveyed.

Truth spent the first thirty years of her life enslaved in the Hudson River Valley ninety miles north of New York City. Her parents, James and Elizabeth Baumfree, named her Isabella, or "Belle," as she came to be known.[1] At an early age she faced the trauma that follows from having little control over one's life. At nine, she was sold away and whipped for the first time. At fifteen, her owner prevented her from marrying the man she loved, though she eventually wed another man and bore five children. Truth once believed slavery to be "right and honorable" and "looked upon her master as a *God*," she wrote in her *Recollections*. She later recalled "with utter astonishment" that she had ever believed in the system that oppressed her.[2] Truth spent much of her adult life trying to shift social consciousness so more people could perceive the subjugation they accepted as normal.

Truth's strong sense of right from wrong, and her determination to enforce the few rights she had, helped shape her destiny. She worked hard—raking and binding hay by day and doing laundry by night—and took pride in her strong character, one that valued truth and despised falsehood. In 1826, when her owner reneged on a promise to free her before the statutory end of slavery in New York, she ran away. And when she learned that her former master sold her five-year-old son Peter to a slaveholder in Alabama in violation of New York state law, she set out to secure his return, even though she had no money and little understanding of the law. She turned to local Quakers, who offered her shelter and advised her to apply to the grand jury for the return of her son. She walked for miles to the county courthouse and lodged her complaint with the "first man she saw of imposing appearance" whom she assumed was the *grand* jury.[3] The actual grand jury listened with solemnity to her words and issued a writ, which she then carried more than eight miles to the local constable, who delivered it to the family of Peter's owner. It took a year, but she won Peter's freedom, although he bore psychological and physical scars inflicted by his cruel owner.

On June 1, 1843, the day of the Pentecost, Truth began her life anew as an itinerant preacher. She left New York City, a place she considered sinful, and wandered through the small towns of New York, Connecticut, and Massachusetts. Along the way, she spoke, sang, and prayed at religious gatherings. When someone offered her lodging, she often stayed for a few days and helped with household chores. She adopted a symbolic name: Sojourner Truth—a traveler who proclaimed the truth of God's message. She believed that the Gospels were influenced by both God and humanity, "that the Spirit of truth spoke in those records, but that the recorders of those truths had intermingled with them ideas and suppositions of their own."[4] She sometimes hired a person to read her passages from the Bible—preferring children, since adults tended to add their own interpretation—and compared "the teachings of the Bible with the witness within."[5]

A year later, Truth joined the Northampton Association of Education and Industry, a transcendentalist utopian experiment founded by abolitionists that did not recognize distinctions in rights based on sex, race, or religion. Truth began making abolitionist speeches, first locally and then, in 1845, to a national anti-slavery convention in New York City, where a newspaper reported she spoke with "good sense and strong feeling."[6] In 1850, Truth joined the British abolitionist George Thompson on a tour through Upstate New York, providing firsthand testimony of the abuses of slavery. Inspired by the success of Frederick Douglass's autobiography, Truth published her own book with the help of a coauthor and then traveled throughout the Northeast to spread the anti-slavery message, often without a prearranged schedule. She also became interested in women's rights as it emerged and attended the Worcester Convention.

Former slave Sojourner Truth, who advocated abolition and women's rights. (Library of Congress)

Truth was one of many black Americans who joined the antebellum women's rights movement. As early as 1832, Maria Stewart, a free woman from Connecticut, spoke against subordination based on race and sex at a public lecture in Boston's Franklin Hall. Though not enslaved, she said, Northern blacks were kept from "rising above the condition of servants."[7] Stewart did not abide by St. Paul's Scriptural admonition that women be silent in the church. "Did Saint Paul but know of our wrongs and deprivations, I presume he would make no objections to our pleading in public for our rights," she said.[8]

Frederick Douglass spoke at the 1848 Seneca Falls Convention, where he urged women to demand the right to vote when it was still controversial. He joined two other black men who attended the second Women's Rights Convention in Rochester a few weeks later. Jermain Loguen served as a vice president of the Convention, and William Nell spoke in praise of the "energies and a rare devotion of women in every good cause."[9] Two sisters from a prominent, well-to-do Philadelphia family, Harriet Forten Purvis and Margaretta Forten, were the principal organizers of the 1854 National Women's Rights Convention in their home city.

Some black proponents of women's rights brought a transnational perspective to the movement. Nancy Prince traveled the world as the wife of a sailor and made her "home" in several countries, including Russia and Jamaica. Living in societies without slavery made living in her home country all the more painful. At the 1854 Philadelphia Convention, Prince said that "she understood woman's wrongs better than woman's rights."[10]

Sarah and Charles Remond, paid lecturers for the American Anti-Slavery Society, attended the 1858 Women's Rights Convention in New York City. Charles had attended the 1840 World Anti-Slavery Convention in London where he joined William Lloyd Garrison in protest when the Convention voted not to seat women delegates.[11] Sarah lectured on abolition in the British Isles and raised funds for the support of freed people after the Civil War. Mary Ann Shadd Cary also participated in the 1858 Women's Rights Convention. She had fled Delaware to the safety of Canada after the Fugitive Slave Act of 1850 threatened the freedom of free blacks. There, Cary established a newspaper, *The Provincial Freeman*, to encourage black emigration from the United States.

When Truth walked to the front of the Ohio Women's Rights Convention in Akron and asked for permission to speak, she brought a lifetime of hard work, self-assertion, and religious devotion. In less than three minutes, "her powerful form, her whole soul, earnest gesture . . . her strong and truthful tones" affected an audience in a way that was "impossible to transfer to . . . paper," a local reporter wrote.[12] With her wide-set eyes, deep mahogany skin, strong mouth and chin, she stood before the audience and argued for women's rights with dry wit and common sense.

Truth said she was as strong as any man, worked as hard in the fields as any man, and ate as much as any man. She reminded the audience that Jesus liked and relied upon women, and that Mary and Martha raised him. If the Savior came from God and was borne by woman, Truth asked, where did that leave man? And if women were responsible for the exile from the Garden of Eden, Truth said, it was time to let them repair the damage. Men seem confused, pressed by the complaints of the slave and women. They would feel much better, Truth said, if they simply gave women some rights as well. Truth made "some of the shrewdest remarks" of the entire Convention, the *New York Tribune* reported.[13]

After the Convention, Truth resumed itinerant preaching for God and for abolition, traveling the next two years in a borrowed buggy on the backroads of Ohio. With no set itinerary, and with faith that God would "always lead to a good place to hold a meeting," Truth would let go of the reins when she came to a fork in the road.

"God," she said, "you drive."[14]

Notes

1. Jacqueline Bernard, *Journey toward Freedom: The Story of Sojourner Truth* (New York: W.W. Norton, 1967), 2.

2. Sojourner Truth, *Narrative of Sojourner Truth: A Bondswoman of Olden Time, with a History of Her Labors and Correspondence Drawn from Her "Book of Life"* (New York, Oxford: Oxford University Press, 1991), 33.

3. Ibid., 47.

4. Ibid., 109.

5. Ibid.

6. *National Anti-Slavery Standard*, May 15, 1845, in Dorothy Sterling, *Ahead of Her Time: Abby Kelley and the Politics of Anti-Slavery* (New York: W. W. Norton, 1991), 212.

7. Maria Stewart in Bert James Loewenberg and Ruth Borgin, eds., *Black Woman in Nineteenth Century American Life: Their Words, Their Thoughts, Their Feelings* (University Park; London: Pennsylvania State University Press, 1976), 192, 198, in Paula J. Giddings, *When and Where I Enter: The Impact of Black Women on Race and Sex in America* (New York: W. Morrow, 1984), 51.

8. Ibid., 53.

9. "Woman's Rights Convention," *North Star*, August 25, 1848, in Martha S. Jones, *All Bound Up Together: The Woman Question in African American Public Culture, 1830–1900* (Chapel Hill: University of North Carolina Press, 2007), 71.

10. *HWS*, 1:384 in Rosalyn Terborg-Penn, *African American Women in the Struggle for the Vote, 1850–1920*, Second Printing (Bloomington: Indiana University Press, 1998), 18.

11. James Oliver Horton and Lois E. Horton, "The Affirmation of Manhood: Black Garrisonians in Antebellum Boston," in Donald M. Jacobs, ed., *Courage and Conscience: Black & White Abolitionists in Boston* (Bloomington: Indiana University Press, 1993), 140.

12. *Antislavery Bugle*, Salem, Ohio, June 21, 1851, in Carleton Mabee, *Sojourner Truth: Slave, Prophet, Legend* (New York; London: New York University Press, 1993), 81.

13. *New York Daily Tribune,* June 3, 1851, 6, in Mabee, *Sojourner Truth*, 78.

14. Lucy N. Colman, *Reminiscences* (Buffalo, NY: H.L. Green, 1891), 65, in Mabee, *Sojourner Truth*, 58.

CHAPTER NINE

Susan B. Anthony

Susan B. Anthony first met Elizabeth Cady Stanton at the age of thirty-one when she visited Seneca Falls in March 1851. She had just listened to speeches by American abolition leader William Lloyd Garrison and British abolitionist George Thompson and was on a street corner talking to her friend Amelia Bloomer when Stanton approached. Anthony's interest in women's rights had grown after reading about the Worcester Convention, and she was excited to meet Stanton. Bloomer introduced her two friends, and after a short exchange, Stanton bade goodbye and left for home. Stanton later recalled that she liked Anthony right away, noting her sincere smile and serious demeanor, and regretted not inviting Anthony home for dinner. It was an inauspicious beginning to a friendship that would last a half century.

In her twenties, Anthony had built a life many young women would envy. She was head teacher at a well-regarded school in Canajoharie, New York, and earned an independent living—though she was still paid far less than a man. Anthony overcame her initial nervousness in the classroom and took pride as her students performed well in annual public examinations. She exuded intelligence and common sense, wore stylish yet modest clothes, and coiled her rich brown hair at the nape of her neck according to the fashion of the times. Suitors accompanied her to town dances and on carriage rides in the countryside, though none impressed her enough to marry. But her life had settled into a predictable routine—comfortable and increasingly meaningless. "I am out of sorts with the world," she wrote to her parents in 1848, "a weariness has come over me."[1] She yearned for something more, something transcendent. "I am tired of theory," she wrote. She wanted to build "a happier and more glorious world."[2]

To those who knew Anthony well, her restlessness of spirit was not a surprise. Her parents Daniel and Lucy, who were Quakers, raised their four daughters and two sons to lead purpose-driven lives. Games, toys, and music were forbidden, and clothing was modest, often of somber gray cloth, although her mother, a former Baptist, occasionally indulged them with a lively plaid. Education was paramount. When Anthony complained that her teacher refused to instruct the girls in long division, her father built a schoolhouse on their property and hired a teacher to homeschool his children and employees. At Deborah Moulson's Female Seminary, a Quaker boarding school near Philadelphia, Anthony and her sister Guelma lived according to its principles of "Humility, Morality and a love of Virtue," though its sometimes-harsh environment fostered Anthony's streak of self-recrimination.[3] After Daniel's cotton mill business failed during the Panic of 1837, the Anthony sisters returned to their home to find it repossessed and all the family's personal belongings at auction, including their clothes, the boys' pocketknives, and their parents' eye-glasses. The Anthonys moved to a farm near Rochester where they were active in the anti-slavery movement. Daniel sold insurance, and Anthony, at the age of twenty-six, moved almost two hundred miles east to teach at the Canajoharie Academy and helped pay off her father's debt.

For a while, Anthony found her transcendent cause in the temperance movement to end the consumption of alcohol. Drinking was deeply embedded in American society, widely seen as healthful and invigorating for men. The earliest temperance advocates were older men who testified to their own descent into debauchery, but Anthony believed women were the key to temperance. Mothers could teach their children the dangers of alcohol, and wives could "keep up such an incessant talking about voting for temperance men, that their husbands and fathers will be compelled for *peace's sake*, if no other, to cast their votes for honest, humane, total abstinence men."[4] In 1848, Anthony helped establish the Canajoharie Daughters of Temperance, and two hundred people showed up for her first speech in a hall festooned with cedar and red flannel, her name spelled out in large evergreen letters. Anthony became known as "the smartest woman that was now or ever was in Canajoharie," a title that both delighted and perplexed her.[5] "I hardly knew how to conduct myself amidst so much kindly regard," she wrote her parents.[6]

Still, Anthony felt an emptiness, a lack of appreciation made worse by misfortune. She was close to her cousin Margaret Caldwell and nursed her for weeks in the spring of 1849 while Margaret was pregnant and after she gave birth. Anthony resented Margaret's husband, who neglected his wife, did no work in the house, and even announced at one point that he was heading to the California gold rush. When Margaret died from complications of childbirth, Anthony believed she lost the only one who deeply knew and loved her. "I often feel that I have not a disinterested friend, not one who loves me for my very self, but many who endure my presence because they may derive some service from me," she confessed to friends.[7]

Anthony quit teaching and continued her temperance work from the family farm in Rochester. Her parents were committed reformers and opened their home to local and itinerant progressives as they passed through the Rochester area, including William Lloyd Garrison, Frederick Douglass, Abby Kelley Foster, Stephen Foster, and John Brown, who at the time was a little-known abolitionist living among former slaves in northern New York.

In January 1852, leaders of the New York Sons of Temperance invited Anthony to attend their general meeting in Albany. When she rose to address the gathering, she was told to sit down—"The sisters were not invited there to speak but to listen and learn," a delegate explained.[8] Stunned, Anthony and a few other women walked out and agreed to form a state women's temperance society. Anthony stayed with Stanton in Seneca Falls so they could prepare for their first convention. Stanton, halfway through her fifth pregnancy, warned Anthony she always expressed her true beliefs, which were sometimes radical, and that "no one may wish to share with me the odium of what I may choose to say."[9]

Three months later, five hundred women gathered at Corinthian Hall in Rochester for the inaugural meeting of the Woman's State Temperance Society, the first statewide women's temperance organization in the country. They adopted a constitution that reserved all offices for women—a necessity, Stanton explained, because women would otherwise defer to men in leadership. Members elected Stanton as president and Anthony as secretary and agent. Stanton praised the delegates for gathering to discuss one of the great questions of the day. It was time for women to throw off their shackles and claim "the dignity of a moral being" to "save man from the slavery of his own low appetites."[10] Then Stanton criticized societal norms regarding marriage and religion, two institutions revered by many women. Arguing that wives should be able to divorce "the confirmed drunkard," Stanton challenged the prevailing idea that divorce should be permitted only for bigamy or desertion. And when she argued that better education and homes for the downtrodden would do more to "prevent immorality and crime in our cities than all the churches in the land could ever possibly do," she fulfilled her warning to Anthony that she would shock people.[11] The *Troy Journal* criticized Stanton's comments for "reviling Christianity" and called the delegates unwomanly. Marriage, it said, was a "divine institution" in which a virtuous wife might reform a "confirmed drunkard."[12]

Susan B. Anthony, a major force in the fight for women's suffrage for more than fifty years. (Library of Congress)

Anthony traveled across the state of New York to build the Woman's State Temperance Society, eventually speaking in over thirty counties. She experienced firsthand the difficulties faced by an organization run by women: a lack of independent finances, a clergy that often did not support female-led organizations, and the belief held by many women that the regulation of alcohol was a man's concern. When Anthony fielded petitions calling for a state law to prohibit the sale of liquor, it was the first time she worked for legal change and later called it "my first declaration for woman suffrage."[13] In the late summer of 1852, Anthony attended her first Women's Rights Convention in Syracuse. More than two thousand people, including Lucy Stone, Antoinette Brown, Paulina Wright Davis, Ernestine Rose, and Lucretia Mott, from eight states and Canada attended. She had been to meetings that discussed the role of women before, but not where it had been the central focus. She came away believing that before women could affect any changes in temperance, teaching, or improving the world, they had to have more power and respect.

Two months later, Anthony and Amelia Bloomer attended the annual meeting of the New York Men's State Temperance Society, which had invited "temperance associations of every name."[14] Just before the meeting opened, Reverend Samuel May, Anthony's friend and strong supporter of women's rights, asked them not to participate. Word of Anthony's attempt to speak at the earlier Sons of Temperance meeting had spread, and several clergy members threatened to leave if the women were there. But Anthony and Bloomer refused to yield. When they took their seats on the platform, Rev. Dr. Henry Mandeville, an Albany minister, set his chair facing the women, sat down with his back to the audience, and glared at them. When a woman leaves her home to attend such conferences, Rev. Mandeville later said from the podium, she sacrifices her womanhood. "She is a hybrid species, half man and half woman, belonging to neither sex."[15] He finished his short speech, snapped his hat on his head, and left.

"Mr. President!" Anthony said, rising to speak. The chair, Rev. Philemon Fowler of Utica, refused to recognize her.

"Let her speak!" some shouted from the audience.

"Order, Order!" Fowler yelled above the din.[16] The room quieted for a moment after he threatened to quit. But then chaos returned. Fowler proclaimed the Society's constitution did not permit women to speak, an interpretation narrowly endorsed by a hasty vote, and all mention of Anthony and Bloomer was removed from the record of the meeting. Twice in six months, Anthony was publicly humiliated by an organization because she was a woman.

In the spring of 1853, at the first annual convention of the Woman's State Temperance Society, Stanton reflected upon the past year as "prophetic of a happy future of strong, united, and energetic action among the women of our State."[17] Over two thousand members had raised $1,761, enough to fund four lecturers and print more than fifty thousand pages of propaganda, and the Society had taken on women's rights, marriage, and the church. Anthony had done much of the Society's work herself, spending long days writing, printing, and posting, and late nights in meetings, strange hotels, and friends' homes while on the road. She acquired the moniker "Little Napoleon" for her determination and organizational skills.[18] Yet, the Society's constitutional prohibition on men holding leadership positions made some members uneasy. Frederick Douglass said it was a sign of weakness—that women could have power only if they mandated it. The organization needed men's help, Rev. Antoinette Brown said. Stanton and Anthony yielded to pressure and agreed to allow men to hold leadership positions, expressing their hope that any male leaders "will modestly permit the women to continue the work they have so successfully begun."[19] Their hope was quickly dashed when a group of conservative men and women tried to take control. Men began to dominate discussions and led a push to rename the organization "The People's League."[20] When it came time to select officers, Stanton's opponents produced a pre-printed ballot containing a list of women candidates whose traditional views stood them in stark contrast to the controversial Stanton. Voters ousted Stanton and overwhelmingly reelected Anthony, who accused men of hijacking the organization and refused to serve. "My soul is no longer in this movement, and what is the use of my body being here?" she said.[21] Both women cut all ties to the organization they had founded and that Anthony had spent an entire year building. Stanton asked Anthony if she finally understood the depths of women's subordination. "Do you see at last?" she asked.[22] "At last, I see," Anthony replied.[23]

Back home in Seneca Falls, Stanton reflected on the debacle. "You ask me if I am not plunged in grief at my defeat at the recent convention for the presidency of our society," Stanton wrote to Anthony. "Not at all," she confessed.[24] Overwhelmed by her domestic duties, Stanton was relieved to be free from the burden of the Society and told Anthony that she would withdraw from public life. She encouraged Anthony to put the entire incident behind her, "to waste no powder on the Woman's State Temperance Society," she said. "We have other and bigger fish to fry."[25]

After Stanton retreated to family life, Anthony joined more than five hundred teachers from around the state who gathered in August 1853 for the New York State Teacher's Convention in Rochester. Two-thirds of the attendees were women who, by custom, sat silently in the back of the meeting while men did all the talking. Anthony seethed with indignation as she looked at the faces of the women who simply accepted their imposed silence. Finally, after listening for several hours to her male colleagues' thoughts on how to bolster the status of the teaching profession, Anthony rose.

"Mr. President," she said.[26]

The delegates sat in silence, stunned that a woman would ask to address the meeting. After a long pause, President Charles Davies, a mathematics professor at West Point, wearing a blue and tan uniform, responded.

"What will the lady have?"[27]

"I wish to speak to the question under discussion," Anthony replied.[28] For the next half hour, male delegates debated whether to permit Anthony to speak and finally decided by a slim margin that she could.

So long as women held low status in society, the entire teaching profession would share that fate, Anthony told the delegates. If women were deemed incapable of being doctors or lawyers, why would anyone respect a profession where they predominate? They were 80 percent of the teachers in New York, yet earned only one-third of the total teacher wages. Women delegates had mixed responses to Anthony's questioning. Some were horrified. "Did you ever see such a disgraceful performance?" one asked.[29] "I never was so ashamed of my sex," said another.[30] Others were thrilled. "You have taught us our lesson and hereafter we propose to make ourselves heard," a delegate told her.[31]

The next day, President Davies addressed the question of women's participation with an aria of flattery. "Behold this beautiful hall!" he said, looking out over the audience seated among the neo-classical columns.[32] "Mark well the pilaster, its pedestal, its shaft, its rich entablature, the crowning glory of this superb architecture, the different parts, each in its appropriate place, contributing to the strength, beauty and symmetry of the whole! Could I aid in bringing down this splendid entablature from its proud elevation and trailing it in the dust and dirt that surround the pedestal? No, never!"[33] Anthony looked around and saw many of the women adjusting their ribbons and lace, looking self-satisfied, as if to say "Beautiful, perfectly beautiful!" she wrote to a friend.[34] But other women delegates felt scorn and contempt. When a teacher from Rochester presented Davies with resolutions calling for women to have equal pay as teachers and equal rights and responsibilities in the organization, Davies replied that other business was more pressing. When Anthony urged that the resolutions be read aloud, he yielded, and to his astonishment, the resolutions passed overwhelmingly. Anthony followed with a rousing speech on women's rights.

A month later, Anthony attended the Women's Rights Convention in New York City at the Broadway Tabernacle. The Convention paused to hear from Rev. Antoinette Brown after she and several other women arrived from the World's Temperance Convention in session a mile north. Brown described how she had tried to speak there but was shouted down by some of the delegates, who believed that women should be silent and were particularly outraged that the woman attempting to speak was a preacher. For more than ninety minutes, Brown stood her ground and refused to leave the platform as delegates heckled her with clenched fists and red faces. "Shame on the woman!" "She shall not speak."[35] When the Temperance Convention ultimately decided that Brown could not speak, she and her supporters left the hall and her opponents rejoiced. They were "now rid of the scum of the convention," Rev. John Chambers, a Philadelphia Presbyterian, said.[36] John Harwell Cocke, a Virginia minister, was glad to "rebuke to this most impudent clique of unsexed females."[37] Providence mayor A. C. Barstow made crude comments about the women that newspaper editors deemed too indecent to publish. William Lloyd Garrison, who had attended conventions for over two decades, witnessed the abuse of Brown and remarked that "on no occasion have I ever seen anything more disgraceful to our common humanity."[38]

Soon, however, the Women's Rights Convention itself was disrupted by a group of male rowdies in the front who began to shout "Shut up," "Sit down," and "Get out," making it impossible to hear Convention speakers.[39]

Mott could not control the crowd and yielded the chair. Wendell Phillips tried to speak but was drowned out with hisses. Then one of the rowdies jumped on stage. Yes, there were "many instances of the tyranny inflicted on women," he said, "but is that a reason that they should vote?"[40] Both sides erupted. "Take a drink." "Bow Wow," the hecklers continued.[41]

As Sojourner Truth ascended the platform to speak, the mob taunted her, Anthony said, because she possessed "the two most hated elements of humanity. She was black, and she was a woman, and all the insults that could be cast upon color and sex were together hurled at her."[42] Unperturbed, Truth scolded the troublemakers for hissing when the women spoke. "If they'd been brought up proper they'd have known better than hissing like snakes and geese," she said. "I can see them a-laughin', and pointin' at their mothers up here on the stage." Women want rights just like Esther in the Bible, and "we'll have our rights," she told them. "You may hiss as much as you like, but it is comin.' "[43] The *Tribune* editor Horace Greeley was in the audience and tried to reason with the rowdies, but had no success. With no other recourse, the Convention adjourned indefinitely. The protestors had silenced leaders of the women's rights movement, and most New York newspapers approved. "We saw, in broad daylight, in a public hall in the city of New York, a gathering of unsexed women," the *New York Herald* reported, opining that the women there probably bore fewer children and neglected their homes.[44]

Anthony's transformation from schoolteacher to women's rights reformer was complete. Her search for a transcendent cause that began in the temperance movement revealed to her the depth of women's subordination. After more than two years of frustration, she pivoted her formidable organizational skills and singular focus to working for women's rights, eventually becoming the movement's most enduring leader. "You stir up Susan," Henry Stanton once said to his wife, "and she stirs the world."[45]

Notes

1. SBA to Parents, May 28, 1848, SL, in Barry, *Anthony*, 50.
2. SBA to Mother, October 15, 1848, SL, in Barry, *Anthony*, 50.
3. Ida Husted Harper, *Life and Work of Susan B. Anthony*, 3 vols. (Salem, MA: Ayer Company, Publishers, Inc., 1983), 1:24 (hereafter cited as *SBA*).
4. SBA to the Editor, *Carson League*, September 20, 1852, cited in *SP*, 1:206.
5. Ward and Burns, *Ourselves*, 46.
6. Ibid.
7. SBA to Brother and Sister McLean, May 14, 1849, SBA Papers, SL, in Barry, *Anthony*, 56.

8. *SBA*, 1:65.

9. Ibid., 1:67.

10. *HWS*, 1:482–83.

11. Ibid.

12. *The Troy Journal,* n.d., in *HWS*, 1:485.

13. SBA, "Woman's Half-Century of Evolution," *North American Review* (December 1902): 806, cited in Barry, *Anthony*, 69.

14. *HWS*, 1:485–87.

15. *The Lily,* July 1852, 60–61, in *SBASB*, 1:10.

16. *HWS*, 1:487.

17. Ibid., 1:494.

18. McMillen, *Stone*, 95.

19. *HWS*, 1:494.

20. *SBA*, 1:95.

21. SBA, *Rochester Daily Democrat,* June 5, 1853; Anne C. Coon, "The Bloomer Costume: Fashion Reform, Folly, and 'Intellectual Slavery,' " *Rochester History* 57 no. 3 (Summer 1995): 3.

22. No citation, in Rheta Childe Dorr, *Susan B. Anthony: The Woman Who Changed the Mind of a Nation* (New York: AMS Press, 1970), 76.

23. Ibid.

24. ECS to SBA, June 20, 1853, in Stanton and Blatch, *Letters,* 2:51–52.

25. Ibid.

26. *SBA*, 1:98.

27. Ibid.

28. Ibid.

29. Ibid., 1:99.

30. Ibid.

31. Ibid.

32. Ibid.

33. Ibid.

34. Ibid., 1:100.

35. Ibid., 1:101.

36. Ibid., 1:89.

37. Clement Eaton, *The Growth of Southern Civilization* (New York: Harper and Brothers, 1961), 322, in Mary Elizabeth Massey, *Women in the Civil War* (Lincoln: University of Nebraska Press, 1994), 23.

38. *HWS*, 1:160.

39. *SBA*, 1:103.

40. *HWS*, 1:573.

41. Ibid., 1:574.

42. Ibid., 1:567.

43. Sojourner Truth, September 7–8, 1853 in *HWS*, 1:567–68.

44. *New York Herald,* September 7, 1953, in *HWS*, 1:556.

45. ECS to SBA, August 20, 1857, in *SP*, 1:351.

CHAPTER TEN

The Woman Question

Elizabeth Smith Miller wore a striking new outfit during a visit to her cousin Elizabeth Cady Stanton one day in the early spring of 1851. The dress was loose at the waist and ended only four inches below the knees, exposing voluminous pantaloons delicately tied together at each ankle, with feet protruding below. Miller created the outfit, she said, after her corseted Victorian dress dragged in the dirt while she was gardening, a nuisance she could no longer tolerate. She had heard health reformers recommended shorter dresses for women so she fashioned a new style of her own. Delighted, Stanton took her cousin to meet the Seneca Falls postmistress, Amelia Bloomer, who liked the outfit so much that she promoted it in her women's rights newspaper, the *Lily*. "Really ladies, will it not be nice?" Bloomer wrote. "We shall no longer have our dresses drabbled in the mud, or half the depth of them wet with snow." Women will be able to breathe and "our forms will be what nature made them."[1] As the style caught on, the new outfit took on her name: "bloomers."

Physicians warned that Victorian women's attire could cause an assortment of maladies, including back pain, fainting spells, internal bleeding, and a prolapsed uterus. A corset worn by a woman narrowed her waist by two to three inches, and "tight lacing" compressed it four inches or more, forcing flesh behind the spine to achieve the ideal waistline of eighteen inches. "If you wish to find all the organs in their normal position," one anatomy professor advised, "procure a male subject."[2] Below the waist, layers of petticoats covered by yards of finished material formed a bell shape. Victorian women's clothing created "the POETRY of dependence," Stanton wrote, because a woman had to rely upon a man to "help her upstairs, and down, in the carriage and out, on the horse, up the hill, over the ditch and fence." To achieve progress, women must change the form of their clothing. "How can we ever compete with a man for equal place and pay with garments of such frail fabrics and so cumbersomely fashioned," she wrote in the *Lily*. And "how can we ever hope to enjoy the same health and vigor with a man, so long as pounds of clothing is hung on the hips, the limbs cramped with skirts, with high heels, and the whole woman out of her true equilibrium."[3]

A few brave women donned the odd-looking bloomers. "However much it lacked in taste," a pioneer woman wrote in her diary after wearing them to cross the hot, dusty plains, "I found it to be beyond value in comfort and convenience."[4] A San Francisco newspaper reported that a woman wearing "a black satin skirt, very short, with flowing red satin trousers, a splendid yellow crape shawl and a silk turban *à la Turque*" was followed by "a large retinue of men and boys, who appeared to be highly pleased with the style."[5] Stone adopted it, as did Stanton, who had her bloomers made from black silk. Some found the style amusing. It made women look like "an ambulatory cotton bale, or a peripatetic haystack," a man said.[6] Others found it immodest. When men surrounded and cheered women in bloomers as they danced at a ball in New York City, one newspaper declared that no "respectable females" would wear them.[7] Some sensed rebellion. Those who wore "the apparel, appurtenances, and insignia of manhood cannot be too severely rebuked or too legally repressed," the *New York Times* wrote.[8] Bloomers promote the "wild spirit of socialism or agrarian radicalism," William Nevin, a classics professor warned. If these "levellers" succeed in "destroying the natural distinctions of character and sex between us," they will also "succeed in destroying all moral and government civilization."[9]

The hostile reaction to bloomers surprised Stanton. Her parents strongly disapproved of them, and her brother-in-law wrote her a critical letter, though her husband Henry took the outfit in stride. "The worst thing about it," he said, was that it exposes women's legs when they sit down—"to the delight of those gentlemen who are curious to know whether their lady friends have round and plump legs, or lean and scrawny ones."[10] Several men told Stanton "they would not vote for a man whose wife wore the Bloomers," and when she accompanied her cousin Gerrit Smith campaigning for election to the House of Representatives, young boys followed her, hissing and shouting "breeches."[11] Stanton stubbornly pledged to "never take it off, for now it involves the principle of freedom."[12] She did not mind being at the center of controversy, and her friends knew it. In April 1851, Bloomer scribbled a note on an envelope she forwarded to Stanton who was visiting at Peterboro, jokingly encouraging her not to stay away from Seneca Falls for too long as "people have nothing to talk about while you are gone."[13]

A woman in a traditional "bloomer costume," 1851. (Library of Congress)

Bloomers provided striking visual evidence that some women were determined to break boundaries set by tradition. They also began to enter occupations long closed to women. While women always worked in family businesses, many people believed that the rough-and-tumble world of public commerce would destroy their femininity. Lucretia Mott's son-in-law, Edward M. Davis, refused to hire twenty-eight-year-old Elizabeth M'Clintock for a clerk's position in his Philadelphia import business. M'Clintock, the eldest child of Mary Ann M'Clintock and a participant at the Seneca Falls Convention, had clerked for years in her father's drugstore. But no one in the wholesale district had ever hired a woman, Davis told Mott when she appealed to him to reconsider. A woman would meet "a miserable circle of antagonisms," he said.[14] In Washington, D.C., the U.S. commissioner of Patents Charles Mason broke ground when he hired thirty-four-year-old Clara Barton as clerk in the new patent building at the same pay as men. Her work ethic and elegant penmanship earned her a comfortable living, but she faced resentful coworkers who catcalled and blew smoke in her face as she walked through the halls. The *New York Tribune* ran exposés outing employers who paid women far less than men for the same work in factories, dry goods stores, and schools. Women were easily exploited because they were restricted to a few occupations, the *Tribune* asserted. Let women choose the occupations best suited for them, just as men do, and this injustice will end.

Educational opportunities for women slowly expanded in the 1850s. Three small coeducational colleges opened within a decade: Lawrence

University in Wisconsin, Antioch College in Ohio, and Bates
Maine. Antioch College president Horace Mann, the Massachusetts education reformer who promoted public schools, said that women deserve
"every right to a full and complete mental development" and believed that
educated women would regenerate society.[15] He created a common cur-
riculum for both sexes and hired the first full-time woman faculty member paid a salary equal to that paid to men. But Mann also believed in a
division of labor based on God-given "innate and connate distinctions"
between men and women. Women should pursue "the more quiet and
retired professions and trades," Mann said, and men should go into "those
of noisy struggle and violent exertion" such as law, politics, and the military.[16] Catharine Beecher, a leader in women's education, shared Mann's
view of divinely inspired spheres. She deplored the subordination of
women and founded the Hartford Female Seminary in 1823 to educate
them. Yet Beecher also believed that women should be educated only for
certain professions, particularly teaching. They would wield influence as
the mothers and educators of future citizens.

When Mann presented his ideas about education and divisions of labor
for men and women to a New York audience in 1852, Ernestine Potowski
Rose despaired. How, she asked, could politicians ever make the right
decision if even "Honorable gentleman" such as Mann espoused such
views?[17] Wendell Phillips agreed. Separate spheres for men and women
was a ruse to lead women into accepting their inferior social status, he
said. Opponents of reform always say, "You are not fit for such a privilege"
and until all avenues are open to women, any discussion of innate sex difference "is mere beating of the air."[18]

Some women sought to enter professions traditionally limited to men.
The Geneva Medical College in Upstate New York accepted Elizabeth
Blackwell as a student in 1847. When she graduated two years later,
Blackwell became the first certified woman doctor in the United States.
Harvard Medical School admitted Harriot Hunt in 1850 after having initially rejected her three years earlier, but she eventually withdrew under
pressure from several faculty and male students who protested that they
would lose respect for "the modesty and delicacy of her sex."[19] At the same
time, two new medical colleges for women were established in Boston and
Philadelphia. Paulina Wright Davis, a leader of the 1850 Worcester Wom-
en's Rights Convention, attempted to reform health care by spreading
knowledge about the female body and encouraging natural healing. After
several physicians turned down her request that they educate women on
anatomy and physiology, she decided to do it herself. She used charts and
drawings to teach about the female body, reproduction, and birth control,

subjects barely mentioned in polite society. At one point in her lecture, Davis uncovered an anatomically correct plaster mannequin of a female she had specially ordered from Paris. While many women were receptive, some bolted for the door, and others demurely deflected their eyes. A few fainted.

Olympia Brown, a twenty-six-year-old graduate of Antioch College who had grown up in a pious family, wanted to become a preacher. The St. Lawrence Theological School in Upstate New York was the only school to accept her. President Ebenezer Fisher did not think that women were "called to the ministry," he wrote her, "but I leave that between you and the Great Head of the Church"—and was surprised when Brown arrived for class.[20] After graduation, Brown became the first ordained woman minister in the nation and found a congregation that welcomed her. Oberlin graduate Antoinette Brown (no relation to Olympia Brown) received a license to preach from the Congregational Church in 1851 and began ministering to an Upstate New York congregation a year later. Religious liberals welcomed the women, but others objected. One woman denounced Antoinette Brown for violating the biblical call for women to be silent in the Church, shouting at her from outside the sanctuary so as not to violate it herself.

Religion was debated at women's rights conventions held nearly every year during the 1850s. At the 1852 Syracuse Convention, Antoinette Brown argued that Scripture could be interpreted to support women's rights and proposed a resolution that the Bible "truly and practically recognizes neither male nor female in Christ Jesus."[21] Paulina Wright Davis believed that religious passions damage a reform movement and had seen abolitionists lose valuable time debating whether Scripture supported slavery. Others argued that women's rights needed no religious sanction since human rights and freedom are self-evident. Two years later at the Women's Rights Convention in Philadelphia, Lucretia Mott and Rev. Henry Grew played out the same debate they had at the World Anti-Slavery Convention in London a dozen years earlier, when Grew insisted that the Bible endorsed women's subordination and Mott disagreed.

The 1850s was also a decade during which many women's rights reformers married and faced the challenges of raising families. Stone had refused several proposals of marriage, but after two years of ardent courtship by Henry Browne Blackwell, a small business owner from Cincinnati, she agreed to wed. Blackwell, a brother to physician Elizabeth Blackwell, was himself a reformer and promised to treat Stone as an equal. When they wed at the Stone home in May 1855, they altered traditional marriage vows. The Stantons had struck the word "obey" from their vows, but Blackwell and Stone went much farther.[22]

This act on our part implies no sanction of, nor promise of voluntary obedience to such of the present laws of marriage, as refuse to recognize the wife as an independent, rational being, while they confer upon the husband an injurious and unnatural superiority investing him with legal powers which no honorable man would exercise, and which no man should possess.[23]

Stone also kept her surname. Stanton had been daring in using "Elizabeth Cady Stanton" or "Mrs. Stanton" instead of the prevailing "Mrs. Henry Stanton." Stone believed a "wife should no more take her husband's name than he should hers."[24] She was and would always be Lucy Stone.

After marriage, Stone kept up her agitation for abolition and women's rights. In Cincinnati, she attended the sensational trial of Margaret Garner, a twenty-three-year-old runaway slave who attacked her own children, killing one of them, when they faced a return to slavery. The court allowed Stone to testify on Garner's behalf. No one talks of the sexual assaults on slave women and girls, yet all know that they happen, Stone told the crowded courtroom. Garner attacked her children to prevent this, and Stone asked if anyone there would not do the same. After a U.S. district court judge ordered Garner and her family returned to slavery, Garner's infant daughter drowned in a boating accident as they traveled south on the Mississippi River. Garner died of typhus two years later. Stone traveled around the upper Midwest to lecture on women's rights and saw firsthand the hardships women faced on the frontier. When she and Blackwell moved to northern New Jersey, she refused to pay taxes on her house until she was granted equal rights. When the township forced a sale of her possessions, Stone vowed to protest again "next year, and the year following, and every year, until the law was changed."[25] If that were the case, the constable who helped her carry her unsold items back into the house said, he hoped that someone other than he would have to enforce the law—and quickly left.

At the age of thirty-seven, Lucy Stone became pregnant with her first child. She feared childbirth, which had killed her sister Eliza Barlow, but gave birth to a healthy girl, Alice Stone Blackwell, in September 1857. When Stone began a limited lecture schedule, she ran into problems that many women encounter when they try to have a family and a career. Her husband encouraged her to stay home and show "womanly self devotion & constancy—*both admirable* & I think *true to nature*."[26] Stone responded with guilt. "I *am* trying to be a good wife and mother. I have wanted to tell you how hard I am trying, but I *have*, and my miserable failures hitherto make me silent now."[27] She enjoyed lecturing but "shrank like a snail into its shell" when she "thought of the possible evil that might befall . . . [Alice] if my guardian eye was turned away."[28] Stone reduced her lectures, and after a stillbirth in the summer of 1859, she restricted them even more.

Stanton gave birth to four more children in the 1850s for a total of seven. She hoisted a flag with each birth—white for a girl and red for a boy—shocking her neighbors by highlighting the act of giving birth, something that was rarely mentioned in public. She took pride in easy deliveries, but found her last pregnancy at the age of forty-three very difficult. "I never suffered so much," she wrote to Anthony three weeks after the birth.[29] The baby cried often, Henry was away, and she struggled to recover. Nine-year old Daniel grew weak and pale with an unknown illness over several weeks. "I am anxious beyond endurance," Stanton wrote Henry.[30] She increasingly resented Henry's absence, who was away ten months a year working in Albany as a New York State senator and in Washington, D.C. as a reporter for the *New York Tribune*. "How rebellious it makes me feel when I see Henry going about where and how he pleases," she wrote to Anthony in 1858. "He can walk at will through the whole wide world or shut himself up alone."[31] Henry often wrote loving letters filled with his longing for home. Yet when he was in Seneca Falls, Stanton said, he often closed himself off with "his God, his evening paper."[32] Isolated, worried, doing the incessant labor of raising young children with none of the stimulation she felt in Boston, Stanton despaired. "I have been compelled to hold all my noblest aspirations in abeyance in order to be a wife, a mother, a nurse, a cook, a household drudge," she complained.[33]

Anthony felt abandoned by fellow women's rights advocates who were pouring their energy into family life. She scolded Stanton for leaving her to fight alone and considered Stone's retreat into domestic life a defection. And when Antoinette Brown married Samuel Blackwell (Henry Blackwell's brother) and began bearing children, Anthony commanded her to stop— "two will solve the problem, whether a woman can be any thing more than a wife and mother better than a half dozen [sic], or [t]en even."[34] How could women claim to work for women's rights if they chose "first to please their husband" and left little time or energy for anything else?[35] "I would not object to marriage if it were not that women throw away every plan and purpose of their own life," she wrote.[36] Stone resented Anthony's dismissal of parenting and implied that, as a childless woman, she could not understand the burden of motherhood. "If you had had measles and whooping cough added to all you have done it would not be *half* as hard as the taking care of a child day and night is—*I know.*"[37]

Anthony pleaded with Stanton to stay active in women's rights. When Stanton promised to help if Anthony would "hold the baby and make the puddings," the two began a cooperative partnership that lasted for decades.[38] In daytime, Anthony would help manage the household while Stanton wrote. At night around the fire, after the children were in bed, Stanton and Anthony planned their strategy for advancing women's rights. The Stanton children found Anthony stern and foreboding and believed that she could see around corners. One of the Stanton boys said that Anthony was the only person other than his mother who ever spanked him. After several days, with a fresh batch of speeches in her suitcase and words of encouragement from Stanton, Anthony set off alone. The children were glad to see her go.

Anthony sometimes eased her own loneliness by reading the novel *Aurora Leigh* by Elizabeth Barrett Browning. Its protagonist is a young woman who longs to escape from a life defined by notions of propriety. She declines an offer of marriage from an attractive, wealthy aristocrat in order to pursue her love of literature. Leigh triumphs in the end as she develops an independent writing career in Rome. "I read and reread it," Anthony said, carrying her well-worn copy of the novel in her satchel wherever she went.[39]

In the 1850s, Stanton focused on resolving inequities imposed by marriage, which she saw as the root of women's subordination. In an address before the New York legislature, she called for marriage to be treated like any other civil contract—requiring the parties to have reached a minimum age for consent, allowing dissolution if the parties desire, and putting an end to the "civil death" women suffered when they married.[40] Her father's harsh rebuke of her address cut her deeply. Stanton could not understand why a family that celebrated its Revolutionary War heritage would condemn her fight for basic rights and freedoms. "To think that all in me of which my father would have felt a proper pride had I been a man is deeply mortifying to him because I am a woman."[41]

Discussing marriage rights invited controversy, but endorsing divorce in the mid-nineteenth century went too far even for many reformers. In the spring of 1860, Stanton debated the topic with Horace Greeley and Indiana politician and reformer Robert Dale Owen in the pages of the *New York Tribune*. When she introduced the topic at the Women's Rights Convention in New York, even long-time supporters were critical. Antoinette Brown Blackwell told the Convention that a woman's duty is to redeem, not divorce. A wife's "highest social obligation" is to reform a wayward husband, and her first motherly duty is "to teach her children to do the same."[42] Wendell Phillips worried that talk of divorce would tarnish women's rights and moved to place the entire discussion off the record. Greeley mocked the 1860 Women's Rights Convention as the "Wives Discontented." Families are sustained by an "expectation of abiding affection" and "permanency," he wrote in the *New York Tribune*. By loosening moral sensibilities liberal divorce would multiply current evils "a thousand-fold."[43] Stanton felt "surprised and humiliated" by Phillips's efforts to suppress discussion of the topic. She retained a brave face in public, but she was deeply upset and wept in private.[44]

Women's rights progressed slowly in the 1850s. The Worcester Women's Rights Convention opened the decade with a probing debate on the nature and capacities of women. Subsequent conventions continued the discussion of what came to be known as "the Woman Question."[45] But much of the momentum came from incremental advancements, such as more women in college, a few women entering professions formerly reserved for men, and the nation's first ordained woman preacher and certified woman doctor. By the end of the decade, national newspapers regularly covered, and often condemned, these debates and advancements, defining anew the public's idea of the meaning of womanhood. Yet just as momentum seemed to be growing, it would be interrupted by war.

Notes

1. *The Lily*, n.d., in Coon, "Bloomer Costume," 18.

2. Gleason 1851: 17 and ECS to *The Sybil*, 1857, in Elizabeth Reitz Mullenix, "Private Women, Public Acts: Petticoat Government and the Performance of Resistance," *The Drama Review* 46, no. 1 (n.d.): 109–10.

3. ECS, *The Lily*, April 4, 1852, 27, in Jennifer Curtis, " 'We'll Fight for Nature-Light, Truth-Light and Sunlight, against a World in Swaddling Clothes.' Reconsidering the Aesthetic Dress Movement and Dress Reform in Nineteenth Century America," *Past Imperfect* 13 (June 2007): 115–16.

4. Louise Barry, "Albert D. Richardson's Letters on the Pike Peak Gold Region," *Kansas Historical Quarterly* (February 1943): 12, in Marion Tinling, "Bloomers Comes to California," *California History* 61, no. 1 (Spring 1982): 23–24.

5. *Alta California*, July 14, 1851, in Tinling, "California Bloomers," 19.

6. Louise Barry, "Richardson's Letters," 12, in Tinling, "California Bloomers," 23.

7. *Spirit of the Times*, 1851, 469, New York City, in Mullenix, "Private Women," 111.

8. "Women's Right's," *NYT*, October 18, 1851, in Curtis, "'We'll Fight," 117.

9. William Nevin, 1852: 252–53, in Mullenix, "Private Women," 104.

10. HBS to ECS, February 15, 1851, 1, Henry Stanton Papers, Women's Rights National Historic Park Collection, Seneca Falls, NY.

11. ECS to Elizabeth Smith Miller, June 4, 1851, Seneca Falls, in Stanton and Blatch, *Letters*, 2:30.

12. Ibid.

13. Note written by Amelia Bloomer on a letter she forwarded from Seneca Falls, in Stanton and Blatch, *Letters*, 2:27, note 1.

14. Elizabeth M'Clintock File, Garrison Family Papers, SCA, in Massey, *Civil War Women*, 7.

15. Horace Mann, "A Word to a Young Woman," *SBASB*, 1:2, n.d.

16. Ibid.

17. Ernestine Rose, no citation, in Yuri Suhl, *Ernestine L. Rose: Women's Rights Pioneer* (New York: Biblio Press, 1990), 126.

18. Wendell Phillips, "Shall Women Have the Right to Vote?" (The Equal Franchise Society of Pennsylvania, reprinted in 1910, 1851), n.p.

19. Ronald Takaki, "Aesculapius Was a White Man: Antebellum Racism and Male Chauvinism at Harvard Medical School," *Phylon* (1960) 39, no. 2 (1978): 129, https://doi.org/10.2307/274507.

20. Olympia Brown, *Olympia Brown: An Autobiography*, Gwendolyn B. Willis, ed., *The Annual Journal of the Universalist Historical Society* 4 (1960): 27.

21. *The Proceedings of the Woman's Rights Convention Held at Syracuse, September 8, 9 & 10, 1852* (Syracuse, NY: J. E. Masters, 1852), 66.

22. Stanton, *Eighty Years*, 72.

23. Marriage Protest in *Liberator*, May 4, 1855, in Kerr, *Stone*, 86.

24. Hays, *Morning Star*, 131.

25. "Lucy Stone and the Collector—Sale of Gerrit Smith and Gov. Chase for Taxes. January 25, 1858, *NYT* (1857–1922), from http://search.proquest.com/docview/91437340? accountid=28588," 5.

26. HBB to LS March 3, 1858, BLC, in Kerr, *Stone*, 104.

27. LS to HBB, May 21, 1858, BLC, in Kerr, *Stone*, 104.

28. LS to ABB, February 20, 1859, BFP, in McMillen, *Stone*, 144.

29. ECS to SBA April 2, [1859], Film, Reel 9 in Lori Ginzberg, *Elizabeth Cady Stanton: An American Life* (New York; London: Hill and Wang, 2009), 95.

30. ECS to HBS December 9, 1850 in Stanton and Blatch, *Letters*, 2:25.

31. ECS to SBA, July 4, 1858, TS-DL, in Griffith, *Stanton*, 95.

32. Ibid., 80.

33. Lois Banner, *Elizabeth Cady Stanton: A Radical for Women's Rights* (Boston: Little, Brown, 1980), 34.

34. *SP,* 1:360. [Underlining in original is removed by the author.]

35. Ward and Burns, *Ourselves*, 83.

36. *SBA*, 2:644.

37. LS to SBA, April 1, 1858, Blackwell Family Collection, LC, in Kerr, *Stone*, 106.

38. ECS to SBA, June 10, 1856, in *SP*, 1:103.

39. Anthony inscription in *Aurora Leigh*, in Leonard N. Beck, "The Library of Susan B Anthony," *The Quarterly Journal of the Library of Congress* 32, no. 4 (October 1, 1975): 332.

40. "Address by ECS to the Legislature of New York," in Gordon, *SP*, 1:246. According to Gordon, this address was submitted in writing. In her memoirs, Stanton recalls personally delivering the speech. See Stanton, *Eighty Years*, 187–89.

41. ECS to SBA, September 10, 1855, Griffith, *Stanton*, 84.

42. Speech of ABB, National Women's Rights Convention Debate, 1860, in Karlyn Kohrs Campbell, ed., *Man Cannot Speak for Her: Key Texts of the Early Feminists* (Westport, CT; London: Praeger, 1989), 2:207.

43. Greeley, May 14, 1860, *New York Tribune*, in *HWS*, 1:740–41.

44. Stanton, *Eighty Years*, 225.

45. Dennis A. Norlin, "The Term 'The Woman Question' in Late Nineteenth Century Social Discourse," *Bulletin of Bibliography* 49, no. 3 (June 1992): 179–93.

CHAPTER ELEVEN

Civil War

When war finally came just before dawn on April 12, 1861, as Confederate batteries along the shores of Charleston Bay opened fire on Fort Sumter, Stanton welcomed it as the only way to end slavery. "The war is music to my ears," a "chorus for freedom," she wrote in its early months, proud to be "one of the mothers of the republic" when her seventeen-year-old son Henry enlisted.[1] Anthony found the war "glorious," but "strange."[2] Mott could not bring herself to approve. Harriet Beecher Stowe saw the war as a reckoning, when the "ill-gotten wealth" of slavery will "be paid back" in "the taxes of war." Northerners who were blind to the cruelty endured by slaves, "whose tears nobody regarded," will see their sons suffer and their mothers share the grief of slave mothers. The reckoning soon came when a mother who lost her son at the First Battle of Bull Run appeared at Stowe's doorstep in Hartford, Connecticut. "Oh, Mrs. Stowe," the grieving mother said, "God only knows what I suffer, but I wanted to see you and tell you about it." Stowe's twenty-one-year-old son Fred enlisted against her wishes and against the advice of his mentor at the Harvard Medical School, Oliver Wendell Holmes, who urged him to finish medical school to join the war as a surgeon. But Fred was eager to fight. "People shall never say, 'Harriet Beecher Stowe's son is a coward,' " he said.[3]

Young men rushed to enlist. The Sixth Massachusetts Regiment reached full complement quickly and was dispatched to Washington, D.C., to protect the nation's capital. On April 19, as they marched from one train station to another in Baltimore, a mob sympathetic to the Confederacy began to throw stones. A full-scale riot ensued and, when it was over, four Massachusetts soldiers and twelve Marylanders lay dead. When the soldiers of the Massachusetts Sixth finally arrived in Washington, D.C., a small group of well-wishers greeted them at the train station, including Clara Barton, who hailed from the same area of Massachusetts and worked as a recording clerk in the U.S. Patent Office. Barton visited them again at their barracks in the Capitol building and found them wanting in necessities. Her appeals for supplies, published in newspapers back home, yielded plentiful donations that she delivered to the appreciative troops, beginning a life of service to people in times of crisis.

As other women headed to Washington, D.C., to serve the war cause, they challenged tradition, expanding work roles and taking on greater responsibilities. Dorothea Dix, a sixty-year-old public health reformer, left Boston as soon as she heard about Fort Sumter. For over two decades, she had worked to transform care for the mentally ill by establishing public health-care institutions and lobbying at the highest levels of the state and federal governments. She and her nurses were ready to help "wherever we may be needed," she told President Abraham Lincoln's private secretary John G. Nicolay.[4] Three days later, Secretary of War Simon Cameron directed that Dix have "all necessary aid in organizing military hospitals" and gave her the title of superintendent of women nurses.[5] Dix advertised in newspapers for women who could witness tremendous suffering and "be calm, gentle, quiet, active, and steadfast in duty."[6] To reduce any hint of sexual impropriety, she specified that applicants should be middle-aged and "plain."[7] She set strict rules of conduct for her nurses. Unless caring for the ill, they were to avoid "any place of amusement in the evening," be in their rooms by taps, and not venture out or allow any private or officer in their rooms "except on business."[8]

Dr. Mary Walker closed her surgery practice in Upstate New York and headed to Washington, D.C., when the war began. By the time she arrived, the surgeon general of the army and his staff of thirty surgeons could barely cope with the rising casualties. Walker applied directly to Secretary of War Cameron for an official commission as a surgeon. It was a standard practice to contract with individual physicians, giving them the rank of lieutenant, decent pay, and more work than they could handle. But Cameron and the surgeon general wanted nothing to do with a woman surgeon. Undeterred, Walker headed to a makeshift hospital in downtown Washington, D.C., where Dr. J. N. Green welcomed her help treating a hundred gravely wounded men, even offering to share his salary, which she declined. Walker had worn bloomers before the war and, in Washington, D.C., assembled her own quasi-uniform: a knee-length military-style jacket festooned with martial braids worn over blue pants with gold stripes on the outside seam. Word spread of the eccentric Dr. Mary Walker.

Several hundred women left their homes to fight, disguising themselves as men when they enlisted. Sarah Collins signed up with a Wisconsin regiment, but she was discovered to be a woman and sent home before the regiment shipped out. Ellen Goodridge fought alongside her fiancé for three years, until he died. Fanny Wilson, from New Jersey, was outed as a woman at the Battle of Vicksburg, after a year of fighting, and later re-enlisted in another regiment. Jennie Hodgers fought the entire war as "Albert Cashier" and collected a veteran's pension until she was revealed to be a woman following an accident after the war. Many women took on greater responsibilities at home when their men left to fight. For some, this meant acquiring new skills as they struggled to maintain family farms and businesses. Letters to their husbands away at war often reflected growing confidence in themselves as they learned to manage on their own.

Dr. Mary Walker, a prominent abolitionist and suffragist, was also a prisoner of war during her time as a Civil War surgeon. She is the only woman who has ever received the Congressional Medal of Honor. (Library of Congress)

In the fall of 1862, when President Lincoln finally issued the Emancipation Proclamation ending slavery in areas still under rebellion, some Northerners felt it was too little, too late. But freed people met the news with joy. On January 1, 1863, Emancipation Day, the freed slaves who comprised the First South Carolina Volunteer Infantry Regiment burst into a thunderous chorus of "My Country Tis of Thee, Sweet Land of Liberty, of Thee I Sing." Twenty-five-year-old Charlotte Forten, a black Philadelphian who traveled south to teach newly freed slaves, joined the celebration at Camp Saxton in South Carolina. "The dawn of freedom which it heralds may not break upon us at once," she wrote in her diary, "but it will surely come, and sooner, I believe, than we have ever dared hope before."[9]

Harriet Tubman, the runaway slave who had guided more than seventy people to freedom before the war, helped free even more serving as a Union scout. In early June 1863, she joined hundreds of black soldiers of the Second South Carolina Volunteer Infantry Regiment on a raid along the Combahee River in South Carolina. Standing on deck of the lead boat, using information from her contraband slave scouts, she helped guide Union boats through treacherous waters as the soldiers destroyed bridges and railroads and cleared torpedoes. As word spread that "Lincoln's gun boats" were passing by, hundreds of slaves fled to the river, children clinging to their mothers, as slave drivers tried to hold them back. The Union boats loaded as many people as they could carry, freeing an estimated 750 slaves.

As the war reached fever pitch, killing and wounding tens of thousands of young men in battles on rolling American farmlands, medical workers struggled to cope. Clara Barton went where she was needed, first to local hospitals and then, as casualties mounted, to the battlefield. Tubman spent several months caring for newly freed slaves and wounded soldiers on the Sea Islands, concocting homemade medicines and washing wounds with water that turned "red as clar blood," she said.[10] Dix directed rising numbers of nurses at Union hospitals, but many chafed under her autocratic leadership. The author Louisa May Alcott served as a nurse and found Dix "a kind old soul, but very queer, fussy and arbitrary; no one likes her and I don't wonder."[11] Secretary of War Edwin Stanton took away Dix's authority to assign nurses and gave it to the medical branch of the army and, later, in the fall of 1863, to surgeons themselves.

Walker treated rising numbers of wounded soldiers in Washington. She assisted many women who came looking for injured husbands and sons and helped establish a home where they could stay as their loved ones recuperated. When a widow whose son was detained and accused of desertion approached her for help, Walker got the boy released to his mother when it was discovered he was a minor. After a young drummer boy under her care succumbed to his injuries, Walker convinced his mother to remain and work at the hospital, knowing she would face a bleak future alone at home. Walker followed the army as it ventured south. In late 1863, Confederates captured her as she attempted to treat wounded Southern civilians. She was kept as a prisoner of war in Richmond for four months, until she was traded in a prisoner exchange. In October 1864, Walker finally received an official appointment as the first woman surgeon ever assigned to a regular army.

The Loyalty League

As the Civil War dragged on, some women lamented that they could not do more. "Think how our boys are all going!" Ellen Wright of New York wrote. "Is it not stifling, irksome work, to remain quietly at home?"[12] When several newspapers and journals criticized Northern women for their complacency, Anthony and Stanton responded that women contributed "in nursing the sick and wounded, knitting socks, scraping lint, and making jellies," and most of all "when a mother lays her son on the altar of her country."[13] Most women's rights leaders put off the idea of holding a convention during wartime, but Anthony chafed at the delay. The New York legislature reversed parts of the Married Women's Property Act, stripping mothers of equal rights to their children and of widow's rights to their husband's property. "I am sick at heart," Anthony wrote to Mott a year into the war, "but cannot carry the world against the wish and will of our best friends."[14]

In 1863, Stanton and Anthony called for the creation of a women's organization that would press for an end to slavery. Even after the Emancipation Proclamation, slavery existed legally in some parts of the nation. Abolitionists wanted a constitutional amendment to eliminate it, and Stanton and Anthony wanted women to have a voice in its undoing. "Woman is equally interested and responsible with man in the final settlement of this problem of self-government," they wrote in the appeal for their new organization and "let none stand idle spectators now."[15] In May, hundreds of women gathered in New York City to form the Woman's Loyal National League. To support a federal anti-slavery amendment, they organized a massive drive using one of the few political tools available to women: a petition. Anthony, however, tried to link women's rights to a proposed anti-slavery amendment by presenting a resolution that referenced the rights of all black citizens and all women. Some members objected to including women in the resolution since the focus of the League was to end slavery. Stone, the Convention's elected president, replied to these objections noting that the League must not repeat the founding fathers' mistake of persuading those who reviled slavery to remain silent in order to forge national unity. Anthony's resolution passed by a large majority, prompting the *New York Herald* to criticize how "the most patriotic and praiseworthy" efforts devolved into "a revolutionary women's rights movement."[16]

A month later, Stanton faced the first of two personal crises that followed one another in short succession. At the start of the war, when her husband Henry received a political appointment to work in the port of New York and then found his son Neil a job checking ships for smuggling activity, the Stantons moved to a home in New York City. In July 1863, when Lincoln called for another draft, thousands of New Yorkers rampaged through midtown Manhattan. They burned the draft building, the mayor's house, and two police stations; they wrecked streetcars, cut telegraph wires, and severely beat the city's police superintendent after recognizing him in civilian clothes. They also targeted black institutions and citizens, killing eleven and injuring dozens. Stanton, who lived in midtown, feared that Henry's work as an abolitionist would make her home a target and took her younger children to the fourth floor, opened a window, and instructed them to escape to the roof if the rioters invaded their home. Finally, they came, "the most brutal mob I have ever witnessed," Stanton wrote.[17] "Here is one of those three-hundred-dollar fellows!" someone shouted as they pulled Stanton's son Neil down the street.[18] The mob eventually let him go after he offered to buy them all drinks and complied with their order to cheer three times for "Jeff Davis."[19] Stanton fled with her family to her sister's home a few blocks away. A few months later, both Henry and Neil lost their jobs at the port after Neil was found to have accepted bribes from shipowners. Newspapers pilloried the Stanton name, and friends shunned them. Neil left for New Orleans where he later became a harbormaster and supervisor of elections, and Henry, who blamed his political enemies for using his "weak boy" to drive him out of the job, was unemployed for nearly a year until Greeley rehired him to work at the *Tribune*.[20]

When the Women's Loyal National League met for a second Convention in 1864, it had grown to over five thousand members and raised enough money to sponsor speakers in New York City and two full-time lecturers in the Midwest. This time, attendees readily passed resolutions that included reference to women's rights, including the demand for equal pay for women in medicine. Its members had made the most successful petition drive in history, gathering nearly four hundred thousand signatures on anti-slavery petitions that Massachusetts senator Charles Sumner dramatically unrolled on the Senate floor as he introduced his proposal for the Thirteenth Amendment. The League had given women a voice on the national stage and maintained the bond between women's rights and abolition.

Women's rights reformers held mixed opinions of Lincoln. Stanton, who had so heartily welcomed war, was now exhausted by it. She wanted peace through a political settlement and rejoiced when she thought Lincoln would lose re-election in 1864. Lucy Stone's husband, Henry

Blackwell, stumped for Lincoln, but Stone herself stayed home. Sojourner Truth thanked Lincoln in person for being "the best President who has ever taken the seat" when she met him in 1864. Others would have done the same, Lincoln replied, "if the time had come." She asked him to sign her scrapbook, which he did: For Aunty Sojourner Truth, Oct. 29, 1864 A. Lincoln. "I felt that I was in the presence of a friend," Truth wrote.[21] Harriet Tubman declined to meet Lincoln. She was angry he delayed deploying black soldiers in the war and paid them only half the wages of white soldiers, but later regretted her decision after realizing that he "was our friend."[22] Lincoln handily won re-election in November 1864, boosted by Union Army victories on the battlefield. In January 1865, the House of Representatives passed the Thirteenth Amendment to abolish slavery as supporters on the floor hugged and danced and shouts of joy rang out from the galleries.

Ten weeks later, on April 9, Robert E. Lee surrendered his army to Ulysses S. Grant at Appomattox Courthouse in southern Virginia. The conflict that began in a battle with no casualties and ended as the bloodiest in American history, receded into history as Southern soldiers laid down their arms and headed home, leaving a deep rift between South and North. Five nights later, John Wilkes Booth assassinated Lincoln at Ford's Theater, shocking a nation already traumatized by war. Anthony was at her brother's house in Leavenworth, Kansas, and felt little sadness when she received a telegram with the news. It was a divine act, she thought, when "God had spoken to the nation in His thunder tone." She had been "sad and sick" over Lincoln's decisions to send Confederates home and to permit them to vote, while black men could not, and to leave freed people in the South to fend for themselves.[23] In religious services in Leavenworth the next day, Anthony observed varying degrees of mourning. The Methodist service made "a stirring word," the Episcopal Church, a mere reference, and the Catholic Mass made no mention at all. In the African Methodist Episcopal and Baptist Churches, the pews were jammed. A week later, at the official mourning ceremony in Leavenworth's largest public building, blacks gathered in the front seats, which "dreadfully shocked & outraged" the "pro Slavery anti-negro people," Anthony wrote.[24] After taking tea with several of the area's leading citizens the next day, she found it "perfectly shocking how few of the Republicans are ready to give euqual [sic] rights to black men."[25]

The Civil War had left 600,000 men dead. Many of those who survived came home from the war permanently altered. Stanton's son Henry returned with an unknown affliction. Fred Stowe, Harriet Beecher Stowe's son who had left medical school to fight, suffered debilitating headaches from a head wound he received at Gettysburg. His mother bought him an orange farm in Florida, which struggled financially. After he struck off alone for San Francisco, his mother never heard from him again. Stowe, who had called the war "God's will," and said both sides "should deeply and terribly suffer" for the sin of slavery, lost her son.

Women gained no new rights during the Civil War, but they expanded the boundaries of their work and earned public recognition for contributions to the war. Dorothea Dix had overseen the appointment of more than three thousand nurses. Clara Barton's service to the wounded became so well known that she was hailed as "the Angel of the Battlefield." Dr. Mary Walker received a Congressional Medal of Honor, the only woman ever awarded one, and a disability pension for her service. Harriet Tubman did not receive a pension until three decades after the war, despite her service as a Union scout. Ordinary women across the nation had sustained homes and farms with extra toil, cared for the sick and wounded, and worked countless hours to raise funds for soldiers. "God bless the women of America!" Lincoln said. If the praise of women by all poets and orators in history had been applied to American women, "it would not do them justice for their conduct during this war."[26] Stone believed that a grateful nation would soon grant women full citizenship and the vote. When Senator Sumner asked her when she thought women's suffrage would come, she replied, "it is at our very doors."[27]

Notes

1. ECS to William H. Seward, September 19, 1861, from Stanton and Blatch, *Letters*, 2:89; ECS, June 7, 1861, in Griffith, *Stanton*, 109.

2. SBA to Wendell Phillips, April 28, 1861, Anthony Collection, HH, in Wendy Hamand Venet, *Neither Ballots nor Bullets: Women Abolitionists and the Civil War* (Charlottesville: University of Virginia Press, 1991), 34.

3. Charles Edward Stowe and Lyman Beecher Stowe, *Harriet Beecher Stowe: The Story of Her Life* (Boston; New York: Houghton Mifflin and Company, 1911), 191–93.

4. Dix to Anne E. Heath, April 20, 1861, in Marshall, *Dorothy Dix*, 203, in Judith Ann Giesberg, *Civil War Sisterhood: The US Sanitary Commission and Women's Politics in Transition* (Boston: Northeastern University Press), 35.

5. Simon Cameron to the Surgeon General, June 10, 1861, Letters Received by the Adjutant General's Office, National Archives; General Orders no. 31, *Official Records*, Set 3, 1:263, in Thomas J. Brown, *Dorothea Dix: New England Reformer* (Cambridge, MA: Harvard University Press, 1998), 290.

6. Dix to Louisa Lee Schuyler, April 29, 1861, reprinted in Sylvia G. L. Dannett, ed., *Noble Women of the North* (New York: Thomas Yoseloff, 1959), 623, in Brown, *Dix*, 283.

7. Holland, *Our Army Nurses*, 19, in Brown, *Dix*, 303.

8. Anna L. Boyden, *Echoes from Hospital and White House: A Record of Mrs. Rebecca R. Pomroy's Experience in War-Times* (Austin, TX: D. Lothrop & Co., 1884), 161–2, in Brown, *Dix*, 293.

9. *Charlotte Forten Diary*, 1863 in Jean M. Humez, *Harriet Tubman: The Life and the Life Stories* (Madison: University of Wisconsin Press, 2003), 55.

10. Sarah Bradford, *Harriet Tubman: The Moses of Her People* (n.p.: Carol Publishing Group, 1997), 97.

11. Martha Saxton, *Louisa May* (Boston: Houghton Mifflin Company, 1977), 256, in Brown, *Dix*, 313.

12. Ellen Wright to Lucy McKim, August 15, 1862, Garrison Family Papers, SSC, in Venet, *Neither Ballots*, 94.

13. ECS, SBA, March 1863, in *HWS*, 2:53.

14. SBA to LM, April 1862, Lutz, *Anthony*, 95, in Griffith, *Stanton*, 110.

15. ECS, SBA, Women's Loyal National League Call, in Stanton and Blatch, *Letters*, 2:198.

16. *New York Herald*, in Mary Elizabeth Massey, *Bonnet Brigades: American Women and the Civil War* (New York: Alfred A. Knopf, 1966), 164–65, in Griffith, *Stanton*, 113.

17. ECS to Gerrit and Ann Smith, July 20, [1863], in *Letters*, 44, in Griffith, *Stanton*, 109.

18. ECS to Mrs. Gerrit Smith, July 20, 1863, in Stanton and Blatch, *Letters*, 94.

19. Ibid.

20. HBS to Carroll, November 1863, HBS-NYHS, in Griffith, *Stanton*, 114.

21. Truth, *Narrative*, 178–79.

22. "Conversation with Sojourner Truth about President Lincoln," in Humez, *Tubman*, 249.

23. "Remarks by SBA at Memorial Service for Abraham Lincoln," April 23, 1865, in *SP*, 1:546.

24. SBA Diary, April 23, 1865, in *SP*, 1:547.

25. SBA Diary, April 24, 1865, in *SP*, 1:547.

26. Mary Livermore, *My Story of the War: A Woman's Narrative of Four Years Personal Experience as Nurse in the Union Army, and in Relief Work at Home, in Hospitals, Camps* (Hartford, CT: AD Worthington, 1890), 112.

27. Hays, *Morning Star*, 190.

CHAPTER TWELVE

The Negro's Hour

After the Civil War, the urgent need to confront rising white supremacy strained antebellum alliances between abolitionists and women's rights reformers. Many Southern whites could not "conceive of the Negro as possessing any rights at all," a Freedmen's Bureau assistant commissioner in Mississippi said.[1] When several state legislatures in the South passed laws that had the practical effect of reinstating aspects of slavery, many reformers believed that black male suffrage had to take precedence over women's suffrage. "This hour belongs to the Negro," Wendell Phillips declared at the first postwar meeting of the American Anti-Slavery Society.[2] To demand suffrage for both women and black men at the same time would not only fail but would also harm black men far more than women, he argued. Giving priority to black men shocked some women's rights supporters. Stanton pointed out to Phillips that "the African race" includes women and questioned whether black men with rights would behave any different from white men.[3] "Why should the African prove more just and generous than his Saxon compeers?" she asked.[4]

In the spring of 1866, after President Andrew Johnson vetoed two civil rights bills, Republican leaders drafted the Fourteenth Amendment to strengthen constitutional protections for individual rights. All citizens would have "the equal protection of the laws," and no state could "deprive any person of life, liberty, or property, without due process of law."[5] But the proposed amendment also contained the word "male" three times and would insert a reference to sex in the Constitution for the first time.[6] It would not prohibit women from gaining the right to vote, but it would make their exclusion from rights afforded to male citizens more explicit. It would penalize states that denied rights to black men but would permit all states to deny protections to women. Stone and Blackwell pleaded with Senator Charles Sumner, one of the amendment's principal supporters, to drop the word "male," but Sumner believed it was necessary and reassured them that rights for women would soon follow.[7]

At the American Anti-Slavery Society meeting in New York City in May 1866, former allies hashed out their loyalties to race and sex. The gathering convened shortly after the Memphis Riots, during which hundreds of Memphis whites rampaged through a black neighborhood, murdering dozens and burning more than ninety homes. Abby Kelley Foster, a long-time abolitionist and women's rights advocate, said that pressing for women's rights at an anti-slavery convention was inappropriate. Her husband Stephen disagreed. "Is liberty an incident of sex?" he asked. "I should despise myself if I asked woman to help me in securing my right to the ballot-box and deny it to her."[8] Robert Purvis, a prominent black abolitionist and vice president of the American Anti-Slavery Society, said the organization should support women as much as black men to "resist all oppression."[9] Garrison, too, stood by women. Yet most attendees disagreed and decided as a group to support the Fourteenth Amendment as drafted, which guaranteed rights to black men but not to women.

Those who wanted to continue working to achieve rights for both blacks and women gathered the next day to create the American Equal Rights Association (AERA), an organization to promote "human rights."[10] Stephen Foster worked thirty-five years to free the slave "because he was a human being," he said, "and for the same reason I demand the ballot for woman."[11] America needs "the peculiar genius that God has given to woman," New York's most prominent preacher Henry Ward Beecher argued.[12] The Association fielded petitions asking Congress for an amendment to "prohibit the states from disenfranchising any of their citizens on the grounds of sex."[13] But the AERA's efforts came too late. A month later, Congress passed the Fourteenth Amendment, and it moved to the states for ratification.

Some women reformers saw the pending enfranchisement of freedmen as deepening their own subordination. Poor, uneducated men formerly at the lowest stratum of society would have the privileges of citizenship they sought. In the fall of 1866, Stanton declared a quixotic independent candidacy to represent New York's Eighth Congressional District. If elected, Stanton said that she would demand universal suffrage so that women of "wealth, education, and refinement" could "outweigh this incoming pauperism, ignorance, and degradation."[14] Her argument had little appeal to voters. The Democratic candidate won handily with 13,816 votes; the Republican received 8,210. Stanton received 24.

As the women's suffrage movement stalled at the federal level, several of its leaders decided to seek suffrage in states that were revising their constitutions. Stone reminded New Jersey legislators that women had voted there for three decades following the Revolutionary War, before a change to the state's constitution shut them out. Anthony and Stanton campaigned in New York. Stanton sarcastically told the New York Judiciary Committee that white males were "the nobility of this country," a "privileged order, who have legislated as unjustly for women and negroes as have the nobles of England for their disfranchised classes."[15] She argued that women should be permitted to vote on changing the constitution since New York twice in the past permitted normally disenfranchised groups to vote at constitutional conventions. For months, Anthony spoke to small groups and large assemblies across the state to urge women's inclusion as voters. She also lobbied prominent citizens, including Mary Greeley, a long-time women's rights supporter married to Horace Greeley, the influential editor of the *New York Tribune*. Horace Greeley headed the Suffrage Committee of the New York Constitutional Convention, which was charged with recommending prerequisites for voter registration under the new constitution. Anthony and Stanton knew they had little chance of persuading Greeley to support a guarantee of women's suffrage—but they could embarrass him. When they presented the last petitions to the Suffrage Committee as submitted by "Mrs. Horace Greeley," the galleries burst into laughter. "You two ladies are the most maneuvering politicians in the State of New York," Greeley fumed later that day, after refusing to shake their hands at a reception. Why, he asked, had they used his wife's married name since Stanton was so insistent on using her own name? "Because I wanted all the world to know that it was the wife of Horace Greeley who protested against her husband's report," Stanton replied. Greeley responded in a deep, measured voice that he now saw their "animus" and vowed never to write well of them again in his newspaper. Any future reference to Stanton would be to "Mrs. Henry B. Stanton."[16] Greeley steered the Suffrage Committee to recommend black male suffrage, while pointing out that women were classified with other groups who could not vote, including "idiots, lunatics, persons under guardianship, felons, and persons convicted of bribery."[17] New York and New Jersey rewrote their constitutions after the Civil War without granting women's suffrage, and the bitterness of the struggle caused suffragists to lose the powerful Greeley as an ally.

When the New York campaign faltered, suffragists held out hope for Kansas, which planned referendums on black male and women's suffrage for the fall of 1867. Charles Henry Langston, a schoolmaster for contraband slaves in Leavenworth, began the push for black male suffrage during the Civil War. Langston was the son of Ralph Quarles, a Virginia planter, and his common-law wife, Lucy Jane Langston, a freed woman. After the death of his parents, Langston moved to Ohio and used his substantial inheritance to attend Oberlin College. Kansas Republican governor Samuel J. Crawford agreed to present the issue to voters in a referendum, and State Senator Colonel Sam N. Wood amended the bill to authorize another referendum on women's suffrage, although some of his fellow Republicans feared that linking the two issues would doom both. A succession of suffragists headed to Kansas in the hope that heavy lobbying of male voters might win them the vote. Stone and Blackwell arrived in April and traveled long stretches by wagon, sometimes more than thirty miles a day, over hills, across muddy-bottomed creeks, buffeted on windy prairies. They found "the most astonishing (and astonished) audiences in the most extraordinary places."[18] One night it was a log school house, the next a stone church, then a store with planked seats. One woman told them "no decent woman would be running over the country talking n***** and woman," and a widower said that if his wife had spoken for suffrage, "he would have pounded her to death."[19] Most audiences and local newspapers, however, supported blacks' and women's right to vote. As Olympia Brown traveled the state, she found "brave and earnest women; kind and true men" and "some of the most dishonest politicians the world has ever seen."[20] Once, when opponents shouted and threw stones at the window of a frontier schoolhouse where she was lecturing, Brown invited them in and yielded the floor. A young frontier lawyer attacked women's suffrage as he slammed the table, waved his arms in the air, and dripped rivulets of sweat. "You had better shut up," the women in the front row told him. "We've no use for you."[21]

Anthony felt certain women would win the right to vote in Kansas. Stone predicted an overwhelming victory. The referendum had strong support from leading politicians, including the governor, two U.S. senators, and several state representatives. But the defeat of suffrage in New York that spring emboldened opponents, and some Republican leaders in Kansas continued to fear that women's suffrage would derail suffrage for black men. Influential newspapers were largely silent. Stone, with tears in her eyes, begged Greeley to give the issue more attention, and the *Tribune* finally published a letter of tepid support signed by several prominent citizens. Greeley himself recommended that Kansas men support suffrage for women as an "experiment."[22] Even the *Leavenworth Times*, edited by Anthony's brother, waited until the day of the referendum to endorse women's suffrage. British Member of Parliament John Stuart Mill exhorted Kansans to lead the fight for women's suffrage, just as they had the fight against slavery. But some Kansans resented meddling from outsiders.

Kansans had a dramatic and exhausting beginning, the editor of the Atchison *Daily Champion* complained, and "need, more than any other people on the globe, immunity from disturbing experiments on novel questions of doubtful expediency." If people from the East want suffrage, have "Massachusetts or New York, or some older State, therefore, try this nauseating dose."[23] If it is found to be wise, Kansans will follow.

In the final weeks of the Kansas campaign, as opposition to women's suffrage hardened, Anthony collaborated with George Francis Train, a wealthy, eccentric Democrat with ambitions to be president. Train earned his initial fortune with a fleet of forty clipper ships during the California gold rush and later earned even more money in mining and transportation around the world. In the final weeks of the campaign, he traveled with Anthony to dozens of Kansas towns, entertaining listeners with his quick wit as he delivered a populist message. The two were an odd pair—Anthony, the serious Quaker in a demure black dress, her hair parted in the middle and tied soberly at the nape of her neck. And Train, ten years younger with curly hair, sported a blue coat with shiny brass buttons, patent leather boots, and lavender kid gloves—an outfit some likened to an opera costume. Train supported progressive causes, including currency reforms, labor unions, and women's rights, but he was also a blatant racist. According to him, if black men gained the right to vote and not women, it would place whites "lower in the scale of citizenship and humanity," he told voters in Ottawa, Kansas. "Woman first, and negro last, is my programme."[24]

Anthony's and Stanton's collusion with Train shocked their allies. Garrison asked Anthony how they could "have taken such leave of good sense, and departed so far from true self-respect, as to be traveling companions and associate lecturers with that crack-brained harlequin and semi-lunatic." Train may attract an audience, he said, "but so would a kangaroo, a gorilla or a hippopotamus."[25] Stanton and Anthony took the low road and defended their association with Train. If abolitionists were willing to shut out women to enhance the likelihood that black males would gain suffrage, then they should be able to oppose black suffrage to promote suffrage for women. "Come forward and talk more strongly and more earnestly in favor of women's enfranchisement," Anthony told her critics, "and we will accept your services as gladly as those of Mr. Train."[26]

On Election Day, Kansas men voted down women's suffrage by a 2–1 margin, 20,234 to 9,091, and defeated black male suffrage by only a slightly smaller margins—19,965 to 10,502. Kansas men seemed more worried about conflicts in the state with Native Americans and a cholera epidemic, and some worried women would use the vote to restrict the sale of alcohol. Women's suffrage referendums also failed that year in Massachusetts, Iowa, Maine, and Michigan. The men of Kansas, like men everywhere in America, Stanton concluded, simply did not want suffrage for women. They were not ignorant or uninformed, they just did not understand the importance of the ballot for women's protection and "did not feel for *her* the degradation of disfranchisement."[27] Stanton saw men's reluctance to permit women to participate in the electoral process as a function of power: rulers rarely see merit in the protests of their subordinates. "The 'white male' is the aristocracy of this country," Stanton said. "We belong to the peasantry."[28]

The Split

After defeat in Kansas, Anthony and Stanton poured themselves into establishing a newspaper, hoping to spread the gospel of women's rights across the nation as Garrison had spread the message of abolition with the *Liberator*. They rented rooms near city hall in New York City, just above the *New York World* and down the street from the *New York Times*. Parker Pillsbury would write most of the articles; Stanton would craft most editorials; Anthony would manage production; and Train, hoping to advance his political ambitions, would pay the bills. They called their newspaper the *Revolution*; its motto "Principle, Not Policy: Justice, Not Favors" was emblazoned across the top of the front page.[29]

The first issue published in January 1868 launched a broad assault on male-centered culture—"Mandom," Pillsbury called it—in which a woman knows herself as a "satellite" of a man, "shining only with his light, cheering only with heat borrowed from him."[30] The issue bemoaned unequal pay, sexual harassment, and the moral double standard. A Boston police officer disguised as a woman was harassed by more than twenty-seven men, including some from respectable society, the *Revolution* reported.[31] If the city of St. Louis required prostitutes to register with the Board of Health, so should it require that brothel customers register their names, addresses, and occupations with the police.[32] After the *New York World* criticized Stanton for scanning a theater audience through her opera glasses and declaring New York senator Roscoe Conkling "the ablest and handsomest man in that body," Stanton accused the paper of promoting a double standard. "Women have been looked at through opera glasses for six thousand years," Stanton wrote, "their faces, forms and fashions that begin variable subject of comment by all men, great and small."[33] The *Revolution* encouraged women to ignore the ridicule used by critics of women's rights. To label a woman strong-minded "is like saying she has a beard," leaving many women to protest "I am no ranter for women's rights."[34]

The *Revolution* also reflected the racism Stanton, Anthony, and Train exhibited in Kansas. Stanton railed against "Sambo" in her editorials, and the *Revolution* reprinted stories of alleged sexual assault of white women by black men.[35] Samuel May, a long-time abolitionist loyal to women's rights, struggled to understand how Anthony could work with Train. Garrison warned that Train was mentally unstable, but Anthony and Stanton defended their work with him. "If the Devil himself had come and said ladies I will help you establish a paper I should have said Amen!" Stanton wrote.[36]

As the Republican Party focused on furthering rights of black men, Anthony sought support from the Democratic Party and attended its National Convention in Tammany Hall in New York City. It was a packed affair, with party loyalists jostling each other in the July heat as they cheered their favored causes. But when Anthony stood patiently on stage as a clerk read her memorial offering a universal suffrage plank, the delegates laughed and jeered. She left, embittered. Neither of the two major parties showed interest in women's suffrage.

After the Fourteenth Amendment was ratified and Republicans proposed the Fifteenth Amendment, which would give black men the right to vote, reformers began to organize the first suffrage organizations for women. The New England Woman Suffrage Association (NEWSA) was created in the fall of 1868, enlisting long-time suffrage stalwarts like Lucy Stone, Henry Blackwell, William Lloyd Garrison, Olympia Brown, Thomas Wentworth Higginson, Frederick Douglass, and Stephen and Abby Kelley Foster. New members broadened the organization's visibility and appeal—Lydia Emerson, the wife of Ralph Waldo Emerson, and her former neighbor Louisa May Alcott, who had recently begun her popular *Little Women* series. Julia Ward Howe, the socially prominent writer and wife of Samuel Howe, the famous reformer for the deaf and blind, became its first president. Garrison reassured the audience that women's rights would come soon. It had already passed through the initial phases of "indifference" and "opposition and ridicule" that every reform movement goes through, and was entering its final phase, when "people are ready to receive the truth."[37] Yet even here, in an association organized specifically to promote women's rights, some members urged that black male enfranchisement take priority. "Woman has a thousand ways by which she can attach herself to the ruling power of the land that we have not," Douglass explained.[38] Brown insisted that NEWSA focus on women's suffrage only and warned that reformers often delude themselves with belief in imminent success when victory may be generations away. Stone successfully pushed for a resolution that favored universal suffrage, but two months later asserted in testimony before Congress that "woman must wait for the Negro."[39] The old guard, Brown complained to Anthony, had "exhausted their fund of heroism in behalf of the Negro" and had "no extra stock of self-sacrificing spirits on hand." Douglass, Garrison, and Higginson "are the last persons in the world to do anything for us: we must look for our support to new men."[40]

Editor, orator, and abolitionist Frederick Douglass, the foremost African American leader of the nineteenth century, and a vocal advocate of women's suffrage. (Library of Congress)

Nor was there much interest in Congress to promote women's rights. Representative George W. Julian, a Quaker from eastern Indiana, offered a constitutional amendment for women's suffrage in December 1868, and Kansas senator Samuel Pomeroy introduced a resolution for a universal suffrage amendment in the U.S. Senate, but both proposals languished in committee.

In May 1869, the American Equal Rights Association (AERA), fractured over giving precedence to rights for black men over women. Francis Ellen Watkins Harper, born free in Baltimore and a supporter of abolition and suffrage, said that "when it was a question of race," she would "let the lesser question of sex go." Whereas for white women, she said they will make "race occupy a minor position."[41] When Stanton was nominated for the vice presidency of the AERA, Stephen Foster denounced her work with Train, which he believed had "repudiated the principles of the society."[42] Anthony defended Train, but Frederick Douglass countered that rights for black men were "a question of life and death." "When women, because they are women, are hunted down through the cities of New York and New Orleans; when they are dragged from their houses and hung upon lampposts; when their children are torn from their arms, and their brains dashed out upon the pavement," Douglass said, describing a litany of horrors, "then they will have an urgency to obtain the ballot equal to our own."[43] The audience thundered with applause.

"Is that not all true about black women?" a voice called out from the audience.[44]

"Yes, yes, yes," Douglass replied. "It is true of the black woman, but not because she is a woman, but because she is black."[45] The audience applauded. Anthony pointed out that "it was the men that clapped and not the women." She noted that Douglass suffered terrible prejudice and hatred, yet even he would not wish to be a woman. When she offered resolutions that opposed the Fifteenth Amendment and supported suffrage only for men and women who were educated, the audience stomped, shouted, and made such a ruckus that the next speaker left the stage. Stone tried to conciliate. Both positions had merit, she told the audience, which quieted as she spoke. Women had "an ocean of wrongs too deep for any plummet," as did the Negro who has "an ocean of wrongs that cannot be fathomed." While they would be lost arguing for the rights of just one group, she would be "thankful in my soul if *any* body can get out of the terrible pit."[46]

The next day, when AERA Convention delegates passed a resolution to support the Fifteenth Amendment, bitterness and division grew. Mary Livermore said, to some applause, that men had been disrespectful. Anthony believed Wendell Phillips and Theodore Tilton had betrayed the movement for women's rights by deeming it in a theoretical phase and not yet worthy of political action. "To think that those two men, among the most progressive in the nation," Anthony said, "should dare to look me in the face and speak of this great principle for which I had toiled, as a mere intellectual theory!"[47]

Two days after the divisive AERA Convention, and after Lucy Stone had already left town, Anthony, Stanton, and Mott joined about sixty others to form the National Woman Suffrage Association (NWSA). It would work for a broad spectrum of rights and liberties, but most importantly, for a federal amendment granting women the right to vote. Men could affiliate with the new organization, but leadership was reserved for women. Stanton was named president. The *Revolution* would be its mouthpiece. Anthony later told Stone that the formation of the NWSA had been spontaneous. But Stone, to whom Anthony had denied rumors of a new organization before Stone left town, believed Anthony had deliberately deceived her and formed the organization without including her.

Six months later, in November 1869, Lucy Stone and moderates from around the country met in Cleveland to form the American Woman

Suffrage Association (AWSA), which they believed would better represent women's concerns. Stone wrote to Stanton that her Association "shall never be an enemy or antagonist of yours in any way," but tried to keep Stanton and Anthony away from the founding convention.[48] Stanton stayed home but accused Stone and her colleagues of "sedulously and malignantly" trying to undermine the NWSA and the *Revolution*.[49] Anthony attended and tried to have Stanton elected head of the new organization, but the delegates instead elected the esteemed New York preacher Henry Ward Beecher. Delighted, Stone said that men were better organizers and women needed their help. AWSA would work for the Fifteenth Amendment, giving black men the right to vote, and use more moderate means than the NWSA to achieve women's suffrage. Sojourner Truth joined, despite her earlier hesitation to have black men gain the vote before women, and Francis Ellen Watkins Harper was a founding member. The *New York Times* applauded its moderate approach, as did Greeley, who hoped that its leaders would "not mistake rashness for courage, folly for smartness, cunning for sagacity, badinage for wit, unscrupulousness for fidelity."[50]

The AWSA grew rapidly. Stone crisscrossed Northern states, organizing new branches and trying to convince existing suffrage organizations to join. Beecher and Howe drew large crowds to its first anniversary meeting, and wealthy Bostonians financed its newspaper, the *Woman's Journal*, which quickly outsold the *Revolution*. In April 1870, Mott and Theodore Tilton tried to unite the two competing organizations, but the leaders could not reconcile their disagreements. Divisions among women's rights supporters had hardened, rendering two major suffrage organizations: the AWSA, with its moderate tactics and broad base, and the NWSA, still pursuing a federal amendment with edgy critiques of male-dominated society. Stone successfully parried a second attempt by Anthony to undermine her leadership at the May 1870 AWSA Convention, and continued the organization's moderate approach by passing uncontroversial resolutions, including one that supported stable marriage.

When the Fifteenth Amendment was ratified in 1870, giving black men a constitutional guarantee of voting rights, Stanton and Anthony sensed that an opportunity to press for women's rights had passed. It was the third constitutional amendment for civil rights in five years, and the nation was exhausted by war and political turmoil. The suffragists had presented petitions to Congress, lobbied former political allies, railed about inequities in the *Revolution*, all to no avail. Women, they learned, must depend upon themselves.

The *Revolution* bled money. Stanton had predicted the paper would have a hundred thousand subscribers, but it never reached more than three thousand, and it lost money every week. Train stopped funding it when he left for England in 1869, so Anthony borrowed to keep it afloat. Her debt reached $10,000 before she sold it to Martha Ballard, a wealthy New Yorker, for the nominal sum of one dollar—which was stolen from Anthony's purse. "I feel a great calm sadness like that of a mother binding out a pet child she could not support," Anthony wrote in the last edition under her management.[51] Anthony returned to public speaking and paid off the enormous debt after several years. Frustrations grew as the nascent movement faltered. "If I were to give free vent to all my pent-up wrath concerning the subordination of women," Lydia Maria Child scolded Senator Sumner in 1872, "I might frighten *you*." [52]

Notes

1. Colonel Samuel Thomas, in Jason Phillips, "Reconstruction in Mississippi," *Mississippi History*, www.mshistorynow.mdah.ms.gov/articles/204/reconstruction-in-missippi.

2. "Thirty-Second Anniversary of the American Anti-Slavery Society," NASS, May 13, 1865, in Faye E. Dudden, *Fighting Chance: The Struggle over Woman Suffrage and Black Suffrage in Reconstruction America* (New York; Oxford: Oxford University Press, 2014), 62.

3. ECS to Wendell Phillips, May 10, 1865, Stanton and Blatch, *Letters*, 2:104–5.

4. ECS to Wendell Phillips, December 26, 1865, in Stanton and Blatch, *Letters*, 2:110.

5. U.S. Constitution, Amendment XIV.

6. Ibid.

7. Leslie Wheeler, *Loving Warriors. A Revealing Portrait of an Unprecedented Marriage. Selected Letters of Lucy Stone and Henry B. Blackwell, 1852–1893* (New York: Dial Press, 1981), 212, and Blackwell, *Growing Up in Boston's Gilded Age*, 230, in McMillen, *Stone*, 164.

8. "Remarks by ECS to the Anti-Slavery Society," May 9, 1866, in SP, 1:581.

9. Ibid., 1:580.

10. *HWS*, 2:172.

11. Ibid., 2:175.

12. Ibid., 2:160.

13. Stanton, *Eighty Years*, 242.

14. "Letter by ECS to the Electors of the Eighth Congressional District." October 10, 1866, in *HWS*, 2:181.

15. ECS Address to the New York Judiciary Committee, January 23, 1867, in *HWS*, 2:273.

16. Ibid., 2:287.

17. Ibid., 2:288.

18. HBB to ECS and SBA, April 21, 1867, in *HWS*, 2:235.

19. Ibid., 2:236.

20. Olympia Brown, *Acquaintances*, 19ff. in Charles E. Neu, "Olympia Brown and the Woman's Suffrage Movement," *The Wisconsin Magazine of History*, 43, no. 4 (Summer 1960): 279.

21. Charlotte Coté, *Olympia Brown: The Battle for Equality* (Racine, WI: Mother Courage Press, 1988), 84.

22. *New York Tribune*, October 1, 1867, n.d., in *HWS*, 2:249–50.

23. John A. Martin, ed., *The Atchison Daily Champion*, n.d., in *HWS*, 2:249–50.

24. George Francis Train, Ottawa, KS, n.d., in *HWS*, 2:244–45.

25. WLG to SBA, January 4, 1868, *Revolution*, January 29, 1868, in *SP*, 2:124.

26. SBA, St. Louis, Missouri, November 25, 1867, in *SP*, 2:109.

27. *HWS*, 2:267.

28. ECS to Thomas W Higginson January 13, 1868, in *SP*, 2:127.

29. See the digital collection of *The Revolution* at http://digitalcollections .lclark.edu/items/ browse?collection=21&sort_field=Dublin+Core%2CDate.

30. Parker Pillsbury, "Mandom," *The Revolution*, July 8, 1869, in Lana Rakow and Cheris Kramarae, *The Revolution in Words: Righting Women 1868–1871* (New York: Routledge, 1990), 121–22.

31. *The Revolution*, March 11, 1869, in Rakow and Kramarae, *Righting Women*, 135–36.

32. "The Social Evil," *The Revolution*, August 11, 1870, in Rakow and Kramarae, *Righting Women*, 88.

33. ECS, *The Revolution*, February 19, 1868, in *SP*, 2:129–30.

34. Mrs. Emily E. Ford, "A Strong-Minded Woman of a Gentlemanly Deportment," *The Revolution*, October 20, 1870, in Rakow and Kramarae, *Righting Women*, 133; F. "I Am Not a . . . ," *The Revolution*, April 7, 1870, in Rakow and Kramarae, *Righting Women*, 237.

35. "Woman's Rights Convention," *Washington Daily Morning Chronicle*, January 20, 1869 and "Woman's Rights Convention," *Washington Evening Star*, January 20, 1869, in *Papers* 13:282, in Dudden, *Fighting Chance*, 169.

36. *Revolution*, January 29, 1868, ECS to Olympia Brown, January 1868, in Olympia Brown Collection, SL, in Kerr, *Stone*, 132.

37. Olympia Brown Papers, SL, in Coté, *Brown*, 100.

38. "Woman Suffrage," *New York World*, November 19, 1868, 5, in Ellen Carol DuBois, *Feminism and Suffrage: The Emergence of an Independent Women's Movement in America, 1848–1869* (Ithaca, NY: Cornell University Press, 1999), 166–67.

39. "LS and the Negro's Hour," *The Revolution* 3, February 4, 1869, 89, in Dudden, *Fighting Chance*, 165.

40. Olympia Brown to SBA, January 3, no year cited, Brown Papers, in Coté, *Brown*, 102–3.

41. *HWS*, 2:347, 383–85 cited in Terborg-Penn, *African-American Women*, 32.

42. *HWS*, 2:382.

43. Proceedings, Anti-American Slavery Society, New York, May 11, 1869, in Kerr, *Stone*, 139.

HWS 2:382. Barry asserts that this account in *HWS* is inaccurate in *Anthony*, 193. In later years, Anthony told her biographer Ida Harper that Stanton had altered the account of this event in order to hide some of the antagonism.

44. *HWS*, 2:382.

45. Ibid.

46. Ibid., 2:384.

47. *SBA*, 1:323–24.

48. LS to ECS, October 19, 1869, BLC, *The Revolution*, October 28, 1869, in Kerr, *Stone*, 146.

49. ECS, "The Cleveland Convention," October 28, 1869, in *SP*, 2:277.

50. *New York Tribune*, November 25, 1869, in Kerr, *Stone*, 147.

51. Quoted by ECS, *The Revolution*, n.d., Rakow and Kramarae, *Righting Women*, 40.

52. Lydia Maria Child to Charles Sumner, July 9, 1872, Sumner Papers, in Eric Foner, *Reconstruction: America's Unfinished Business, 1863–1877* (New York: Harper Perennial, 1988). Updated edition published in 2014, 473.

CHAPTER THIRTEEN

The New Departure

In October 1869, Missouri suffragist Virginia Minor made a new argument for women's rights. "I believe that the Constitution of the United States gives me every right and privilege to which every other citizen is entitled," Minor told delegates to the National Woman Suffrage Association (NWSA) Convention in downtown St. Louis, and if legislatures did not recognize those rights, then women should turn to the courts to enforce them.[1] The Fourteenth Amendment made all people born and naturalized in the United States citizens. No state "shall abridge the privileges or immunities of citizens" or "deprive any person of life, liberty, or property, without due process of law."[2] These protections were designed for former slaves, but women's rights advocates seized upon them to bypass exhausting struggles at the state and national levels. NWSA delegates endorsed Minor's "New Departure" resolutions, declaring that states did not have "the right to deprive any citizen of the elective franchise," and that they could "regulate" but not "prohibit" voting.[3]

The New Departure tactic brought new hope to suffragists. "We no longer beat the air—no longer assume merely the attitude of petitioners," Minor said.[4] Anthony sent copies of the New Departure resolutions to each member of Congress. The logic of the approach was "unanswerable," she said, and predicted that the battle for women's suffrage would now "be short, sharp and decisive."[5] Stanton employed the New Departure argument when she testified in late 1871 before the Congressional Committee on the District of Columbia. So many women came to hear her testify that the committee had to move to a larger room, with one senator remarking that he had never seen so much interest in a committee meeting in his twenty years in office. Maine senator Hannibal Hamlin, the chairman of the committee and a suffrage opponent, presided over the hearing. Massachusetts senator Charles Sumner, a veteran of the antislavery struggle and a suffrage supporter, noted that he was "fatigued and worn," but "listening with alert attention."[6] Flanked by rows of women and facing a semi-circle of committee members at the opposite end of a large table, Stanton calmly stated that women already had the right to vote. States can regulate but not prohibit the right of a citizen to vote, and full citizenship came with personhood. "Are not women people?" she asked.[7] A month later, Anthony advanced the New Departure argument when she testified before the Senate Judiciary Committee. "Although I am a Quaker and take no oath," Anthony said, "I have made a most solemn 'affirmation' that I will never again beg my rights, but will come to Congress each year and demand the recognition of them under the guarantees of the National Constitution."[8]

Bradwell v. Illinois

In 1871, thirty-eight-year-old Myra Bradwell applied for admission to the Illinois State bar using the New Departure argument. She had passed the bar exam with high honors, and her application contained all necessary documents, including a certificate of qualification and written testimony to her good character. Since no woman had been admitted to the Illinois bar, she added a memorandum addressing the question many people were thinking: "Does being a woman disqualify her under the laws of Illinois from receiving a license to practice law?" No, she wrote, answering her own question. The Illinois legislature never intended to exclude women when they used the word "he" in the statute regulating admission, citing several instances where it used the pronoun "he" to denote both men and women.[9]

If any woman deserved to gain admission to the Illinois bar, it was Bradwell. She had assisted her husband James in his successful Chicago legal practice for years and published the *Chicago Legal News*, a weekly newspaper that reported on the city's frothy politics and state legal news. Bradwell used her publication to scold lazy lawyers and inept prosecutors, and to call out jury bribery and judges selected for their politics over their competence—some even having no legal experience at all. She criticized laws that treated women as dependents, whether of a husband or the state, and lobbied legislators to pass a bill to hold husbands *and* wives equally responsible for family expenses. Yet Bradwell also enjoyed being a wife and mother and made frequent references to godliness. "I often wish all those excellent folk who picture me as a fanatic destroyer of domesticity and the sweetness of true womanhood could see my two daughters and our home life," she said.[10]

But the Illinois Supreme Court rejected Bradwell's application to the bar—twice. She could not perform the duties of a lawyer as a married woman since she needed her husband's consent to sign a contract, the court held. And when the Illinois legislature passed the statute regulating bar admission, it did not intend to include women as potential lawyers.

Bradwell appealed her case to the U.S. Supreme Court, where her friend Wisconsin senator Matthew Hale Carpenter, a charismatic orator and supporter of women's rights, argued the case for free. The Fourteenth Amendment opens to all citizens "the honorable professions as well as the servile employments of life," Carpenter asserted before a packed gallery. "Intelligence, integrity, and honor" should be the only qualifications for the job.[11] Then, in an astonishing twist, Carpenter said that Bradwell's claim of constitutional privileges did not include suffrage. Although he had long advocated the right to vote, Carpenter believed that the court would be more likely to concede a right to employment if it were separate from the more contentious issue of women's suffrage. Carpenter had undermined the New Departure argument for suffrage before the Supreme Court. Anthony was furious. Carpenter made a "school boy pettifogging speech," she complained to Bradwell.[12]

U.S. v. Susan B. Anthony

Ten months later, on the morning of November 2, 1872, Anthony walked with her sisters Mary, Hannah Mosher, and Guelma McLean to a polling station in a barbershop near her home in Rochester, looking like a "prim spinster with no thoughts of girlish or coquettish wiles," an observer noted.[13] They insisted that the three young registrars add their names to the voting rolls and, when the registrars balked, Anthony read aloud the Fourteenth Amendment and a portion of the New York Constitution, pointing out that neither referenced sex. The registrars still hesitated.

"If you still refuse us our rights as citizens, I will bring charges against you in Criminal Court and I will sue each of you personally for large, exemplary damages," Anthony threatened.[14] She then produced a letter from Henry Selden, a prominent local judge, attesting that citizenship gave women the right to vote. Flummoxed, the registrars consulted a prominent local lawyer, who advised them to enroll the women, which they did. Over a hundred women across the nation had already tried to vote. Sojourner Truth was turned away from her polling place in Battle Creek, Michigan. Victoria Woodhull and her sister were not permitted to vote in New York. Several women in New Jersey and Massachusetts were allowed to fill out ballots, but their votes were not counted. Mary Ann Shadd Cary, a Howard Law School graduate, and sixty-three women were turned away from the polls in Washington, D.C., but obtained affidavits attesting to their attempt to vote. A wealthy New Hampshire widow voted with no resistance. A Detroit widow was allowed to vote, while her married friend was turned away. There was little rhyme or reason as to why some women's attempts to vote were successful and others were not, but Anthony's high profile as a leading suffragist made her attempt a symbolic challenge to the entire system.

Word spread quickly of the women's registration in Rochester. Afternoon newspapers reported it as an act of public defiance, and some called for Anthony's prosecution. Anthony returned to the barbershop to bolster the registrars and assure them that she would pay for any legal costs they incurred. Three days later, on November 5, Anthony and fourteen other women voted as soon as the Rochester polls opened. "Well, I have been and gone and done it, positively voted this morning at 7 o'clock, and swore my vote in at that," Anthony wrote to Stanton. "Not a jeer, not a rude word, not a disrespectful look has met one woman."[15]

Three weeks later, the Anthony sisters were at home when a tall gentleman dressed in gloves and a high hat knocked at their door. He was deputy U.S. marshal E. J. Keeney, he explained a bit shyly, and he had come to place Anthony under arrest. Anthony was shocked. She thought that the registrars might face legal action, but not her. "Is this your usual method of serving a warrant?" she asked Keeney to his obvious discomfort.[16] He showed her the warrant, but Anthony was indignant. She was not "dressed properly to go to court," she told him, and when the marshal said she could present herself at the courthouse, Anthony replied that she had committed no crime and would not go alone. The marshal waited in the parlor while Anthony changed dress. When she came down the steps, she held out her wrists to be cuffed like a common criminal. The marshal declined. They walked together to the courthouse where she found the three registrars and fourteen other women voters already under arrest.

Anthony knew her arrest would get national attention and hoped to gain public support for the rationale of the New Departure argument. In the weeks before her trial, she spoke in every village in the county. "Friends and fellow citizens," she began, "I stand before you tonight, under indictment for the alleged crime of having voted at the last Presidential election, without having a lawful right to vote." She had broken no laws, but "simply exercised my *citizen's right*, guaranteed to me and all United States citizens by the National Constitution, beyond the power of any States to deny."[17] The government, she reminded her audiences, was founded not to bestow rights but rather to protect rights already rooted in natural law and granted by God. She ended with an appeal that juries acquit law-abiding citizens who vote. Speaking in a modest black dress with her graying hair twisted in a knot, Anthony seemed less a threat to the Republic than a model of principled defiance. When the state moved her trial to Canandaigua, the Ontario Country seat in Western New York, Anthony quickly moved there and spoke in sixteen of the twenty townships before her trial began.

In the meantime, the Supreme Court ruled in an 8–1 decision in *Bradwell v. Illinois* that women *are* citizens and that while states may not abridge the privileges and immunities set forth in Article IV and the Fourteenth Amendment, admission to the state bar is not among them. Citizenship merely implies "the idea of membership of a nation, and nothing more."[18] Justice Joseph P. Bradley went further, opining that admitting a woman to the bar would defy the "law of the Creator." Woman's "timidity and delicacy," he wrote, "unfits it for many of the occupations of civil life."[19] Because an independent career may harm the family, it was justifiable for a state to bar women from some occupations. Chief Justice Salmon Chase, who thirty-six years before had protected abolitionist James Birney from an Ohio mob, cast the sole dissenting vote. However, due to declining health, Chase did not file a dissenting opinion and died the following year.

The *Bradwell* decision, Anthony said, was a defeat for the New Departure argument, a "virtual concession of all we fought for in the late War— the supremacy of the National Gov't to protect the rights of all persons—all citizens—against the states' attempts to deny or abridge."[20] The courts "are so entirely controlled by prejudice and precedent we have nothing to hope from them but endorsement of dead men's actions."[21]

Anthony's trial began on June 17 in the district courthouse in downtown Canandaigua, which was packed with observers. Judge Ward Hunt, an outspoken opponent of women's rights, determined that Anthony could not take the stand to testify in her own defense since her sex made her an incompetent witness. Anthony's attorney, Judge Henry R. Selden, who had written the letter supporting her registration, argued on her behalf. The Fourteenth Amendment, he told the jury, gave women the right to vote. Her intent was not to break the law, but to exercise what she believed were her rights as a citizen. Anthony committed no crime "if she voted in good faith believing that she had such right." The prosecution, Selden said, must show "not only that the defendant knowingly voted, but that she voted *knowing that she had no right to vote*." U.S. district attorney Richard Crowley countered that Anthony's state of mind should have no bearing on the verdict. She had broken the law, and "whatever Miss Anthony's intentions may have been she did not have a right to vote."[22]

At the end of the trial, Judge Hunt took the unusual step of endorsing the prosecution's position on "questions of law," that Anthony's state of mind was irrelevant and that the Fourteenth Amendment did not grant her the vote. "If I am right in this," Hunt told the jury, "the result must be a verdict on your part of guilty, and I therefore direct that you find a verdict of guilty." Selden jumped to his feet. "That is a direction no court has power to make in a criminal case," he objected. Judge Hunt ignored the objection, and the clerk proceeded. "Gentlemen of the jury, hearken to your verdict as the Court has recorded it. You say you find the defendant guilty of the offense whereof she stands indicted, and so say you all?"[23] The jury agreed. Outside the courtroom, some of the jurors said they wanted to find Anthony not guilty. Selden protested that Judge Hunt made jurors "silent spectators," which "substantially abolishes the right of trial by jury."

At sentencing, Judge Hunt ordered Anthony to rise. "Has the prisoner anything to say why sentence shall not be pronounced?" he asked. "Yes, Your Honor, I have many things to say," Anthony replied, ready to make the most of the opportunity to speak. "You have trampled underfoot every vital principle of our government," she said, including her natural, civil, political, and judicial rights. "Robbed of the fundamental privilege of citizenship, I am degraded from the status of the citizen to that of the subject; and not only myself individually but all of my sex are, by your honor's verdict, doomed to political subjection under this so-called republican form of government."[24]

"The Court cannot listen to a rehearsal of argument which the prisoner's counsel has already consumed three hours in presenting," Judge Hunt interjected.

Anthony continued. Judge Hunt had denied her right to vote and a trial by jury, thus "my sacred rights to life, liberty, property, and——."

"The Court cannot allow the prisoner to go on," Judge Hunt ordered.

Anthony protested "high-handed outrage upon my citizens' rights." Since her arrest in November, this was the first time that she had been allowed to defend herself in court.

"The prisoner must sit down," Judge Hunt said, "the Court cannot allow it."[25]

Anthony demanded a trial by her peers. The jury was all-male, and regardless of their race, ethnicity, education, income, or state of sobriety, she said, they were her political superiors. "Under such circumstances," she added, "a commoner of England, tried before a jury of lords, would have far less cause to complain than have I, a woman, tried before a jury of men."[26]

"The Court must insist—the prisoner has been tried according to the established forms of law," Judge Hunt replied.

"Yes, Your Honor, but by forms of law all made by men, interpreted by men, administered by men, in favor of men and against women."[27]

"The Court orders the prisoner to sit down," Hunt declared. "It will not allow another word."[28]

Anthony ignored him until she finished, then sat down. Hunt announced her punishment: a hundred dollar fine and the cost of prosecution. Anthony vowed never to pay and urged all women to follow "the practical recognition of the old Revolutionary maxim, 'Resistance to tyranny is obedience to God.' "[29]

Hunt declined to send Anthony to jail, which would have given her the right to appeal to the Supreme Court. Found guilty and sentenced, yet not imprisoned, Anthony was in a legal purgatory with no avenue for appeal. But the trial did generate public sympathy. When Judge Hunt repeatedly interrupted Anthony, even many suffrage opponents perceived a gross injustice and bestowed a begrudging respect. Several newspapers called for the removal of Judge Hunt. "Such a case never before occurred in the history of our courts," opined the *Utica Observer*.[30] Judge Hunt also railroaded the three young registrars, even barring their defense attorney from addressing the jury. They were found guilty and fined twenty-five dollars plus costs. Like Anthony, however, they refused to pay and instead went to jail. Anthony appealed to powerful friends in Washington, D.C., who convinced President Ulysses S. Grant to pardon the offenders, who, during their week in jail, had been well cared for by suffrage supporters.

Anthony's New Departure argument, that states did not have the right to deprive any citizen of the right to vote, had failed. She and the registrars had been found guilty, and no appeal to the Supreme Court was possible. But in one sense, her tactic succeeded. Her imposed silence during the trial highlighted women's vulnerability in the courts, and many Americans were moved by the plight of a citizen arrested for the simple act of voting.

Minor v. Happersett

The last hope for the New Departure legal theory lay with its originator, Virginia Minor, who also tried to vote in the fall of 1872. As a taxpaying citizen, she told St. Louis registrar Reese Happersett, she had the right to vote. When Happersett refused to register her, Virginia and her husband Francis filed suit in the St. Louis Circuit Court, using the New Departure argument. Happersett did not contest the facts of the Minors'

Virginia Louisa Minor, a suffragist best remembered for her role in *Minor v. Happersett*, an 1875 U.S. Supreme Court case in which Minor contended that the Fourteenth Amendment to the Constitution afforded women the right to vote. She did not win her case. (Library of Congress)

argument, but explained that he was simply following the law. When the circuit court for St. Louis County and the Missouri Supreme Court unanimously decided against the Minors, they appealed to the U.S. Supreme Court. In 1875, Francis Minor joined two well-respected Missouri attorneys, John Krum and John Henderson, to press their case before the U.S. Supreme Court. They added an unusual argument: that the interpretation of the law in Missouri was not a reflection of justice, but of culture. The limits on women are a "popular idea," and "men accept it as a matter of fact, and take for granted that it must be right," just as slavery had once been thought so. Without the vote, governance for woman is a form of "Despotism, and not a Republic."[31]

Francis Minor nervously argued the case before the Supreme Court in February 1875. The justices tried to engage him, but he failed to present a convincing argument. "So you hold that citizenship confers the right to vote?" Justice Stephen J. Field, the Court's foremost intellectual, asked. "Yes, Sir," Minor answered without elaboration.

"Have children within the right to vote?" Field continued. "Yes, Sir," Minor responded with noticeable discomfort.[32] When the Court asked Minor to elaborate, his awkwardness grew. The justices stopped asking questions.

A month later, the Supreme Court issued its decision: the Missouri restrictions on women's suffrage were constitutional, for citizenship conveys "the idea of membership of the nation, and nothing more." The Fifteenth Amendment had barred voting discrimination on the basis of "race, color, or previous condition of servitude," but not sex, for there was no legislative willpower to include women.[33] Chief Justice Morrison Waite added that the Court had carefully considered the merits of this important case—in contrast to previous courts that simply dismissed the issue—but that the Court's duty is "to decide what the law is, not to declare what it should be." Someday, he wrote, "such arguments may induce those having the power, to make the alteration."[34]

The *Minor v. Happersett* decision sounded the death knell for the New Departure strategy. Bradwell had argued that the Constitution permitted women the right to pursue any profession. Anthony had claimed it gave her the right to vote. Minor had asserted that citizenship granted full political rights. Initial hopes that the courts might find women's rights in the Constitution were lost. A generation earlier, in a case stemming from the same Missouri court as Minor, the Supreme Court decided that Dred Scott, as a slave, had no citizenship and no rights. Now, the Supreme Court decided that Minor was a citizen with no voting rights. Nor was there any political will to reinterpret the Constitution. The New Departure reached a dead end.

Notes

1. *Missouri Democrat*, October 7, 1869, in Laura Elizabeth Howe Staley, "The Suffrage Movement in St. Louis during the 1870s," *Gateway Heritage* 3, no. 4 (1983): 38.

2. Ibid.

3. *HWS*, 2:408.

4. Ibid.

5. SBA to Laura De Force Gordon, February 9, 1871, Box 1, Laura De Force Gordon Collection, Bancroft Library, UC Berkeley, in Rebecca J. Mead, *How the Vote Was Won: Woman Suffrage in the Western United States, 1868–1914* (New York: New York University, 2006), 37.

6. *HWS*, 2:417.

7. Ibid., 2:412.

8. Francis Minor, October 14, 1869, *The Revolution*, in N. E. H Hull, *The Woman Who Dared to Vote: The Trial of Susan B. Anthony* (Lawrence: University Press of Kansas, 2012), 187; SBA testimony before the Senate Judiciary Committee, January 12, 1872, in *HWS*, 2:410.

9. *Chicago Legal News*, February 5, 1870, 145, in Nancy T. Gilliam, "A Professional Pioneer: Myra Bradwell's Fight to Practice Law," *Law and History Review* 5, no. 1 (Spring 1987): 109.

10. Bradwell, *Chicago Tribune*, May 12, 1889, 26, in Jane M. Friedman, *America's First Woman Lawyer: The Biography of Myra Bradwell* (Buffalo, NY: Prometheus Books, 1993), 172.

11. Carpenter's Brief in U. S. Supreme Court, *Chicago Legal News*, 4 (January 20, 1872): 108, in Friedman, *Lawyer*, 24, 22.

12. SBA to Myra Bradwell, July 30, 1873, in the possession of Friedman, in Friedman, *Lawyer*, 23.

13. E. T. Marsh, November 4, 1922, Bergen, New York, Sophia Smith Collection, SCA, in Barry, *Anthony*, 249–50.

14. Ibid., 250.

15. SBA to ECS, n.d., in *SBA*, 1:424.

16. *SBA*, 1:426.

17. "Address of Susan B. Anthony," in Susan B. Anthony, United States, and Circuit Court (New York : Northern District), *An Account of the Proceedings on the Trial of Susan B. Anthony, on the Charge of Illegal Voting, at the Presidential Election in Nov., 1872, and on the Trial of Beverly W. Jones, Edwin T. Marsh, and William B. Hall, the Inspectors of Election by Whom Her Vote Was Received* (Union, NJ: Lawbook Exchange, 2002), 151.

18. *Minor v. Happersett*, 88 US 162 October 1874; Opinion by Chief Justice Waite, in Charles L. Zelden, *Voting Rights on Trial: A Handbook with Cases, Laws, and Documents* (Santa Barbara, CA; Denver; Oxford: ABC-CLIO, 2002), 194.

19. 83 U.S. at 141 in Gilliam, "Pioneer," 126.

20. SBA to Hon. Benjamin Butler, April 27, 1873, in http://law2.umkc.edu/faculty/projects/ftrials/anthony/voteletters.html, accessed May 20, 2011.

21. SBA to Myra Bradwell, 30 July 1873, in the possession of Friedman, in Friedman, *Lawyer*, 23.

22. Anthony, United States, and Circuit Court, *Trial of Susan B. Anthony*, 6, 51–52.

23. Ibid., 68.

24. Ibid., 82.

25. Ibid.

26. Ibid., 83.

27. Ibid.

28. Ibid., 84.

29. Ibid., 85.

30. *Utica Observer*, n.d., in *SBA*, 1:443.

31. Hull, *Woman Who Dared*, 201.

32. Ibid., 202.

33. Ibid.

34. Ibid., 208.

CHAPTER FOURTEEN

Wyoming and Utah

In the summer of 1868, Congress cobbled together parts of the Idaho, Utah, and Dakota Territories to create Wyoming Territory, a fifty-eight thousand square mile rectangle of high, arid land. With little to offer by way of employment except low-paying jobs in mines, and a paucity of arable soil, few chose to settle there. When President Grant at one point proposed to divide Wyoming among its neighbors, even some Wyoming residents approved.

Then the railroads and a gold rush came. General Grenville Dodge, chief engineer for the Union Pacific Railroad, determined that the best route for a transcontinental railway line was through the South Pass in southwestern Wyoming, which rose gently to 7,550 feet and had an ample supply of coal. Towns like Rawlins Springs and Laramie emerged almost overnight along the line when gangs of men appeared on the high plain to work on the railroad. Settlers called Cheyenne the "Magic City of the Plains" when it grew from a tent city to a collection of wooden structures in a matter of months.[1] Saloons sprang up everywhere, and prostitution, bar brawls, and gunfights abounded. South Pass City's half-mile business area had seven hotels, three breweries, a wholesale liquor dealer, and a cluster of saloons. In Laramie, its first mayor quit after just three months in office, and outlaws took over the town until vigilantes, and a few hangings, restored order. Drunken men flashed knives and revolvers as they patrolled the polls on Election Day in South Pass City, threatening a handful of black men who wanted to vote, and beating a white man nearly unconscious when he tried to intervene. A U.S. marshal drew his revolver and escorted the black men through the crowd, swearing to shoot anyone who interfered. Despite the roughness of frontier life—or maybe because of it—many in Wyoming cherished the trappings of civilization. Laramie boasted the first county library in the territory and had electric lights before Denver. Cheyenne had an Opera House, two newspapers, and a capitol building with steam heat, an elevator, elaborate frescoes, and stained glass windows. Its "Millionaire Row," lined with mansions built by cattle barons, rivaled exclusive neighborhoods in the East.[2]

As the gold rush waned and railroad workers moved on, Wyoming's population declined. Some towns survived, others did not. Cheyenne became the capital with a permanent population. The number of inhabitants in South Pass City peaked in the thousands in 1868 but shrank to only a few dozen seven years later.

As in most frontier areas, women were scarce in Wyoming, numbering just one in nine residents. Newspapers debated how to attract more women to sustain a permanent population. Women from the East "have no idea how quick they will be snapped up" and "have the satisfaction of civilizing just so many men who are relapsing into barbarism for the want of such society and home discipline as they can furnish," one newspaper wrote.[3] Western ideals of womanhood reflected a frontier ethos, which valued strength and hard work. "A rough took occasion to insult a lady on Seventeenth Street this afternoon," the *Cheyenne Leader* reported in November 1869, and she responded by firing a pistol at him but "unfortunately she was not well-enough skilled in the use of arms to aim well, and he escaped."[4] Wyoming does not need "soft-eyed hyenas," wrote one newspaper editor, but rather women who could wash "heavy underclothing in soapsuds" in winter and "make a pie that will not taste like a stove lid veneered with cod liver oil."[5] Granting women the right to vote, some suggested, would entice hard-working women to move to Wyoming where their votes would counter those of the irresponsible "roving man."[6]

Yet there was little momentum for women's suffrage. It was stalled at the federal level and the neighboring Dakota territorial legislature had defeated it by one vote. In Wyoming, there were no suffrage organizations, no organized protests, and no petitions. A handful of national suffragists gave speeches as they passed through the territory. Anna Dickinson spoke during a trip to California and persuaded many in the territory to drop their opposition to suffrage, though a crowd of ogling men on the street drove her into a nearby coach for refuge. "The irrepressible 'Annie D' " should settle in Wyoming, the *Cheyenne Leader* wrote. "We'll even give her more than the right to vote—she can run for Congress."[7]

Two men took the lead on women's suffrage in Wyoming Territory. Secretary of the Territory Edward M. Lee asked his friend William Bright, president of the Territorial Council, Wyoming's upper house, to introduce a suffrage bill. Years earlier, Lee had tried unsuccessfully to add a suffrage amendment to the Connecticut state constitution when he served in its legislature. He knew it would be easier to pass suffrage in a territory that required only a majority vote of the legislature and a governor's signature rather than the two-thirds of the legislature and a majority of voters for a state constitution. Though Bright had never been to a suffrage lecture, or even heard a woman speak in public, he vowed his full support, prodded by several Wyoming women and his wife Julia, whom he "venerated" and "submitted to her judgment and influence more willing than one could have supposed," a friend observed.[8] "It was just," Bright said, and added that if black men could vote, so should women "like my wife and mother."[9] It was also good politics. If Republican governor John Campbell were to sign the bill into law, he would go against his party's position on suffrage. A veto would pit him against the legislature dominated by Democrats.

On November 27, 1869, eight days before the legislative session ended, the Territorial Council passed the suffrage bill without discussion by a 6–2 vote. In the House, however, Ben Sheeks, a young South Pass City attorney, tried to sabotage the bill. First, he moved to postpone its consideration "indefinitely" or until July 4, when the legislature was in recess. Then, he attempted to replace the word "woman" with the phrase "all colored women and squaws." After that, he tried to amend the bill to require that voting women "perform all other duties as citizens."[10] Finally, he sought to raise the voting age for women to thirty-five, calculating that no woman would ever admit to being that old. But his efforts failed, and the House passed the suffrage bill by a vote of 7–4. Governor Campbell, however, hesitated to sign it. He opposed suffrage and thought it might be improper for a territorial government to decide the issue. After four days of prodding by two territorial Supreme Court judges, several local women, and his own wife, Campbell finally signed the bill into law on the evening of December 10, the last day the Wyoming legislature was in session.

On the next Election Day, according to informal observation, most of Wyoming's thousand eligible women voters showed up at the polls. Laramie officials opened a booth early so Louisa A. Swain, a seventy-year-old well-respected citizen, could vote first. Cheyenne men doffed their hats as an eighty-year-old woman alighted from her carriage at her polling place. After she voted, the men cheered "so rousingly," a newspaper reported, "that they were heard for several squares."[11] Many believed women's suffrage improved decorum on Election Day, with fewer fights and less intimidation by ruffians. "No rum was sold, women rode to the polls in carriages furnished by the two parties, and every man was straining himself to be a gentleman because there were votes at stake," a Laramie editor noted.[12] The Republican candidate newly elected to the U.S. House of Representatives credited his victory to these dynamics.

The Wyoming legislature did more than grant women the right to vote—it also gave them equal pay when employed by the territorial government, the right to their earnings and property when married, and the right to hold public office. Lawmakers elevated women's status, Lee said, because it was "a 'first-class advertisement'" that would yield "increased immigration and large accretions of capital to their new and comparatively unknown Territory."[13] Susan B. Anthony said she would go there herself and run for the U.S. Senate were she not already engaged in the East. Wyoming soon got its first woman public official when Sweetwater County's Justice of the Peace James W. Stillman resigned to protest women's suffrage, and several prominent men prodded fifty-seven-year-old Esther Morris to apply for the job, even posting the required five-hundred-dollar bond for her. Nearly six feet tall and physically robust, Morris was an outspoken optimist. "She had courage to do what would have been easier to avoid," an acquaintance said, though some thought her "blunt and often cutting."[14] Orphaned at eleven and a widow at thirty, her early life was one of struggle. She supported her family with a millinery shop and, by fifty, she had remarried and given birth to several sons.

Morris hesitated to accept the justice of the peace position because of her limited legal knowledge, but eventually agreed, hoping her common sense would suffice. In February 1870, Morris was sworn in and began holding court in her small, dirt floor log cabin in South Pass City. She appointed two of her sons as clerks. Her first act was to issue a warrant for the arrest of her predecessor, who refused to turn over official documents because he objected to a woman justice of the peace. When the prior Justice's lawyer pointed out a defect in the warrant, she ruled it invalid and promptly issued a new one. Morris was quick to squelch small talk and petty squabbling by lawyers and meted out particularly harsh sentences for public drunkenness, even jailing her own husband, a heavy drinker, when he disrupted her courtroom. Crying in the courtroom to gain sympathy from the judge "did no more good than pouring whiskey down a rathole," one defendant said.[15] In her nine months on the bench, Morris oversaw twenty-six cases and issued seventy decisions, mostly dealing with debt collection and assault and battery. The *South Pass News* applauded her. She "advocated the elevation of women," it reported, but "does not wish the downfall of man."[16]

Wyoming also seated the nation's first mixed-sex jury when Albany County called up several women for three weeks of jury duty, a summons that surprised and amused some of them. "The eyes of the whole world are today fixed upon this jury," Judge J. H. Howe said in his courtroom as eight men and four women sat for a murder trial in March 1870.[17] Judge Howe confessed to doubts about allowing women to sit as jurors but was determined to see it through. Women had long been the victims of the "vices, crimes and immoralities of man" without power to defend themselves, he said.[18] Now they would be pioneers. Eventually, after mixed-sex juries returned convictions in cases involving first-degree manslaughter, cattle and horse theft, and wrongful branding, Judge Howe announced that they were the best juries he had seen in his twenty-five-year legal career. The women "acquitted themselves with such dignity, decorum, propriety of conduct and intelligence as to win the admiration of every fair minded citizen of Wyoming," he said.[19] Some felt that the presence of women cleaned up the courts. Jury trials used to be a "farce," the *Laramie Sentinel* reported, with "the jury taken up with the telling of vulgar and obscene stories." Mixed-sex juries were more determined to enforce blue laws, and some defense lawyers believed women were too likely to convict. "We can't clear a client if he is guilty, before a woman jury," one complained.[20]

Yet some disapproved of women serving as jurors. The *Cheyenne Daily Leader* reported that the women jurors looked unwell and hoped that they "do not sink under the weight of their privations and return to their homes with shattered nerves and ruined health."[21] Greeley's *New York Tribune* deemed the mixed-sex jury "indecorous and not suitable."[22] After rumors spread of questionable sleeping arrangements, Judge Howe explained to the newspapers that the men and women slept in separate rooms and that a female bailiff escorted the women as they traveled in a group between their hotel and the courtroom.

Democratic legislators had granted women suffrage but found that Wyoming

A newspaper illustration showing women at the polls in Wyoming Territory in September 1870, when Wyoming became the first government in the world to grant the vote to women. (Library of Congress)

women voted largely Republican. Partisan newspapers turned against women voters. Normal women would not oppose losing their right to vote, the Democrat-leaning *Laramie Sentinel* wrote. Only "the suffrage shriekers, the unsexed and uncultivated, one had almost said unchaste, of the Territory" would object.[23] In November 1871, legislators voted along party lines to repeal suffrage, but Governor Campbell, a Republican, vetoed the attempt, noting in his diary that someone offered him a two-thousand-dollar bribe to change his mind. Women voters "have conducted themselves with as much tact, sound judgment and good sense as the men," he told the legislators. If women lost their rights, "what is to prevent a future Legislature from depriving certain men, or classes of men, whom, from any consideration, they desire to disfranchise, of the same rights?"[24] When a lone Democrat later proposed again to repeal suffrage, no other legislator joined him, and his constituents even talked of lynching him.

Two months after Wyoming women got the vote, the territorial government of Utah granted suffrage to women. Wyoming and Utah Territories were similar in size and shared a common border. Yet Utah had 87,000 residents, ten times the number of Wyoming, and more than nine in ten of Utah's residents were Mormon. The Mormons—members of the Church of Jesus Christ of Latter-day Saints—settled in Salt Lake City nearly a quarter-century earlier, seeking refuge in the high desert after the murder of their founder Joseph Smith in 1844. With a strong communal ethos and strict social norms that kept many vices at bay, the Mormon community flourished under the leadership of Brigham Young, Smith's successor. Yet as the Mormon community grew, so did controversy over its practice of polygamy. Smith began it in secret sometime in the 1830s, when he married Fanny Alger, a teenager, over the objections of his wife Emma. After five years with two wives, Smith married again and, in the following three years, wed thirty more women. Church leaders made polygamy public in 1852 when they endorsed the "doctrine of the plurality of wives."[25] The majority of Mormons were not polygamous—at most one-in-four engaged in the practice—but nearly all of the leadership were, and about a third of all Mormon women were married to polygamous husbands. Young eventually married fifty-five women and fathered fifty-six children. He lodged most of his large family in two houses in central Salt Lake City: the Beehive House, a substantial home where he resided, and the Lion House, a dorm-like structure next door with twenty gabled bedrooms. Polygamy's defenders said it provided women who would otherwise remain single with the protection of a home and the dignity of marriage. Heber Kimball, the husband of forty-five women and father of sixty-five children, said polygamy was "not to have women to commit whoredoms with, to gratify the lusts of the flesh, but to raise up children."[26] Young believed the practice was superior to the monogamous ideal promoted by gentile society, where married men often had mistresses. Defenders cited the Bible in support of polygamy—Abraham had several wives—and Martin Luther and St. Augustine approved the practice.

Most Americans found polygamy abhorrent. The Republican Party declared it one of the "twin relics of barbarism"—the other being slavery—and Republican legislators passed a federal law in 1862 to make the practice illegal.[27] U.S. vice president Schuyler Colfax campaigned against polygamy in lectures and newspapers. The chaplain of the U.S. Senate, Rev. J. P. Newman, a Methodist, traveled to Salt Lake City and challenged Young to a public debate. The popular speaker Anna Dickinson gave lectures on "Whited Sepulchres" and "Women's Cry from Utah" that portrayed Mormon women as haggard and somber, their unquestioning obedience the result of a cruel system.[28] Indiana representative George W. Julian called polygamy "a system of unmitigated sensuality & lust on the part of the men, & of degradation & superstition on the part of the women."[29] He believed women in Utah would vote to end polygamy and sponsored legislation to grant them suffrage.

Brigham Young was initially undecided on whether women should have the right to vote. He knew outsiders criticized polygamy and wondered aloud whether women would end it if they could. Other Utah leaders supported women's rights. The *Deseret News*, a leading Mormon newspaper, supported suffrage, and the *Utah Magazine* argued that a nation without women having an important role in "all the vital concerns of humanity, is barbaric in its notions and estate."[30] When Illinois congressman Shelby Cullom submitted a bill in late 1869 to disenfranchise male voters who supported polygamy, Mormon women responded with mass protests, including a "Great Indignation Meeting" of six thousand women at the Salt Lake Tabernacle.[31] The legislation, Sarah Kimball said, "would also deprive us, as women, of the privilege of selecting our husbands, and against this we most unqualifiedly protest."[32] Eliza Snow, a wife of Brigham Young who lived at the Beehive House, said Utah women were misunderstood and it "is high time that we should rise up in the dignity of our calling and speak for ourselves." Mormon women support "plural marriage" and oppose any legislation that would make them adulterers and their children illegitimate. Polygamy was not the exploitation of women, she said, but God's plan "to restore and preserve the chastity of woman."[33] Snow was a leader among Mormon women and founded several organizations, including the Female Relief Society, which built granaries and staffed hospitals with nurses and a woman surgeon. But she also encouraged women to obey male authority at home and in the Church and let men speak last at Female Relief Society meetings, so "that if we say anything that needs correcting it can be corrected."[34]

Young eventually supported women's suffrage, partly to defend against critics who said his religion exploited women and partly to enhance the Church's political power by adding voters who were disproportionately Mormon. The all-Mormon Utah legislature unanimously approved women's suffrage on February 12, 1870, enabling over fifteen thousand women to vote in the fall elections, although unlike Wyoming, Utah did not permit women to hold public office.

Young was proud of Utah's leadership in women's suffrage and invited Elizabeth Cady Stanton and Susan B. Anthony to present a series of talks for women at the Mormon Tabernacle. Anthony and Stanton agreed to speak but suspected Young would disapprove of what they had to say. Women's rights, Young once said, should give wives the right to ask husbands for help at home, and women's "privilege," he said, was "to stop all folly in your conversation."[35] When Anthony and Stanton reached Salt Lake City in June 1871, they planned to make all of their controversial statements in one talk in case Young shut them down. Anthony watched as the women filtered in and found "scarcely a sunny, joyous countenance in the whole three hundred, but a vast number of deep-lined, careworn, long-suffering faces—more so, even, than those of our own pioneer farmers' and settlers' wives," she said.[36] For five hours, the women discussed rights, marriage, birth control, and other issues with "such free talk as those women had never heard before," Stanton said. Mormon women defended their religion, "yet they are no more satisfied than any other sect," she observed.[37] Young canceled the remaining speeches. Anthony joined most other suffragists in denouncing polygamy, but Stanton refused to condemn it. It was no worse than tolerating men with mistresses, she said.

In less than three months, Wyoming and Utah gave women the vote with little turmoil and minimal campaigning by women's rights activists. These successes were partly possible because it was much easier to pass suffrage in territorial legislatures than in state legislatures. Although granting suffrage in Wyoming and Utah enfranchised fewer than thirty thousand women in a nation of thirty-eight million people, it was a symbolic breakthrough. As Anthony and Stanton headed west over the plains on a prairie schooner pulled by oxen on their way to California, they awoke at 4 A.M. to note the exact moment they crossed into Wyoming and entered "the land of the free and home of the brave."[38] Some people in the West had said they needed women to civilize their society, Anthony told a Cheyenne audience, but by granting women suffrage, she said, westerners were as far above the East in civilization as they were in altitude.

Notes

1. Lori Van Pelt, "Cheyenne, Magic City of the Plains," https://www.wyohistory.org/ encyclopedia/cheyenne-magic-city-plains.
2. "Cheyenne, Wyoming," http://plainshumanities.unl.edu/encyclopedia/doc/egp.ct.012.
3. "Come Along Girls," *Wyoming Tribune* no. 7, January 1, 1870 Edition, 2 pluto.wyo.gov/ awweb/main.jsp.
4. "No Title," *Cheyenne Leader* (November 27, 1869): 4, at http://pluto.wyo.gov/ awweb/ main.jsp?flag=browse&smd=2&awdid=12.
5. Bill Nye, cited in T. A. Larson, "Dolls, Vassals, and Drudges: Pioneer Women in the West," *The Western Historical Quarterly* 3, no. 1 (January 1972): 8.
6. E. A. Curley, *The Territory of Wyoming: Its History, Soil, Climate, Resources, etc.* (Laramie, WY: Board of immigration, December 1874), in T. A. Larson, *History of Wyoming* (Lincoln; London: University of Nebraska Press, 1978), 88.
7. Ibid., 83.
8. *HWS*, 3:730; William H. Bright, *Revolution* 5 (January 13, 1870), 21, in Larson, "Dolls," 7.
9. T.A. Larson, "Woman Suffrage in Western America," *Utah Historical Quarterly* 38 (Winter 1970): 12.
10. Miriam Gantz Chapman, *The Story of Woman Suffrage in Wyoming, 1869–1890* (MA Thesis, University of Wyoming, 1952) 12; T. A. Larson, *Wyoming: A Bicentennial History* (New York: W.W. Norton and Company, 1977), 79–80.
11. "Women at the Polls," *Burlington Iowa Hawkeye*, n.d., in Matilda Joslyn Gage Scrapbook, LC, Box 1, Folder 7.
12. Bill Nye, "Bill Nye's Experience Tells What He Knows about Woman Suffrage," *Annals of Wyoming* XVI (1944): 66, in Dee Brown, *The Gentle Tamers: Women of the Old Wild West* (New York: G.P. Putnam's Sons, 1958), 246.
13. Edward M. Lee, "The Woman Movement in Wyoming," *The Galaxy* XIII (June 1872): 755–60, in Larson, *History of Wyoming*, 81.
14. Grace R. Hebard, *How Woman Suffrage Came to Wyoming* (Laramie, WY, 1920), 6, in Chapman, *Wyoming Suffrage*, 16; Note 138 in Marcy Lynn Karin, "Esther Morris and Her Equality State from Council Bill 70 to Life on the Bench," *American Journal of Legal History* 46 no. 3 (July 2004): 324.
15. Chapman, *Wyoming Suffrage*, 326.
16. *South Pass News*, March 19, 1870, in Virginia Scharff, "The Case for Domestic Feminism: Woman Suffrage in Wyoming," *Annals of Wyoming* 56 (1984): 36.

17. Judge J. H. Howe to Myra Bradwell, *The Chicago Legal News*, in HWS, 3:736.

18. Ibid., 3:733.

19. Howe, *Chicago Legal News*, in HWS, 3:736.

20. *Laramie Sentinel*, February 27, 1871, in Chapman, *Wyoming Suffrage*, 29.

21. *Cheyenne Daily Leader*, March 14, 1870, in Chapman, *Wyoming Suffrage*, 26.

22. *The New York Tribune*, n.d., in Larson, *Bicentennial History*, 85.

23. *Laramie Sentinel*, December 12, 1871, in *Laramie Sentinel*, November 21, 1871, cited in Amanda Frisken, "Sex in Politics: Victoria Woodhull as an American Public Woman, 1870–1876," *Journal of Women's History* 12, no. 1 (Spring 2000): 102.

24. *Laramie Sentinel*, December 12, 1871, in Chapman, *Wyoming Suffrage*, 75.

25. B. Carmon Hardy, *Doing the Works of Abraham: Mormon Polygamy: Its Origin, Practice, and Demise* (Arthur H. Clark Co.: Norman, Oklahoma, 2007), n.p.

26. No citation, Irving Wallace, *The Twenty-Seventh Wife* (New York: Signet, 1961), 13.

27. Republican Party Platform of 1856, http://www.digitalhistory.uh.edu/disp_textbook. cfm?smtID=3&psid=4028.

28. See "Anna Dickinson's 'Whited Sepulchres,' 1869–1870," in Angela G. Ray, ed., *The Lyceum and Public Culture in the Nineteenth-Century United States* (East Lansing: Michigan State University Press, 2005), 143–72.

29. Personal Journal of George Washington Julian, June 13 or 17, 1869, in Patrick W. Riddleberger, *George Washington Julian Radical Republican* (n.p.: Indiana Historical Bureau, 1966), 254.

30. Edward W. Tullidge, "Woman and Her Sphere," *The Utah Magazine*, III (June 26, 1869): 119, cited by Thomas G. Alexander, "An Experiment in Progressive Legislation: The Granting of Woman Suffrage in Utah in 1875," in Carol Cornwall Madsen, ed., *Battle for the Ballot: Essays on Woman Suffrage in Utah, 1870–1896* (Logan: Utah State University Press, 1997), 108.

31. Lola Van Wagenen, "In Their Own Behalf: The Politicization of Mormon Women and the 1870 Franchise," in Madsen, *Battle for the Ballot*, 67.

32. *Deseret News* (January 14, 1870), in Madsen, *Battle for the Ballot*, 67.

33. Jill Mulvay Derr, "Eliza R. Snow and the Woman Question," in Madsen, *Battle for the Ballot*, 83.

34. Eliza R. Snow, "Degradation of Woman in Utah," Provo Stake Relief Society Minutes, May 27, 1881, in *Woman's Exponent*, July 1, 1881, in Derr, "Snow," in Madsen, *Battle for the Ballot*, 86.

35. *Deseret Evening News*, August 14, 1869, in Larson, "Dolls," 11.

36. SBA, 1:390.

37. Stanton, *Eighty Years*, 284.

38. SBA, 1:388.

CHAPTER FIFTEEN

Scandal

In early January 1871, in a crowded room in the U.S. Capitol, Victoria Woodhull stood before the House Judiciary Committee to speak on behalf of women's rights, the first woman ever to do so. She wore a blue velvet dress with a white rose pinned at the neck, her brown hair neatly tucked into a stylish Alpine hat. Her younger sister Tennessee Claflin sat nearby watching calmly. Popular opinion held that no respectable woman would present herself so publicly. "Quiet and pure lights" stay out of the newspaper columns, except those "devoted to marriages and deaths," the *New York World* proclaimed the year before.[1] Politicians and newspaper reporters packed the room to see how Woodhull would do. She looked pale and held onto the large mahogany table as she spoke. Her voice trembled, and she stopped every few words—some thought she might faint. "Women constitute a majority of this country," pay taxes, and perform "the most vital responsibilities of society" by bearing, training, and inspiring men to their "noblest impulses," she said. Yet men fear women who "propose to carry a slip of paper with a name upon it to the polls," her voice steadied as she spoke.[2] The United States led in sweeping away old prejudices and ignorance, Woodhull concluded, and she urged Congress to champion women's rights. Woodhull bowed to the committee members and sat down.

Anthony watched from two rows behind Woodhull. Women's rights leaders tried for years to address Congress, and here, suddenly, a woman with scant attachment to the movement held the limelight. Isabella Beecher Hooker, chief organizer for the National Woman Suffrage Association (NWSA) annual Convention, learned of Woodhull's testimony only the day before and initially declined to attend. Dark rumors hovered over Woodhull, and Hooker wanted to shield NWSA from potential controversy while she tried to heal the breach between NWSA and the American Woman Suffrage Association (AWSA). Anthony, too, initially hesitated to attend, but her Washington host, Senator Samuel Pomeroy of Kansas, told her that if they delved into everyone's past, nothing would get done in politics. Woodhull impressed listeners with her forceful arguments and graceful style. She confounded popular notions of women's intellectual frivolity. "All the past efforts of Ms. Anthony and Mrs. Stanton sink to insignificance beside the ingenious lobbying of the new leader," the *New York Tribune* reported.[3]

After hearing her speak, Hooker proclaimed Woodhull was "Heaven sent for the rescue of woman from the pit of subjection" and placed her on the platform at the NWSA Convention that afternoon.[4] Anthony felt more hopeful than ever. The battle for women's rights, she predicted, would be "short, sharp and decisive."[5] Sympathetic politicians sent Woodhull's Memorial, her strongly worded statement in support of women's rights, to thousands of constituents across the nation, and President Grant invited her to his office. "Some day you will occupy that chair," Grant said as he offered his seat.[6] People visited Wall Street just to see Woodhull and Claflin, the brokerage house headed by the two sisters, and the first ever run by women. The poet Walt Whitman described them as "a prophecy of the future."[7]

Woodhull and Tennessee Claflin garnered wealth and influence through their connections with powerful men. They befriended Cornelius Vanderbilt, who consulted Woodhull for her purported skill as a medium while he grieved the deaths of his beloved mother and a cherished son, George Washington Vanderbilt, who was killed in the Civil War. Vanderbilt sponsored their Wall Street brokerage house and passed them stock tips, enabling them to earn huge profits and live lavishly. The sisters purchased a brownstone mansion in a fashionable Manhattan neighborhood where they frequently entertained influential New Yorkers amid sophisticated blue silk furnishings and imported carpets. They also befriended Massachusetts congressman General Benjamin Butler, one of the keenest political operators on Capitol Hill. Short, stooped, chomping on an unlit cigar as he roamed the halls of Congress, Butler was "the smartest damn rascal that ever lived," Lincoln's Secretary John Hay said.[8] But Butler's wife was in Germany seeking treatment for cancer, and he was lonely. Butler visited Woodhull and Claflin after long days on Capitol Hill, and it was he who arranged Woodhull's appearance before the Judiciary Committee. Yet, for all the attention that Woodhull generated with her testimony, the committee's majority report concluded that only states had the right to set voting requirements and recommended no further action.

As Woodhull's influence grew, whispers of a sordid past became louder, particularly as reported in sporting newspapers that catered to young men.

Woodhull openly practiced spiritualism, claiming to contact the dead, and was rumored to support the doctrine of Free Love. She lived with her husband and twelve other relatives, including her former husband whom some said she never divorced. When Horace Greeley called on NWSA and AWSA to denounce Woodhull and Free Love, Woodhull struck back in the newspaper she and her sister published, *Woodhull & Claflin's Weekly*. She branded his two top reporters as hypocrites for criticizing Free Love by "a light reflected from the gaiety of the night's amours." She described the Greeley home as a "domestic hell"

American feminist reformer Victoria Woodhull, the first female U.S. presidential candidate, 1872. (The New York Public Library)

where the famous editor squelched his intelligent wife and treated his vivacious daughters with "senseless indifference."[9] "It is the same old game," Anthony vented in her diary—society condemns women for transgressions that it tolerates in men.[10] "When we shall require of the men, who shall speak—vote, work for us—to prove that they have never been unduly familiar with any woman—never guilty of trifling with or desecrating womanhood—it will be time enough for us to demand of the women to prove that no man has ever trifled with or desecrated them."[11] Stanton wrote to Mott that men set women against each other. "He creates the public sentiment, builds the gallows, & then makes us hangman for our sex," she said. "If Victoria Woodhull must be crucified, let men drive the spikes, & plaite the crown of thorns."[12]

Stanton saw the rumors of Woodhull's sexual impropriety as simply "a new scare to keep rebellious womanhood in check," but Woodhull's endorsement of Free Love during a speech in November 1871 horrified most suffragists and tainted their cause.[13] Woodhull claimed an inalienable right to love whom she wished without interference by law or society.

Yet it was one thing to criticize the double standard—it was another thing entirely to challenge the institution of marriage itself. Oregon suffragists declared in a local newspaper "we are not advocates, but on the contrary, are opponents of the Free Love Doctrine."[14] The Connecticut Woman Suffrage Association withdrew from NWSA, and Iowa suffragists asked Anthony and Stanton to stay away from their state. While NWSA stood by Woodhull, leaders of AWSA tried to distance themselves from her. "My one wish, in regard to Mrs. Woodhull," Stone wrote in late 1871, "is, that [neither] she nor her ideas, may be so much as heard at our meeting."[15] Harriet Beecher Stowe advised that "the Boston women have only now to be quiet, patient, firm, and discreet and they may save the cause."[16]

In the spring of 1872, unable to gain support of the major political parties, Anthony and Hooker lobbied a new party, the Liberal Republicans, formed partly by Republicans disgusted with the corruption scandals of the Grant administration. Anthony's friends Theodore Tilton and George W. Julian welcomed the women to their Liberal Republican Convention and seated Anthony on the platform with other dignitaries. But when the Convention delegates selected Horace Greeley as their candidate for president, Anthony and Hooker walked out. Stanton said she "would sooner cut off my right hand than use my influence in behalf of this enemy to the woman cause."[17] She vowed never again to "ask favors or pocket insults" from "the white male conventions."[18]

A week later, Anthony faced a crisis at the NWSA Convention in New York when Woodhull tried to unite labor and reform groups into a new political party. Woodhull had already convinced the American Section of the International Working Men's Association to elect her as their leader by railing against monopolies and absentee landlords, and calling for the nationalization of banks. She also persuaded the American Association of Spiritualists to elect her as its president, even though she had no prior connection to the organization. Now she was attempting to take control of the NWSA Convention. Stanton supported the idea of a new party. The two major parties ignored suffrage, and the Liberal Republicans, she believed, had selected an enemy of women's rights as their candidate for the highest office in the land. Suffragists had "culture refinement, social influence, but no political power," Stanton said, while workers had the votes. Together they could "strike a blow that will be felt by politicians."[19] Anthony believed that creating a new party was futile.

Attendees of the NWSA Convention included many new faces and more men than usual. Woodhull supporters interrupted the morning speeches and complained that the Convention should address human rights. Woodhull then took the stage and moved that the meeting join a larger convention at Apollo Hall. When Anthony, as chair, refused to call the question, Woodhull demanded a vote and won. Anthony shouted them out of order. When Woodhull grabbed the podium, Anthony left the stage and directed the janitor to turn off the lights, which abruptly ended the meeting. Most of the attendees departed to join Woodhull at Apollo Hall. Anthony thwarted an outright hijacking of the organization but lost many of her supporters in the process. She did not know if it was she or the others who had gone mad. "I am feeling today that life doesn't pay," she confided to her friend Martha Coffin Wright, "the way seems so blocked up to me on all sides."[20]

Woodhull's supporters created the Equal Rights Party and nominated her as its candidate for president of the United States, making her the first woman ever to run for that office. They also nominated Frederick Douglass as vice president even though he was not present and did not seek the office. The platform called for the destruction of monopolies, direct taxation, adequate compensation for labor, representation for minorities, women's suffrage, and an end to capital punishment. "Women waved their handkerchiefs and wept," while "men shouted themselves hoarse and perfect confusion prevailed," the *Sun* reported.[21] But all the noise and enthusiasm failed to make up for a lack of money, organization, and viability. The labor movement ultimately rejected Woodhull because she advocated women's suffrage, Free Love, and claimed to communicate directly with spirits of the deceased. Vanderbilt withdrew his support, and Woodhull's finances dried up. The New York media increasingly ignored her.

Although Stanton stayed loyal to NWSA and did not endorse the Equal Rights Party, Anthony was furious that she supported Woodhull for as long as she did, and for calling the New York meeting a "People's Convention" instead of a Women's Rights Convention. It was a "perfect fiasco," she wrote in her diary, "never did Mrs. Stanton do so foolish a thing—all came nearer being lost."[22] Stanton tried to find something positive in the experience. "All the agitation has helped in some way," she wrote to Lucy Stone, asserting that the Free Love scare had made "some suffrage respectable."[23] Hooker, too, tried to find something of value. The new party, she reasoned, placed NWSA as the "binding link between the extremes of respectability and mobocracy," and the party members would work with suffragists because "they want the prestige of our social position."[24] Most suffragists just hoped the Woodhull problem was behind them.

A few minutes after noon on November 2, 1872, as Woodhull and her sister traveled along Broad Street in Manhattan with three thousand copies of their newspaper, *Woodhull & Claflin's Weekly*, U.S. marshals stopped their carriage, confiscated the papers, and arrested the sisters. One of the marshals sat on Claflin's lap to restrain her while the sisters were transported to the Ludlow Street Jail, where they spent the next two nights. Police raided the *Weekly* headquarters and confiscated all remaining copies of the paper.

The next day, the sisters were taken to the federal building where, at their insistence, the court proceedings were conducted in public. The U.S. government charged them with obscenity for an exposé they published in the *Weekly*, which described alleged wild debauchery at an annual New York dance featuring "three thousand of the best men and four thousand of the worst women."[25] In the report, Claflin claimed to have seen two men having sex with an intoxicated woman who lay on a couch with her skirts thrown over her head. Luther Challis, a successful Wall Street broker, and other men corrupted "two fresh-faced young schoolgirls perhaps fifteen or sixteen years of age," she wrote.[26] Amid wild drinking and frenzied dancing, Challis refilled the girls' wine glasses until they were in a stupor and then shouted "Let them alone!" when Claflin tried to intervene.[27] Then Challis and his friends took the girls to a house of prostitution "where they were robbed of their innocence," the *Weekly* stated. And Challis, "to prove that he had *seduced a maiden, carried for days on his finger, exhibiting in triumph, the red trophy of her virginity*" before handing over the girls to more than a hundred of his friends.[28] The court cited in particular as evidence of obscenity "the red trophy of her virginity."

Woodhull's lawyer, William F. Howe, argued that the arrest of Woodhull and her sister was to protect "certain persons in high station, who dare not come forward and face public opposition."[29] The exposé had been the stated reason for arrest, but the real impetus, Howe said, was another *Weekly* article that alleged an affair between Rev. Henry Ward Beecher and Elizabeth Tilton, a parishioner who was the wife of Beecher's assistant, Theodore Tilton. Beecher, the most prominent preacher in the nation, seemed to exemplify Protestant morality. Married for nearly thirty years, with four surviving children, he celebrated his silver anniversary at the Plymouth Church where he had preached to every sitting president during the past twenty-five years. Noah Davis, a Beecher parishioner and the U.S. attorney for the Southern District of New York, accused the *Weekly* of "atrocious, malicious, gross and untrue libel upon the character of the gentleman whom the whole country reveres, and whose character it is well worth the while of the government of the United States to vindicate."[30]

Months before, Theodore Tilton, Beecher's close friend and publisher, shared with Stanton the painful details of his wife's affair. He had confronted Elizabeth and, after she confessed, removed her wedding ring in a rage, ripped a portrait of Beecher off the wall, and questioned the paternity of their child. Elizabeth became hysterical and blamed her husband for her miscarriage at six months. Their family life was in shambles. Stanton told Woodhull about the affair, and Woodhull published the story, she said, to expose the hypocrisy of her critics—and threatened to reveal the names of hundreds more. Despite government efforts to squelch the *Weekly*, the sensational news made it into the public realm. More than a hundred thousand copies of the ten-cent paper sold out immediately, and New Yorkers bought all available new copies as soon as they hit the streets. Eager readers paid as much as $2.50, and some, it was rumored, paid forty dollars. Beecher's supporters went to newsstands in Brooklyn and purchased or destroyed all the papers they could find.

The scandal divided the Beecher family. Henry's sisters Catharine and Harriet Beecher Stowe believed in their brother's innocence, but his youngest sister Isabel Beecher Hooker believed Woodhull and wrote to her brother asking him to be truthful. In private, Anthony condemned the famous preacher and tried to console Hooker. "When God shall take up his old plan of punishing *liars*," Anthony wrote her, "there will be a good many people struck dead in Gotham and its suburbs."[31]

While awaiting trial, Woodhull made her case to the public in a series of sensational speeches that made news around the country. Harriet Beecher Stowe persuaded the governor of Connecticut to ban Woodhull's planned speech in Hartford. In New York City, Woodhull climbed on stage at the Cooper Institute disguised as an old Quaker woman, and then dramatically revealed herself to a thousand spectators, waving her arms in defiance and heaving with emotion. At the end of the speech, Woodhull walked to the edge of the stage and extended her arms to the three marshals who were waiting to arrest her. The audience shouted its disapproval as they hauled her off to jail.

Released on bail, Woodhull wrote to suffrage leaders and heavily promoted their cause in the *Weekly*. But Anthony did not respond to Woodhull's letters or invite her to the NWSA Convention in May 1873. Even Stanton was discouraged, tired of conventions and feeling "like a fallen angel," she wrote to a friend.[32] Anthony resented Stanton's withdrawal from the movement. "Mrs. Stanton failed to be present at my lecture," she wrote in her diary. "She has never yet heard me give a lecture."[33]

Woodhull's obscenity trial began in June 1873. The anti-vice crusader Anthony Comstock testified that obscene materials in the *Weekly* had been sent through the mail, thus violating federal law. But Woodhull's attorney argued that newspapers were exempted from obscenity laws and the judge agreed, ordering the jury to find Woodhull not guilty. Woodhull kept up her campaign to expose powerful men who she saw as moral hypocrites. She became a popular speaker on the lyceum circuit, earning nearly $300 per lecture. Audiences came expecting to hear shocking assertions, and Woodhull did not disappoint them. Every woman has a right to sexual pleasure, she said, and the sexual emancipation of women would produce happier marriages and healthier children. She blamed her eldest child's severe mental impairment on her unwilling and ignorant submission to her first husband at the age of fourteen. After moving to England in 1877, Woodhull continued her public lectures and eventually married a wealthy banker, whose entire family refused to attend the wedding. Woodhull later reflected that the Beecher scandal overshadowed everything else she had done and that had she known the consequences, she would "have fainted by the wayside."[34]

Beecher's church and denomination exonerated him, and, for another decade, he was the nation's most influential preacher before passing away in his sleep in 1886. Beecher escaped the scandal with little damage, Stanton said, because he was "the soul and center" of powerful religious and financial networks that would suffer if his reputation were tarnished.[35] Parishioners at his Plymouth Church stood by him to the end. "They act nobly," Beecher wrote to a friend a year after the scandal broke, "and I knew they would."[36]

The Woodhull scandal damaged the suffrage movement. Woodhull's emergence on the national stage as a suffrage leader and her open promotion of Free Love the next year linked the two movements in the minds of many Americans. Suffrage opponents had long predicted moral decay if society altered the traditional roles of men and women. Woodhull and the chaos she inspired seemed to confirm their worst fears. Stone and AWSA tried to distance themselves from Woodhull from the start, and Anthony belatedly tried to separate Woodhull from NWSA, but a murky link between social chaos and the suffrage movement would linger for more than a generation.

Notes

1. *New York World*, January 2, 1870, cited in Frisken, "Sex in Politics," 95.
2. "The Memorial of Victoria C. Woodhull," *HWS*, 2:446, in Lois Beachy Underhill, *The Woman Who Ran for President: The Many Lives of Victoria Woodhull* (Bridgehampton; Lanham, MD: Bridge Works Publishers, 1995), 102–3.

3. *New York Tribune*, n.d., in Underhill, *Woodhull*, 104.

4. Isabella Beecher Hooker to Anna Savery, November 12, 1871, IBH, in Barbara Goldsmith, *Other Powers: The Age of Suffrage, Spiritualism, and the Scandalous Victoria Woodhull* (New York: Harper Perennial, 1999), 251.

5. SBA to Laura De Force Gordon, February 9, 1871 in *SP*, 2:417.

6. *New York Tribune*, January 16, 1871, in Underhill, *Woodhull*, 105.

7. Walt Whitman, Walthall Papers, Boston Public Library, Southern Illinois University, in Underhill, *Woodhull*, 66–67.

8. No citation, in Underhill, *Woodhull*, 96.

9. Victoria Woodhull, *Woodhull and Claflin's Weekly*, n.d., in Underhill, *Woodhull*, 146.

10. SBA Diary, March 18, 1871, in note 2, *SP*, 2:426.

11. SBA to Martha Coffin Wright, March 21, 1871, in *SP*, 2:425.

12. ECS to LM, April 1, 1871, in *SP*, 2:428.

13. ECS, "The Greatest Bugaboos," August, 1871, in *SP*, 2:443.

14. "The Free Love Cry," *New Northwest*, January 5, 1872, in Frisken, "Sex in Politics," 101.

15. LS to John K. Wildman, November 7, 1871, BLC, in Kerr, *Stone*, 168.

16. Harriet Beecher Stowe to Thomas Wentworth Higginson, May 24, 1871, Antislavery Collections, BPL, American Anti-Slavery Society Collection, in Kerr, *Stone*, 166.

17. Interview of SBA by Anne E. McDowell in Philadelphia, c. June 11, 1872, in *SP*, 2:508.

18. ECS to HB and LS, May 31, 1872 in *SP*, 2:505.

19. ECS to IBH, February 2, 1872, in *SP*, 2:479.

20. SBA to Martha Coffin Wright, May 22, 1872, in *SP*, 2:496.

21. Woodhull was too young for the constitutional age requirement of thirty-five; *The Sun*, May 11, 1872, 1, in Mary Gabriel, *Notorious Victoria: The Life of Victoria Woodhull, Uncensored* (Chapel Hill, NC: Algonquin Books, 1998), 170–71.

22. SBA Diary, May 10, 1872, in *SP*, 2:494.

23. ECS to HBB, September 15, 1872, NAWSA Collection, LC, in Kerr, *Stone*, 172.

24. IBH to ECS, May 12, 1872, in Gabriel, *Notorious Victoria*, 172.

25. *New York World*, December 24, 1869, in Goldsmith, *Other Powers*, 339.

26. Goldsmith, *Other Powers*, 340. Source citation in *New York World*, December 24, 1872; *Woodhull Claflin's Weekly*, November 2, 1872; and *Argus*, November 19, 1872, and testimony in the trials of Woodhull and Claflin.

27. Ibid.

28. *Woodhull and Claflin's Weekly*, November 2, 1872, in Goldsmith, *Other Powers*, 342.

29. William F. Howe, November 4, 1872, in Underhill, *Woodhull*, 231. See Notes 230–233 (p. 334) for source citation.

30. Noah Davis, US Attorney for the Southern District of NY, November 2, 1872, in Underhill, *Woodhull*, 230.

31. SBA to IBH, July 14, 1873, in *SP*, 2:618.

32. ECS to Martha Coffin Wright, in *SP*, 2:597.

33. SBA Diary, May 6, 1873, in *SP*, 2:606.

34. Victoria Woodhull, n.d., Holland-Martin Family Archives, London, in Underhill, *Woodhull*, 227.

35. ECS, Letter in *The Chicago Tribune*, August 24, 1874, in Underhill, *Woodhull*, 248.

36. Henry Ward Beecher to S.B. Chittenden, November 2, 1872, Beecher Family Papers, Sterling Memorial Library, Yale University, in Debbie Applegate, *The Most Famous Man in America: The Biography of Henry Ward Beecher* (New York: Doubleday, 2006), 423.

CHAPTER SIXTEEN

Setbacks in the West

The West was the first region in the nation to grant women suffrage, but, in the 1880s, women faced serious setbacks as they lost the vote in two territories, saw it challenged in a third, and failed to gain it in a hard-fought referendum in a new state.

When Utah women gained suffrage in 1870, some hoped they would use it to end polygamy. But when women voters helped reelect Utah's congressional delegate William H. Hooper, a polygamist who defended the practice, it hardened the perception that women were the "catspaw of the priesthood."[1] Kate Field, a popular lyceum lecturer who lived in Salt Lake City for nearly a year, told audiences that she had seen women "work like galley slaves" to support a lazy husband, and that when Mormon leaders preach church before state, the federal government tolerates "organized treason."[2] Harriet Beecher Stowe likened polygamy to "a cruel slavery whose chains have cut into the very hearts of thousands of our sisters—a slavery which debases and degrades womanhood, and the family."[3] Eliza Webb, Brigham Young's nineteenth wife, became one of the harshest critics of polygamy. She married the sixty-eight-year-old Young when she was twenty-four and lived for a while in the Lion House with several other wives and their many offspring. But Webb was unhappy and, after filing for divorce in 1873, wrote an exposé of women's hardships in polygamist life and delivered damning lectures to packed houses in the East.

Anti-polygamy sentiment intensified over time. President Rutherford B. Hayes called for "preventing as well as punishing" polygamy and threatened to revoke the rights of citizenship in Utah.[4] First Lady Lucy Webb Hayes headed a missionary organization to assist the "suffering sisters in Utah."[5] Women's groups spread anti-polygamist sentiment at the grassroots level. In 1878 gentile women organized the Ladies Anti-Polygamy Society of Utah "to fight to the death that system which so enslaves and degrades our sex."[6] The Women's Christian Temperance Union joined the anti-polygamy crusade as it broadened its activities beyond the prohibition of alcohol. Polygamy reflects women's powerlessness, WCTU president Frances Willard said, and if women were in the House of Representatives, polygamy "would not be even thinkable."[7]

By the late 1870s, the federal government had outlawed polygamy and placed local Utah courts under federal control. After the U.S. Supreme Court decided in 1879 that anti-polygamy legislation was constitutional, the federal government began to prosecute polygamists. Over 1,300 were jailed, including Utah's sole congressional Representative George Q. Cannon, one of the Mormon Church's Twelve Apostles and a husband to five wives. The harshest anti-polygamy legislation was the result of an unlikely alliance: Republican senator George Edmunds of Vermont, a cantankerous Union veteran and chairman of the Senate Judiciary Committee, and Democrat John Randolph Tucker, a jovial Virginia congressman who had been his state's attorney general during the Civil War. Tucker supported states' rights even after the Civil War but pressed for federal intervention in Utah because he saw traditional marriage as the root of civilization. The Edmunds-Tucker Bill proposed draconian measures to restrict the power of the Mormon Church, including requiring that voters, jurors, and public officials take an anti-polygamy oath, mandating civil marriage licenses, compelling wives to testify against their polygamous husbands, designating the children of polygamists as illegitimate—and ending women's suffrage. Utah women had been "enfranchised for church ends alone," Edmunds said, "to make the church impregnable to outward attack, independent and hostile in civil attitude."[8]

Mormon women protested as the Edmunds-Tucker Bill worked its way through Congress. In March 1886, hundreds of women filled the Salt Lake Theater to hear speakers denounce those who would deprive women of the vote "for no other reason than that we do not vote to suit our political opponents."[9] It was religious persecution, they said. Colorado senator Henry M. Teller agreed. By prosecuting polygamists, the government was only creating martyrs among a people who already promoted a narrative of persecution, he said. "You cannot expect that the president of the Church who married his wives more than a generation ago will put them from him and declare that they are prostitutes."[10] Mark Twain agreed and rebuffed lecturer Kate Field when she asked him to support her anti-polygamy efforts. Polygamy was appalling, he told her, but "the Mormon religion *is* a religion." Polygamy should be "extirpated," he said, "but always by fair means, not the Congressional rascalities."[11]

Suffragists divided over polygamy. Stone and AWSA published testimonials to its evils and criticized NWSA when its leadership invited Mormon women to their annual convention in 1879. But Stanton and New York suffragist Matilda Joslyn Gage believed outrage against polygamists was hypocritical. Many unfaithful men were accepted in gentile society, and infidelity affected many lives, including "Lucy Stone's own married life," Gage wrote, referencing Henry Blackwell's rumored affair.[12] Yet as anti-polygamist sentiment intensified across the nation, Anthony carefully distanced NWSA. When Attorney Belva Lockwood spoke in support of the Mormons and their "freedom of religious convictions," Anthony interrupted her to make clear that NWSA did not share such views.[13] They should support woman suffrage in Utah but leave the question of polygamy to Congress.

Despite all the protests and principled opposition, Congress passed the Edmunds-Tucker Bill and President Grover Cleveland signed it, even after meeting Utah gentile women at the White House who asked him to veto it for the sake of women's suffrage. After participating in elections for seventeen years, Utah women lost the right to vote.

Washington

In 1888, a year after the Edmunds-Tucker Act ended women's suffrage in Utah, women in Washington Territory also lost the right to vote. They had won the vote in 1883, after thirty years of "almost" winning it. Reformers in Washington mostly welcomed women's political involvement as a positive influence on law and order, but some worried that politically active women might alienate powerful interests, particularly the alcohol industry. When a Tacoma gambler sought to reverse his conviction by claiming that his jury had improperly included women, local men affiliated with saloons and brothels supported him. So did the courts. In another case initiated by the wife of a saloon owner, the Washington Supreme Court determined that when the U.S. Congress passed the Washington Territorial Organic Act in 1853, the word "citizen meant and still signifies male citizenship and must be so construed."[14] Associate Justice George Turner added that women were unfit to vote for they lack the "bone and sinew equal in strength to that with which nature had provided man."[15] The decision caught many Washington women off guard. It was a "war on women," one said.[16]

In the summer of 1889, delegates to the Washington Constitutional Convention ignored women's suffrage as they prepared for statehood. Henry Blackwell was there, trying to resurrect suffrage for women, but found Washington men generally opposed and "the whiskey interest" working to prevent it. "I am fighting against odds," Blackwell wrote.[17] Washington male voters defeated a suffrage referendum by a 2–1 margin in the fall of 1889, and two months later, Washington became a state without suffrage for women. The first Washington state legislature made a concession: women could vote for the trustees and directors of local schools—but not for school superintendents.

Wyoming

When Wyoming Territory prepared for statehood in the late 1880s, its women had been voting for two decades. A handful of delegates to the Constitutional Convention tried to undermine women's suffrage by proposing to hold a referendum, but they were voted down by 20–8. "No man has ever dared to say in the territory of Wyoming that woman suffrage is a failure," former governor John Wesley Hoyt said. "We stand today proud, proud of this great experiment."[18] And if Congress should object because of woman suffrage, another delegate proclaimed, "we will stay out forever."[19] In November 1889, voters overwhelmingly approved a state constitution that included women's suffrage.

Yet the effort to gain statehood for Wyoming snagged on party politics in Washington, D.C. Democrats who were reluctant to see another Republican state admitted to the Union attacked women's suffrage. New Jersey Democrat William McAdoo said suffrage would undermine morality, and Georgia Democrat George Barnes called it "antagonistic to republican institutions."[20] Alabama Democrat William Oates said that Wyoming had suffrage because of "certain strong-minded women who overcame a lot of weak minded-men."[21] Illinois Democrat William Springer proposed three amendments: first, to call a new Wyoming Constitutional Convention in which only men could vote; second, to limit voting in the first election after statehood to men only, who would then vote on women's suffrage; and finally, to insert the word "male" into the Wyoming Constitution.[22] All three proposals narrowly failed.

Congress approved the admission of Wyoming by a vote of 139–127 in the House and 29–18 in the Senate. When President Benjamin Harrison signed the bill granting statehood on July 10, 1890, Wyoming citizens set off fireworks and rang bells in churches, trains, and fire halls. At the official celebration two weeks later, more than five thousand people turned out for a parade that included a float carrying forty-two young women representing the existing states, followed by a small carriage with three little girls representing recently admitted Idaho, Wyoming, and the

Goddess of Liberty. The first official speech, given at the base of the Capitol, was by Theresa A. Jenkins, who spoke on women's suffrage. Esther Morris, the former Justice of the Peace from South Pass City, presented the governor with a U.S. flag as a gift from the women of Wyoming. The *Woman's Journal* hailed Wyoming's admission with women's suffrage as "the greatest event that has occurred in American history since the Declaration of Independence and the adoption of the Federal Constitution."[23]

South Dakota

Anthony heard the good news from Wyoming while speaking in Madison, South Dakota, and shared it with a delighted audience. She was there campaigning for a suffrage referendum and urged Wyoming women to help make South Dakota "the second free state for women."[24] But Wyoming suffrage passed with a simple majority vote of elected officials; success in South Dakota depended on male voters, and referendums on women's suffrage had never succeeded in the state. Suffragists from the South Dakota Equal Suffrage Association asked the national suffragists for assistance. It was the first state campaign in which the new National American Woman Suffrage Association would participate, and many of its most talented speakers went to South Dakota eager for victory.

Anthony spent months traveling around South Dakota, trying to build public support for suffrage, in the company of Anna Howard Shaw. Shaw had immigrated from England as a little girl and grew up on the Michigan frontier in a hard-working family with high ideals. Like Anthony, she became a high school teacher and temperance speaker, before becoming a preacher and physician, and then joining Anthony in her suffrage campaigning in the late 1880s. Their carriage wheels crunched over dried grass and sank deep in dusty soil parched by three years of drought. They met settlers returning east on wagons pulled by sullen animals. "Everyone," Shaw recalled, "had the forsaken, desperate look worn by the pioneer who has reached the limit of his endurance."[25] In one day alone, they rode thirty miles to give a speech and then another forty to catch a train, keeping warm with buffalo overcoats and heated wood blocks under their feet. When their train arrived at its next stop four hours late, they discovered that local preachers had tried to sabotage their lecture, which "aroused Miss Anthony's fighting spirit," Shaw said.[26] They quickly rented a theater; distributed handbills; and gathered help for introductions, collections, and music. That night people crowded the theater, sitting in the aisles and along the stage, as Anthony and Shaw gave fiery speeches. At the hotel, Shaw collapsed on her bed, too tired to remove her hat and shoes and awoke nine hours later to Anthony shaking her by the shoulder, telling her that it was time to move on. Another evening, a drunken man in the front row repeatedly interrupted Anthony, demanding that she stop talking so much about women and say more about George Washington. "Put him out," the crowd shouted as several men stepped forward. "No, gentlemen," Anthony said. "He is a product of man's government and I want you to see what sort you make."[27]

Lucy Stone remained home, convinced that South Dakota was a lost cause. Her husband Henry Blackwell delivered nearly three dozen lectures in six weeks, sometimes joining Anthony on stage, but often giving them on his own. Blackwell complained to his wife that Anthony and other suffragists alienated men with sarcastic censure and complaints about foreigners. "If only our women would not follow Stanton's foolish counsel & would use *womanly conciliation,* we should be much more successful," he said.[28]

New York suffragist Matilda Joslyn Gage worked for suffrage in South Dakota while staying with her daughter Maud and son-in-law L. Frank Baum, who had settled in Aberdeen just a year before. Frank supported women's suffrage and pressed for its passage as the editor of the *Aberdeen Saturday Pioneer.* "We must do away with sex prejudice and render equal distinction and reward to brains and ability, no matter whether found in man or woman," he wrote.[29] Women would clean up politics, he believed, especially humble, hard-working western women.

Two midwestern women who would become major leaders in the suffrage movement joined the South Dakota campaign. Emma Smith DeVoe, originally from Illinois, first became enthused about women's rights at the age of eight, when she saw Anthony speak. Known for her poise and elegance, DeVoe campaigned for suffrage in the final weeks. Carrie Chapman Catt, too, showed an interest in women's equality during her childhood in Iowa. After discovering at the age of thirteen that women could not vote, Catt talked so much about suffrage that her father worried "she never in the world will get married."[30] At Iowa State Agricultural College, where she became her class valedictorian, she organized a Ladies Military Company, began a debate club for women, and won the right for women to speak at the literary society. After graduation, Catt became a respected high school superintendent; married; wrote a book to raise the status of housekeeping; and got all but ten citizens in Mason City, Iowa, to sign a women's suffrage petition. After her first husband's early death, she married George Catt, a prosperous hydraulic engineer who shared her progressive ideals and agreed to support her as she pursued suffrage activities. Catt impressed others with her orderliness and self-confidence, exemplified by her dignified bearing and hair neatly parted in the middle and pinned to the sides. When Lucy Stone heard Catt speak in Iowa the year before, she remarked that Catt "will be heard from yet in this movement."[31]

Despite the exhaustive efforts of national and local suffragists, South Dakota voters turned down women's suffrage by a 2–1 margin in November 1890. Catt and other leaders blamed immigrants. On Election Day, Catt had watched as young men brought in groups of illiterate immigrants, marked their ballots for them, and then gave them a dollar or two "in plain sight."[32] She learned lessons from the debacle that served her for the next thirty years: that a prohibition referendum offered at the same time as a suffrage referendum links the two in the minds of male voters, the importance of money, and the need for support of political parties. The Farmers Alliance and the Knights of Labor had pledged their support, but then formed a new party that refused to include suffrage in its platform.

Anthony headed east to fight again. DeVoe headed west and would soon begin work for suffrage in Idaho. Catt headed to the West Coast and contracted typhus, mumbling delirious speeches from the South Dakota campaign as she lingered for weeks on the edge of death. Henry Blackwell went home to Massachusetts. Gage returned to New York, while her daughter and husband Frank Baum moved to Chicago. In his spare time, Frank wrote a children's book, naming the protagonist "Dorothy" after their beloved niece who died in infancy. Frank's story, *The Wizard of Oz*, would become an iconic work of American fiction.

Stanton once predicted that suffrage would come from the West and "roll East."[33] But in the 1880s women lost the vote in Utah and Washington. Wyoming suffrage survived when it became a state only after its supporters refused to yield. The hard-fought South Dakota defeat in 1890 embittered many of the suffragists who had toiled for months. They had used "all the great maxims of Republican government, which the fathers had stated so clearly," Stanton wrote, and yet nearly forty-six thousand men "went to the polls and denied every one of them." Those men were now "responsible for every act of violence or injustice inflicted on the women of that State, for every insult offered to his mother, sister, wife, or daughter."[34]

Notes

1. *The Woman's Journal*, January 26, 1876, in Lola Von Wagenen, "Sister-Wives and Suffragists: Polygamy and the Politics of Woman Suffrage, 1876–1890," PhD. Dissertation, New York University, 1994, 182, cited in note 37, Sarah Barringer Gordon, *The Mormon Question: Polygamy and Constitutional Conflict in Nineteenth-Century America* (Chapel Hill: University of North Carolina Press, 2002), 279.

2. "Muchly Married Women," *Cincinnati Enquirer,* February 8, 1886, 4, and *Ogden Standard Examiner,* June 20, 1884, 2, in Gary Scharnhorst, *Kate Field: The Many Lives of a Nineteenth-Century American Journalist* (New York: Syracuse University Press, 2008), 162.

3. Wallace, *Twenty-Seventh Wife,* 14.

4. James D. Richardson, *A Compilation of the Messages and Papers of the Presidents, 1789–1897* (Washington: Government Printing Office, 1898), 560.

5. "Memorial of the Woman's Home Missionary Society of the General Conference of the Methodist Episcopal Church" (Philadelphia, PA, May 1, 1884), in Joan Iversen, "The Mormon-Suffrage Relationship: Personal and Political Quandaries," in Madsen, *Battle for the Ballot,* 156.

6. "Our Policy," *Anti-Polygamy Standard* (April 1880), 4, in Scott, Patricia Lyn, "Jennie Anderson Froiseth and the Blue Tea," *Utah Historical Quarterly* 71 no. 1 (Winter 2003): 30.

7. Frances E. Willard, "Introduction," in The Women of Mormonism (Detroit, 1882), xvi, in Sarah Barringer Gordon, " 'The Liberty of Self-Degradation': Polygamy, Woman Suffrage, and Consent in Nineteenth-Century America," *Journal of American History* 83 no. 3 (December 1996): 823.

8. "Sen. Edmunds Speech on 'Woman Suffrage in Utah'; Senate Record 49th Congress, 1st Session Misc. Doc. No. 122," June 8, 1886, 5, Suffrage Collection, Series 1: Congressional Documents, SCA.

9. Resolution titled, "Appeal for Freedom, Justice, and Equal Rights" (n.p.: n.d.), cited in Kathryn MacKay, "Chronology of Woman Suffrage in Utah," in Madsen, *Battle for the Ballot,* 315.

10. U.S. Congress, Senate, Congressional Record, 49th Congress, 1st Session, January 6, 1886, pp. 460–61, in M. Paul Holsinger, "Henry M. Teller and the Edmunds-Tucker Act," *The Colorado Magazine* 48, no. 1 (1971): 7.

11. Lilian Whiting, *Kate Field: A Record* (Boston: Little, Brown, 1899), 448–49, in Scharnhorst, *Kate Field,* 164–65.

12. "Polygamy Degrades Womanhood," *WJ,* 10 (29 March 1879): 97, in Iversen, "Quandaries," 154; Matilda J. Gage, "The Brand of the Slave," *National Citizen and Ballot Box* 4 (May 1879), 2, in Scharnhorst, *Kate Field,* 155.

13. Ibid., 159.

14. *Bloomer v. Todd,* 3 Washington Territory 599 1888, in Shanna Stevenson, *Women's Votes, Women's Voices: The Campaign for Equal Rights in Washington* (Pullman, WA: Washington State University Press, 2009), 28.

15. *Rosencrantz v. Territory of Washington,* 2 Washington Territory 267 (1884), in Stevenson, *Women's Votes,* 25.

16. Note 56, in Mead, *Western Suffrage,* 49.

17. Stevenson, *Women's Votes,* 29 (note 121), 31.

18. No citation, Larson, *History of Wyoming,* 249.

19. Ibid.

20. Congressional Record, v. 21, Part 3, 51st Congress, 1st Session, March 7 to April 4, 1890, p. 2666, and Congressional Record, Ibid, p. 2685, in Chapman, *Wyoming Suffrage,* 101.

21. Ibid., 103–4.

22. Ibid.

23. *Woman's Journal* 20, September 8, 1889, 305, in Larson, *Bicentennial History*, 100–101.

24. SBA to Women of Wyoming, forwarded to Mrs. M. E. Fost, June 29, 1899, sent from Madison SD, printed in *Laramie Boomerang*, July 7, 1890, 8.

25. Anna Howard Shaw, D.D., M.D., *Anna Howard Shaw, the Story of a Pioneer* (New York; London: Harper and Brothers, 1915), 200.

26. Ibid., 203.

27. "Susan B. Anthony as an Epigramist," *Utica Observer*, February 13, 1900, in *SBASB*, 30:67.

28. HBB to LS, September 2, 1890 in note 7, in *SP*, 5:323.

29. *Aberdeen Saturday Pioneer*, February 1, 1890, in Nancy Tystad Koupal, "The Wonderful Wizard of the West," *Great Plains Quarterly* 9 (Fall 1989): 208.

30. "Carrie Chapman Catt Dies, 88, Active for Feminism to the End," *New York Tribune*, March 10, 1947, CCC Papers, SCA.

31. *Woman's Journal* (November 9, 1889): 356, in Jacqueline Van Voris, *Carrie Chapman Catt: A Public Life* (New York: The Feminist Press, 1987), 18.

32. Undated Speech, SL, in Van Voris, *Catt*, 25.

33. Stanton Diary, April 4, 1888, in Stanton and Blatch, *Letters*, 2:251.

34. ECS to LS and the Massachusetts Woman Suffrage Association, January 15, 1891, in *SP*, 5:349–50.

CHAPTER SEVENTEEN

The New Woman

In the 1880s, the lyceum lecturer Mary Livermore gave a popular talk she called "What Shall We Do with Our Daughters?"[1] Younger women were no longer content with a purely domestic life, she said. Women's colleges and coeducational state universities provided an advanced education and sometimes offered young women the opportunity to reimagine their future. It was the New Woman—a more confident generation with expectations of greater independence, whose "very look, step, and bearing is free," a prominent professor observed.[2] But many of them felt useless and frustrated, encouraged to improve the world but constrained by their limited role in society.

Some women pressed against limitations by pursuing careers traditionally reserved for men. By the end of the century, women were one in ten medical students, three in four teachers, and almost all nurses and social workers. Some even worked in professions formerly closed to women. Ellen Swallow Richards became the first woman chemistry major and a graduate of the Massachusetts Institute of Technology; she was later a pioneer in the fields of municipal sanitation and domestic science. Alice Freeman Palmer graduated from the University of Michigan after it became coeducational and, at the age of twenty-six, became president of Wellesley College, the first woman to head a nationally regarded institution of higher learning. Belva Lockwood won admission to law school and, after completing the course of study, fought to get her degree when the law school refused to grant it. Then, after being repeatedly denied permission to practice before the Supreme Court Bar, she lobbied Congress to pass a law permitting women lawyers to appear in federal courts. In 1880, Lockwood became the first woman to argue before the Supreme Court and, four years later, ran for U.S. president as a candidate of the Equal Rights Party.

Black women forged their own version of the New Woman. Anna Julia Cooper attended a Freedmen's School in North Carolina and earned a master's degree in mathematics from Oberlin College, and later in life, a PhD from the University of Paris-Sorbonne. As a teacher and principal at the prestigious M Street High School in Washington, D.C., Cooper worked to uplift black students, many of whom went on to elite colleges and universities. She founded several institutions to assist the needy, including the first black Young Women's Christian Association, the Colored Women's League, and the Colored Settlement House. In her 1892 book, *A Voice from the South,* Cooper argued that black women were essential to progress and should not be ignored as they were in the

Belva Lockwood, a prolific attorney and politician who fought for women's suffrage both in and outside of the courtroom. (Library of Congress)

Fourteenth Amendment and in the women's suffrage movement. Black men sometimes "drop back into the sixteenth-century logic" on the woman question, she wrote, and white women think that they represent all women and shun cooperation with others.[3] Mary Church Terrell, Cooper's colleague at the M Street High School, also earned a master's degree at Oberlin College and had a distinguished career in teaching and reform. She was a cofounder of the National Association of Colored Women and later the National Association for the Advancement of Colored People.

Southern white women became more involved in promoting civic progress, though they still mostly accommodated or even encouraged the rise of white supremacy. Kate and Jean Gordon, sisters from an influential New Orleans family, established the Equal Rights Association Club to press for women's rights and public improvement in Louisiana. Kate later became a national suffrage leader, and Jean became a factory inspector and pushed for compulsory education and the end of child labor. Mary Barr Clay, daughter of the famous abolitionist Cassius Clay,

Educator and civil rights activist Anna Julia Cooper. (Library of Congress)

became president of the American Woman Suffrage Association in 1883. Together with her sister Laura, she organized the Kentucky Equal Rights Association, which lobbied for juvenile courts, property rights for married women, greater access to higher education and other progressive reforms.

One of the most powerful manifestations of the New Woman was the rise of clubwomen. As family size declined in the late nineteenth century, women had more leisure time and joined clubs in droves. Some were social clubs, but many worked to improve society through good works such as building libraries or playgrounds or pressing for reform. Large clubs, whose memberships sometimes numbered in the hundreds or even thousands, trained women how to organize, project a public voice, and pressure the political system. The largest club, the Women's Christian Temperance Union (WCTU), developed an extensive grassroots network and held conventions that drew women from across the nation. Like many other clubs, it claimed moral superiority for women. "Organized womanhood," as some called it, would elevate society and enable women to enter the public sphere. Mary Livermore, active in the suffrage and temperance movements, called it "a necessary step in the evolution of women." It was "an unconscious protest against the isolation in which women have dwelt in the past, a reaching out after a larger and fuller life," she said, "a desire to keep in touch with other women who are thinking and acting independently."[4] The belief in feminine delicacy and purity that some men used to justify keeping women close to home became a reason for them to venture from it.

Anthony saw clubwomen as potential allies as she sought to expand the suffrage base. Frances Willard, elected to head the WCTU in 1879, endorsed suffrage under the banner of "Home Protection."[5] The ballot, Willard told her followers, was necessary to defend the home from the liquor industry and corrupt politicians. Anthony drew closer to Willard as WCTU members became many of the suffrage movement's foot soldiers. Women "screeching for the ballot to fight whiskey is a tremendous power on our side," she said.[6] She guided NWSA to reduce its focus on a federal amendment and, beginning with the 1882 Nebraska referendum, started working on state campaigns with the WCTU. Yet as Anthony drew closer to the highly religious WCTU, Stanton pulled away, convinced that religion was a source of women's subordination. "You may go over the world, and you will find that every form of religion that has breathed upon this earth, has degraded woman," she told the NWSA Convention in 1885.[7] Men wrote Scripture to suit their own interests, Stanton said, and announced a project to reinterpret the Bible from the perspective of women.

Anthony and Stanton sought to strengthen NWSA by placing it at the center of the suffrage movement in public perception. Over the course of a decade, Anthony, Stanton, and New York suffragist Matilda Joslyn Gage wrote the first three volumes of what would be a six-volume *History of Woman Suffrage*. It was a compilation of newspaper clippings, documents, reminiscences, and essays from the previous forty years. Stone initially objected that it was too soon to write a history and that it would reflect a bias toward the NWSA's role in the suffrage movement—which it did—and initially submitted a mere two-sentence summary of her work to be included in the book. Anthony preferred to make history, not write it, and detested the many hours of tedious work at the writing table. Nevertheless, Anthony and Stanton worked together on the *History*, at times arguing over its contents. "Sometimes these disputes run so high that down go the pens, one sails out of one door and one out of the other, walking in opposite directions around the estate," Stanton's daughter recalled of the many conflicts between Anthony and her mother. Then, "just as I have made up my mind that this beautiful friendship of forty years has at last terminated, I see them walking down the hill, arm in arm."[8]

In 1888, NWSA commemorated the fortieth anniversary of the 1848 Seneca Falls Convention with a large gathering in Washington, D.C., implicitly highlighting it as the start of the women's rights movement and not the 1850 Worcester Women's Rights Convention as some others believed. The same anniversary gathering also launched the International Council of Women, intended to develop transnational cooperation among women reformers. Stanton, 72 years old, stout, with curly white hair, looked "as if she should be the Lord Chief-Justice," the *Washington Star* reported.[9] The subordination of women was universal, Stanton told delegates from the British Isles, Germany, Scandinavia, and the United States. "Whether our feet are compressed in iron shoes, our faces hidden with veils and masks; whether yoked with cows to draw the plow through its furrows, or classed with idiots, lunatics and criminals in the laws and constitutions of the State, the principle is the same."[10] President and Mrs. Grover Cleveland received the anniversary attendees at the White House, and public receptions for them were so popular that there was little room to move. The call for suffrage had made little progress in the past four decades, but it was no longer a radical idea that shocked polite society. An aging Frederick Douglass expressed his great satisfaction at having stood for women's rights since its earliest years. "When I ran away from slavery, it was for myself; when I advocated emancipation, it was for my people; but when I stood up for the rights of woman," Douglas told the gathering, "self was out of the question, and I found a little nobility in the act."[11]

Stone, Henry Blackwell, and the American Woman Suffrage Association (AWSA) continued to use moderation in the pursuit of suffrage. Stone emphasized the "purity" of women as justification for the vote, urging her *Woman's Journal* readers to support the anti-vice crusader Anthony Comstock as he targeted explicit sexual materials and public figures who transgressed moral boundaries. When Democratic presidential candidate Grover Cleveland acknowledged fathering a child out of wedlock as a young man, Stone called upon her followers not to vote for him, though most other reformers still supported Cleveland over his corrupt Republican opponent. Cleveland's debauchery and the accepting attitude of his supporters only showed why women must get involved in politics, she told readers. But AWSA was losing money and members, and *Journal* subscriptions were dropping. Lucy and Henry found it ever harder to sustain the organization and their own morale. The first generation of suffragists were aging and dying. Mott passed away in 1880, and Sojourner Truth in 1883. When Stone read of Wendell Phillips's sudden death a year later, she was so overcome that she lifted her head up and sobbed, her daughter Alice later recalled. Nor were there suffrage victories to sustain hope. Rhode Island voters defeated a suffrage referendum by a 3–1 margin in 1887, and legislators in Vermont and Massachusetts refused even to give women the right to vote in municipal elections. Younger suffragists, including Rachel Foster Avery and Alice Stone Blackwell, had not experienced the bitter divisions after the Civil War, and even Lucy began to favor unifying AWSA and NWSA. In late 1887, Anthony and Avery began merger talks with Stone and her daughter Alice. However, some NWSA members worried that a single organization with a broader focus might dilute efforts to achieve a federal amendment at a time when most state suffrage initiatives were failing.

The proposed new organization, the National American Woman Suffrage Association (NAWSA), would campaign for suffrage at both the state and national levels. Aware that some of her colleagues bitterly opposed unification, Anthony portrayed herself as a victim of circumstance. "The pressure the other leaders brought to bear upon me was overwhelming," she stated. "I simply could not fight them any longer."[12] NWSA's final convention, held in February 1890, was the most contentious in its history. Stanton, still the president, decided at the last moment not to attend. Upon learning this, Anthony let her anger subside for a day and then penned a letter to Stanton that Anthony hoped would "start every white hair in her head."[13] When Stanton arrived at the last moment with no speech, Anthony posted a guard outside her room until she wrote one. Stanton gave her speech and left for England the next day. Widowed after Henry's death in 1887, Stanton would live with her daughter Harriot Stanton Blatch and her family for nearly two years.

As vice president, Anthony presided over every session of the Convention without prompting the negative reactions Stanton's stridency often elicited. Anthony "was the life and soul of the meetings," the *Washington Star* reported. "She does not make much noise with her gavel, nor does she have to use it often, but she manages to keep the organization over which she presides in the state of order that puts to shame many a convention of the other sex."[14] On the Convention's final evening, when the Executive Committee voted 30–11 to create NAWSA, Anthony succeeded in all her goals. The two rival organizations had merged with Stanton as the titular leader, they paid homage to the movement's elders both living and deceased, they engaged new members and inspired new leadership, and they appealed to Washington political elites. Yet NAWSA was more moderate. With more than ten thousand members and an ambitious agenda to win suffrage in multiple state referendums, Anthony wrote to Stanton, "We can only hold them together to work for the ballot by letting alone their whims and prejudices on other subjects."[15]

To assuage sore feelings, Anthony purchased lifetime NAWSA memberships for Olympia Brown and Matilda Joslyn Gage. Gage, however, left the organization and formed the Woman's National Liberal Union to work for a broad range of rights. Stanton worried that NAWSA was too religious and afraid to confront power. Be wary of conservatives who sought to take over the organization and snuff out "whoever else dares to differ," she wrote to Clara Colby after arriving in England. "Frances Willard needs watching," she added. "She is a politician."[16] But Anthony had always believed that suffrage can come "only through the assistance of all religious bodies and political parties." For suffrage leaders "to identify themselves with the other issues of the day is to create animosities and alienate supporters."[17]

After returning from England, Stanton appeared before the House Judiciary Committee more than three decades after her first appearance there and gave what she and others considered one of her best speeches. Stanton told the array of men before her that she would not repeat the usual arguments for suffrage that all were familiar with, but instead addressed the philosophical reasons why women should share in the broad array of life's opportunities and responsibilities. The most important reason to treat women equally, she said, was that a woman "must rely on her self." Women and men go through life as individuals, Stanton said, and they face its darkest moments alone, in the "solitude of self." Men are better prepared to cope since they are encouraged to develop their strengths and abilities. Denying a woman the right to achieve her full potential leaves her unprepared and unable "in the emergencies of life to fall back on herself for protection." Chivalry cannot protect women in life's most difficult moments, for they are experienced alone. The human soul, the individual, is eternal, singular, vulnerable, and unknowable to the outside. "Who can take, dare take, on himself the rights, the duties, the responsibilities of another human soul?" she asked.[18] North Carolina senator Zebulon Vance told Stanton that the suffrage speeches that day were better than any he had ever heard, and that if it only were up to logic, their efforts would succeed.

Stanton's public statement before the Judiciary Committee reflected her own internal struggles as she faced the end of life in the "solitude of self." Seventy-seven years old, weary of infighting, and finding it increasingly difficult to move about, Stanton resigned the presidency of NAWSA after two years. A stoic acceptance of aging and wistful reflection on life gone by crept into her thinking. "I cannot clamber up and down platforms, mount long staircases into halls and hotels, be squeezed in the crush of receptions, and do all the other things public life involves," she wrote in her diary. "That day is passed for me."[19] On a visit to the Peterboro mansion where she and her cousin Elizabeth Smith Miller had spent many childhood summers together and where she first met her husband Henry, Stanton felt like one who walks the deserted halls of times past, tenderly remembering family and friends who had gathered there for years, but who had all passed away. It is best for the elders to help the next generation emerge, "for they have a big work before them—much bigger, in fact, than they imagine," Stanton reflected. "We are only the stone that started the ripple, but they are the ripple that is spreading and will eventually cover the whole pond."[20]

In 1893, two events advanced the cause of the New Woman. The Chicago World's Fair offered an impressive Women's Pavilion in the White City, the main complex of buildings open to visitors. During the six months of the Fair, many of the twenty-seven million attendees saw the Women's Pavilion's exhibits, which highlighted the accomplishments of women in a building designed by Sophia Hayden, the first female architecture graduate from the Massachusetts Institute of Technology. That same year, more than five hundred delegates from twenty-seven countries and 126 organizations gathered at the Fair's auxiliary building in downtown Chicago for the World's Congress of Representative Women. The Congress addressed topics of concern for women around the world, ranging from suffrage to family to health. On the final day of the gathering, as part of a religious service conducted entirely by women, Anna Howard Shaw gave an ecumenical sermon, drawing inspiration from Christianity, Buddhism, Zoroastrianism, and other faiths. "I do not stand here this morning to define God to you," Shaw told the crowd. "I do not undertake to tell you just how you shall believe in God or just what your conception of God may be." But God does exist, she said. A reformer must have "faith in God, and know that ultimately she shall see somewhere, at some time, the triumph of the truth, but she herself must become uncompromisingly obedient to the higher laws of God everywhere."[21] Delegates warmly embraced the broad appeal of Shaw's sermon, and she considered it one of only two that ever met her own high expectations.

After a week, the Women's Congress disbanded, and the delegates from around the nation and the world returned home. Over 150,000 visitors had attended eighty-one sessions to hear more than three hundred speakers. At any one time during the Congress, at least seven meetings were ongoing, sometimes as many as eighteen. Even though the venue could accommodate ten thousand people, hundreds had to be turned away at the popular sessions. Any visitor could see that women were astir. The Congress significantly strengthened international connections among women's rights activists and breathed fresh life into the movement at home. Anthony thought it "advanced the cause by twenty-five years."[22] Catt thought it helped place suffrage within a broad framework of reform, making it appear less radical. She noticed that newspaper cartoons of women reformers changed from mockery—being "made to look like escapers from the insane asylum"—to more humane depictions.

Suffragists had been well represented and prominent, speaking nearly three dozen times. "We did a whizzing business," Catt said.[23]

In the fall of 1895, more than three thousand people celebrated Stanton's eightieth birthday with a grand gala at the Metropolitan Opera House in New York City. Stanton sat on stage in an elevated chair lined in roses, her name spelled out in carnations as many testified in tribute to her, and live musicians serenaded between speeches. Stanton slowly made her way to the podium using canes for support as the audience applauded and waved handkerchiefs. Women's rights was unstoppable, she declared, the "principle is practically conceded," the battle "nearly finished."[24] Yet women would never get equality unless they challenged religious presumptions of their inferiority. The next day, tired, Stanton played the piano in her spacious apartment, singing old songs in "a voice and manner so beautiful, so sad," her nephew Rob Stanton thought. "She seemed so far away from us and the throngs that greeted her with so much enthusiasm the night before, and was living over and over again the days of her youth, seeing life as it was sixty or seventy years ago." Then she stopped, "not from exhaustion, but as if she were overcome with emotion and the memories of her youth," he thought. "Bob," she said, turning to her nephew with tears in her eyes, "life is a great mystery."[25]

Two weeks later, the first part of *The Woman's Bible* was published. Written collaboratively by Stanton and twenty-six other women, it offered commentary and revisions of biblical passages that referenced women. Eve, *The Woman's Bible* stated, was a woman of high character, a seeker of knowledge who embodied "the courage, the dignity, and the lofty ambition of the woman."[26] Adam neither protected her nor took responsibility for his own act of eating the forbidden fruit—thus did he "shield himself at his wife's expense."[27] St. Paul's admonitions that women keep silent in the church were "bare-faced forgeries, interpolated by unscrupulous bishops" determined "to reduce women to silent submission, not only in the Church, but also in the home and in the state." A bride's pledge to "obey" her husband was the result of a poor translation that, if properly done, would require a woman simply to "defer."[28] The Bible, they wrote, assumes that women were created as inferior beings subject to male authority. But this was a historical misinterpretation made after the original scriptures were destroyed in the sixth century B.C. to give a husband authority over his wife.

To almost no one's surprise, *The Woman's Bible* met a formidable backlash. A Southern Presbyterian bishop called it "a pernicious and dangerous book" that questions Christ's authority as the head of the church and man as the head of the family. "If woman saps the foundation of the family," he said, "how can society and the state continue to stand?"[29] *Godey's Lady's Book*, the most popular women's magazine of the era, defended Scripture and its separate spheres for men and women. God created woman as a guardian and guide of "home, honor, and happiness," and men to be "the worker, inventor, and maker of things from earth; the provider and protector for the household; the lawgiver and defender of social, moral, and political rights, the sustainer of moral and religious duties." The few suffragists who "ignored the great and radical differences between the sexes" do not speak for most women.[30] *The Woman's Bible* even offended most suffragists. Catt was horrified to find herself listed as a coauthor and insisted that Stanton remove her name. Anthony found it "flippant and superficial" and did not blame women's subordination on religion.[31] "The trouble is in ourselves today," she wrote to Stanton, "not in men or books thousands of years ago."[32]

The Woman's Bible roiled the next NAWSA Convention held just weeks after its publication. Stanton's old opponents from AWSA allied with younger members to accuse her of damaging suffrage through her irreverence. Southern delegates described how much *The Woman's Bible* offended people back home, and Rachel Foster Avery, Anthony's close ally, said it was "without either scholarship or literary value, set forth in a spirit which is neither that of reverence or inquiry."[33] Another delegate called for a resolution to condemn the work. Although Stanton was absent, her supporters defended her. Anthony was silent through much of the debate but finally stepped in to argue for her old friend. She had lived long enough to see that Stanton was often ahead of her time, Anthony said. Mott had criticized Stanton's initial call for suffrage at Seneca Falls but "had sense enough not to bring in a resolution against it."[34] And when Stanton called for easier divorce in 1860, fellow reformers said she "had killed the woman's cause." Anthony would "be pained beyond expression" if they passed the resolution to condemn *The Woman's Bible*. And if delegates began to pass resolutions against individual members then they should be beware. "This year it is Mrs. Stanton; next year it may be I or one of yourselves who may be the victim."[35] In the end, despite Anthony's efforts, delegates passed Catt's resolution that NAWSA "has no official connection with the so-called 'Woman's Bible' or any theological publication."[36] Anthony had defended Stanton but saw the whole episode as a distraction. "The religious part has never been mine, you know, and I won't take it up," she wrote to Stanton shortly before publication of *The Woman's Bible*. "So go ahead in your own way and let me stick to my own."[37]

The Woman's Bible controversy highlighted the emergence of a new, more conservative generation of suffragists. Stanton never again attended a NAWSA meeting, and Anthony assumed the real and symbolic leadership of the movement. Partly to appease Southern members, NAWSA placed increasing emphasis on state suffrage and began holding its annual convention outside of Washington, D.C., every other year. NAWSA leaders also endorsed state suffrage efforts to enfranchise only educated women, a tactic employed by some Southern suffragists to reinforce white supremacy. The merger of NWSA and AWSA suffrage organizations into NAWSA created a unified movement, but it dampened the pressure for broader social reform championed by NWSA.

NAWSA may have changed its focus, but the large number of young women moving from the home into the broader world continued to grow, along with their expectations. The author Henry James remarked that "the situation of women, the decline of the sentiment of sex, the agitation on their behalf" was the most remarkable development of the era.[38] President Cleveland considered women's restlessness and discontent as "perversions of a gift of God to the human race." The best club for a woman, he wrote, "is her home."[39] But despite the sentiments of Cleveland and others, the rise of women would continue. "Of one thing men may be assured," Stanton wrote, "the next generation will not argue the question of women's rights with the infinite patience we have displayed this past half-century."[40]

Notes

1. Mary Livermore, "What Shall We Do with Our Daughters?" in Jean V. Matthews, ed., *The Rise of the New Woman: The Women's Movement in America, 1875–1930* (Chicago: Ivan R. Dee, 2003), 39–40.

2. G. Stanley Hall, in Matthews, *New Woman*, 51.

3. Anna Julia Cooper, *A Voice from the South* (New York, Oxford: Oxford University Press, 1988), 75.

4. No citation, Matthews, *New Woman*, 23.

5. Ruth Birgitta Bordin, *Frances Willard* (Chapel Hill: University of North Carolina Press, 1986).

6. SBA to Robinson, November 5, 1881, Robinson/Shattuck Papers, SL, in Ruth Ellen Williamson Drish, "Susan B. Anthony De-Radicalizes, Re-Organizes, and Re-Unites AWSA Woman Suffrage Movement, 1880–1890" Thesis (The University of Iowa, 1985), 30.

7. ECS, January 20–21, 1885, in *SP*, 4:396.

8. Margaret Stanton Lawrence, "The New Era," November, 1885, in *SP*, 4:560.

9. Venet, *Ballots nor Bullets*, 161.

10. ECS, Opening Address to the International Council of Women, in *HWS*, 4:133–34.

11. "International Council of Women," 329, in Wellman, *Seneca Falls*, 225.

12. Coté, *Brown*, 132.

13. Dorr, *Anthony*, 297.

14. *Washington Star*, n.d., in *HWS*, 4:173.

15. SBA to ECS, 1897, in Leila R. Brammer, *Excluded from Suffrage History: Matilda Joslyn Gage, Nineteenth-Century American Feminist* (Westport, CT; London: Greenwood Press, 2000), 101.

16. ECS to Clara Colby, March 6, 1890, Colby Manuscripts, HEHL, in Griffith, *Stanton*, 200.

17. SBA, "Woman's Half Century of Evolution," *North American Review* 172 (1902), 807, in Brammer, *Excluded*, 93.

18. " 'The Solitude of Self' Speech by ECS to the House Judiciary Committee," in *SP*, 5:423–34.

19. ECS Diary, November 1, 1892, in Stanton and Blatch, *Letters*, 2:290.

20. ECS Diary, February 25, 1892, New York, in Stanton and Blatch, *Letters*, 2:282–83.

21. AHS Sermon, May 21, 1893, in Sewall, *The World's Congress of Representative Women* (Chicago; New York: Rank McNally & Co., 1894), 865–66.

22. SBA, Dorr, *Anthony*, 306.

23. CCC, "The Worth of An American Ballot," *Woman's Journal*, May 28, 1892, 174 in Van Voris, *Catt*, 32.

24. "Speech by ECS to Reunion of the Pioneers and Friends of Women's Progress," November 12, 1895, in *SP*, 5:724.

25. R.B. Stanton, "Reminiscences," in Griffith, *Stanton*, 209–10.

26. Stanton et al., *The Woman's Bible*, 1:24, in Kathi Kern, *Mrs. Stanton's Bible* (Ithaca, NY: London: Cornell University Press, 2001), 159.

27. Ibid., 160.

28. Ibid., 154.

29. "A Striking Sign of the Times: A Chapter from the Woman's Bible," *Our Hope* 2 (1896), in Kern, *Bible*, 174.

30. Editor's Table, "Invention and Intuition," *Godey's Lady's Book and Magazine*, 1893, in Kimberly A. Hamlin, *From Eve to Evolution: Darwin, Science, and Women's Rights in Gilded Age America* (Chicago; London: University of Chicago Press, 2014), 32–33.

31. SBA to Clara Colby, December 13, 1895, in Kern, *Bible*, 180.

32. SBA to ECS, December 2, 1898 in Kern, "Free Woman Is a Divine Being, the Savior of Mankind: Stanton's Exploration of Religion and Gender," in Ellen Carol DuBois and Richard Cándida Smith, eds. *Feminist as Thinker: A Reader in Documents and Essays* (New York: New York University Press, 2007), 100.

33. *Woman's Journal*, February 1, 1886, in Kern, *Bible*, 34.

34. *HWS*, 4:263–64.

35. Ibid.

36. Rachel Foster Avery, ed. *Proceedings of the Twenty-Eight Annual Convention of the National American Woman Suffrage Association*, held in Washington, DC, January 23–28, 1896 (Philadelphia: Alfred J. Ferris, 1896), 91, cited in Kern, *Bible*, 184.

37. SBA to ECS, July 24, 1895, Anthony Family Papers, Huntington Library, in Kern, *Bible*, 60.

38. Henry James (1883), in Matthews, *New Woman*, 3.

39. *The Spokesman Review*, Spokane, Washington, May 12, 1905.

40. ECS to SBA, January 8, 1887, in *SP*, 4:539.

CHAPTER EIGHTEEN

Colorado

On a Saturday afternoon in late July 1893, Katharine Lee Bates, the thirty-three-year-old chair of the English Department at Wellesley College, traveled with several others up Pikes Peak in a covered prairie wagon with "Pikes Peak or Bust" painted on the side.[1] The ride took several hours, slowly winding back and forth over parched western soil, climbing nearly eight thousand feet above the town of Colorado Springs. Some of the passengers became sick from heat and high altitude, the party fell silent, and their picnic lunch went untouched. When they stopped at an overlook three miles up, two of the group fainted. Their worried driver told them they could stay only half an hour.

Bates was a popular professor, a rotund and gregarious figure often seen walking the Wellesley campus with a stack of books in her arms and a pince-nez perched on her nose "as by a miracle," her friends said. Her grandfather was valedictorian of his class at Harvard and president of Middlebury College. Her father was a congregational minister with a penchant for literary reflection, and her mother was one of the first women to attend college at the Mount Holyoke Female Seminary. Calling herself "a shy, nearsighted child, always hiding away with a book," Bates turned her love of literature into a career.[2] One student recalled her "passion for justice" as Bates criticized animal traps and fur coats, the class hierarchy of Europe, and capital punishment.[3] The United States, Bates believed, was destined for international leadership as the "Land of Hope," a "Pioneer of Brotherhood among the nations."[4] A poet by nature, "a singing soul," one of her colleagues said, Bates saw rhythm in everyday life, "feeling it with a zest or a poignancy far beyond the general."[5]

Bates was lured west by the promise of an exciting job and adventurous travel. The ambitious president of Colorado College at the foot of Pikes Peak hired several high-profile academics to teach summer courses. Among the hires were Hamlin Garland, a popular novelist and biographer of Ulysses S. Grant, who would later win the Pulitzer Prize; William J. Rolfe, a Shakespeare scholar; Elisha Andrews, the president of Brown University and a fervent proponent of silver coinage; the English journalist and anti-prostitution reformer William T. Stead, who would later perish on the *Titanic*; Katharine Coman, a Wellesley history professor with whom Bates shared a home; and a promising political scientist from Princeton University and future president of the United States, Woodrow Wilson. Bates began her trek west at the end of June, heading by train to Niagara Falls, then on to see the Chicago World's Fair, where "all men were poets for one brief, bright space in the White City," she wrote.[6] On the train ride from Chicago to Denver, looking out from her comfortable bench and sleeping berth of a Pullman car, she wrote of the "Fertile prairies. Hot run across western Kansas" and the "purple range of the Rockies."[7]

As Bates recovered from the Pikes Peak expedition in the splendor of the Antlers Hotel, one of the finest in the West, with hot and cold running water and a rare elevator, she opened her notebook and penned a few lines on the "most glorious scenery I ever beheld."[8]

O beautiful for halcyon skies,
For amber waves of grain,
For purple mountain majesties
Above the enameled plain!
America! America!
God shed his grace on thee
Till souls wax fair as earth and air
And music-hearted sea![9]

At the end of her trip, in her comfortable home in Wellesley getting ready for another semester of teaching, Bates reviewed her writings from the summer. "Consider my verses," she wrote in her diary as she put them away for a year, "disheartening."[10] It would be two more years before they were published in the local paper and later paired to a church hymn by an enterprising publisher. "America the Beautiful" became wildly popular. Asked to explain its appeal, Bates replied that it was because "Americans are at heart idealists, with a fundamental faith in human brotherhood."[11] Colorado became a testing ground whether that "fundamental faith" would include voting rights for women.

Below Pikes Peak, the state of Colorado was in trouble. Silver, its top commodity, was dropping in value. Colorado had enjoyed boom years supplying almost half of the nation's silver. Aspen, the leading silver producer and home to more than 2,200 miners, had alone produced one-sixteenth of the world's silver; supported six newspapers, several banks, a railroad; and bustled with new houses, schools, churches, and many children. However, as silver from other countries entered the market and governments demonetized silver, the price began to fall. In 1891, the last good year, silver was ninety-nine cents per ounce; a year later, it was eighty-seven cents. In April 1892, when the price dropped by two cents in less than a day, panic set in. Mines shut down, and customers ran to banks before they closed. Nine out of ten Aspen miners lost their jobs.

Some felt it was time for a new political party. "Don't offer them the antiquated excuse that you have always been a Democrat or Republican," the *Rocky Mountain Daily News* proclaimed. "No man, in the past ten years, has been able to demonstrate the difference between them."[12] In the fall of 1891, disaffected Coloradans formed a Populist Party to address their economic strain and selected as their candidate for governor Davis Hanson Waite, a sixty-five-year-old, white-haired newspaperman from Aspen. Rapacious capitalism and "plutocratic oligarchy" had taken over America, Waite believed. Millions were out of work, and millions more were destitute, while a few thousand lived in luxury. He saw cabals of all kinds—a "land monopoly, patent monopoly, liquor monopoly, and any or all other monopolies"—sustained by major parties and protected by newspapers that suppressed news to fit their interests.[13] Working people must unite to struggle for an eight-hour workday, the direct election of senators, the monetization of silver, the income tax, and against vice and gambling, which thrived in several Colorado cities. Waite's fieriness made even some Populists nervous. The *Rocky Mountain News* endorsed the entire slate of Populist candidates except for Waite, who lacked the "dignity, self-restraint, wisdom, business tact, and force of character" that the office of governor required.[14] The *Rocky Mountain Sun* deemed him "a good, quiet, peaceable citizen, but erratic in his ways and garrulous in the extreme."[15]

In the summer of 1892, when Populists enthusiastically welcomed a dozen women to their Convention in Denver, suffragists believed they finally found a party that would promote their cause. They trusted the Populists to deliver a suffrage referendum after the election. Waite was not an egalitarian, though. He believed black people were incapable of self-rule and spoke openly of "Jew extortioners."[16] He supported suffragists, not as equals, but as opportune political partners.

The Populists won big, gaining twenty-seven seats in the House and twelve in the Senate, a stunning success in Colorado's short political history. Waite won the gubernatorial race with nearly half the vote in a three-way race, performing especially well in the mining counties, where his support reached as high as 77 percent. However, Waite surprised suffragists when he endorsed only municipal suffrage, permitting women to vote only at the local level. Nor did the Populists hold enough seats in the legislature to pass a referendum proposal. When a suffrage bill finally came up in the House and Senate, women sat in the visitors' galleries to watch, hissing when a legislator insulted suffrage supporters. Finally, on April 3, the last day of the legislative session, enough Republicans and Democrats in both houses joined the Populists to pass a bill for a suffrage referendum that, if voters approved, would grant Colorado women the right to vote.

Yet the Colorado suffrage referendum scheduled for the fall of 1893 seemed unlikely to pass. All previous referendums had failed, including Michigan (1874), Colorado (1877), Nebraska (1882), Oregon (1884), Rhode Island (1886), Washington (1889), and South Dakota (1890). A generation earlier, Stone and Anthony campaigned for a referendum in Colorado that failed by a 2–1 margin and failed again four years later. But a nationwide depression that began in February 1893 with the collapse of the Philadelphia and Reading Railroad and led to a run on gold that depleted the nation's reserves in April heightened Populist appeals for dramatic changes in the political system.

Colorado suffragists launched a small, but determined, effort to convince men to share the vote. Beginning with just two dozen members, twenty-five dollars, and donated space in the Denver Opera House, the Colorado Equal Suffrage Association grew to include many of the state's most prominent women. Led by Elizabeth P. Ensley, a black suffragist originally from Massachusetts, the group remained nominally nonpartisan, although many members openly supported the Populists. When Denver permitted women to participate in municipal elections, the number of voters quadrupled and a woman was elected to the Denver school board, the first woman to hold office in Colorado. As the depression in Colorado worsened, suffragists argued that it harmed women as well as men, and that they, too, would vote to end politics as usual. "The merciless power of plutocracy that crushes you crushes us also," one woman wrote to the *Denver Republican*. "Without a vote you would be powerless; without a vote we are powerless."[17]

In May, Colorado suffragist Ellis Meredith traveled to the Chicago World's Fair to plead with the National American Woman Suffrage Association (NAWSA) leaders for help. Meredith told Anthony and Stone that success in Colorado would begin a suffrage landslide all across the West. "Are all those Mexicans dead?" Anthony asked Meredith, still bitter over the suffrage defeat in Colorado a generation earlier.[18] She had blamed the failure on Mexicans, Irish, and German Catholics, and was particularly disappointed by a small number of black men in Denver who she believed voted against suffrage. Stone sent Meredith $300, but thought privately that with "no money and only one small society," Colorado was "a hopeless case."[19] Catt was equally skeptical but explained her reasons with more tact. The movement was focused on winning suffrage in Kansas, she told Meredith, because it was the one state where victory seemed possible. Meredith continued her appeal for help even after returning to Colorado and expressed disappointment in their lack of support. She explained to Catt that the political process in Colorado offered advantages not present in other states—the requirement that an amendment needed only a simple majority of votes to pass, the secret ballot, no organized opposition, and the suffrage movement's support of the silver issue. "I dislike to feel that you think we have been rash and premature," she wrote Anthony. "A word of encouragement from you would go a long way."[20]

Catt finally conceded that NAWSA leaders were under-supporting Colorado suffragists and personally headed west to help the cause. She advised the local suffragists to focus solely on gaining the vote and keep a low profile until late in the campaign. Catt would meet with small groups and then address large crowds just before the referendum. "I have a voice like a foghorn and can be heard in out-of-door meetings," she wrote. And for those who are religious and conservative, "I have a Sunday school speech—'the Bible and Woman Suffrage.' "[21]

In the summer of 1893, some in Colorado sensed growing support for suffrage. Albina Washburn, a Denver columnist for the *Labor Enquirer*, reported that "seldom have we a public meeting here that is not more or less tinged with the spirit looking toward woman's enfranchisement."[22] Two-thirds of Colorado's thirty-three newspapers favored it. So did many political organizations. The Knights of Labor and the Farmers Alliance each appointed a committee to support suffrage, and Republicans and Democrats endorsed it in most counties. A state senator from southern Colorado who had voted against the suffrage bill faced a crowd of hostile women who "threatened to run him out of the County," Meredith told Anthony.[23]

When Catt arrived in Denver in early September, she was surprised by the favorable prospects, noting more men in her audiences than ever before. She visited nearly half of the state's counties, mostly those where support was already strong, traveling more than a thousand miles on bumpy, dusty roads, using transportation networks that did not always connect. Once, after missing a train that would have taken her thirty miles down-mountain to her next engagement, she found the only alternative transportation was a rail handcart—a small flatbed on a wheeled chassis with no seats or shock-absorbing springs, and open to the wind and weather. A large man of few words offered her a ride. They made a mad dash down the mountain, the handcart lifting on two wheels as it sped around corners. Catt's hat blew off, pins in her neatly done hair fell out, and she clung to the platform, expecting death at any moment. "There wasn't a mortal thing to hang on by except the legs of the navvy," she wrote a friend, "who for the first fifteen minutes or so displayed a taciturnity of demeanor that forbade such a liberty." Hair askew, gasping, and shaken to the core, she got to her meeting on time, but vowed to "never ride down a mountain on a handcart again if Congress were waiting to hear me."[24]

Colorado suffragists pursued a "quiet campaign" to "arouse as little opposition as possible."[25] Anthony advised Meredith to seek support at the precinct and ward level through September and then in October, to "take the cities with big & rousing meetings."[26] Only men should propose sympathetic resolutions at party meetings. "Don't let us say anything about purifying politics, don't say the ballot given to women will destroy the liquor traffic," a Colorado suffragist advised. "Woman's ballot will make the wheels of government go round with less friction and added force," she added, "yet we need not say much about it just now."[27] Like Catt, Anthony also warned against tying the movement to the free silver cause and cautioned against endorsing a particular party. But in a state where sentiment was passionately pro-silver, it was hard not to use the issue. Even Catt sometimes started her talks endorsing free silver.

Anti-suffragists began a belated campaign to spread fear of drastic social change if Colorado women acquired the vote. Wyoming suffrage had reduced women "to the depths of all that low politics imply," one leaflet stated.[28] Utah women upheld polygamy. Kansas, where women voted at the municipal level, was "in worse shape than ever before." One pamphlet warned young men "if you don't want a female lawyer, doctor or politician for a wife, but would prefer a woman who will be a good companion, home maker, wife and mother, then vote and induce all your friends to vote against EQUAL SUFFRAGE." But the anti-suffrage cause was damaged when it produced pamphlets that were openly sponsored by the Denver Brewer's Association, a smoking gun in a state whose voters were highly suspicious of corporate manipulation of politics. "We got out nearly 150,000 pamphlets," Meredith wrote, "but not one was so valuable as theirs."[29]

On Election Day in December 1893, Denver suffragists were present at polling stations, passing out instructions on how to mark the bottom of the ballot to cast a vote for suffrage, while suffrage leaders raced by carriage from one precinct to another, cajoling, cheering, and keeping an eye on the process. In downtown Denver, a local newspaper reported, women formed a gauntlet where "every man was button-holed, exhorted and almost compelled to promise that he would cast his ballot for equal suffrage."[30] Male voters passed the suffrage referendum with 55 percent of the vote, with particularly strong support from miners in central Colorado and farmers in the Northern counties. Joyous suffragists, some surprised that they won, streamed into their Denver headquarters decorated with flags depicting a W, for Wyoming, and a C for Colorado. They ended their celebrations singing "Praise God from Whom All Blessings Flow."[31] "Well—I can't yet believe it is true," Anthony proclaimed when she heard the news. "It is too good to be true! [32]

In the fall of 1894, Colorado voters elected the nation's first woman state legislator and the state's first black legislator. They also voted Governor Waite out of office. As conditions had worsened, Waite intensified his battle against the establishment. Instability peaked in the spring of 1894 during the Cripple Creek strike near Pikes Peak, when Waite sent the state militia to defend worker rights, he said, and when he personally negotiated on behalf of the miners. Newspapers across the state criticized Waite, and Republicans waged a "Redeemer" campaign to oust him. Waite blamed his defeat on women's suffrage, which "brought to the polls at least 30,000 ignorant hired girls" who voted against him.[33] He urged Populists in other states to oppose giving women the right to vote. The truth was, many women *had* voted against Waite. As the Panic of 1893 eased, many Colorado voters shunned Populist politics and returned the Republican Party to power.

After five months of work and a big victory in Colorado, Catt returned to the East Coast. Her fellow suffragists gave her much of the credit for the success and elected her to the position she most coveted: "National Organizer" for NAWSA. Colorado broke the long string of referendum failures, and three years later, voters in Idaho would also extend suffrage to women by a 2–1 vote. Some Colorado women resented eastern suffragists who belatedly gave their support. Western suffragists had followed their own path to victory, allying with temperance workers, supporting free silver, and endorsing, on occasion, the Populist Party. When easterners sent "discouraging prophecies" to the women of Colorado," other western women had "sent words of hope and encouragement" and money, one local woman said. "Colorado women will not forget these things when their turn comes to help their sisters in Nebraska."[34]

Notes

1. Lynn Sherr, *America the Beautiful: The Stirring True Story behind Our Nation's Favorite Song*, First Edition (New York: Public Affairs, 2001), 32.

2. Ibid., 16.

3. Ibid., 76.

4. Ibid., 20.

5. Ibid., 72–73.

6. Ibid., 29.

7. Dorothy Whittemore Bates Burgess, *Dream and Deed: The Story of Katharine Lee Bates*, First Edition (Norman: University of Oklahoma Press, 1952), 101.

8. Sherr, *America*, 34.

9. Katharine Lee Bates, *America the Beautiful* (Boston: Oliver Ditson Company, 1917). Available at the Library of Congress.

10. Sherr, *America*, 37.

11. "'America the Beautiful,' 1893 | The Gilder Lehrman Institute of American History," July 15, 2012, 1, http://oa.gilderlehrman.org /history-by-era/art-music-and-film/resources/%E2%80%9Camerica-beautiful%E2%80%9D-1893.

12. "Defense of the Home," *Rocky Mountain Daily News*, October 15, 1891, 3, in Suzanne M. Marilley, *Woman Suffrage and the Origins of Liberal Feminism in the United States* (Cambridge, MA; London: Harvard University Press, 1996), 130.

13. Waite Speech, "Mission of the Populist Party," Waite Papers, and *Aspen Union Era*, November 19, 1891, in John R. Morris, *Davis H. Waite: The Ideology of a Western Populist* (n.p.: University Press of America, 1982), 44.

14. *Rocky Mountain News*, July 29, 1892, in Morris, *Waite*, 13.

15. *Rocky Mountain Sun*, July 30, 1892, in Malcolm J. Rohrbough, *Aspen: The History of a Silver-Mining Town, 1879–1893* (New York; Oxford: Oxford University Press, 1986), 217.

16. David B. Griffiths, "Far-Western Populist Thought: A Comparative Study of John R. Rogers and Davis H. Waite," *The Pacific Northwest Quarterly* 60, no. 4, (October 1969): 190.

17. "Read This to Your Husband," 8, no citation, in Caroline J. Stefanco, "Pathways to Power: Women and Voluntary Associations in Denver, Colorado, 1876–1893," PhD Dissertation Duke University, 1987, 225.

18. *HWS*, 4:514.

19. LS to HB, May 21, 1893 in Wheeler, *Loving Warriors*, 351.

20. Alice Ellis Meredith to SBA, June 14, 1893, in *SP*, 5:524.

21. Stephen J. Leonard, "'Bristling for Their Rights: Colorado's Women in the Mandate of 1893," *Colorado Heritage* (Spring 1993): 13.

22. Albina Washburn, "Public Sentiment in Colorado," *WJ*, July 8, 1893, 212, in Marilley, *Woman Suffrage*, 142.

23. Meredith to SBA, June 14, 1893, in *SP*, 5:523.

24. CCC, *Woman Standard*, 101, in Van Voris, *Catt*, 36.

25. Meredith to SBA, June 14, 1893, in *SP*, 5:522.

26. SBA to Meredith, July 16, 1893, in *SP*, 5:536.

27. Mrs. M. E. Wrigley, "Excellent Advice" September 23, 1893, 300, in Marilley, *Woman Suffrage*, 144–45.

28. "Document 19: 'Anti-Woman Suffrage: Don't Fail to Read This,' Leaflet, 1893 (Women. Suffrage. Newspaper Clippings), Western History Collection, The Denver Public Library, Denver, Colorado," n.d., http://womhist.alexander street.com/colosuff/doc19.htm.

29. Leonard, "Bristling," 13.

30. "The Heavens Intact," *Denver Republican*, November 8, 1893, 7, in Stefanco, "Pathways to Power," 226–27.

31. Van Voris, *Catt*, 36.

32. Leonard, "Bristling," 13.

33. Davis R. Waite to Ignatius Donnelly, December 11, 1894, Donnelly Papers in Morris, Waite, 103.

34. Caroline Nichols Churchill, "Suffrage Enthusiasm: Western Women Wild With Joy over Colorado's Election," *The Queen Bee* 15 (November 29, 1893): 1.

CHAPTER NINETEEN

Transitions

On a hot day in the summer of 1899, Anthony stood in the shadows of the round tower at Windsor Hall, Queen Victoria's residence just outside London. She was in England for a meeting of the International Council of Women (ICW) and had asked an aristocrat acquaintance if the delegates could "secure some recognition from the Queen."[1] After enjoying cakes and fresh fruits served by the queen's livery in the enormous St. George's Hall, the guests waited behind tall soldiers in bearskin hats and gentlemen-in-waiting wearing long coats and white spats, hoping to see the queen as she went for her daily ride around Windsor Park. After more than an hour, a sudden flurry of maids appeared at the door, followed by the queen, perched in a chair carried by a kilted Scot and a turbaned Indian. Anthony was a bit surprised to see "a very human looking woman—a good, motherly woman."[2] Waves of women curtsied as the carriage arced along the gravel drive, the queen pausing to acknowledge their discomfort in the hot sun, and then drove off as the English sang "God Save the Queen" and the Americans sang along with the words to "America."[3] Anthony was delighted with the brief visit, yet wondered why the most powerful woman in the world did so little to advance women's cause "when a word from her would have turned the scales."[4] Queen Victoria ruled her empire with a firm hand and ably managed the largest household in the world. Her love for Prince Albert and their children would "refute the oft repeated assertion that public life destroys the feminine instincts and unfits women for home duties."[5] The queen, Anthony reasoned, held a faulty understanding of progress that did not link women's advancement to improving social conditions.

Three thousand delegates from Europe and the United States attended the ICW meeting in London. When it was founded in 1888 under the leadership of the National Woman Suffrage Association (NWSA), Anthony was initially pleased to see many conservative groups join. But after a decade, she was increasingly frustrated that the ICW would not endorse suffrage. Women "might as well beat the air as go on talking" about governance when they "had no voice in it," she told the gathering.[6] May Wright Sewell, the council president, replied that the vote was not the only means to influence a society. Still, Anthony was the "the colossal figure" at the meeting, a symbol of dedication and grit after decades of labor.[7] Delegates gave her a five-minute standing ovation when she arrived, and Lady Rothschild honored Anthony with a reception at her grand estate, where guests mingled in striped tents pitched on well-cropped lawns, as servants in pale blue uniforms offered trays of exquisite food and acrobats and equestrians provided entertainment.

Six months later, in February 1900, Anthony announced her retirement after eight years as president of the National American Woman Suffrage Association (NAWSA). Dozens of women and men paid tribute, and hundreds of supporters stood in line for two hours to shake her hand. Anthony told the crowd that when she joined the women's rights movement a half-century before, she was "the most despised and hated woman in all the world." Now, "it seems as if I had lived through it to be loved by you all."[8] Anthony's popularity, the *Chicago Times Herald* wrote, came from her "marvelous mixture of optimism and persistence," qualities even her opponents often acknowledged.[9] The choice of Anthony's successor surprised some. Many assumed it would be Anna Howard Shaw, NAWSA vice president and a talented speaker who had worked closely with Anthony for years. But Carrie Chapman Catt had the skills and temperament to develop a mass movement, Anthony believed, and introduced her to NAWSA delegates as "my ideal leader."[10] Catt told the delegates that a large, diverse organization would advance the cause better than a narrow group with limited membership. The individual non-conformists of the past, the "long-haired man and the short-haired woman with a straight waist and blue stockings," were yielding to a broader array of reformers, including "women of culture, social position and wealth, representatives of conventional ideas and mothers of families."[11] Twenty-nine-year-old Maud Wood Park attended the Convention and noticed very few young women there. A recent graduate of Radcliffe College, she was determined to recruit younger, educated women. Together with Inez Haynes Gillmore, Park founded the College Equal Suffrage League and began traveling to college campuses to build chapters.

Anthony retired to Rochester, but she still fought battles close to home. Trustees at the University of Rochester had reluctantly agreed to admit women if supporters raised sufficient funds within two years to cover the added costs of admitting them. On the morning of September 8, 1900,

Anthony read that the deadline was at four o'clock that afternoon, and fundraisers were still $8,000 short. Her sister Mary offered to donate $2,000, the "hard earnings of years" from her "steady, plodding labor" as a teacher, she said.[12] Anthony then raced around the city by cab seeking the remaining funds from prosperous donors and delivered the money with a half-hour to spare. When a few trustees objected that one elderly donor might die before fulfilling his pledge, Anthony took the paper and scrawled her name across it. "I am good for it, if the gentleman who signed it is not."[13] The next term, thirty-three women entered the university.

In June 1902, Anthony packed up her scrapbooks and donated them to the Library of Congress in Washington, D.C. The thirty-four volumes of neatly clipped newspaper articles covered a half-century of the suffrage struggle. In the accompanying note, Anthony wrote that the donation was made so "future generations of women may see and learn of the struggles that the pioneers went through." History making and history writing was now for "my younger friends and coworkers—Mrs. Carrie Chapman Catt—Mrs. Anna Howard Shaw and others," who stood on the shoulders of the earliest suffragists. "May they not have to work to the end of their days to secure the rights to represent themselves—as have so many who began this public movement."[14]

Anthony then headed to the Upper West Side of Manhattan, where Stanton lived in a comfortable apartment with her children Robert, Margaret, and Harriot, and her granddaughter Nora. Stanton was eighty-six years old. Her world had narrowed as her eyes weakened, and she found it difficult to get in and out of a carriage. She despaired that NAWSA had become too religious and women's suffrage seemed still far away. "All my fifty years' work seem to have borne little fruit," she wrote to a friend, blaming "women themselves."[15] Anthony shared Stanton's exasperation that the struggle had taken so long. "We little dreamed when we began this contest, optimistic with the hope and buoyancy of youth, that half a century later we would be compelled to leave the finish of the battle to another generation of women," she wrote to Stanton shortly before their meeting.[16] But Anthony was certain of its inevitable success. Old prejudices were giving way, and younger, more confident and better-educated women, Anthony wrote, "will carry our cause to victory."[17] The two old friends talked for a while, holding hands at the end. "Shall we meet again, do you think?" Anthony asked before she left. "Oh, yes, if not here, then in the hereafter, if there is one," Stanton replied. "And if there isn't we shan't know it."[18] Anthony promised to return in November for Stanton's eighty-seventh birthday.

Stanton still promoted the cause from her desk. In mid-October, she offered a rebuttal to Harvard University president Charles Eliot's complaint that college women produced small families. It was a good thing they did, Stanton replied, since Harvard men often made poor fathers. A week later, she urged President Theodore Roosevelt to support suffrage, just as he had as governor of New York. Lincoln had liberated four million slaves, and he could do the same "by bringing about the complete emancipation of thirty-six million women."[19] It was her last letter. Her children noticed a rapid decline in her health and on October 26, Stanton was too tired to dress. At one point, she stood for a few minutes, assisted by her nurse and a doctor, resting her hands on the table and staring out as though making a speech, Harriot thought. Stanton sat down, dozed off, and died in her sleep two hours later. Harriot telegrammed Anthony at her home in Rochester, "Mother passed away at three o'clock."

Anthony was at her desk when the telegram arrived. She sat alone in her room, absorbing the news until her sister Mary gently called her downstairs as darkness settled in. "I am too crushed to speak," Anthony told a reporter who came by for a comment that night. Stanton would have made eloquent utterances had she died first, "but I cannot put it into words."[20] They had not always agreed, she said, but they never believed rumors of disloyalty and never faltered on the importance of gaining suffrage for women. Anthony most enjoyed the early years in Seneca Falls when she and Stanton often plotted strategy deep into the night, "when the whole world was against us and we had to stand closer to each other."[21] "Oh, this awful hush!" she wrote her friend Ida Harper the next day. How strange that the world "goes on and on just the same no matter who is or who dies!"[22]

Stanton's memorial service was a small, private affair held in her New York City apartment. Anthony sat in Stanton's armchair, gazing at her friend lying in an open coffin, the table that first held the Declaration of Sentiments standing nearby. "A lighthouse on the human coast is falling!" the old abolitionist Reverend Moncure D. Conway eulogized. "To vast multitudes the name of Elizabeth Cady Stanton does not mean so much a person as a standard inscribed with great principles."[23] Antoinette Brown Blackwell offered religious remarks after which Stanton was buried at Woodlawn Cemetery in the Bronx. Two weeks later, on Stanton's birthday, a day Anthony had originally planned to spend with her old friend, she instead met with friends and suffragists, including Anna Howard Shaw, Lucretia Mott's sister Martha Coffin Wright, and Stanton's cousin Elizabeth Smith Miller. Stanton's granddaughter Nora accompanied Anthony on the train upstate and saw that Anthony cried most of the way. The suffrage movement was in decline, Nora thought, with no recent victories and an aging membership whose efforts seemed limited to "polite little drawing-room meetings for years." The signs, Nora said, were "ominous."[24]

The suffrage movement in the South had its own dynamic. After the Civil War, as state legislatures there rewrote their constitutions, several of them considered granting suffrage to women, often as a measure to ensure white supremacy. In the 1890s, NAWSA decided "to give especial attention to suffrage work in the Southern states."[25] In the space of a dozen years, NAWSA held three of its national conventions in the South: Atlanta in 1895, New Orleans in 1903, and Baltimore in 1906. It sponsored lecture tours in the South by high-profile speakers from the North and South, including Kentucky suffragist Laura Clay and Mississippi suffragist Belle Kearney. It appointed a vice president in each state to drum up support by encouraging the creation of state and local suffrage organizations, which grew in number and were often led by elite women who sought the vote to improve society.

In courting the South, NAWSA acceded to white supremacy. It accepted all Southern suffrage organizations as affiliates, including those that limited membership to whites. To appease Southern racists, Anthony asked Frederick Douglass not to attend the Atlanta Convention. At the New Orleans Convention, NAWSA approved states' rights and clarified that a state auxiliary organization could organize "in accordance with its own ideas and in harmony with the customs of its own section."[26] Coralie Franklin Cook, a professor of elocution at Howard University and a leader in the National Association of Colored Women, publicly reminded Anthony that black women "wait and hope with you for the day when the ballot shall be in the hands of every intelligent woman," and that enfranchised women should work "in behalf of thousands who sit in darkness."[27] Anthony visited black suffragists who met separately from NAWSA's gathering in New Orleans, but she did not try to end the segregationist policies of NAWSA's affiliates. Although Anthony and other NAWSA leaders accepted white supremacy at the state level, they resisted it at the highest level of NAWSA's national leadership. When Catt resigned the presidency of NAWSA in 1904 to care for her ill husband, Anthony opposed making Laura Clay head of the organization because Clay was "negro equality-hating," and "we should never have another colored woman on our stage if she could have her way."[28] Instead, Anthony and her followers selected Anna Howard Shaw to lead the organization.

In 1904, international cooperation among women's rights activists was enhanced when women from Europe and the United States created the

International Woman Suffrage Alliance. Its founders were frustrated that the ICW would not endorse suffrage. Delegates met in Berlin to discuss progress in their countries and to share strategy. German law forbade women from attending political events, so they held meetings under the auspices of Hamburg, a free city. Two police officers sat on stage, one taking notes, the other holding a billy club, ready to end the meeting should anyone speak improperly of the Kaiser. Mary Church Terrell, first president of the National Association of Colored Women and a close friend to Anthony, gave a well-received suffrage speech in fluent German and French. Charlotte Perkins Gilman, a leading thinker on women's roles and author of the highly influential book *Women and Economics*, was a popular speaker. Gilman believed that women could achieve equality only if they were freed from domesticity and childrearing, a message that often divided her audiences. When Social Democrats at the conference announced that women's liberation could come only through them, Catt, the Alliance president, asked that women not affiliate themselves with any particular party, which would use them as pawns. Anthony asked women to ignore differences of party or religion.

The mayor of Berlin toasted the alliance members, the first women's group ever welcomed in Berlin's town hall. The German empress received them in the ornate banquet hall of the Royal Palace. Wearing a richly embroidered white silk dress, splendid pearl earrings, a diamond-studded gold chain, and a small hat adorned with pink roses, the empress made brief, intelligent remarks in several languages as she moved along a receiving line. "Miss Anthony, you are the honored guest of this occasion," the empress said upon meeting Anthony. Anthony replied that she hoped the empress broached the subject of women's rights with her husband. "The gentlemen," the empress replied, "are very slow to comprehend this movement."[29] Afterward, the American delegates debated whether they were better received by Queen Victoria, who served them tea in her grand hall but did not speak with them, or the German empress who spoke warmly, but with minimal engagement. The opinions were divided, but they all agreed that they were as well or better received by the British and European leaders than by their own president.

NAWSA recognized the growing number of young suffragists at a college evening at its 1906 Convention. M. Carey Thomas, president of Bryn Mawr College, said women were already more than one-in-three college students and "steadily gaining on men."[30] Thomas believed educated, public-spirited women were the drivers of suffrage since they would not tolerate subordination, and educated men would support their demands. When Thomas introduced Anthony, the audience rose and applauded, some even cried. Eva Perry Moore, president of the Association of Collegiate Alumnae, lauded Anthony's "invincible honor" and said her work had made "a larger life and higher work possible to other women."[31] Pale and gaunt after being bedridden with an illness for days, Anthony thanked the crowd and agreed that college women "will someday be the nation's greatest strength." She was too weak to attend congressional hearings on suffrage, something she had done for decades. Shaw visited Anthony in the beautiful room management always reserved for her at the Shoreham Hotel and came upon her as she gazed wistfully at the Washington Monument. This would be Anthony's last trip to the nation's capital.

At an event in Washington to celebrate her eighty-sixth birthday, Anthony "sat there just as she had so many times before—and yet there was a difference," Shaw said. Dressed in her usual black dress and red shawl, her silver hair parted down the middle, "the great reformer, the orator, the planner of campaigns, seemed to have faded into the background and left instead only the beautiful, beloved woman, with an expression so spiritual that to every heart gave the thrill of sorrowful thought—This is the last!" Shaw begged Anthony to stay seated, but Anthony insisted on standing, resting her hand on Shaw's shoulder. She spoke of Shaw and the other officers seated on the stage near her, stretching her hand to grasp them and telling the audience how much they buoyed her over the years. "There have been others also just as true and devoted to the cause—I wish I could name everyone—but with such women consecrating their lives," she stopped and looked off into the distance, brought her hands to her side and said, "failure is impossible!"[32]

Those were her last public words. Too ill to attend a planned large birthday celebration in New York City, Anthony took the overnight train to Rochester with her nurse and sister Mary. Pneumonia set in and spread to both lungs. Notes of gratitude for her life's efforts poured in as newspapers reported her decline. Janet Jennings, a well-regarded journalist in the nation's capital, wrote that she was a shy, fearful western girl until Anthony inspired her. "I owed everything to you and your teachings—everything which helped me to grow, to lift myself to a broader plane of self-support, to a higher sense of the dignity of labor," she wrote. "It is due to you that I am what I am—not much perhaps but never lacking in moral courage, in truth, in sense of justice."[33]

Anthony spent her final days in her room, visited by friends and family. She clasped Shaw's hand, recalling the many challenges they had faced together and extracted a promise that Shaw would carry on as head of the suffrage movement. Anthony warned that she had been unchallenged in part for her age and years of work but that Shaw would likely face resistance to her leadership. Anthony encouraged her to do what is right and be brave. Keep agitating, Anthony advised, even when others show no gratitude. Anthony stopped eating and drifted in and out of consciousness, calling out the names of her associates, "all seemed to file past her dying eyes that day in an endless, shadowy review," speaking to each "as if in a final roll-call," Shaw said.[34] At the end, family and friends surrounded Anthony's oak-framed bed with its simple carved design. Her sister Mary sat next to her. Shaw kneeled, took Anthony's hand and pressed her face into it. Anthony clasped Shaw's hands, drew them to her lips and kissed them, and then slipped into unconsciousness, never to wake again.

More than a thousand newspapers reported her death. Suffragists around the world "claimed her and looked up to her as their leader, courageous, loyal and far-sighted," a British suffragist noted.[35] "All womanhood will shed bitter tears," a Dutch woman wrote, "we loved her so much."[36] The New York Senate recognized her as "one of the most famous and remarkable women of her time."[37] For two days, hundreds of friends came to pay their respects as Anthony lay in a plain Quaker casket wearing her black satin dress and a flag pin with four small diamonds as stars to represent the four suffrage states. On the day of the funeral, although frigid winds and heavy snow swept through the streets of Rochester, thousands of people lined the sidewalks, sometimes spilling onto the streets as Anthony's bier passed. Ten policemen worked to keep order outside the Presbyterian Church, which reached its 2,500 capacity audience in less than fifteen minutes. Rochester's prominent citizens were there, including the mayor and the president of Rochester University, but most of the mourners were ordinary people, single women, mothers who brought their children, working men and women, business leaders, young, old, rabbis, priests, and preachers. One elderly black woman hobbled in on a crutch, her shoulders covered with fresh-fallen snow, and sobbed before the open casket. Another plucked a leaf from a cluster of violets "to 'member Miss Anthony by," she said.[38] For nearly two hours, people streamed in to pay their respects, and hundreds were still outside when the funeral began. During the service, William Lloyd Garrison's son recalled that when he was a boy, Anthony was always a welcome guest in the Garrison home, prized for her simplicity and her willingness to help. Mrs. R. Jerome Jeffrey spoke on behalf of "the colored people of Rochester," recalling Anthony's support for them long ago "when it meant a great deal to be a friend to our poor, down-trodden race."[39] Shaw praised her as the most "harmonious" person she had known, who "blended into oneness with all humanity.[40]

Anthony was an excellent organizer, the *North American Review* wrote, but what set her apart from other suffrage leaders was her dedication to women's suffrage, giving "every hour of her time and every power of her being."[41] It was her work and her recreation: her politics and her religion. Future generations would remember her as "the Liberator of Woman," the *April Review of Reviews* declared.[42] Several newspapers opined that her death would doom suffrage. "Miss Anthony's peculiar views on this question would be soon forgotten," the *New York Observer* predicted. The *Brooklyn Eagle* called suffrage "one of the world's lost causes."[43]

No one had supported Anthony more than her sister Mary, who sat near the casket stifling her sobs with a handkerchief. Mary had joined the women's rights movement three years before her more famous sister. She worked as a public school math teacher and principal for three decades and spent much of her free time attending to others. In later years, she cared for her parents, including six years spent bathing, dressing, and feeding her invalid mother before heading off to work in the morning and sleeping next to her on a sofa at night. She volunteered for the Red Cross, sewed old clothes into usable garments for the poor, and nursed the sick who had no one to care for them. She taught as a substitute teacher for free, so ailing teachers would not lose their pay. She packed for Anthony, warmed her overshoes for winter trips, prepared her bath, and tended her when she was ill. For decades, she carefully pasted thousands of newspaper articles about her sister and women's rights into thirty-four tidy scrapbooks. After the death of her parents, Mary ventured out more with her sister, accompanying her to the western United States and to Europe, but always stayed in the background and chose the simplest accommodations.

Anthony acknowledged Mary's efforts in the dedication of her 1888 biography: "To my youngest sister, Mary, without whose faithful and constant homemaking there could have been no freedom for the outgoing ever grateful and affectionate sister."[44] Yet after Anthony's death, Mary reproached herself for not doing more. Nine days after the funeral, Mary and Shaw boarded a train and headed west for another suffrage battle. "I never saw a more beatific smile that was on Aunt Mary's face as the train pulled out of the station," her niece wrote.[45] In Oregon, Mary suffered a bout of vertigo and injured herself in a fall, and her health quickly deteriorated after she returned to New York. In February, three months after her sister's death, Mary died at home. "For half a century the name of Mary Anthony was hardly known outside this city, while her sister was famous on two continents," the *Rochester Post-Express* wrote after Mary's death. "But later the world learned what was known here—that the extraordinary energy which Susan B. Anthony displayed in public was possible only through the unselfish loyalty, the unflinching devotion and the unremitting labor of her sister at home."[46]

Notes

1. *SBA*, 3:1143–44.
2. Ibid., 3:1157.
3. "Miss Anthony at Windsor," no newspaper cited, February 11, 1906, in SBASC, 31:178.
4. *SBA*, 3:1143.
5. Ibid., 3:1156–57.
6. Ishbel Aberdeen, ed., International Council of Women Report of Transactions of the Second Quinquennial Meeting Held in London, July 1899 (London: Fisher Unwin, 1900), 153, in Allison L. Sneider, *Suffragists in an Imperial Age: U.S. Expansion and the Woman Question, 1870–1929*, First edition (New York: Oxford University Press, 2008), 113.
7. *SBA*, 3:1140.
8. "The National American Woman Suffrage Association—A Report of the Proceedings of Its 32nd Annual Convention," in *HWS*, 4:394.
9. "Retirement of the Great Suffrage Leader," *Chicago Times Herald*, February 7, 1900, in *SBASB*, 30:55.
10. *HWS*, 4:387–88 in Sara Hunter Graham, *Suffrage and the New Democracy* (New Haven, CT; London: Yale University Press, 1996), 7.
11. "The Women Storming," *Pittsburg Post*, February 14, 1900, in *SBASB*, 30:9.
12. Mary Anthony to Ellen C. Eastwood, Treasurer of the Fund Committee for the University of Rochester, in *SBASB*, 3:1495.
13. Shaw, *Pioneer*, 220–21.
14. *SBASB*, 1:1.
15. ECS to Victoria Woodhull Martin, October 4, 1898, in *SP*, 6:245.
16. SBA to ECS, Before October 26, 1902, in *SP*, 6:451.
17. Ibid.
18. Dorr, *Anthony*, 327.
19. ECS to Theodore Roosevelt, October 25, 1902, Stanton and Blatch, *Letters*, 2:369.
20. *SBA*, 3:1262.
21. Ibid., 3:1263.
22. Ibid.
23. Ibid., 3:1264.
24. Ellen Carol DuBois, *Spanning Two Countries: The Autobiography of Nora Stanton Barney* (London: History Workshop 22, 1986), 146.

25. *HWS*, 4:184 in Elna C. Green, *Southern Strategies: Southern Women and the Woman Suffrage Question*, First edition (Chapel Hill: University of North Carolina Press, 1997), 8.

26. *HWS*, 5:59.

27. Coralie Franklin Cook, "National Convention of 1900," in *HWS*, 4:399.

28. SBA to the Garrisons, January 1904, in Trisha Franzen, *Anna Howard Shaw: The Work of Woman Suffrage*, First Edition (Urbana: University of Illinois Press, 2014), 100.

29. *SBA*, 3:1319–20.

30. Ibid., 3:1393.

31. Ibid., 3:1487.

32. Ibid., 3:1409.

33. Ibid., 3:1454.

34. Shaw, *Pioneer*, 233–34.

35. *SBA*, 3:1448.

36. Ibid., 3:1449.

37. Ibid., 3:1446.

38. Ibid., 3:1431.

39. Ibid., 3:1437.

40. Shaw, *Pioneer*, 236.

41. *SBA*, 3:1485–86.

42. *April Review of Reviews*, in ibid., 3:1485.

43. *SBA*, 3:1474.

44. Ibid., 3:1500.

45. Ibid., 3:1503.

46. Ibid., 3:1510.

CHAPTER TWENTY

Sisterhood

On an October day in 1909, a thick ribbon of humanity trailed for two blocks from Carnegie Hall in mid-Manhattan. When the doors opened, people quickly filled the three thousand seats and disappointed hundreds were turned away. The audience, mostly women, included box makers, bookbinders, hat trimmers, textile workers, waitresses, teachers, librarians, society women, lawyers, and engineers, including Nora Stanton Blatch, the granddaughter of Elizabeth Cady Stanton and the first woman to earn a civil engineering degree at Cornell University. All were there to see Britain's most famous suffragist, Emmeline Pankhurst, a fifty-one-year-old mother of five whose militant tactics for women's rights had garnered international fame. She and her followers disrupted parliamentary speeches, smashed windows at the prime minister's residence, and drew hundreds of thousands to their rallies. The year before, Pankhurst was arrested trying to enter Parliament and arrested again when she slapped a police officer, twice. Many Americans were wary of Pankhurst's militancy. "Noise, obstruction, agitation are bread and butter to her," the *New York Times* chided. Pankhurst's methods, if used in America, would secure "nothing but ridicule."[1]

When Pankhurst took the stage in a fashionable, purple velvet dress trimmed in white lace, many in the audience were surprised. She was a petite woman who looked "more like a nice, home-keeping mother than a political leader," one newspaper reported.[2] "I know you have not all come here tonight because you are interested in suffrage," she began, knowing that some in the audience were just curious to see a radical. "I am not a hooligan."[3] British suffragists had turned to militancy only after men in power ignored their questions, forcibly removed them from public meetings, and hauled them off to prison, she said. Prime Minister Arthur Balfour had suggested to Pankhurst that suffragists would succeed only when they forced their cause into the center of politics—so they did.

"The movement is where no political party can afford to overlook it," Pankhurst told the cheering crowd. She urged American women to make their movement politically powerful by uniting across class lines, to "value our womanhood before everything else in the world." Rich or poor, "we are all outclassed because we are women."[4]

New York, home to some of the wealthiest Americans and to masses of working poor, was a testing ground for women's ability to unite. Six years prior, the Women's Trade Union League (WTUL) was founded to promote the unionization of trades where women predominated through a coalition of working women and middle-class "allies."[5] Although women as a group were paid much less than men, traditional unions often ignored them. Rose Schneiderman and Leonora O'Reilly, organizers for the WTUL who had worked in low-paying jobs since their early teens, visited factories and immigrant neighborhoods to recruit women into unions. Mary Dreier, head of the New York WTUL, appealed to middle-class audiences for support, though she often found them suspicious of organized labor. Recognizing that women voters would lend strength to their cause, the WTUL established a Suffrage Bureau in 1908. It organized suffrage leagues for working women and tried to convince working men that voting women could join them to fight for higher pay and better conditions.

The WTUL's efforts increased the number of pro-union and pro-suffrage women working in factories, but mostly ignored women in white-collar jobs. Harriot Stanton Blatch, Elizabeth Cady Stanton's daughter, established the Equality League of Self-Supporting Women in 1907 to unify all women in the workforce, including rising numbers of teachers, librarians, office workers, and other white-collar workers. Equality League members employed new tactics that took the battle for suffrage to the streets. On one occasion, members drove between polling places on Election Day, some riding on the sideboards of Model T Fords bedecked with suffrage banners, drawing more attention than "a white elephant," Blatch said.[6] Blatch and labor activist Maud Malone toured Upstate New York to promote the cause. Albany's mayor failed in his attempts to stop them from holding an open-air meeting, and when Vassar College president James Monroe Taylor barred them from campus, they met with students in a cemetery off campus. Vassar's vivacious and popular student leader, Inez Milholland, encouraged other students to join the suffrage movement. Blatch arranged for working women to testify before the New York Senate Judiciary Committee and recruited society women for their money and influence, including Anne Morgan, the youngest daughter of millionaire financier J. P. Morgan who had founded the elite Colony Club. Yet these wealthy new members were hardly "self-supporting"—they lived off fortunes earned by others. In 1910, Blatch changed the name of the Equality League to the Women's Political Union (WPU).

Katherine Duer Mackay, a prominent socialite who owned one of the finest homes on Long Island, founded the Equal Franchise Society to work for suffrage through education and persuasion. She appointed other society women to the executive board, along with Blatch, who though not wealthy was at ease in such company. Mackay decorated her Madison Avenue headquarters with expensive furniture and sent invitations to their meetings at the Colony Club on Tiffany stationery. Annual dues for the Society were five dollars, an entire week's wages for a working woman. The best suffragists, Mackay said, were mothers devoted to children "in order to make them citizens worthy of our great country."[7]

Alva Vanderbilt Belmont, one of the richest women in the country, put her tremendous energy and resources into the suffrage cause. After marrying William K. Vanderbilt in 1875, Belmont vaulted the Vanderbilt family into the highest echelons of New York society through lavish entertaining at the family's plush mansions in New York City and Newport, Rhode Island. In 1895, she divorced William over his infidelity, a scandal that damaged her social standing. She regained her footing when she finessed the marriage of her daughter Consuelo to Charles Spencer-Churchill, the Ninth Duke of Marlborough, in an exchange of money for title. The next year, she married wealthy investment banker Oliver Belmont. After her husband's death, Belmont was inspired by an electrifying meeting of Pankhurst's Women's Social and Political Union in London. But her growing involvement in the movement, she said, was "a slow-gathering inner harvest of thoughts which had taken years to ripen."[8] In 1909, Belmont established her own suffrage organization, the Political Equality Association, and recruited members across race and class lines. Suffrage will fail unless it "means freedom and equal rights to all women of every race, of every creed, rich or poor," she told a black audience.[9] She opened Marble House, her sumptuous Newport mansion, to more than five hundred paying guests who listened to suffrage speeches as Belmont strolled among the crowd holding a parasol and handing out pamphlets. Some reporters likened her to captains of industry who were forthright, impatient with formalities, and keen observers. She was "a serious, practical, masterful woman with an uncommon amount of brain and a great fund of energy and ambition for driving power," one reporter wrote.[10] Yet few knew that Belmont feared public speaking, often canceling engagements at the last minute or appearing flushed when she addressed audiences large and small.

Carrie Chapman Catt, who moved to New York after the death of her husband, believed these suffrage organizations lacked a critical element for success: the ability to apply political pressure. Women needed to play the game of politics like any other group. She and eight hundred women formed the Woman Suffrage Party (WSP) in 1909 to develop an organization with widespread, ground-level appeal. With a tightly organized hierarchy modeled on Tammany Hall, the WSP monitored New York politicians; offered classes and study groups; and produced a suffrage journal, the *Woman Voter*, edited by Mary Ritter Beard. Members visited immigrant neighborhoods to distribute suffrage literature and win support through community projects, even constructing replicas of a Chinese tea garden and German villa. Catt was a political moderate who eschewed publicity-driven proselytizing and even refused to speak at the nation's first open-air suffrage meeting in Madison Square.

By the fall of 1909, when Pankhurst arrived in New York, the city had a kaleidoscope of suffrage organizations, each with its own vision of how to press for women's right to vote. A strike by the city's textile workers over low pay and poor working conditions would test Pankhurst's call for unity and coordinated action by women. More than fifty thousand women in New York produced over half of all clothes manufactured in the United States, yet earned wages barely high enough to survive. The Triangle Shirtwaist Factory alone employed hundreds of women who toiled over sixty hours per week—at below poverty–level wages. When the strike began on November 23, the WTUL stepped in with money and press coverage. A plainclothes officer arrested WTUL leader Dreier as she picketed outside the Triangle Shirtwaist Factory—and quickly released her after realizing who she was—prompting newspaper reports on the abuses of women picketers. But it was Clara Lemlich, a twenty-three-year-old garment worker, who ignited the strike into a mass movement. At a meeting in early December, she listened to labor leaders' debate for four hours whether other workers should join the walkout. Lemlich suddenly climbed on stage and demanded that workers join the strike. "I am tired of listening to speakers who talk in generalities," she shouted as the crowd roared with approval.[11] The next day, twenty thousand workers stayed home or walked the picket lines, and the garment industry ground to a halt. Factory owners hired "scabs" to cross picket lines and thugs and prostitutes to harass the strikers. In the first month of the strike, police arrested more than seven hundred workers, including Lemlich, whose ribs were broken from the rough handling.

Some wealthy sympathizers joined strikers on the picket lines. Elsie Cole, an eloquent Vassar graduate, encouraged the picketers and urged passers-by to support the strike. After her third arrest, the *New York Times* reported, she "pleaded her case so effectively that the policemen on duty have no mind to interfere with her again."[12] When a factory boss shows up at the police station, "she can make a full-fledged argument and win her point while the boss is struggling for the words to form a single sentence."[13] Inez Milholland, the former Vassar College student leader who was attending law school in New York, advised picketers to avoid arrest by shouting "strikebreaker" rather than "scab" and once leaped out of a car to confront a police officer who was arresting a striker.[14] "For once," the *New York Times* commented, "the factory girl and the college girl are making a fight together."[15] Colony Club members listened to working women of the WTUL describe their low pay and horrible conditions and donated $1,300. The Shubert family pledged to support strikers with the following week's profits from their family's theater chain.

Belmont supported strikers by financing the largest labor rally in New York history, held at the Hippodrome Theater with the stipulation that one hour be devoted to suffrage. She saw herself as a "female knight," a protector of vulnerable women, and visited a Greenwich Village courthouse to see for herself whether police and prison guards mistreated strikers under arrest.[16] Newspaper reporters watched as her elegant carriage pulled up in front of the courthouse, and Belmont emerged dressed in fashionable French broadcloth and a velvet hat. She sat directly in front of the judge, leaning in and cupping her ear to hear the proceedings as the picketers appeared one by one, nodding her head in approval when she was satisfied and displaying scorn when she was not. Once, angered by some action of the judge, she stood to speak, hesitated, then sat down. When the judge ordered a woman not to wear a sign in support of the strike, Belmont jumped to her feet, "I'll wear one too," she blurted out. "I'll wear one on the street if I want to."[17] Word of Belmont's assistance spread. "Belmont's all right," one working woman said. "Take it from me, she's a peach."[18]

Some Socialist labor organizers resisted working with Belmont and other suffragists. They "are only interested in us because they think through us they can get the working girls," one said.[19] Some believed one could be a Socialist or a suffragist, but not both. You cannot "serve two Gods," a prominent Socialist told labor organizer Ruth Schneiderman.[20] Labor men threw rotten tomatoes at Clara Lemlich as she appealed to working women outside factories to support suffrage. "Why don't you go home and wash the dishes?" they shouted.[21] But Socialist suffragists denied that they did the bidding of rich women and defended their suffrage work. "Mrs. Belmont and Mrs. Morgan can no more control the women of the working class when they get the ballot, any more than the same Belmont-Morgan crowd can control the men of the working class."[22]

Despite some mistrust, solidarity among women strikers and their supporters remained until the Shirtwaist Strike ended in February 1910, when most factory owners agreed to improve wages and conditions. Membership in the International Ladies' Garment Workers Union exploded, and Lemlich became a hero. To celebrate, Belmont took the strike leaders to Delmonico's, one of New York's finest restaurants in the heart of the financial district. Lemlich and Dreier were there, as were a sprinkling of prominent New Yorkers and members of the "mink brigade," wealthy supporters who had donated nearly $50,000.[23] Rev. Percy Grant expressed thanks to participants on both sides for ending the strike peacefully and praised the manufacturers for being "good citizens" by providing better terms for their workers. Two years ago, he said, a British suffragist criticized American women for their disinterest in "public questions" and suggested they did not deserve the vote until they got involved. Now "our women are showing that they do take an interest in the life, labors, and demands of thousands of working women and girls."[24]

New York suffragists devised more ways to take their message to the streets. They lobbied with "sandwichettes," carrying sandwich boards emblazoned with slogans about the vote.[25] They hawked suffrage souvenirs and sold affordable lunches "to reach the head and heart by way of the stomach."[26] They sponsored an organ grinder concert that began with the song "No Wedding Bells for Me."[27] A suffragist gave a "voiceless speech" in a Fifth Avenue shop window, shedding placards to the floor as she mouthed the words.[28] In May 1910, thousands of women marched along Fifth Avenue, holding signs and yellow flags accompanied by a hundred cars bedecked with daisies, yellow jonquils, and suffrage banners. "New York State Denies the Vote to Idiots, Lunatics, Criminals, and Women," one stated. "Taxation without Representation Is Tyranny," said another.[29] Organizers were elated. Women had united across class lines, and the suffrage movement had become more public, more aggressive, even "militant," Blatch said—and permanently so.[30] When Blatch's daughter Nora divorced in 1911, her husband sued for custody of their young daughter on the grounds that Nora neglected the toddler's education other than to teach her to say, "Votes for Women" and "Hurrah for Woman Suffrage."[31]

In 1912, Blatch and the WPU organized a spectacular parade, with three thousand marchers who walked the entire four-mile route to highlight suffragist discipline and unity. Inez Milholland led the parade astride a white horse, her self-confident radiance providing a dramatic contrast to the stereotype of the withered, angry suffragist. Three women followed representing the WPU, the Woman's Suffrage Party, and the Collegiate Equal Suffrage League. Scottish bagpipers symbolized ways of old, followed by a woman in a sedan chair, "The Lady of Yesterday." Then came representations of women performing work in the home, spinning and weaving, followed by masses of factory workers, secretaries, teachers, doctors, and lawyers, all grouped according to their profession, making it "impossible for an intelligent onlooker to contend that woman's place is in the home," Blatch said.[32]

Suffragists also inserted themselves into the mechanics of voting. Blatch and several others began poll watching on Election Day for the hotly contested New York mayoral race of 1909, though a ward heeler scolded her that it was "no place for a woman."[33] At the next primary election, police arrested women poll watchers, sometimes forcibly. Upon release, the women immediately returned to the polling sites and the authorities gave up trying to stop them. Politicians will change "as soon as they understand that they can't play with us and smooth this down anymore," Blatch said.[34] The WPU also hired professional lobbyists in Albany and actively campaigned against suffrage opponents, including Artemus Ward, a Judiciary Committee member who kept the women's suffrage bill bottled up in committee. "We must make them see that they must reckon with us as they do with men," Blatch said.[35]

Belmont threw more energy and resources into suffrage. She financed the relocation of NAWSA headquarters from Ohio to New York City and hired three employees to run a Press Bureau, which quadrupled the production of suffrage propaganda. She purchased two midtown buildings for the Political Equity Association, sponsored a suffrage lunchroom in a working-class neighborhood, and hired a "Santa Clausette" to hand out more than a thousand gifts.[36] She modified her Madison Avenue mansion to hold suffrage lectures, opened her Long Island estate to more than twenty volunteer "farmerettes," established an affordable hospital managed by women, and created a Department of Hygiene to educate women on health and personal care.[37] "Mrs. Belmont is everywhere," a reporter wrote. "One minute she is giving instructions to the peach-faced girl who sells liquid shampoo," he wrote, "the next she is watching Chloe of the kitchen range steaming rice."[38] Catt criticized Belmont's high-profile tactics. Some measure progress by the number of newspaper articles, Catt noted; "I think we should make more progress if we had considerably less."[39]

For all the effort expended to unite women across class lines, many working-class suffragists still felt alienated. Middle-class women had "the best intentions in the world," WTUL organizer Leonora O'Reilly told Dreier, but they "rub the fur the wrong way, they really don't speak our language." They use working women "and then throw them over," she said.[40] On March 22, 1911, O'Reilly and others formed a suffrage

A sign in the Ohio headquarters of the women's suffrage movement in 1912 exhorts men to "come in and learn why women ought to vote." The National League of Women Voters was not formed until 1920, so this sentence is best left out. I try to stay "in the moment" with photos. (Library of Congress)

organization of and for working women—the New York Wage Earners' Suffrage League. Three days later, on a dreary Saturday afternoon, fire broke out at the Triangle Shirtwaist Factory in lower Manhattan, killing 146 people—123 women and 23 men, mostly young Jewish and Italian immigrants. Doors locked to prevent workers from stealing or taking breaks, a faulty fire escape, an inept response by the fire department, and managers who escaped while others perished inside—all reflected the callous exploitation of which workers had long complained. After the fire, Dreier served on the New York Factory Investigating Commission, empaneled to scrutinize hundreds of factories, hold dozens of hearings, and propose new legislation on worker safety. While the New York legislature passed most of its proposals for improving worker health and safety, male labor leaders' condescending attitudes toward working women changed Dreier from "an ardent supporter of labor to a somewhat rabid supporter of women," she said.[41] The WTUL increasingly turned away from militant strikes and toward promoting legislative reform for women workers, including suffrage.[42]

In early 1912, as the New York Senate Judiciary Committee debated a bill for women's suffrage, the WPU posted "silent sentinels" outside, pairs of women signifying "the patient waiting that the women of the Empire State have done since Elizabeth Cady Stanton made the first demand for our enfranchisement in 1848."[43] They tried to enter the Assembly Chamber holding banners with the names of anti-suffrage legislators. They chased reluctant senators through the capitol corridors, even following one into the Senate Majority Leader's office and then escorting him back to the Judiciary Committee meeting, one suffragist on each side of him and one behind. The senator told Blatch he would "never forgive this."[44] Yes, he would, Blatch said, and someday he would recall it with pride. When the New York Senate once again voted down the suffrage referendum bill by 24–17, an exasperated senator asked Blatch if the suffragists would leave him alone. "You will never get peace," Blatch replied.[45]

Over 150 WPU volunteers canvassed the legislative districts of two suffrage opponents, encouraging constituents to reject them at the polls. One was defeated and the other was barely reelected. "Why gentlemen, the cunning and shrewdness, and the deception and underhanded way they will go round to secure votes to defeat a member for office!" the latter

Harriot Stanton Blatch speaking on Wall Street, ca. 1915–1920. (Library of Congress)

told his fellow legislators. "Woman is dangerous when she wants to gain a point," he said. "She will stop at nothing."[46] Blatch and others watched from the gallery with amusement and a sense of their growing power. "No candidate could meet our fire, unscathed," she said.[47]

Some working women allied with the Collegiate Equal Suffrage League to confront the "sentimentality" of New York legislators. Thousands of hat trimmers, cap makers, shirtwaist sewers, laundresses, and young college women filled the Cooper Union Auditorium "just to show the gentlemen we have arrived."[48] A few working women turned to British-style militancy. Maud Malone interrupted Theodore Roosevelt and Woodrow Wilson with indignant questions about suffrage as they campaigned for the presidency in 1912. Even Belmont began to favor American women developing "their own militant methods," comparing the suffrage movement to other patriotic struggles. Yet most suffragists and Americans were still wary of militancy. When Belmont told the press that technology made women equal to men and that modern warfare "requires more brain than muscle," the *New York World* reported her remarks under the banner "Women to Kill Men to Get Vote, Says Mrs. Belmont."[49]

By 1912, New York suffragists had brought the movement out of front parlors and auditoriums and into factories, foundries, immigrant neighborhoods, college campuses, and the streets. With their bold demands and creative tactics, suffragists had forced the public to pay attention. Yet class divisions in the movement persisted. The "cultured" ladies were sincere but "narrow," Schneiderman told a fellow WTUL member after NAWSA hired her to work on an Ohio referendum. But they "are beginning to see the necessity of having a working girl tour a State rather than some professor," she said.[50] Maggie Hinchey, a laundry worker who attended a NAWSA conference in New York, remarked that she felt "as if I have butted in where I was not wanted." A schoolteacher who represented workers said she found "not a word of labor spoken at this convention so far" and left early.[51] To succeed, the suffrage movement needed to become a mass movement with women from different backgrounds. In New York, women collaborated across class lines, but Pankhurst's call for women to value their unity above everything else had its limits.

Notes

1. "The Advent of Mrs. Pankhurst," *NYT (1857–1922)*, October 22, 1909, 6, 96975212, ProQuest Historical Newspapers: *NYT*.

2. "Suffrage Cheers for Mrs. Pankhurst," *NYT (1857–1922)*, October 22, 1909, 1, 96975212, ProQuest Historical Newspapers: *NYT*.

3. "Great Throng Hears Mrs. Pankhurst," *NYT* (*1857–1922*), October 26, 1909, 1, 96939059, ProQuest Historical Newspapers: *NYT*.

4. "Great Throng," 1; "Mrs. Pankhurst's Farewell Address," *WJ*, December 11, 1909, 199, in Ellen Carol DuBois, *Harriot Stanton Blatch and the Winning of Woman Suffrage* (New Haven, CT; London: Yale University Press, 1997), 115.

5. Nancy Schrom Dye, "Creating a Feminist Alliance: Sisterhood and Class Conflict in the New York Women's Trade Union League, 1903–1914," *Feminist Studies* 2 no. 2/3 (1975): 27.

6. Harriot Stanton Blatch, *Challenging Years: The Memoirs of Harriot Stanton Batch* (Westport, CT: Hyperion Press, 1976), 98.

7. "Militant Suffrage Not for Mrs. Mackay," *NYT* (*1857–1922*), October 14, 1909, 9, 96937231, ProQuest Historical Newspapers: *NYT*.

8. "Why I Am a Suffragist," *The World To-day*, October 21, 1911, 1171–72, in Peter Geidel, *Alva E. Belmont: A Forgotten Feminist,* PhD Dissertation, Columbia University, 1993, 70.

9. No article title, *NYT*, February 7, 1910, 4, in Geidel, *Belmont*, 153–55.

10. Kate Carew, "Kate Carew Asks Mrs. Belmont about the Baby and the Ballot," *New York World*, December 2, 1909, in Geidel, *Belmont*, 187.

11. Ann Schofield, *"To Do and To Be": Portraits of Four Women Activists, 1893–1986* (Boston: Northeastern, 1997), 50; John Thomas McGuire, "From Socialism to Social Justice Feminism: Rose Schneiderman and the Quest for Urban Equity: 1911–1933," *Journal of Urban History* 35 (2009): 1001.

12. "College Girls as Pickets in a Strike," December 19, 1909, 96930926, ProQuest Historical Newspapers: *NYT*.

13. Ibid.

14. Ibid.

15. Ibid.

16. *New York World*, December 18–20, 1909, in Geidel, *Belmont*, 137.

17. Ibid.

18. Ibid.

19. Theresa Malkiel, no citation in Geidel, *Belmont*, 142.

20. Max Fruchter to Rose Schneiderman, March 5, 1911, in Annelise Orleck, *Common Sense & a Little Fire* (Chapel Hill; London: University of North Carolina Press, 1995), 99.

21. Newman, interview by Wertheimer; Scheier, "Clara Lemlich Shavelson," in Orleck, *Common Sense*, 99.

22. Malkiel, no citation in Geidel, *Belmont*, 142.

23. Schneiderman, *All for One*, 8.

24. "Mrs. Belmont to Buy Only Union Waists," February 8, 1910, 5, *NYT* 97046266, ProQuest Historical Newspapers: *NYT*.

25. Bzowski, Frances Diodato, "Spectacular Suffrage; Or, How Women Came Out of the Home and into the Streets and Theaters of New York City to Win the Vote," *New York History* 76, no. 1 (January 1995): 69–70.

26. Ibid.

27. Ibid.

28. Ibid.

29. Blatch, *Challenging Years*, 130.

30. Blatch, *Jus Suffragii*, June 15, 1910, 79 in Patricia Greenwood Harrison, *Connecting Links: The British and American Woman Suffrage Movements, 1900–1914* (Westport, CT: London: Greenwood Press, 2000), 133.

31. "Deforest Blames Suffrage," *NYT*, October 19, 1911, 9, in Joanna Newman, *Gilded Suffragists: The New York Socialites Who Fought for Women's Right to Vote* (New York: New York University Press, 2017), 118.

32. "The Uprising of the Women," *NYT*, May 5, 1912, Suffrage Scrapbook v. 1, VCA.

33. "Fair Sex on Guard," *New York American,* November 3, 1909, n.p., in DuBois, *Blatch*, 127.

34. *New York Sun*, March 1910, n.p., HSB—NY in DuBois, *Blatch*, 132.

35. Ibid.

36. Geidel, *Forgotten Feminist*, 210.

37. "Women Farmers Arrive," *NYT*, March, 5, 1911, 10, in Sylvia D. Hoffert, *Alva Vanderbilt: Unlikely Champion of Women's Rights* (Bloomington, IN: Indiana University Press, 2011), 82.

38. Donnelly, "My Experiences with a Society Suffragette," *New York Press*, December 10, 1911, in Geidel, *Belmont*, 277.

39. CCC to Ida Husted Harper, March 11, 1910, in Geidel, *Belmont*, 181–82.

40. Leonora O'Reilly to Margaret Dreier Robins, September 23, 1912, Robins Papers, University of Florida, in Jacoby, "The Women's Trade Union League and American Feminism," *Feminist Studies* 3 (Autumn 1975): 134.

41. Note 43, in Ann Schofield, *To Do and To Be, Portraits of Four Women Activists, 1893–1986* (Lebanon, NH: Northeastern University Press, 1997), 69.

42. See Orleck, *Common Sense*, 129–34.

43. Women's Political Union 1911–12 Annual Report, 23–24, in DuBois, *Blatch*, 138.

44. Blatch, *Challenging Years*, 163.

45. Ibid., 172.

46. Ibid., 175.

47. Ibid., 155.

48. "Senators vs. Working Women," Reel 12, O'Reilly Papers, in Orleck, *Common Sense*, 102.

49. *New York Evening World*, March 16, 1912, in Geidel, *Belmont*, 298–99.

50. Schneiderman to Pauline Newman, July 26, 1912, in Jacoby, *American Feminism*, 131.

51. Margaret Hinchey to Leonora O'Reilly, 1913(?), O'Reilly Papers, U. of Florida, in Jacoby, *American Feminism*, 134. A misspelling in the original quote is corrected by the author.

CHAPTER TWENTY-ONE

Success in the Pacific West

In 1909, eighty-five NAWSA delegates in three designated train cars headed west for their annual Convention in Seattle. Many of the "Suffrage Special" passengers had spent years working for the vote, including Anna Howard Shaw, Henry Blackwell, Charlotte Perkins Gilman, and Fanny Garrison Villard, the daughter of William Lloyd Garrison and wife of the railroad baron Henry Villard. When the train arrived in eastern Washington, the delegates found the state suffrage movement deeply divided, riven by two powerful women with opposing approaches to winning the vote.

May Arkwright Hutton, a suffrage leader in eastern Washington, left behind a life of hardship when she headed west in 1883 at the age of twenty-three. Born out of wedlock to a mother who abandoned the family, her grandfather provided stability in her childhood but little love. Arkwright married a coal miner and took in boarders to make ends meet. After the death of her husband, the stout, robust Arkwright, a woman who "never knew a stranger anytime, anywhere," boarded the Northern Pacific Railroad for California. Jim Wardner, a fellow passenger and miner, heard she was a good cook and offered to set her up with a restaurant if she would settle in the small Idaho town named after him.[1] Arkwright agreed and soon found that her new "restaurant" was a stove and a few pieces of cookware in the rear of a saloon. She made a living, though, and married one of her customers, Levy Hutton, a railroad engineer. The Huttons invested in several local mines, including the Hercules Mine, which made them very wealthy after the largest deposit of silver in the West was discovered there in 1901. In 1904, Hutton became a Democratic candidate for the Idaho state legislature, where she campaigned "just like any man," she said. "I gave away cigars—and hustled."[2] Hutton then moved with her husband to a mansion in Spokane, Washington, the nearest "big" city, where she became involved in helping other women and the downtrodden. She established a boarding house for young workingwomen and helped track down wayward fathers to make them support their children. Hutton was flamboyant and outspoken—she "did and said what she liked, and she had no inhibitions," someone said—and dashed around Washington in a chauffeured red car.[3]

Emma Smith DeVoe, the state's leading suffragist, moved to Tacoma, Washington, after the successful 1896 suffrage campaign in Idaho. Slender, elegant, and known for her gentle voice and gracious style, DeVoe advocated a suffrage tactic called the "still hunt"—to seek the vote by quietly lobbying and not demanding it. They would confront suffrage opponents and try to convert them to the cause "with sincere and tolerant consideration, or—in the case of irrationally prejudiced persons whom it is impossible to answer," with gentle teasing. "The more womanly we can be," DeVoe said, "the better for our cause."[4] To highlight suffragists' concern for domesticity, DeVoe wrote a "Kitchen Contest" newspaper column that offered prizes for the best short essay on home care and encouraged local suffrage groups to promote home economics in their schools.[5] In 1909, Washington suffragists produced *The Washington Women's Cookbook*, featuring recipes interspersed with suffrage quotes and short histories of the movement. At a dollar apiece, it raised money and "made us friends among the men," DeVoe said.[6]

At first, DeVoe and Hutton worked well together as president and vice president of the Washington Equal Suffrage Association (WESA). Hutton believed DeVoe was doing "splendid work on the other side of the Range," and wrote to NAWSA leaders "if we had raked the nation with a fine-tooth comb we could not have found Mrs. Emma Smith DeVoe's equal as an organizer, state president and presiding officer."[7] But Hutton's brash style and crude language alienated fellow suffragists and powerful politicians. The senator in charge of a state suffrage bill said Hutton's meddling in Olympia damaged his work, and "it became necessary to ignore her entirely."[8] Hutton's "aggressiveness and her peculiar methods," DeVoe wrote, "nearly ruined our cause." Hutton came to resent the "self-centered, exclusive, ultra-conventional" suffragists who were "content to rest upon their college-earned laurels, and little heard of outside their 'frat' clubs and organizations," she said. The vote was needed most by eight million working women, "who not only support themselves, but their fathers, mothers, sisters, brothers and husbands."[9]

Hutton tried to engineer a leadership coup d'état at the 1909 WESA Convention by quietly recruiting new members loyal to her and luring them to the Convention with the promise of an all-expenses paid trip to the Alaska-Yukon-Pacific Exposition that was being held in Seattle at the same time. When DeVoe and WESA treasurer Dr. Cora Smith Eaton discovered Hutton's plan, they rejected the new members and tried to smear Hutton's reputation. Eaton wrote to Carrie Chapman Catt claiming that Hutton had been a prostitute known as "Bootleg Mary" when she lived in Idaho. Eaton also threatened Hutton that if she came to the state convention, they would release evidence of her sordid past. Hutton fought back. She informed Eaton that she would attend the Convention with her supporters and publicly read Eaton's "threatening and blackmailing letter," which she had already sent to her lawyer.[10] Hutton then accused DeVoe and Eaton of being careless with money and drawing a salary when suffrage leadership should be voluntary. As president, DeVoe was paid a hundred dollars each month, though it was not enough even to cover her living expenses.

When the NAWSA delegates on the Suffrage Special arrived in Spokane, their first stop in Washington, Hutton welcomed them with an elaborate banquet, which she paid for herself. As a commemoration of western pride, the mayor presented Shaw with a gavel made of Idaho silver and wood from each of the four western states where women could vote. About fifty Spokane delegates boarded the train for Seattle, making several stops to campaign for suffrage. Along the way, Hutton and her followers gave NAWSA delegates their explanation for the rift that existed between the Washington suffrage groups. When Eaton refused to seat the Spokane women at the WESA Convention and accused Hutton of bribing members to join, Hutton and her followers appealed to NAWSA leadership. NAWSA refused to recognize either faction at their convention, but seated both without voting privileges.

Despite divisions at the top, the fragmented Washington suffrage movement effectively promoted the cause. At the Alaska-Yukon-Pacific Exposition, suffragists rented space at the Women's Building and networked with other organizations, particularly the State Federation of Women's Clubs and the National Council of Women. They handed out suffrage ribbons and hired a dirigible to trail a banner with the message: "Votes for Women."[11] Outside of Seattle, suffragists lobbied farmers and successfully convinced union members, the Farmers Union, the Grange, and the state Federation of Labor to support suffrage. Catholic clergy were silent, while Protestant clergy gave strong support for suffrage, perhaps anticipating women's future political support of temperance. Some Washington suffragists used political campaign tactics. They systematically canvassed the state, making note of each voter's nationality, employment, and stance on suffrage. They hung posters and banners, held parades, spread flyers, and published the suffrage newspaper *Votes for Women*.

Suffrage groups around the state assigned women to influence local media, but most newspapers already supported the effort, often highlighting the differences between the militant English suffragists and their own mild, domestic suffragists.

In November 1910, Washington voters approved women's suffrage by a vote of 52,000 to 30,000, winning a majority of votes in each of the state's thirty-eight counties. Governor M. E. Hey congratulated DeVoe on the "ladylike, quiet campaign you conducted, with appeals to reason and not to prejudice or passion."[12] On the same day, however, male voters in adjoining Oregon rejected a suffrage referendum by almost the same margin as in Washington.

Two months later, DeVoe formed the National Council of Women Voters to spread the successful methods used in Washington to other states. Some westerners mistrusted NAWSA. "A large number of our Citizens resent the advent of women coming in our state organizing and telling us how to help other women secure the ballot," Margaret Roberts of Idaho explained. "We feel that the western women are better fitted to come into the east and help and tell eastern women how to organize." Some members prided themselves on the "still hunt" tactic. "We do not care to do anything that will antagonize our men," Roberts told Catt.[13] DeVoe prevailed upon Governor James Brady of Idaho, a suffrage supporter, to convene the first Convention of the new National Council of Women Voters, with delegates from five western states. Although struggles over leadership and membership between Hutton and DeVoe marred the Convention, both agreed that western women should lead their own suffrage struggles. "We are having no quarrel with our brilliant sister coworkers of the Eastern States," Hutton wrote, but "they do not understand the freedom-loving, patriotic spirit of our Western men."[14]

In California, prospects for a suffrage victory had improved since the failed campaign of 1896 as many new organizations that supported it emerged. Some were based on ethnicity and race. Italian American women in the Vittoria Colonna Club worked for suffrage as did black clubwomen who formed groups in Los Angeles and Oakland. Other organizations reflected class divisions. The San Francisco Wage Earners League, for example, sought the vote in part to change working conditions. Middle-class women and men who crusaded against corrupt governance, the spread of disease, and pressed for public playgrounds and the creation of a juvenile justice system increasingly saw women's suffrage as a tool for civic improvement. In the 1908 San Francisco "war on rats," for example, women volunteers were essential to reducing the exploding rat population that spread the bubonic plague after a devastating earthquake.[15]

In 1911, the California Federation of Women's Clubs endorsed suffrage after years of hesitation, adding its twenty-five thousand members to the effort. Progressives who worked to strengthen democracy through political initiatives, referendums, and the secret ballot saw women as allies. Men in the San Francisco Citizens' League of Justice encouraged women to attend court and watch for evidence of corruption. And reform politicians in Los Angeles welcomed women's support in the hotly contested municipal elections of 1909. When Progressives gained control of the Republican Party and won the governorship and a host of state legislative seats in 1910, they put a state constitutional suffrage amendment before voters in October 1911.

Many of the movement's foot soldiers were temperance supporters who kept a low profile because many men would vote against suffrage if it were linked to prohibition. Several suffragists formed the California Woman Suffrage Party modeled on Catt's New York organization that used political tactics and organization to sway voters. Working women were more likely to hold outdoor public meetings or parade in the streets. In the first such meeting in July 1911, suffragists circumvented a city ordinance against political speeches in parks by singing suffrage songs and handing out donuts tagged with "Votes for Women" slogans.[16] As the campaign heated up, suffragists became more visible with parades, public banners, open-air meetings, a speech by British suffragist Sylvia Pankhurst, and in the end, a rally in San Francisco that drew over ten thousand people. As in Washington, California suffragists were sometimes leery of help from the East. They declined Harriot Stanton Blatch's offer to assist, but enthusiastically welcomed NAWSA speaker Jeannette Rankin from Montana.

In October 1911, California voters approved suffrage by fewer than four thousand votes, a margin of less than 2 percent. Support from labor and rural areas offset heavy opposition in Northern California, particularly near San Francisco. The victory highlighted the importance of the Progressive movement in creating a sense of good citizenship that included voting women who could work with men to improve governance. "The victory in California was a victory for Progressives all along the line," Alice Stone Blackwell wrote in the *Woman's Journal*, shortly after the success.[17]

After the California victory, Oregon suffragists pointed out that all surrounding states had suffrage and, despite holding more referendums than any other state, Oregon women still could not vote. Membership and confidence in suffrage organizations had declined after the failed 1906 referendum. Abigail Scott Duniway, active in Oregon suffrage for forty years, blamed the defeat partly on NAWSA, which had sent organizers who pursued a vocal public campaign, and partly on opposition from the liquor industry.

Suffragists successfully petitioned to place an equal suffrage initiative before Oregon voters in the fall of 1912. Seventy-seven-year-old Duniway and her followers practiced the "still hunt" method by quietly lobbying to win the vote. Yet Duniway alienated many working-class and Progressive suffragists when she also supported an initiative that would give the vote only to women who were taxpayers. Though ill and bedridden, Duniway still rejected NAWSA's assistance. The only place she would welcome Anna Howard Shaw was "in Hell," the elderly Duniway said. "Poor Old Bluffer," Shaw responded when she heard of her words. Shaw said she hoped never to visit hell, and, even with all of Duniway's flaws, "I hope she will not."[18]

This time, many new suffrage organizations joined the cause, including nearly two dozen in Portland alone and more than seventy state wide. In January 1912, two influential groups formed in support. The Men's Equal Suffrage Club of Multnomah County had many well-connected citizens who were active in politics. The Portland Equal Suffrage League drew from the highest echelon of Portland society and grew to more than three hundred members. In February, students formed the first state chapter of the College Equal Suffrage League. And in May, black women formed the Colored Women's Equal Suffrage Association, with many members from Portland's black churches. Chinese American suffragists formed groups, buoyed by the expectation that women in the Republic of China would soon get the vote. Others formed the Everybody's Equal Suffrage League, a group "free from all cliques and class distinctions and open to all."[19] Its leader, Esther Pohl Lovejoy, said members were welcome to "scorn any rules and regulations."[20] These grassroots, diverse groups made it more difficult for opponents to counteract the push for suffrage.

Many Oregon suffragists employed modern campaign tactics. During the Portland Rose Festival, they sponsored a lunch wagon decorated with suffrage bunting and signs that said, "Oregon Next." When a suffrage opponent shouted out criticism, they rang a bell as onlookers applauded. Many younger suffragists welcomed NAWSA, and Shaw arrived in late September after getting assurances that her presence would not damage the cause. Lovejoy credited Shaw with reaching a wider audience by speaking to hundreds in the streets and at other public venues. In November 1912, a year after California and two years after Washington, Oregon voters approved suffrage. The victory was as slim as in California,

52 percent, but demonstrated a 15 percent increase in support since a failed referendum six years earlier. The numerous, diverse approaches to winning support for suffrage—what one leader labeled a "neither head nor tail" campaign—had succeeded.[21]

Success in Washington, California, and Oregon ended a fourteen-year period of failed efforts at the state level, since Idaho granted women the right to vote in 1896. In the fall of 1912, Arizona voters approved a suffrage initiative, and Kansas voters approved a suffrage amendment, adding two more states with full suffrage, and the first from the Midwest. Western women were proud to be in the suffrage vanguard, and women in the East felt buoyed by their success.

Notes

1. Benjamin H. Kizer, "May Arkwright Hutton," *The Pacific Northwest Quarterly* 57, no. 2 (April 1966): 49–50.

2. Clippings, Scrapbook 3, Box 3, Hutton Collection, EWSHS, in Mead, *Western Suffrage*, 108.

3. Kizer, "Hutton," 50.

4. *Spokane Evening Chronicle*, February 22, 1908, in Jennifer Ross-Nazzal, "Emma Smith DeVoe: Practicing Pragmatic Politics in the Pacific Northwest," *Pacific Northwest Quarterly* 96, no. 2 (Spring 2005): 78.

5. Frances M. Bjorkman, "Women's Political Methods," *Collier's*, August 20, 1910, 22, in Ross-Nazzal, "Emma Smith DeVoe," 79.

6. *Woman's Journal*, October 22, 1910, in Ross-Nazzal, "Emma Smith DeVoe."

7. Laura Arksey, "In No Uncertain Terms: From the Writings of May Arkwright Hutton," *The Pacific Northwesterner* 52, no. 1 (April 2008): 33.

8. T. A. Larson, "The Woman Suffrage Movement in Washington," *Pacific Northwest Quarterly* 67, no. 2 (Summer 1976): 57.

9. Letter from May Arkwright Hutton to AHS, June 2, 1909, on digitum .washingtonhistory.org.

10. Arksey, "Hutton," 39–40.

11. Ibid., 33.

12. Hay, *Woman's Journal*, November 26, 1910, in Ross-Nazzal, "DeVoe," 80.

13. Margaret Roberts to CCC, February 27, 1919, Roberts Collection, in Rosemary Wimberly, 'The Ballot in the Hands of a Good Woman': Margaret S. Roberts, Municipal Housekeeping, and Idaho Partisan Politics, 1890–1952," *Idaho Yesterdays* 41, no. 3 (December 1997): 13.

14. Abigail Scott Duniway, *Path Breaking: An Autobiographical History of the Equal Suffrage Movement in Pacific Coast States* (London: Forgotten Books, 2012), 250.

15. Guenter B. Risse, " 'A Long Pull, a Strong Pull, and All Together': San Francisco and Bubonic Plague, 1907–1908," *Bulletin of the History of Medicine* 66

(1992): 260–86, in Gayle Ann Gullett, *Becoming Citizens: The Emergence and Development of the California Women's Movement, 1880–1911* (Urbana; Chicago: University of Illinois Press, 2000), 155.

16. *LA Times* July 2 and 13, and August 22, 1911, in Gullet, *Citizens*, 184.

17. Alice Stone Blackwell, "Drawing the Lines," *Woman's Journal* 42, October 21, 1911, 332 in Gayle Gullett, "Constructing the Woman Citizen and Struggling for the Vote in California, 1896–1911," *Pacific Historical Review* 69, no. 4 (2000): 203, https://doi.org/10.2307/3641225.

18. AHS to Esther Pohl, June 6, 1912, Suffrage folder, Khedouri Collection, in Kimberly Jensen, " 'Neither Head nor Tail to the Campaign': Esther Pohl Lovejoy and the Oregon Woman Suffrage Victory of 1912," *Oregon Historical Quarterly* 108, no. 3 (2007): 369.

19. *Oregonian*, October 28, 1912, 1, in Jensen, "Neither Head nor Tail to the Campaign," 368.

20. Ibid.

21. Esther Pohl-Lovejoy, "Oregon's Sudden Conversion," *Woman's Progressive Weekly*, February 15, 1913, 8–9, in Jensen, "Neither Head nor Tail to the Campaign," 350.

CHAPTER TWENTY-TWO

Alice Paul

A thin young woman dressed in a fitted brown suit and a tri-cornered hat walked down the gangplank of the steamship *Haverford* as the sun set in Philadelphia in late January 1910. The black-hulled ship had just arrived from Liverpool after a rough passage, and twenty-five-year-old Alice Paul was glad to be home. Alice's mother Tacie and her fifteen-year-old brother Michael waited to greet her, along with a phalanx of reporters who rushed forward to ply her with questions as soon as she stepped ashore.

"Will you take part in the movement here?" one asked.

"If the opportunity arises I shall certainly do what I can," Paul replied.

Would the American suffrage movement become as divisive as it was in Britain, the reporters asked? Would she support it if it did?

American women would get the vote sooner than in Britain and without British-style militancy, she predicted. But nothing was for certain.

"If it becomes necessary to fight to win," she said, "I believe in fighting."[1]

Paul had left for England two and a half years earlier looking to improve the world. The eldest of four children from a wealthy Quaker family, she grew up on a farm near Moorestown, a small, tightknit community in New Jersey, fourteen miles east of Philadelphia. Her father was a respected banker and gentleman farmer known for his sober temperament and experimentation with the latest farming techniques. Her mother, a descendent of William Penn, was well educated and admired for her gentle demeanor. "Paulsdale," their family estate with a book-filled house, groomed grounds, and wandering peacocks, was an ideal place to grow up, but for Alice Paul it was not enough.[2] From her early years, she displayed unusual determination and gave her high school valedictorian's speech on Florence Nightingale, the British reformer who founded modern nursing as she cared for soldiers in the Crimean War. "When there is a job to be done," Alice's father remarked, "I bank on Alice."[3]

Paul widened her circle at Swarthmore College, where she studied social reform, and in lower Manhattan, where she volunteered at a settlement house and studied at the New York School of Philanthropy. New York City was an exciting contrast to the quiet of Paulsdale and the moral orderliness of Swarthmore, but Paul did not believe her efforts as a social worker would address the core of society's problems. In the United Kingdom, Paul studied Fabian Socialism at the London School of Economics and activism at the Woodbrooke Quaker Study Centre. But it was British suffragist Christabel Pankhurst who inspired Paul to work for the vote. When she first saw Pankhurst speak in November 1907, Paul found her a "quite entrancing and delightful person, really very beautiful" and was shocked when several men yelled, sang, and blew horns to disrupt her speech.[4]

Paul joined Pankhurst's Women's Social and Political Union for a march on the British Parliament and was promptly arrested. At the police station, she met another young American woman under arrest, Lucy Burns. Like Paul, Burns was the daughter of a wealthy bank president inspired by her college professors to pursue social reform and study abroad. But they were opposite in temperament. Burns was quick-witted and charming, a vivacious redhead who "over-runs with a winning Irishness."[5] Paul was restrained, even shy, "with the quiet of a spinning top."[6] They were later arrested together for interrupting a speech by the British foreign minister. When Paul disguised herself as a cleaning woman and smashed a window in London's majestic Guild Hall, shouting "votes for women" as Prime Minister Herbert Asquith began to speak, she was sentenced to a month of hard labor.[7] Paul refused to wear prison clothes, so the warden ordered prison matrons to undress her, and when she resisted, newspapers reported, male guards took over. When she went on a hunger strike, the prison doctor and two assistants fed her by force, pushing a tube in through her nostrils and down her throat to pump in liquid food. "I never went through the experience without weeping and sometimes crying aloud," Paul said.[8] Friends were shocked when they later saw her gaunt physique.

By the time Paul arrived in Philadelphia, American newspapers had depicted her as a militant suffragist. Weighing barely a hundred pounds and answering reporters with forthrightness, Paul seemed more a study-abroad student than a radical. "There is nothing about Miss Paul's appearance that would lead one to suppose that she could possibly raise disturbance enough," a reporter wrote.[9]

Three months after her return, Paul was listening to National American Woman Suffrage Association (NAWSA) president Anna Howard

Shaw present her address at the annual convention in Washington, D.C. when the audience began to stir. Shaw fell silent as six-foot tall, 350-pound president William Howard Taft lumbered toward the stage, greeted by hundreds of delegates who flicked their handkerchiefs in salute. He was the first sitting president to address their organization. Shaw greeted the president warmly and yielded the stage as Paul watched from a few yards away.

"I am not entirely certain that I ought to have come tonight," Taft began, "but your committee who invited me assured me that I should be welcomed even if I did not support all the

Alice Paul, a feminist and suffragist who penned the Equal Rights Amendment in 1923. (Library of Congress)

views which were here advanced." As a young man he supported suffrage, he said, but had changed his mind. Few women wanted to vote, and those who did were "less desirable" as political constituents. He rejected "the theory that the Hottentots or any other uneducated, altogether unintelligent class is fitted for self-government."[10] The Hottentots were a southern African people who were widely viewed as unintelligent in the racist context of the times. The delegates were stunned. Most of them were well educated, and Taft's words "struck those women in the face with a whip," Alice Stone Blackwell said.[11] Loud hisses resonated across the hall. Shaw sprang to her feet. "Oh, my children," she implored as the audience quieted. Taft smiled, "unperturbed," Paul thought.[12]

"Now, my dear ladies," Taft continued, "you must show yourselves equal to self-government by exercising, in listening to opposing arguments, that degree of restraint without which self-government is impossible."[13] Suffrage, where it existed, had not failed, he said, but had made little difference, and women themselves seemed little interested in getting the vote. Taft finished his brief speech; thanked NAWSA for the invitation; shook hands with Shaw, who politely thanked the president for coming; and retreated through the audience. Most delegates rose to bid a respectful farewell, but Shaw was horrified to see some remain seated. It was "one of the saddest hours that I have ever spent in connection with one of our national conventions," she scolded the members after the president left.[14] She later wrote to Taft expressing "the keenest possible regret" over "an unwise and ungracious act." Taft wrote back to assure her that he regretted the audience reaction, "but only because much more significance has been given to it than it deserves and because it may be used in an unfair way to embarrass the leaders of the movement." He hoped it "may soon be entirely forgotten."[15]

At the same 1910 NAWSA Convention, Paul gave a talk about the British suffrage movement to an overflowing crowd with many young women. Most people in Britain welcomed suffrage, she said, but elite legislators resisted change and the newspapers misrepresented the movement. Women were growing bolder, finding their own path with little need "to comfort men." "The cringe was gone from their souls," she told the cheering crowd; "woman the suppliant had become the rebel."[16] Paul also observed NAWSA leaders present petitions and plead for suffrage before House and Senate committees on Capitol Hill, as they had done for more than forty years. "It is not revolutionary on our part to ask a share in our Government," Shaw told the politicians, who listened politely and thanked the presenters before they left.[17] Paul, who had once predicted that a responsive American leadership would make British-style militancy unnecessary, had seen the president of the United States boldly state his opposition and Congress, though it had some sympathizers, ignore their pleas.

That summer, Paul and Burns tried out militant tactics on the streets of Philadelphia while Paul pursued graduate work. They held open-air protests at random locations, unannounced at first to avoid arrest for public disorder. When they realized the police would leave them alone, they announced their protests in the newspapers, drawing hundreds of mostly polite, curious onlookers. In late September, more than two thousand people came to their rally at Independence Square. At one gathering, young boys held up their homemade placards and shouted "VOTES FOR BOYS," but eventually gave up.[18] Their bold tactics garnered free publicity—no rented halls and no advertisement costs—reaching Philadelphians who had little interest in suffrage, but would stop for a few minutes to take in the spectacle of a street protest. When Paul earned her doctorate degree from the University of Pennsylvania in 1912—the first woman to do so— she had in hand her blueprint for action. Suffrage was the only path to equality, she asserted in her dissertation on "The Legal Position of Women in Pennsylvania," and women needed a dynamic leader to focus their energy on destroying an inherited system of inequality.[19]

As suffrage groups became more vocal, more visible, and more successful, suffrage opponents increased their own efforts. Two weeks after the 1911 victory in California, a group of women gathered in the Park Avenue home of Josephine Jewell Dodge to form the first national anti-suffrage organization, the National Association Opposed to Woman Suffrage (NAOWS). The state was like a "household" with a division of labor, Dodge told the gathering, and politics is for men. Women have "civic duties" that do not require the vote, and they did not want political responsibilities "thrust upon them." Women "can do more without the vote than with it." Dodge, NAOWS's new president, was a leader in the day nursery movement to provide affordable day care and a mother of six sons. Most of the members were prosperous, and many had powerful husbands. Dodge herself was the daughter of a Connecticut governor and married to Arthur M. Dodge, the scion of a wealthy family who was active in national politics. Their fears of suffrage melded

The headquarters of the National Association Opposed to Woman Suffrage in the United States, 1911. The organization, known as the "Antis," was comprised of influential women, some clergymen, and a number of men from industry and politics. (Library of Congress)

with wider concerns about rapid social changes brought on by immigration and urbanization. In California, Dodge told her followers,"The lower element among the women were registering," and they "were going to vote the Socialist ticket." The NAOWS women would quietly lobby influential men but rejected the public role that so many suffragists had taken on in recent years. Their new motto was "Down with the Yellow Peril, Women's Votes!"[20]

Many suffragists were encouraged when voters in Arizona, Kansas, and Oregon gave women the vote in the fall of 1912. But Paul and Burns believed that winning suffrage state-by-state wasted time and energy and sought control of NAWSA's moribund Congressional Committee, which was charged with lobbying for a federal amendment. Elizabeth Thacher Kent, the wife of a Progressive California representative, had reluctantly assumed leadership of the Congressional Committee two years earlier with the presumption that there was "no danger of the amendment being passed."[21] She had no staff, no records, no office, no plan, an annual budget of ten dollars that she never fully spent—and she wanted to retire. After NAWSA leaders reluctantly appointed Paul chair and Burns as vice chair, Paul rented a three-room basement, just blocks from Capitol Hill and quickly began to recruit workers. Three young women promised Paul a monthly quota of work and money after she asked them, though moments before, they said, "they had no more idea of contributing so much money or work than of flying."[22] Recruits differed on describing Paul's allure. Some said it was her "Quaker integrity."[23] Another cited "her expectation that you will understand that she is not asking for herself but for Suffrage."[24] Yet another said it was the "gentleness of her personality and the inflexibility of purpose which gives that gentleness power." Either way, "it is very difficult to refuse Alice Paul."[25] Soon the headquarters hummed with three salaried stenographers, four typewriters, and more than twenty volunteers—a mix of wealthy socialites, high school and college students, and housewives.

The Congressional Committee lobbied members of Congress and distributed over 120,000 pamphlets, but its chief project was a grand spectacle for suffrage at the federal level: a parade on the day before Woodrow Wilson's inauguration that would take the same route as his procession. NAWSA President Anna Howard Shaw believed that a parade was too risky and costly. A march should "not be a spectacular demonstration of that which has nothing to do with suffrage and suffrage work," she said.[26] NAWSA members from the South threatened to boycott the parade if black women participated. Ida Wells-Barnett, a black Chicago-based activist, knew it would fall upon Northern suffragists to resist. "If Illinois women do not take a stand now in this great democratic parade then the colored women are lost," she said.[27] NAWSA leadership assuaged Southern demands: black suffragists could participate in the parade, but only if they marched at the rear. Yet as the parade began, several black women and their white colleagues partly undermined this segregation.

On the afternoon of March 3, 1913, thousands of marchers lined up near Union Station. At 3:25 P.M., the starting gun rang out and the parade commenced along Pennsylvania Avenue. A V formation of police vehicles and mounted officers led the procession, followed by the parade marshal, Jane Walker Burleson, and several other leaders. Inez Milholland, "by far the most picturesque figure in the parade," the *New York Times* reported, rode astride a tall, white horse, wearing a triangular crown topped by a gold star that jutted upward from her wavy auburn hair.[28] Her scrolled, white broadcloth Cossack suit extended over pants and white leather boots; a generous blue cape fell nearly to the ground as she gripped the reins with long white leather riding gloves. Representing the future of women, her banner read, "Forward into the Light."

Next came the color guard and a half-dozen marshals who escorted the flag on shiny dark steeds. Then came a wagon with large white broadsides and a sign,

WE DEMAND AN AMENDMENT TO THE CONSTITUTION OF THE UNITED STATES ENFRANCHISING THE WOMEN OF THIS COUNTRY.[29]

Fifty women dressed in blue and gold escorted Shaw, Jane Addams, and other NAWSA officers, followed by thousands of women organized by category. Catt headed "The World-Wide Movement for Woman Suffrage," with women from countries where they could vote dressed in their national attire. Then came marchers from individual states, men who supported suffrage, and floats that depicted the advancement of women throughout history. Just as the parade began, Wells-Barnett joined the Illinois delegation marching between two white women who supported her participation. Black women also marched in the delegations from Delaware, New York, West Virginia, and Michigan. Mary Church Terrell marched with over twenty women dressed in academic regalia from Howard University. Next were teachers, nurses, federal employees, the Women's Bar Association, the Medical Women's National Association, and others. Service clubs, including the Red Cross, the Parent Teacher Association, the Women's Christian Temperance Union, and the National

Consumers' League, followed. There were Catholic, Jewish, and Quaker clubs as well as Democrat, Republican, Socialist, and Progressive groups. There were floats that depicted women working next to men in factories and fields. A dozen senators and representatives walked behind, including Daniel Read Anthony, Jr., the nephew of Susan B. Anthony. At the end of the parade, a float carried a large map of the United States highlighting the nine states that permitted women to vote. Altogether, the parade had ten bands, more than two dozen floats and over six thousand marchers, "an astonishing demonstration," the *New York Times* concluded.[30] Not long after the parade commenced, Woodrow Wilson was surprised to find Union Station mostly empty when his train arrived from New Jersey. People were watching the suffragists, someone explained.

At first, the parade went well. But as marchers reached downtown, the number of spectators swelled into the thousands, sometimes thirty deep on the sidewalks, making them impassable. Unruly crowds spilled onto Pennsylvania Avenue, halting the procession for more than an hour and breaking it into segments. Many parade watchers were drunk, propped up by their friends as they hurled insults. Some jumped on running boards of cars and snatched flags. Others shouted, "Granny! Granny! We came to see chickens, not hens! Go home and sit in the corner!" or "Say, what you going to do tonight? Can we make a date?"[31] A few tried to pull younger women off the floats. Some spat at and hit the marchers. The police stood by. One officer pulled lint from his sleeve as the women were attacked. "I have never heard such vulgar, obscene, scurrilous, abusive language as was hurled at us that day by men," a marcher said, "and it amused the police."[32] First Lady Helen Taft and her daughter left the viewing stand in front of the White House because of the commotion. More than two hundred people were taken to local hospitals for treatment.[33]

When word reached Secretary of War Henry Stimson that the police could not restore order, he called out Troop C of the Fifteenth Cavalry to clear a path for the parade. The soldiers, joined by the police, Boy Scouts, and male suffrage supporters in the Committee of One Hundred and Fifty Club, pressed the crowd back. At the end of the parade route, thousands of shocked women straggled into Constitution Hall near the White House. Newspapers across the nation gave scathing reviews of the police. They were "either derelict or incompetent," the *New York Evening Post* wrote.[34] A congressional investigation eventually resulted in the removal of the police chief and censured the entire force for their neglect of duty that day.

With the parade, Paul and Burns had delivered a resounding success in the form of a bold, public display that disrupted normal politics and brought public sympathy and support to the cause. Even Catt began to defend Pankhurst-style militancy. Since some members of the government had a "long continued succession of discrimination against the suffragettes wholly out of keeping with the 20th century," the situation was escalating to "war," a new kind of war without death.[35] Pankhurst, Catt said, was the "John Brown" of the suffrage movement.[36]

Paul and Burns established the Congressional Union, an organization dedicated solely to passing a federal suffrage amendment. To join, one had to agree to focus on federal work and prioritize suffrage above all other causes. With Paul designated as leader and her aggressive plan of action, some drew parallels with the Union and militant British suffragists. Even the Union's F Street Headquarters bore only the Pankhurst colors of purple, white, and green until NAWSA pressed Paul to fly their blue and yellow flag. When the Congressional Union applied for auxiliary status in NAWSA, members from the South objected, but NAWSA leaders reluctantly agreed, insisting that Paul keep the Union's budget separate from that of the NAWSA Congressional Committee. Some of the tension was generational. One of Paul's colleagues said that Shaw was "utterly incompetent to win votes, more still, is as destructive as an elephant walking on eggs."[37] Eighty-year-old Olympia Brown criticized "uneducated, half-baked women" who joined the suffrage movement only after it became respectable and safe. "Those dear old performers of the last generation are gone," she said.[38]

Strains between NAWSA leaders and Paul and Burns increased as the latter's militancy grew. In October 1913, Emmeline Pankhurst visited the United States on a speaking tour in the wake of heightened militancy by British suffragists who had burned public buildings, destroyed communication cables, smashed a jewel case at the Tower of London, seared suffrage slogans into private golf greens, and poured ink and tar into mailboxes. When immigration officials at Ellis Island detained Pankhurst, Alva Belmont sent a lawyer to secure her release. In November, Burns was arrested for chalking a public sidewalk and refused to pay the fine. In December, when President Wilson postponed a meeting with suffragists, seventy-three women marched to the White House and waited. Wilson finally met with two leaders and promised to give suffrage special attention, but in his first annual address to Congress a few weeks later, he made no mention. The Congressional Union then adopted the British suffrage movement's "party in power" tactic—to work against any politician from the party that controlled Congress, even if the individual member of Congress supported suffrage. NAWSA leaders feared Paul and Burns would campaign against Democrats in eleven states where votes on suffrage were pending. Catt was also working hard to build rapport with President Wilson, a Democrat. "People guilty of so untactical a blunder cannot be trusted to lead in so delicate a situation as the peace question in our own country is at this time," Catt concluded.[39]

NAWSA leaders cut ties with Paul and Burns in January 1914 after Paul conflated the Congressional Committee and the Congressional Union in her annual report. Some accused Paul of mismanaging funds. Shaw was furious and compared Alice Paul to Judas Iscariot. "I want to ignore their existence," she said.[40]

While Paul pressed for a federal amendment, Southern women from eleven states and the District of Columbia met in New Orleans to form their own organization: the Southern States Woman Suffrage Conference. They would press for suffrage at the state level, but only for white women. They believed they could win in the South only if women's enfranchisement did not permit a rise in the black vote. "White supremacy is going to be maintained in the South by fair or foul means," its president Kate Gordon predicted.[41] Not all Southern suffragists agreed to this strategy. The Tennessee Equal Suffrage Association, led by Sue Shelton White, passed a resolution stating that Gordon did not "speak for the women of the South."[42]

Partly to appease Southerners, in January 1914 NAWSA endorsed the Shafroth Amendment, a proposal by Senator John Shafroth of Colorado that would mandate a state suffrage referendum when at least 8 percent of the registered voters in a state petitioned for it. The amendment would allow citizens to bypass a reluctant state legislature and take the issue of suffrage directly to voters. Ruth Hanna McCormick, head of the Congressional Committee after Paul left, believed the Shafroth Amendment was a realistic path that could achieve a measure of success at the state level, rather than rely upon a Congress that showed little interest in a federal suffrage amendment. Senator Shafroth submitted the amendment after the Senate soundly defeated a proposed federal suffrage amendment in March 1914. Paul, and many NAWSA members, objected to a return to a state-level strategy. She called the Shafroth Amendment "an equivocating, evasive, childish substitute for the simple and dignified suffrage amendment now before Congress." By pursuing a course requiring victory in thirty-nine state referendums, "women would vote," the *Suffragist* commented, "the day after never."[43]

The Congressional Union headquarters hummed with activity as it expanded to ten rooms at its F Street location. Paul worked late into the night, keeping the rooms cool during the winter to stay alert. One volunteer said three months passed before she saw Paul take off her hat and was surprised at the volume of her hair. Some members chafed at the highly centralized leadership of Paul and Burns, who appointed the entire executive board from a cadre of disciplined and dedicated activists. A California suffragist resigned from the Congressional Union's Advisory Council over her belief that Paul's autocratic control was "submerging the individuality of the worker into a blind following under hypnotic leadership."[44] Congressional Union members in Ohio called for "a representative body more in accord with American ideals."[45] Paul was unmoved, convinced it was better "to have a small united group than an immense debating society."[46] She believed elections, conventions, delegations, pleading, testifying, and cajoling all dissipated an organization's energy and focus. She continued to appoint officers and believed it unnecessary to account for money. When a member suggested that leadership be more democratic, Paul told the woman to resign.

Without NAWSA backing, Paul recruited wealthy, influential women, including Phoebe A. Hearst and Louisine W. E. Havemeyer, to support the Union. But the most important recruit was Alva Belmont, who was exasperated with NAWSA and conservative suffragists. Paul visited Belmont's Newport mansion, talking with Belmont deep into the night, and offering her a seat on the Union's Executive Committee. Belmont notified NAWSA of her switch in allegiance and sent the Union a check for $5,000. She immediately set to work on its behalf. She organized a ball at the Willard Hotel in downtown Washington in late April 1914, a rally in early May, and a national suffrage convention at her Newport Marble House over the summer, to be attended by her daughter, the Duchess of Marlborough. By the end of 1914, Belmont provided nearly half of the Union's operating funds.

But Paul could not control Belmont, who set up a second Union headquarters in Newport and ran her own events. With the help of her Newport neighbor Molly Brown, Belmont held a "Conference of Great Women," where more than 150 socialites and progressives gathered amid the ornate artwork and well-tended grounds of Marble House. Suffragists from across the nation spoke, including Katharine Houghton Hepburn, whose daughter Katharine would one day become a Hollywood star. Amid the splendor, there were also angry words. Burns denounced both the Democrats, who were unreliable, and NAWSA, which she described as the Democrats' stooge. Burns made clear that the Union would work against

Democrats in the eleven states west of the Mississippi River where women could vote. Some suffragists felt alienated by Belmont's vast wealth. Rose Schneiderman, a labor leader who promoted suffrage among working men and women, found it too "high-faluting" and left after the first day.[47] Mary Ritter Beard, a member of the Congressional Union's executive committee, shied away from a Marble House meeting. "I can't do the Newport stunt," she wrote Paul.[48]

When the winds of war swept across Europe in 1914 after the assassination of the heir to the Austro-Hungarian throne, they seemed to many Americans, a distant stirring from a troubled part of the world. Catt first learned of the war while returning from London after a month of work for the International Woman Suffrage Association (IWSA). When she arrived in New York in early August, she saw small crowds roaming the streets of Manhattan with British flags in their hats, singing the Marseilles and carrying an elderly Belgian on their shoulders. Catt and another IWSA official met President Wilson at the White House to suggest that the United States, as a neutral power, broker peace. Wilson received them politely but offered no assurances. The war was unnecessary, Catt told reporters, and never would have happened if women had political power. "It shows that men, as I have always believed, are as hysterical as women, only they show it in a different way. Women weep and men fight."[49] Three weeks later, fifteen hundred women wearing black armbands walked in silence down Fifth Avenue in a Women's Peace Parade. The crowds, too, watched in silence.

In January 1915, five months into the war, several thousand women formed a Woman's Peace Party and nominated Jane Addams as president. They demanded suffrage for women in all nations to prevent war and proposed that neutral nations unite to disrupt the flow of armaments and combat militarism. Three months later, Addams and several members traveled through hostile waters to attend the Women's International Congress for Peace and Freedom at The Hague in the neutral Netherlands, where more than a thousand delegates passed resolutions for peace and disarmament. In London, Catt had struggled to keep IWSA from falling apart under the pressure of war. The organization remained neutral, and British members initially protected German women in Britain, but as the conflict deepened, British suffragists agitated against the Germans. Catt tried to stay above national grievances, fearing they would taint the entire movement. She sensed the war would get worse. "There is no power on earth that is going to stop that war," Catt wrote to Addams in 1915, "until there has been perhaps the most terrible battle that the world has ever seen."[50]

Paul and the Congressional Union ignored the specter of conflict that haunted the nation. Focused on a national suffrage amendment, they were determined not to be distracted by any other issue—not even war.

Notes

1. "Miss Alice Paul Back," *PL*, n.d., in J. D. Zahniser and Amelia R. Fry, *Alice Paul: Claiming Power* (Oxford; New York: Oxford University Press, 2014), 106–7.

2. Ibid., 9.

3. Anne Herendee, "What the Hometown Thinks of Alice Paul," *Everybody's* 41 (October 1919): 45, in Zahniser and Fry, *Paul*, 9.

4. AP to Tacie Paul, December 12, 1907, in Zahniser and Fry, *Paul*, 46.

5. Inez Haynes Irwin, *The Story of the Woman's Party* (New York: Harcourt, Brace and Company, 1921) reprint by Forgotten Books, 2012, 17.

6. Ibid., 15.

7. Katherine H. Adams and Michael L. Keene, *Alice Paul and the American Suffrage Campaign* (Urbana: University of Illinois Press, 2007), 14.

8. "Suffragette Tells," in Adams and Keene, *Alice Paul and the American Suffrage Campaign*, 15.

9. "Miss Alice Paul Back," *PL*, January 21, 1910, in Zahniser and Fry, *Paul*, 106.

10. *Washington Post*, April 15, 1910, in Mary Walton, *A Woman's Crusade: Alice Paul and the Battle for the Ballot* (New York: Palgrave Macmillan, 2010), 39–40.

11. *HWS*, 5:274.

12. Ibid., 5:269; *Conversations with Alice Paul*, 62, in Walton, *Paul*, 40.

13. *HWS*, 5:270.

14. Ibid., 5:272.

15. William Howard Taft to Mrs. Potter, April 16, 1910, in *HWS*, 5:273.

16. Paul Speech, NAWSA Convention, Washington DC, April 1910 in Linda G. Ford, *Iron-Jawed Angels* (Lanham, MD: London: University Press of America, 1991), 45.

17. *HWS*, 5:291.

18. Caroline Katzenstein, *Lifting the Curtain: The State and National Woman Suffrage Campaigns in Pennsylvania as I Saw Them* (Philadelphia: Dorrance, 1955), 51.

19. "The Legal Position of Women in Pennsylvania" (PhD Dissertation, Univ. of Pennsylvania, 1912), in April 1913, Zahniser and Fry, *Paul*, 123.

20. "Anti-Suffragists in a National Union." *NYT*, November 29, 1911. http:// rose.scranton.edu.ezp.scranton.edu/login?url=https://search-proquest-com.ezp .scranton.edu/docview/97199476?accountid=28588.

21. Elizabeth Thacher Kent, 7, 9, Women's Suffrage Series, Claremont College Libraries; CAP, 645–65, in Zahniser and Fry, *Paul*, 124.

22. Irwin, *Woman's Party*, 19.

23. Ibid.

24. Ibid.

25. Ibid.

26. AHS to AP, January 22, 1913, Reel 1, in Zahniser and Fry, *Paul*, 132.

27. *The Chicago Daily Tribune*, March 4, 1913, in Wandra A. Hendricks, "Ída B. Wells-Barnett and the Alpha Suffrage Club of Chicago," in Marjorie Spruill Wheeler, ed., *One Woman, One Vote: Rediscovering the Woman Suffrage Movement* (Troutdale, OR: New Sage Press, 1995), 269.

28. Robert P. J. Cooney, Jr., *Winning the Vote: The Triumph of the American Woman Suffrage Movement*, Limited Edition (Santa Cruz, CA: American Graphic Press, 2005), 193.

29. Zahniser and Fry, *Paul*, 145.

30. *NYT*, n.d., in Cooney, Jr., *Winning the Vote*, 192.

31. "Government Disgrace, Asserts Suffragists," *New York Tribune*, March 6, 1913, n.p., Suffrage Scrapbook v. 1, VCA.

32. "Suffrage Marchers Jeered and Insulted," *News Press*, March 4, 1913, n.p., ibid.

33. *Washington Post*, March 5, 1913, 38 in Christine Lunardini, *From Equal Suffrage to Equal Rights: Alice Paul and the National Woman's Party, 1910–1928* (New York: New York University, 1986) reprint by Excel Press, 30.

34. Annual Report 1913, NWP Papers, box 1, Tray 25, in Loretta Ellen Zimmerman, *Alice Paul and the National Woman's Party, 1912–1920*, Thesis, Tulane University (1964), 44. Tulane University Special Collections.

35. CCC, "Suffrage Militancy," April 17, 1913, CCC Papers (Box 3), New York Public Library, in Edith F. Hurwitz, "Suffrage Militancy," *Signs: Journal of Women in Culture and Society* 3 (Spring 1978): 743.

36. Ibid.

37. Cora King to Alice Paul, December 17, 1913, in NWP Papers, Box 1, Tray 1, in Zimmerman, *Alice Paul*, 84.

38. Brown to Ida Husted Harper, quoted by Harper to Brown, 1917 (no month), Brown Papers; Acquaintances, 92, in Charles S. Neu, "Olympia Brown and That Woman's Suffrage Movement," *Wisconsin Magazine of History* 43 no. 4 (Summer 1960): 284.

39. CCC to Jane Addams, January 4, 1915, CCC Papers, LC in Van Voris, *Catt*, 125.

40. AHS to Marie Moore Forrest, March 31, 1914, in NWP Papers, Box 3, Tray 1, in Zimmerman, *Alice Paul*, 89.

41. Kate Gordon to Katherine McCulluch, August 19, 1915, Woman Suffrage Papers, Manuscripts Department, TUL.

42. "Resolution adopted by the 1915 state convention of Tennessee suffragists, Jackson," Sue Shelton White Papers, SL, in Marjorie Spruill Wheeler, "The Woman Suffrage Movement in the Inhospitable South," in Marjorie Spruill Wheeler, *Votes for Women: The Woman Suffrage Movement in Tennessee, the South, and the Nation* (Knoxville: University of Tennessee Press, 1995), 43.

43. *The Suffragist*, March 21, 1914, 4, in Zimmerman, *Alice Paul*, 120–21.

44. Charlotte A. Whitney to Mrs. William Kent, September 26, 1915, in NWP Papers, Box 2, Tray 7, Zimmerman, "Paul," 102.

45. Virginia Hitchcock to AP, February 5, 1914, in NWP Papers, Box 2, Tray 4, in Zimmerman, "Paul," 95.

46. Alice Paul to Eunice R. Oberly, February 19, 1914, in NWP Papers, Box 3, Tray 4, in Zimmerman, "Paul," 98.

47. Schneiderman, 123–24, in Hoffert, *Belmont*, 103.

48. Mary Beard to AP August 15, 1914, in Nancy F. Cott, ed., *A Woman Making History: Mary Ritter Beard through Her Letters* (New Haven, CT: Yale University Press, 1991), 79, in Hoffert, *Belmont*, 103.

49. "Paraders Cheer Times War News," 8. *NYT*, August 6, 1914.

50. CCC to Jane Addams, November 12, 1915, LC4, in Robert Booth Fowler, *Carrie Catt: Feminist Politician* (Boston: Northeastern University Press, 1986), 138.

CHAPTER TWENTY-THREE

The Winning Plan

On a pleasant night in September 1915, under orange lanterns and purple, white, and gold banners that waved in gentle San Francisco breezes, hundreds of women crowded onto a terrace at the Panama-Pacific International Exposition, a world's fair to celebrate the completion of the Panama Canal. It was the end of the first Women Voters' Convention, where three thousand western suffragists had gathered to demonstrate their power as a voting bloc. "The western woman will give to her enslaved sister justice and freedom," Alva Belmont told the cheering audience when she opened the Convention.[1] In the middle of the mass of women, illuminated by bright light, was the "Suffrage Flier," a large Overland automobile about to embark on a cross-country journey to deliver a massive suffrage petition to Congress and President Wilson.[2]

Four women climbed into the Suffrage Flier. Two Swedes, Maria Kindberg, the driver, and Ingeborg Kinstedt, the mechanic, sat in front. Sara Bard Field, a suffragist from Oregon, dressed in a stylish, fur-trimmed brown suit, and California suffragist Frances Jolliffe got into the back. As a band struck up rousing music, tall white gates opened and the crowd surged forward, cheering as the Suffrage Flier rolled out into the night. The four travelers had packed mechanic's tools, cases of clothing, the 18,000-foot suffrage petition signed by a half million supporters, and a buffalo skin to keep themselves warm. But no one thought to bring a map.

Over the next eleven weeks, the Suffrage Flier zigzagged across the country, stopping in cities along the way for speeches, parades, parties, and even a ball, planning to arrive in Washington at the start of the next congressional session. Cross-country automobile treks fascinated the public. Six years earlier, four women crossed the nation in sixty-nine days to advertise the dependability of the Maxwell-Briscoe Touring Company car. A year later, the Overland Company shaved three days off that record, in part by equipping their car with an on-board toilet. Paramount Pictures Corporation had recently sent a young star on a solo cross-country trip, a publicity stunt designed to introduce her to the public and to promote the studio. Newspapers reported that she had to fend off a wolf, a hobo, a rancher, and a girl who wanted to follow her back to Hollywood. Even the fastest transcontinental trip, a drive sponsored by the American Automobile Association the year before, had taken nineteen days, eighteen hours, and fifteen minutes.[3]

It did not take long for the Suffrage Flier to find trouble. "As the car rolled through the great gates, I was pretty shaken by it all inside," Field said, who had only reluctantly agreed to make the trip. She thought the Swedes "were strange ones, rather grim-looking" and suspected that Jolliffe would abandon her, which she did after a few days, rejoining the journey weeks later.[4] At one point, the trio got lost in the desert east of Reno, Nevada, when the highway disintegrated into grit. They finally happened upon a ranch, where hot coffee and a cowboy breakfast in front of a kitchen fire restored their spirits.

Their first major stop was Salt Lake City, where their advance person Mabel Vernon had arranged a grand welcome. As the Suffrage Flier rolled into town, a half-dozen cars carrying Salt Lake's best-known women escorted it to the state capitol where the travelers were greeted by the governor, the mayor, the local congressman, and a host of enthused supporters. Heading northeast, they battled blizzards and impassable snowdrifts in Wyoming as drivers coming from the other direction shouted warnings about the dangers ahead. Field, a mere ninety pounds, "a dot of a woman," one newspaper wrote, shivered in the back seat under the buffalo skin. "Every now and then," she later recalled, "we would get out and stomp our feet and keep circulation in motion." After the Wyoming governor and a senator signed the petition, they headed south to Denver, where twenty cars carrying prominent local women escorted the now-battered automobile to the governor's office, and to Colorado Springs, where a women's choir dressed in purple and gold serenaded them with suffrage songs.

On a country road in Kansas, the Overland suddenly plunged into a deep mud hole. The women shouted themselves hoarse calling for help. Field finally got out of the car and promptly sank to her waist. She trudged two hours to a farmhouse they had passed earlier to get help. The astonished farmer obliged, hitching his workhorses to the sunken car and pulling it free shortly after midnight. "Well," he said, "you girls got guts." When the Flier made it to Emporia, the nearest city, the women were visited by William Allen White, editor of the *Emporia Gazette* and one of the most well-regarded journalists in the country. White's writing voiced the soul of rural America, depicting the worst aspects of exploding cities—the vice, the anonymity, and the crass individualism—and beseeched the nation in eloquent prose to hold onto its small-town values and sense of community. White interviewed the intrepid suffragists in their hotel room, while Field was in bed with blankets pulled up to her chin to achieve what she hoped was "the proper covering" while her mud-soaked suit was being cleaned. A married father of two and an ardent defender of public morality, White was amazed at the circumstances. "This is very French," he told them.[5]

In Topeka, sixty miles northeast, the women missed the celebrations planned for their arrival, waylaid by engine and tire troubles. Mabel Vernon had worked her usual magic to ensure the Flier would be greeted with enthusiasm. A crowd waited with a band ready to strike up an energetic greeting, and newspapermen stood by to record it all. Local suffragists had letters of endorsement from every official they could find, including the Kansas state printer. The appointed arrival time came and went. Vernon spoke for two hours, holding the crowd as best she could, but still no car. Hours later, deep in the night, long after everyone had gone home, the Overland rolled into town.

Though black and blue from the rough ride on uneven roads, Field worried most about Kindberg, the Swede in the front seat who glared and growled at her on the long, lonely stretches of road between cities. Envious of the attention Field received, Kindberg wanted to address the crowds, too, though her English was so poor that it was a struggle to understand her. Kindberg had told no one that she had been recently released from a mental hospital.

They passed through Kansas City, Missouri; Lincoln, Nebraska; and Des Moines and Cedar Rapids, Iowa. Illinois women were buoyed by their recent winning of the right to vote in national elections—a partial victory, but a victory, nonetheless. Chicago police closed several streets near Michigan Avenue to accommodate the large crowd that gathered to meet them, which included Mayor Big Bill Thompson. As the Suffrage Flier rolled in, a choir singing the "Hymn of Free Women" greeted the travelers, and Field gave a speech in front of the Art Institute of Chicago, where suffragists had met for the Congress of Representative Women during the Chicago World's Fair a generation earlier.[6]

The Suffrage Flier left Chicago and made its way through cornfields to Indianapolis and then continued east to Columbus and north to Field's hometown of Detroit, which greeted it with fireworks. Then on to Cleveland and northeast to Buffalo and Syracuse as the Flier collected even more dents and souvenir stickers. Alice Paul issued a steady stream of updates to the newspapers. "I thought you would be ten feet tall," New York governor Seymour Whitman told Field when the women reached Albany.[7] In Massachusetts, a state with fervent passions on both sides of the suffrage cause, Governor David Walsh hedged his bets. He ceremoniously greeted the women with a letter of endorsement, but as Field spoke and the newspaper reporters looked on, Walsh discreetly leaned over to Vernon. "Don't ask me to sign the petition," he whispered. "Don't ask me to sign!"[8]

As the Suffrage Flier headed toward the nation's capital, suffragists in Massachusetts, Pennsylvania, and New York campaigned for referendums to be held in the fall of 1915. Ninety-year-old Antoinette Brown Blackwell, the nation's first ordained minister in a mainstream Protestant church, spoke at an anniversary celebration of the Worcester Convention she had attended sixty-five years earlier. Florence Luscomb, one of the first women graduates of the Massachusetts Institute of Technology, rode through Massachusetts in Lucy Stone's carriage dressed in nineteenth-century attire. Pennsylvania suffragists lugged a Liberty Bell replica around the state on a flatbed truck adorned with yellow flags, sounding the horn as they pulled into towns. "We're with you miss," said a hefty miner from Northeast Pennsylvania as he stepped forward to greet them. "All you folks want is a square deal and you can gamble that we'll give it to you."[9] Pennsylvania governor Martin Brumbaugh predicted certain success.

A victory in New York, the nation's most populous state with the largest congressional delegation, would spur the entire movement. Woman Suffrage Party members canvassed virtually all homes of registered voters in New York City, and Catt dropped her resistance to street protests and held a suffrage parade on the East Side, with banners in six languages. As marchers dressed in yellow walked several miles along shop-lined First Avenue, butchers, grocers, and bakers in their aprons came out to watch. One marcher who joined though her husband had opposed, felt thrilled to be "a part, a singing, swinging part of a great stream, all flowing in the same direction toward the same goal."[10] Suffragists held a "Dollar Day" at Party headquarters on E. 34th Street urging supporters to place a dollar in a blue, white, and gold box guarded by women who wore suffrage badges, buttons, and dollar bills pinned to their dresses. Money "poured into it like raindrops," the *New York Times* reported.[11] One woman bedecked with suffrage regalia and accompanied by a bugler to announce her arrival brought in a hundred dollars collected in Brooklyn. Six Minnesota suffragists sent six dollars in an envelope. The former first lady of New Mexico sent ten. A San Francisco suffragist telegraphed a promise for a hundred. By the end of the day, the collection topped a thousand dollars.

Thomas Edison and Theodore Roosevelt wrote public letters to reassure men that suffrage would not damage the family. Socialist Party leader Eugene Debs actively campaigned for suffrage. President Wilson, although he opposed a federal suffrage amendment, announced he would vote for suffrage in New Jersey. The New York *Evening Post* endorsed women as "Partners at the Polls."[12] The *New York World* called suffrage "inevitable."[13] Yet many influential people still opposed it. Elihu Root, president of the Carnegie Endowment and former secretary of state, called politics "modified war" and said it would ruin "the sweet and noble influences" of a woman's character.[14] New Jersey governor James F. Fielder believed that most women did not want the vote. James Cardinal Gibbons, the archbishop of Maryland, said suffrage would violate God's will and "rob woman of all that is amiable, gentle, tender and attractive."[15]

In the six months before the referendums, suffragists held over ten thousand meetings and handed out forty thousand pounds of propaganda. In the final week, they plastered theaters with American flags and yellow bunting, handed out matchbooks emblazoned with "Vote Yes on Woman Suffrage November 2," walked the streets holding sandwich boards, sat on subways with messages scrawled on lap boards, and gave away toys from a "Suffrage Baby Truck."[16] Buglers blared tunes on the street corners of Manhattan. A woman cartoonist drew suffrage cartoons near Times Square as she bantered with the crowd. A "Monster Victory Rally" at Carnegie Hall featured speakers from around the world, a hundred-piece symphony orchestra played at an outdoor rally at Madison Square, and more than a thousand celebrants lunched at the Astor Hotel on the centennial of Elizabeth Cady Stanton's birthday.[17] In the financial district, speakers handed out fliers, buttonhole badges, posters, horns, and little yellow fans printed with "Votes for Women."[18] Workers at a subway excavation site cheered when they saw suffragists carrying Irish, Italian, and Greek flags. "Hey, fellows! It's candy, and they're giving it away," a young newsboy shouted to other boys as a suffragist unloaded boxes of specially marked candy from her car. "This candy is for the commuters," the woman admonished. "Well, can't kids commute?' one asked as a group of boys surrounded her, grabbing the candy, blocking traffic, and then scattering before the police arrived. "Rah for suffrage!" some shouted as they ran away.[19]

Thousands of women volunteered to be poll watchers, more than two thousand in Manhattan alone. "Flying squadrons" of suffrage organizers drove ten high-powered automobiles through Upstate New York.[20] Bonwit Teller, John Wanamaker, Lord and Taylor, Gimbel Brothers, Bloomingdales, and B. Altman granted employees a half-day holiday so they could join a suffrage parade. More than twenty-five thousand suffragists marched in a parade so long that they had to use torches when the sun went down. "Well, boys," one man remarked watching from a window at the Union League Club on 39th Street, "it looks as though they mean it."[21] On the day of the referendum, the Women's Political Union held a 24-hour rally at Times Square, handing out sample ballots to men indicating the correct way to vote. Shaw predicted victory. Catt believed they would win if there were no voter fraud. Blatch thought that Upstate New York would deliver a four thousand to five thousand vote margin of victory.

Carrie Chapman Catt, one of the leading voices in favor of the Nineteenth Amendment, which gave women in the United States the right to vote in 1920. (Library of Congress)

Belmont predicted defeat. "I am surprised at the favorable reports that come in daily," she told the *New York Sunday Herald* two days before the referendum.[22] Republicans and Democrats were silent, but their leaders quietly anticipated defeat. Suffragist hoopla made it seem that pro-suffrage sentiment was prevalent, some New York politicians told the *New York Times,* but suffrage opponents were mostly quiet.

On Election Day, suffragists went to watch polling places, many of them trained in suffrage workshops to spot fraud. Blatch scoured the voter lists at a polling station on the Lower East Side and found only four Anglo-Saxon names. She was not against immigrant men, she said, but "resent their having the license to enslave me," echoing the nativist sentiments of her mother, Elizabeth Cady Stanton.[23] Reporters waited at polling stations to ask prominent New Yorkers how they voted. Governor Whitman, who voted in midtown in 3½ minutes, told them he supported suffrage, as did city mayor John Mitchel, who took 4½ minutes to vote on the Upper West Side. John D. Rockefeller, the richest man in America, pulled up at Herald Square in a limousine with four women and his valet, spent ten minutes in the booth, and refused to reveal how he voted.[24]

As 1.3 million votes were counted, women crowded into the Women Suffrage Party headquarters on East 34th Street and NAWSA headquarters on Fifth Avenue. The Women's Political Union headquarters had set up special communication wires to relay reports from poll watchers. Late that night, they all learned that the referendum lost by a margin of 15 percent. Only five upstate counties voted in favor of suffrage, and all five New York City boroughs voted against it. Suffrage referendums in Massachusetts, New Jersey, and Pennsylvania failed as well.

Suffrage leaders tried to salvage morale at a rally in lower Manhattan. Suffrage is not dead, "it is the resurrection," Anna Howard Shaw told a cheering crowd, as donors pledged thousands of dollars for the next fight, and a band played "Onward Christian Soldiers."[25]

The 1915 referendums became a pivot point. The devastating losses in New York, Massachusetts, and Pennsylvania convinced many suffragists that state referendums were a waste of time. Blatch vowed never again to speak on a street corner and became a delegate to the Congressional Union's first national convention. Alva Belmont became its state chairman. NAWSA announced that it was dropping the Shafroth Bill that focused on state referendums and would work to pass a federal amendment. Discontent over the unsuccessful referendums focused on Shaw, who had promoted the state referendum strategy partly to appease Southern resistance to a federal suffrage amendment. Others complained that while Shaw was a great speaker, she

Dr. Anna Howard Shaw and Carrie Chapman Catt, leaders in the women's suffrage movement, at a suffrage parade in New York City on October 27, 1917. (Library of Congress)

was a poor manager. Shaw announced her intention to step down as NAWSA president in late 1915 after serving for nearly a dozen years. Catt's talent for organization and her mainstream appeal made her Shaw's obvious successor. She wanted to focus on a federal amendment, but repeatedly refused offers to lead NAWSA, too absorbed by the International Woman Suffrage Alliance and work in New York. "It will kill me, I think," she said at NAWSA's December Convention, "but if the New York women will release me from my application to them, I will do it."[26] Catt finally agreed to lead NAWSA and then returned to her hotel room, and wept.

Three weeks later, when the battered Suffrage Flier led nearly a hundred cars in a procession along Fifth Avenue, it symbolized the Congressional Union's pursuit of a federal amendment. During a crowded reception, Representative William S. Bennet greeted Field and Jolliffe on behalf of New York City's twenty-three congressmen. But Mayor John Mitchel refused to sign the suffrage petition. Its "demand" for the vote was ungracious, he said. Field and Jolliffe explained that when women previously "asked," they were denied, so it was time to demand. Mitchel still balked, until Field and Jolliffe created a separate petition with the phrase "We urge."[27]

On Sunday December 5, after traveling nearly five thousand miles over the course of eighty-one days, the Suffrage Flier finally reached Washington, where hundreds of supporters escorted the cross-country travelers to the Capitol. Field and Jolliffe slowly climbed the steps of the Capitol Building to greet a waiting congressional delegation as a dozen girls unfurled the petition behind them. The procession then traveled down Pennsylvania Avenue to the White House, where three hundred invited guests met President Wilson in the East Room. They unfurled the petition again until it snapped to a halt at the opposite wall. Field appealed to Wilson to support a federal suffrage amendment. Wilson replied that their efforts were "impressive" and promised to "consider very carefully what is right for us to do," then bent over and helped two suffragists reroll the petition.[28] Field left the White House buoyed by the hope that Wilson had begun to change his mind. He had not. At his State of the Union address a few weeks later, he made no mention of suffrage.

The National Woman's Party

As the membership of the Congressional Union swelled, its headquarters moved to a large, historic house so near the White House that Wilson could see its fluttering purple, white, and gold banners when he looked out across Lafayette Square. Nicknamed "The Little White House" for the many politicians and presidents who had visited over the years, it had a homey feel, with easy chairs and a fireplace where devout party activists mixed with curious visitors.[29] Paul continued to promote spectacles across the county to draw attention to the suffrage movement. In March, twenty-three suffragists boarded a train called the "Suffrage Special" to campaign in western towns and cities. Sometimes the train moved on from a stop after a half-hour speech. Other times, it stayed for days, while the women held rallies, attended teas, and met politicians. "Everywhere I went," Blatch wrote, women wanted to meet Elizabeth Cady Stanton's daughter. "I wanted to shake hands with you and tell you that you are not nearly as good looking as your mother," one old-timer told her.[30]

As the 1916 national election approached, NAWSA pressed both major parties to include a platform plank calling for a federal suffrage amendment. Ten thousand suffragists marched in a torrential rainstorm to the Republican Convention in Chicago and cheered when Senator Henry Cabot Lodge announced that the Convention favored suffrage. Then Lodge turned to wink at Republican chairman Warren G. Harding and prompted a laugh from Melville Stone, head of the Associated Press, seated nearby, as Lodge added that each state would decide the issue for itself. Anti-suffrage delegates laughed and cheered, recognizing Lodge's trick "to fool the old girls without giving them anything."[31] A week later, six thousand NAWSA suffragists formed a double line along the streets of St. Louis from the Democratic Convention Hall to the main hotel, a massive physical display to dispel any notion of women's apathy. After ninety minutes of "a good old-fashioned lively row," with "statesmen getting red in the face, with galleries in a yellow frenzy, with delegates in uproar," the *New York Sun* reported, the Democratic Party endorsed only a states' rights suffrage plank.[32] Catt tried to put the best face on the defeat. It was the first time that both parties included a suffrage plank in their platform, she said, and it did not prohibit a federal amendment or mean that they *only* supported states' rights. But privately Catt believed that the Democrats used the states' rights planks to "shut us out from the Congress forever."[33] Dudley Field Malone, a Wilson confidante, appealed to women by highlighting Wilson's "He Kept Us Out of War" policy, saving their sons from the horrors of war in Europe.[34]

In June 1916, two thousand women gathered in Chicago to form the National Woman's Party under the auspices of the Congressional Union. It was not a typical political party that adopted a platform and ran campaigns, but rather a voting bloc of women from twelve western states with suffrage that held a quarter of all electoral votes. Suffrage will win,

Belmont told the Convention, "if the women who vote will make it clear, emphatically and unmistakably, that they will vote against every man who does not solemnly pledge himself to work for a national law freeing women."[35] The National Woman's Party adopted the "Party in Power" tactic used by suffragists in Britain: they pledged to vote against any politician from a party that opposed suffrage, even if the individual candidate himself supported it.[36] The National Woman's Party would later merge with the Congressional Union in March 1917.

President Wilson still opposed a federal suffrage amendment. When Blatch led a delegation to the White House in July, he told her that it would increase the number of black voters in the South. When Blatch reassured him that suffrage would actually increase the proportionate advantage of the white vote, Wilson smiled indulgently. "In two states the blacks would still preponderate," he said quietly. Blatch concluded after her visit with Wilson that for suffrage to succeed, "the only alternative was to change presidents."[37]

In the fall of 1916, National Woman's Party organizers headed west for a campaign to convince enfranchised women—and men, if possible—to vote against Democrats. As they canvassed from house to house, passed out handbills, and held meetings in front parlors and on the streets, they were encouraged by the reception they received. Arizona volunteers found all political candidates pledged to support suffrage and were particularly surprised to find "how chivalrous all the men were," one wrote.[38] Travel in the West was exhausting. "I can only say that if the conditions are like the ones I have lived in the past week, I could not stand up under them." Blatch wrote from Colorado as she contemplated quitting the campaign.[39] Even Alice Paul acknowledged, "the few who are working are absolutely worn out and in very bad physical shape."[40] Large crowds gathered to see renowned beauty Inez Milholland, who worked tirelessly in California, despite suffering from pernicious anemia. In late October, in the middle of a speech in Los Angeles, Milholland raised her arm as she said "President Wilson, how long must this go on?"—and then collapsed and died a month later in the hospital.[41]

The candidacy of Jeannette Rankin, a thirty-four-year-old Progressive Republican running for one of two at-large congressional seats in Montana, looked promising. The eldest of six children born near Missoula to a schoolteacher and rancher, she had been a NAWSA field secretary when Montana passed women's suffrage two years before. During her campaign, Rankin traveled six thousand miles by train, fifteen hundred by car, and unknown miles on horseback to visit mines, farms, and towns. She promoted herself as a blend of traditional womanhood and progressivism. Rankin "is a very feminine woman" who dances well, makes her own hats, and bakes a famous lemon merengue pie, her campaigners reassured reporters, but if elected, she would fight for pensions for mothers, child labor laws, compulsory education, and women's suffrage.[42]

The Winning Plan

At the NAWSA Convention in Atlantic City in September 1916, Catt dramatically unveiled the "Winning Plan," her strategy to pass a federal amendment with a "nation-wide campaign of agitation, education, organization and publicity."[43] It would require hundreds of paid organizers, professional lobbyists on Capitol Hill, and a publicity staff at the national and state levels. Its focus on the federal level would alienate some suffragists, particularly those in the South who only supported suffrage at the state level. NAWSA would still fund state campaigns if they met strict guidelines, but Catt was determined to avoid "the stupid inability of newly-formed, untrained committees to put speakers and workers to the best use."[44] The plan was comprehensive and expensive, costing a million dollars, but with a massive base of support and an army of committed suffragists, they could win, Catt said. She later confessed that she would have resigned as head of NAWSA had the Executive Committee not supported it.

President Wilson spoke to delegates near the end of the Atlantic City Convention. Elections were just two months away, and he needed the votes of western women and Progressives. Wilson and his wife Edith walked through hallways lined with women dressed in suffrage colors and entered the theater to over two minutes of sustained applause. "I have not come to ask you to be patient, because you have been," Wilson began.[45] Suffrage is inevitable, but the nation is not yet ready, he said. Suffragists have gone ahead and they must wait for others to catch up. Victory will come state-by-state. Shaw was unconvinced by Wilson's analysis. "We have waited long enough for the vote, we want it now," she said after Wilson finished speaking, pivoting to look him in the face. "We want it to come in your administration!"[46]

Two months later, Wilson narrowly won reelection, carrying ten western states. Pundits in Arizona, Idaho, Utah, and Washington credited women with providing Wilson's slim margin of victory. In Illinois, which recorded votes by sex, women voted for Wilson in the same proportion as men. Montana voters elected Rankin to Congress, but the "Party in Power" tactic had failed. Wilson's pledge to keep the country out of World War I trumped the suffrage issue. Publicly, Paul claimed victory for defeating a Nevada Democrat and weakening another, but some in the National Woman's Party were so discouraged that they feared their efforts might collapse. Paul needed a new tactic.

The White House

On a mid-January morning in 1917, several women left the Congressional Union headquarters, crossed Lafayette Square, and stopped in front of the White House gates to unfurl their pro-suffrage banners. So began the practice of picketing the White House, "a place where the President and public could not fail to see it," Paul said.[47] They knew it would antagonize the public—even Paul initially rejected the tactic as too radical—but it was necessary, she believed, to pressure Wilson and shift public opinion.

Wilson accommodated the picketers at first, sending them tea and warm bricks, which they refused. In early March, suffragists waved flags in Wilson's face as he left a Washington hotel and chanted, "no state can exist half slave and half free."[48] Edith Wilson laughed it off, but the president stared straight ahead, stone-faced. As the car neared the White House, two women threw suffrage banners in his car. The next day, March 4, Wilson's inauguration day, police were posted every fifty feet around the White House perimeter. A band played, buglers blared, and picketers pressed in as Wilson drove through the White House gates. For the first time, both Wilsons looked straight ahead, not smiling or acknowledging the picketers as they had before.

Women from around the country joined the pickets, including eighty-two-year-old Olympia Brown, the seasoned suffragist from Wisconsin. In high winds and freezing rain, she carried a banner that read, "We cannot any longer delay justice in the United States."[49] When several Wisconsin suffragists criticized Brown for her militant tactics, she told the women that suffragists had been "dignified for over sixty years and we still do not have the vote."[50] After decades of struggle, she was ready for militancy. "Ladies will never get the vote if they don't demand," Brown said.[51]

Notes

1. Amelia Fry, "Along the Suffrage Trail: From West to East for Freedom Now!," *American West* 6, no. 1 (1969): 18.
2. Adams and Keene, *Paul*, 106.

3. Fry, "Suffrage Trail," 19.

4. Ibid.

5. Ibid., 21.

6. Ibid., 22.

7. Ibid.

8. Ibid.

9. *Blairsville PA Enterprise*, September 24, 1915, n.p., Collection of Woman Suffrage Clippings by Mrs. Oliver P. Belmont, v. 15, archived at the Belmont-Paul Women's Equality National Monument (hereafter cited as BSC).

10. *NYT*, October 30, 1915, 4, in Bzowski, "Spectacular Suffrage," 87.

11. "Dollar Day Yields $1,000 for Suffrage," *NYT*, October 2, 1915, BSC, v. 15.

12. "Father and Mother—They Are Partners at Home," *New York Evening Post*, October 23, 1915, BSC, v. 15.

13. "Toryism and Equal Suffrage," *New York World*, October 15, 1915, n.p., BSC, v. 15.

14. "A Loss to All Women; An Injury to the State," n.d., n.p., M.M. Breckinridge Papers. Box 1, Folder 1, UKSC.

15. "Cardinal Gibbons Assails Suffrage," *Chicago Tribune*, April 30, 1913, n.p., BSC v. 15.

16. Bzowski, "Spectacular Suffrage," 87.

17. "Suffrage Campaign to End in a Whirl," *NYT (1857–1922)*, October 29, 1915, 5, 97760715, ProQuest Historical Newspapers: *NYT*.

18. "Suffrage Campaign Is at High Pressure," October 30, 1915, 4.

19. "Boys Capture Suffrage Candy," *New York Tribune*, July 9, 1916, BSC v. 15.

20. Memoirs of Zara DuPont, dictated to Edna Stantial, April 1943, NAWSA Papers, reel 7, LC, in Graham, *New Democracy*, 61.

21. Peter Lyon, "The Day the Women Got the Vote," *Holiday*, 11 (1958): 121 BSC v. 15.

22. "Suffrage Leaders Fear Defeat, But Hope for Victory," n.p., BSC v. 15.

23. "Women in Rousing Campaign Finish," *New York Saturday Evening Post*, October 30, 1915, n.p., BSC, v. 15.

24. "Suffrage Women Tame an Election," *NYT (1857–1922)*, November 3, 1915, 4, 97743234, ProQuest Historical Newspapers: *NYT*.

25. "$100,000 Pledge as Suffrage Fund: Big Mass Meeting in Cooper Union Scents Victory Afar and Gives $405 Cash." *NYT*, November 5, 1915, n.p., BSC, v. 15.

26. Gertrude Brown, *On Account of Sex*, Chapter 11, 3, in Van Voris, *Catt*, 130.

27. "Mayor Aids Suffragists: Signs Petition Asking Congress to Give Women Vote," *NYT*, 1915, 8.

28. Fry, "Trail," 24–25.

29. Irwin, *Woman's Party*, 123–24.

30. Blatch, *Challenging Years*, 259–60.

31. Republican Convention in Chicago, June 6, 1916, *The New York Journal*, June 9, 1916; Christine A. Lunardini and Thomas J. Knock, "Woodrow Wilson

and Woman Suffrage: A New Look," *Political Science Quarterly* 95, no. 4 (January 1980): 661.

32. *New York Sun*, June 17, 1916, BSC v. 16.

33. Irwin, *Woman's Party*, 27; CCC, Speech to an Emergency Convention of NAWSA in September of 1916. *WJ*, September 16, 1916, in Van Voris, *Catt*, 133.

34. Doris Stevens to Harriot Stanton Blatch, August 11, 1936-NY-AL, in Dubois, *Blatch*, 196.

35. The National Woman's Party was briefly named the Woman's Party of Western Voters; "The Women Voters: Address Delivered by Mrs. O.H.P Belmont at the Convention of the Woman's Party," June 6, 1916, n.p., 6, BSC v. 16.

36. DuBois, *Blatch*, 195.

37. Blatch, "Points for Speech," HSB-NY, in DuBois, *Blatch*, 197.

38. Irwin, *Woman's Party*, 83.

39. Harriot Stanton Blatch to Hill, October 13, 1916, reel 34, NWP-SY in DuBois, *Blatch*, 200.

40. AP to Ella Riegel, September 21, 1916, reel 32, NWP-SY, in DuBois, *Blatch*, 201.

41. "Faints at Her Highest Point," *Los Angeles Times*, October 24, 1916, pt. 2, 5, in Linda J. Lumsden, *Inez: The Life and Times of Inez Milholland* (Bloomington: Indiana University Press, 2004), 163.

42. "Miss Rankin's Vote a Personal Triumph," *NYT*, November 12, 1916; "Miss Rankin's Talk: A Montana Eulogy," *Brooklyn NY Eagle*, March 6, 1917, in BSC v. 17:568.

43. *HWS*, 5:510.

44. Van Voris, *Catt*, 134.

45. *HWS*, 5:498–99.

46. Ibid.

47. AP, in Katzenstein, *Lifting the Curtain*, 204–5, in Zimmerman, "Paul," 224.

48. "Wilson Annoyed by Suffragists," *News Press*, March 6, 1917, n.p., Suffrage Scrapbook v. 1, VCA.

49. Charles E. Neu, "Olympia Brown and the Woman's Suffrage Movement," *The Wisconsin Magazine of History* 43, no. 4 (July 1, 1960): 285.

50. Ibid.

51. *The Suffragist*, August 11, 1917, in Brown Papers, in Coté, *Brown*, 161.

CHAPTER TWENTY-FOUR

War

On the morning of March 4, 1917, Carrie Chapman Catt, Alice Paul, and two hundred suffragists gathered for breakfast at the Shoreham Hotel in downtown Washington, D.C., to celebrate the first day in office of Jeannette Rankin, the newly elected Republican representative from Montana. Now that a suffragist was entering Congress, Paul was more hopeful, and Catt called for full suffrage by 1919. After breakfast, Rankin addressed a gathering at National American Woman Suffrage Association (NAWSA) headquarters, where she rented a room. "There will be many times when I make mistakes and I need your encouragement and support," she told them. "I know I will get it."[1] Suffragists escorted Rankin to the Capitol, where she and Catt met with House Speaker Champ Clark in his office. At 11:55 A.M., five minutes before Congress convened, Rankin walked into the House chambers carrying yellow flowers. Democrats and Republicans stood and applauded as she entered, some shouting congratulations and reaching out to grab her hand. Hundreds of women in the visitors' galleries cheered as she took her seat on the Republican side near the center. Rankin laughed lightly, amused at the hubbub.

Rankin's first month as a congresswoman was no ordinary time. The United States had been on the sidelines of World War I for nearly three years, but German aggression had brought the country to the brink. On April 2, as the sun set over the nation's capital, President Wilson appeared before a joint session of Congress to ask for a declaration of war. "It is a fearful thing to lead this great peaceful people into war, into the most terrible and disastrous of all wars," Wilson told Congress, but civilization itself was in the balance. Victory would not only defeat a dangerous enemy but also create a postwar world order to protect the rights of small nations and foster peace and prosperity. The world, he said, must be made "safe for democracy."[2]

All through the night, the House debated a war resolution, as more than half the members spoke. Most Americans still thought it was a European War, to be fought in Europe by Europeans. Americans had long followed George Washington's warning not to "entangle our peace and prosperity in the toils of European ambition."[3] Why go now? Loud claps of thunder from a raging storm outside reached deep into the chamber, a fitting echo to the moment. Finally, after seventeen hours of debate, the House voted. Rankin, a committed pacifist, sat through the first roll call in silence. On the second call, she stood to speak. "I want to stand by my country, but I cannot vote for war," she said in a hesitating voice, some newspapers reporting that she wept. "I vote no."[4] Forty-nine others joined Rankin, but the final tally of 373 to 50 was a decisive commitment to war.

Suffrage leaders divided over Rankin's vote. Maud Malone said it represented all women, who were "always against war and its crop of legalized murder, disease, a living rotting death and rape."[5] Blatch supported going to war but admired Rankin's courage for casting an unpopular vote. Catt called it "an honest conviction" and defended Rankin against claims that she wept during the vote. Another representative sobbed, and no one mentioned him, she told the press.[6] Catt pressed NAWSA leaders to support the war effort through the work of its more than two million members, partly in the hope that their patriotic work would advance suffrage. Yet by guiding suffragists to support the war, Catt violated principles of pacifism, and the Woman's Peace Party ejected her from its membership.

Jeannette Rankin of Montana, speaking from the balcony of the National American Woman Suffrage Association, April 2, 1917. (Library of Congress)

A new mood emerged as soldiers went off to war. "The country was no longer quiet, no longer reflective," the muckraker Ida Tarbell observed as she traveled through the South and Midwest. "On every street corner, around every table, it was fighting the War, watchfully, suspiciously, determinedly." Newspapers covered it incessantly, libraries featured more military books, and citizens chattered patriotic talk.[7] In a time when people were rallying around the flag, some viewed suffragist protest as disloyal. For the first time, bystanders attacked suffrage pickets at the White House, ripping their banners, pulling their hair, sometimes knocking them to the ground. A few turned their anger on the National Woman's Party headquarters at the north end of Lafayette Square. After a soldier fired a gun through an open window, nearly killing three volunteers, a suffragist bought a 38-caliber revolver and fifty bullets. Military men became so prominent in the attacks on the picketing suffragists that Secretary of the Navy Josephus Daniels ordered all naval personnel to stay away from them.

In June, five months after the White House protest began, police made their first arrests for unlawful assemblage and obstruction of traffic. Wilson initially intervened to have the women released, a gesture he perhaps believed would earn their appreciation. The next morning, however, several women left the National Woman's Party headquarters, walked a

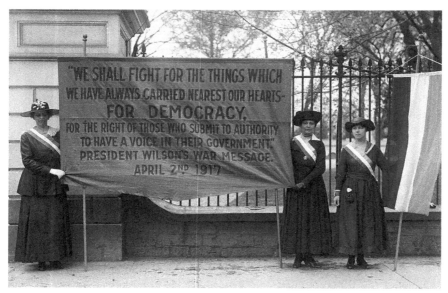

Female suffragists picket at the White House in Washington, D.C., in 1917. (Library of Congress)

hundred yards to the White House gates, unfurled fresh banners—and were arrested, giving impromptu speeches on human rights at the police station. This time, Wilson ignored them, and when they refused to pay fines, the judge sent them to the Occoquan Workhouse, an old prison farm a few miles outside of the capital with cold, damp cells and rats "as big as puppy dogs."[8] More suffragists picketed and were arrested, pursuing the strategy of drawing attention to their cause through civil disobedience. When the suffragists shouted day and night at Occoquan, bothering other prisoners, the superintendent moved them to another jail. When Paul and several others began a hunger strike, D.C. commissioner Louis Brownlow ordered a half dozen cooks to fry ham around the clock next to the women's cells, "convinced that the fragrance of frying ham was the greatest stimulus to the appetite known to man."[9] When that failed to end the hunger strike, the superintendent moved the women to the psychiatric ward and force-fed them. The police eventually arrested more than two hundred women, and ninety-seven were sentenced to jail, some for as long as sixty days. Most newspapers applauded the rough treatment, sometimes likening suffragists to supporters of the German Kaiser or the Industrial Workers of the World, a radical labor organization. The *New York Times* said the White House protests were "not merely unlawful," but also "scandalous and offensive."[10] Some newspapers, including William Randolph Hearst's syndicate of twenty-seven newspapers, covered the picketers with sympathy. Many suffragists believed that the picketers tainted the entire suffrage movement.

Alice Paul felt triumphant in commanding attention at a time when congressional leaders had pledged to consider only war measures. She planned a prolonged campaign and warned volunteers that they may face months of imprisonment. The National Woman's Party membership and donations surged. "What a pity we cannot have a perfectly ladylike organization to raise funds, and another to raise hell!" a suffragist wrote Lucy Burns after the arrests.[11]

Front Door Lobbying

As the picketers pressured Wilson from outside the White House, Maud Wood Park led NAWSA's efforts on Capitol Hill, which they called the "Front Door Lobby."[12] Their headquarters, "Suffrage House," was a former French embassy a mile north of the White House.[13] Its grand entrance hall was flanked by a Susan B. Anthony room containing some of her personal items and the table on which she drafted the suffrage amendment. A sweeping circular staircase led to a grand dining room with a massive fireplace and heavy wooden chairs covered in red velvet, a setting the suffragists dubbed the "throne room." On the third floor were a dozen bedrooms, including one set aside for Catt when she was in town and another for Park, a small, quiet room at the back she selected for the peace of mind it gave her after a day of lobbying. At breakfast, the women gathered in an alcove near the throne room to plan the day, and at night, gathered again before the fireplace to share their experiences on the Hill, often with laughter and mimicry.

The Front Door Lobby kept twenty-two cards with personal and political information on each senator and representative and tailored their approach to individual politicians, creating one of the first modern lobbying systems. They developed a multi-tiered lobbying effort, planning each encounter to best effect. Park arranged for Southern women to talk to Southern politicians while she sat mostly silent, introduced as "a resident of the District of Columbia."[14] She found Southern women excessive in their flattery of the legislators and worried at first that members of Congress would think "we had deliberately sent a honey-tongued charmer."[15] But a lobbyist explained that "southern men were so accustomed to that sort of persiflage they would think a woman unfeminine if she failed to use it."[16] Park's shortest encounter was with Congressman Fiorello LaGuardia, the son of Italian immigrants who represented a poor district in East Harlem. "I'm with you; I'm for it; I'm going to vote for it," he blurted as he rushed through the halls of Congress. "Now don't bother me."[17] Park avoided asking members whether they supported the Nineteenth Amendment if she did not already know, since doing so might prompt an undecided member to take a stand—perhaps against suffrage—and thereby solidify his opposition in his own mind.

Sometimes the Front Door Lobby pressured politicians by asking a state organization to launch a letter-writing campaign. Other times, "when we needed to have 'backfires' built in the case of a wobbly member of the Congress," Park said, they called upon their ninety-five congressional aides or fourteen-member Congressional Committee.[18] These groups were made up of influential women, often connected to powerful men, including Mrs. William Jennings Bryan of Nebraska, Mrs. J. Borden Harriman of New York, and Mrs. Medill McCormick of Illinois. Suffrage lobbyists became so numerous that one legislator complained, "The corridors have resembled the shopping district in the days of a millinery opening."[19] Even sympathetic Capitol Hill staff assisted the suffragists by gathering useful documents, passing along the location of members, and providing space to use a telephone or wait for appointments. When Park learned that Judiciary Committee chairman Edwin Y. Webb erroneously believed that only he could introduce the suffrage amendment, she gave his secretary information on congressional procedure to pass to Webb after they left. This multilayered lobbying effort became common practice in later years, but at the time, suffrage opponents believed it was a new threat to good governance. "If it succeeds," they warned, "states will be governed by secret lobbies instead of by legislatures, and the nation will be governed by the private office in the cloak room rather than by the voters at the polls."[20]

While Park and the Front Door Lobby worked Capitol Hill, NAWSA vice president Helen Gardener tried to gain the confidence of President Wilson with a mixture of politeness, deference, and appeal to reason she thought would work best. Although Wilson supported suffrage only at the state level and had no formal role in passing a constitutional amendment, NAWSA needed his assistance to move a suffrage amendment through Congress. Gardener pressed Wilson to urge House leaders to circumvent Judiciary Committee chairman Webb. Wilson agreed and, in September 1917, the House voted 181–107 to create a new Committee on Woman Suffrage.

New York

In 1917, New York once again put women's suffrage before voters in a state referendum. The Woman Suffrage Party (WSP) approached the effort like a party machine. Mary Garrett Hay, Catt's long-term companion and a veteran of many suffrage struggles, directed the effort from her office lined with maps of the five boroughs and, a "suffrage bible" on her desk containing useful data on New York politics listed by district.[21] The WSP headquarters, which occupied two floors, hummed with the activity of forty paid employees and dozens of volunteers. Five traveling trainers taught local activists in "suffrage schools" how to work with the press, canvass the public, and argue for suffrage.[22] The party's publishing branch produced over a million flyers, and its news office reached out to six thousand newspapers.

Many influential New Yorkers endorsed the referendum as well, including Theodore Roosevelt, Governor Whitman, former mayor John Purroy Mitchel, and Tammany mayoral candidate Judge John F. Hylan. Even Wilson urged its passage and hosted more than a hundred New York suffragists at the White House a week before the vote. Opponents dragged out their old objections and added a few more. New York senator Elon R. Brown said suffragists had too few children and linked them to "birth control agitation."[23]

Three suffragists casting votes in New York City, ca. 1917. (Library of Congress)

When Hay predicted victory, Catt—still haunted by their surprise defeat two years earlier—told her that she was the only person who did. This time, however, all five boroughs of New York City supported the referendum, with strong showings from northern European and Jewish neighborhoods. These produced a 92,000-vote surplus in New York City, enough to overcome upstate opposition, and the referendum passed. Voters in Indiana, Nebraska, North Dakota, Ohio, and Rhode Island also passed referendums that granted women the vote for some elections, and doubled the number of electors from suffrage states. Many began to see women's suffrage as inevitable. "I was somewhat slow in making up my mind with regard to Women's Suffrage," a Wheeling, West Virginia banker wrote to his senator in early 1918, "but I am convinced now, that it is coming sooner or later," admitting that his earlier opposition was "due more to sentiment than logic."[24] "The politically wise," Maud Wood Park wrote, saw it "as the handwriting on the wall."[25]

The chain of suffrage victories came as women stepped up their support for the war effort. Wilson appointed Anna Howard Shaw and several other prominent suffragists to the Woman's Committee of the Council of National Defense, a volunteer board to promote cooperation on the war effort. Blatch directed the Woman's Land Army, a traveling group that helped family farms bring in the harvest. Belmont became vice president of the Woman's Navy League. Others served in the Liberty Loan Campaign and Red Cross. NAWSA urged its members to grow their own food wherever they could, and many did in backyards and vacant lots. Suffrage headquarters in New York solicited women volunteers. In one day, suffragists used eighty donated autos to post nineteen thousand navy recruitment posters around the city. A department store lingerie employee volunteered to drive a truck; a clerk in the Manhattan Borough President's office wanted to serve in aviation; another woman wanted to serve on a battleship; several women signed up for cooking, office work, and offered to provide childcare for mothers who had to work. But Alice Paul and the National Woman's Party remained neutral. Suffrage comes first, Lucy Burns said, finding it "astonishing" that women were asked to contribute while "we must devote all our efforts towards freeing the women of the United States."[26]

Wilson's Endorsement

When the new Woman's Suffrage Committee reported the federal suffrage amendment out and the House scheduled a vote for January 10, 1918, Wilson finally endorsed it. He invited undecided Democrats to the White House and urged them to vote yes "as an act of right and justice."[27] Wilson never clearly explained his reasons, but as a politician, he recognized the changing calculus in the nation's capital as more representatives and senators arrived from states with women's suffrage. NAWSA's tactful lobbying and women's loyal war service gave suffrage the respectable veneer that Wilson still expected from women. The White House picketers who so irritated him were increasing their agitation.

On the long afternoon of January 10, 1918, fifty-four representatives debated the suffrage bill; some had made extraordinary efforts to be present. Tennessee Democrat Thetus W. Sims delayed treatment for a broken shoulder, Illinois Republican James R. Mann left his hospital bed, Indiana Democrat Henry A. Barnhart was carried to the House floor on a stretcher, and New York Republican Frederick C. Hicks, Jr., left his wife's deathbed—at her insistence—to cast the deciding vote. The House passed the suffrage amendment by 274 to 136, one vote more than the two-thirds threshold, as ecstatic suffragists in the gallery burst into singing "Praise God, From Whom All Blessings Flow."[28] Fifty-six representatives changed their positions since the last vote, including thirty from recent suffrage states and twelve who had visited Wilson at the White House the day before. Representatives from six states, all

Southern—Alabama, Delaware, Georgia, Louisiana, Mississippi, and South Carolina—opposed it as a bloc.

If the Senate passed the amendment by the required two-thirds vote, it would go to the states and begin the ratification process. Wilson urged reluctant senators to support the amendment to boost morale during war. On June 27, confidant suffragists and anxious anti-suffragists packed the Senate gallery. Yet several senators threatened to filibuster over what they considered improper interference by Wilson after he sent a letter urging the Senate to pass the amendment and leaders delayed the vote until October 1. The National Woman's Party resumed picketing the White House after a half-year hiatus and targeted the Senate in August, wearing black armbands to symbolize "the death of justice" and holding suffrage banners.[29] "We Deplore the Weakness of President Wilson in Permitting the Senate to Align Itself with the Prussian Reichstag By Denying Democracy to the People," one banner stated.[30] Police arrested forty-eight protesters, including Alice Paul, and charged them with "holding a meeting on public grounds with no permit" and "climbing a statue."[31] Some police used force as women clung to their banners; a few suffered broken wrists. About half were sentenced to ten to fifteen days in jail. Supportive politicians secured their early release, but there was little public sympathy. It was clear that Wilson had done all he could to help the cause. Even Paul's uncle tried to reason with her. "To force the President to use autocratic authority—to force the Senate to pass the Anthony Amendment,—thee would at least see that—such course makes enemies—against suffrage—and have a tendency to discourage its friends," he wrote.[32] A NAWSA member complained that all their work was "being undermined and brought to naught by those asinine women!"[33]

Two days before the Senate vote scheduled for October 1, and still lacking the votes needed for victory, Catt wrote to Wilson "in sheer desperation" to ask for a final public endorsement.[34] Wilson's son-in-law and Secretary of the Treasury William McAdoo advised him to address the Senate in person. Even if his speech did not convince any senators, McAdoo reasoned, it would encourage the election of pro-suffrage politicians. If he did not try, McAdoo warned, the Republicans might get credit for women's suffrage. Wilson reluctantly agreed, but worried that senators might resent his interference—no president had ever appeared before Congress to press for a single issue. With just half an hour's notice, Wilson addressed the Senate. Struggling people around the world looked "to the great, powerful, famous democracy of the West to lead them to the new day for which they have so long waited," Wilson said. The United States must be at the forefront of making men and women political equals.[35] Most senators gave Wilson a polite reception, several were enthusiastic, but Senators James Reed of Missouri and Ian Hardwick of Georgia remained seated as Wilson left the Chamber.

The next day, October 1, the Senate voted 62 to 34 to pass the suffrage amendment, a clear majority, but two votes shy of the two-thirds constitutional requirement. Everyone had someone to blame. NAWSA blamed Republican New England and the Democratic South, which together accounted for twenty-eight of the thirty-four negative votes. The National Woman's Party blamed Democrats for their disproportionate opposition. Arizona senator Marcus Smith blamed the National Woman's Party militants who worked against him and other politicians in the last campaign "merely because some other Democrat was opposed to woman suffrage."[36] Belmont said she was tired of seeing "the same determination to hold under one-half of the human race for the benefit of the other, themselves" and vowed never again to watch from the gallery while politicians debated her right to vote.[37]

Suffragists targeted four senators in the next elections—three Republicans and one Democrat, including Idaho senator William Borah, who Catt said "bears the brunt of the responsibility" for the October defeat.[38] Two weeks before his reelection, Borah discreetly visited Alice Paul at the National Woman's Party headquarters and signed a pledge to support suffrage after the election in return for Paul's promise to "no longer oppose his election."[39] But Paul did not trust Borah and instructed Idaho suffragists to ask him in public if he did indeed support a federal suffrage amendment. When Borah denied it, Paul vowed "to cast all our strength against him."[40] Idaho suffragists strung a banner across Boise's Main Street stating, "Vote against Sen. Borah. He defeated the National Suffrage Amendment," but his supporters quickly tore it down.[41] Suffragists put up another banner the next day—and their opponents shot it down. Suffragists then pledged to fly kites with a suffrage message, "but unfortunately," one woman admitted, "no one knows how to make a kite in this town."[42] When Idaho voters reelected Borah by a 2–1 margin, Catt concluded that working against him was futile. "He seems to think he owns the state and I expect he does," she wrote.[43] But the other two senators targeted by suffragists—Republican senator John Weeks of Massachusetts and Delaware Democrat Willard Saulsbury—lost to pro-suffrage candidates. Several previous congressional opponents changed their minds, including some from New York who needed the votes of newly enfranchised women. One of those enfranchised women, 102-year-old Rhoda Palmer, had signed the Declaration of Sentiments at Seneca Falls seventy years before.

Wilson's aggressive support for suffrage shocked Kate Gordon and Laura Clay. A Southerner by birth, Wilson clearly had some white supremacy sympathies when he re-segregated the District of Columbia as president. Both Clay and Catt believed Wilson privately favored states' rights but supported the federal amendment for political reasons. Some Southern suffragists still tried to reassure their politicians that women's suffrage posed no political threat to white supremacy. "One need not worry about the Negro vote," Tennessee suffragist Anne Dudley said, for only in two states were they a majority, many were moving north, and literacy tests would keep them out of politics and power.[44] Gordon and the Southern Women's Conference lobbied for a suffrage referendum in Louisiana to "vindicate the spirit and sacrifices of the men who in the dark days of reconstruction fought and died to maintain white supremacy."[45] Louisiana governor Ruffin Pleasant and the state's largest newspaper supported state suffrage, but New Orleans mayor Martin Behrman opposed it, and the referendums lost by 3,500 votes—and with it the Southern strategy stalled. Dudley expressed "the intense feeling of humiliation Southern women experience because the South is the greatest opponent to suffrage."[46]

Yet three other states passed suffrage referendums—Michigan, Oklahoma, and South Dakota—increasing the number of voting women to seven million and the number of presidential electors to 336. A week later, the Great War ended.

The Nineteenth Amendment

During the winter and spring of 1919, suffragists kept pressure on politicians in Washington. The National Woman's Party burned Wilson's speeches on freedom and democracy after the war, and, when Wilson arrived in France to negotiate a peace treaty, they built a fire at the base of the Lafayette Monument across from the White House, using wood from Philadelphia's Independence Square to symbolize the destruction of liberty. In January, they celebrated Joan of Arc, the hero of the Hundred Years' War, one of many women, they said, who "offer sacrifice and service and are humiliated and denied."[47] They pledged to ring a bell every hour until women got the vote, but stopped when a senator complained that it kept his children awake at night. The protests spread. Suffragists in Boston and New York burned Wilson in effigy. In mid-February, over two dozen National Woman's Party members boarded a private railroad car dubbed the "Prison Special" for a month-long journey through the South to California and then returning east through the upper Midwest and

New England.[48] Each time they spoke, they appeared in prison clothes. Many women from around the country traveled to Washington to take part in the protests, and the National Woman's Party membership swelled to 48,000. Olympia Brown came from Wisconsin. "I have fought for liberty for seventy years and I protest against the President leaving our country with this old fight here unwon," she said.[49] "It seemed so degrading to me to have to plead for suffrage!" journalist Louise Bryant said. "I had almost overpowering un-ladylike desire to break somebody's head, by way of relief."[50]

The Front Door Lobby kept up pressure on Capitol Hill. Louis Brownlow, a commissioner of the District of Columbia and a long-term observer of national politics, thought Maud Wood Park "one of the ablest political diplomats I have ever known, man or woman," with an uncanny knowledge of political factions and problems in members' districts.[51] Yet suffrage failed again in the Senate in February 1919, this time by just one vote. In March, anticipating certain victory, NAWSA leaders launched its successor organization, the National League of Women Voters, to inform the newly enfranchised and all voters on political issues.

The 66th Congress convened on May 19, 1919, with a new political calculus. Fifteen states had full suffrage, another dozen had suffrage in presidential elections, and women participated in voting for two-thirds of the Electoral College. In a special session dominated by the Republican Party, its leaders wanted to claim credit for suffrage. Wilson worried the Democratic Party would be blamed if a suffrage amendment was not passed and lobbied remaining opponents while still in Paris. Newly elected Georgia senator William J. Harris pledged support. So did Ohio representative Clement Brumbaugh, who then privately asked Catt to continue her suffrage campaign "as of your own initiative, just as though you were acting without any word from me in the matter."[52] Theodore Roosevelt's appeal for suffrage, published shortly after his death, said it was absurd "to higgle about the matter."[53] The new chair of the Woman's Suffrage Committee, Republican James R. Mann of Illinois, introduced the women's suffrage bill in House Joint Resolution No. 1 and quickly moved it out of committee. The next day, the House passed it by an overwhelming margin: 304–89, forty-one more votes than the year before.

When the Senate began debate two weeks later, momentum had clearly shifted. Anti-suffragist senators made their usual complaints, but eleven of the thirteen new senators supported suffrage, and several former opponents announced a change of heart, including Henry W. Keyes of New Hampshire, and Frederick Hale of Maine. Senators from Mississippi and South Carolina, the two states with a black majority, voted against suffrage as did most from North Carolina, Louisiana, and Alabama. Thirteen Southern senators supported Mississippi senator Byron Harrison's amendment that only white women should vote. Senators from Maryland and Missouri split evenly. Senator James A. Reed of Missouri spoke in support of states' rights for nearly five hours, but the state's junior senator, Selden P. Spencer, voiced his disagreement, to rousing cheers from the gallery.

On June 4, after two days of debate, the Senate finally passed the Nineteenth Amendment by a vote of 56–25. Anticipating victory, its supporters had shortened the debate. Indiana senator James Watson, the new chair of the Suffrage Committee known for his verbosity, held his endorsement to one minute. Senator Robert La Follette of Wisconsin said one word, "vote."[54] At suffrage celebrations that night, one woman remarked she had never seen Catt so joyous and relaxed; she "spoke easily and pleasantly, no oratory, and in a heart-to-heart way as though we were all one family."[55]

It had taken Congress a half-century to approve women's suffrage. Now it was up to the states to make it a part of the U.S. Constitution through the ratification process. If they did so quickly enough, women across the nation could vote in the momentous elections of 1920. Rather than support a federal suffrage amendment, Laura Clay resigned from the Kentucky Equal Rights Association, the organization she founded, and joined other Southern woman who quit NAWSA. Suffrage supporters and opponents prepared for new battles.

Notes

1. "Congress Cordial to Miss Rankin," *New York World*, April 3, 1917, BSC v. 17, 5712.

2. President Wilson's Declaration of War Message to Congress, April 2, 1917; Records of the United States Senate; Record Group 46.

3. Carl C. Hodge and Cathal J. Nolan, ed., *U.S. Presidents and Foreign Policy—From 1789 to the Present* (Santa Barbara, CA: ABC-CLIO, 2007), 388.

4. "Only Congresswoman Voted 'No' on War," Jersey City, *NJ Journal*, April 6, 1917, BSC v. 17.

5. Letter to the editor, April 10, 1917, *NY Tribune*, ibid.

6. "Miss Rankin's Tears Puzzle Suffragists," April 7, 1917, *NY Tribune*, ibid.

7. Ida M. Tarbell, *All in the Day's Work: An Autobiography* (Urbana: University of Illinois Press, 2003), 330.

8. Speech by Mrs. Weed, July 8, 1917, and WP Papers, Box 5, Tray 13, in Zimmerman, *Alice Paul*, 229.

9. Brownlow, A Passion for Anonymity, II, 79–80, in Zimmerman, *Alice Paul*, 232.

10. *NYT*, July 19 and 20, 1917, in Zimmerman, *Alice Paul*, 237.

11. Katherine R. Fisher to Lucy Burns, July 14, 1917, and WP Papers, Box 2, Tray 45, in Zimmerman, *Alice Paul*, 244.

12. Maud Wood Park, *Front Door Lobby* (Boston: Beacon Press, 1960).

13. Bernadette Cahill, *Alice Paul, the National Woman's Party and the Vote: the First Civil Rights Struggle of the 20th Century* (Jefferson, GA: McFarland & Company, 2015), 26.

14. Park, *Lobby*, 27.

15. Ibid.

16. Ibid.

17. Ibid., 41.

18. Ibid., 37.

19. The Woman's Protest, VIII, January 1916, 3, in Zimmerman, *Alice Paul*, 220.

20. *Woman Patriot*, III September 20, 1919, 2, in Zimmerman, *Alice Paul*, 267.

21. CCC, " 'The Inheritance of the Woman Movement' Speech at Vassar College," April 14, 1933, CCC Papers, SCA.

22. N.p., 1917, BSC, v. 17.

23. "Senate Passes Suffrage Act; Opponents Birth Control," March 13, 1917, *New York Tribune*, ibid.

24. W. B. Irvine to Howard Sutherland, March 6, 1918, Sutherland Papers, West Virginia Regional History Collection, in Anne Wallace Effland, "Exciting Battle and Dramatic Finish: The West Virginia Woman Suffrage Movement, Part 1, 1867–1916," *West Virginia History* 46 (March 1985): 75.

25. Park, *Lobby*, 121.

26. Lucy Burns, *The Woman's Protest*, II, July–August 1917, 6, in Zimmerman, *Paul*, 252.

27. *Washington Post*, January 9, 1918, in Lunardini and Knock, "Wilson," 666.

28. Van Voris, *Catt*, 148.

29. *Suffragist,* November 23, 1918, 11, in Ford, *Angels*, 233.

30. NWP Press Release, August 6, 1918, Reel 91, NWPP, in Ford, *Angels*, 230.

31. *NYT*, August 31, 1918, 9; *Suffragist*, August 31, 1918, 5, in Ford, Angels, 230.

32. Micke Paul to AP, August 16, 1918, in and WP Papers, Box 1, Tray 16, in Zimmerman, *Paul*, 274.

33. "Mabel Willard [DE Suffragist] to CCC," August 7, 1918, CCC Papers, SCA.

34. Lunardini and Knock, "Woodrow Wilson and Woman Suffrage," 668.

35. Appeal of President Wilson to the Senate of the U.S. to Submit the Federal Amendment for Woman Suffrage, September 30, 1918, in *HWS*, 5:761.

36. "Sen. Marcus A. Smith [AZ] to CCC," October 2, 1918, CCC Papers, SCA.

37. "Address by Mrs. Belmont at Mass Meeting in Washington, DC," December 15, 1918, 2, BSC v. 18.

38. *The Woman Citizen*, October 26, 1918, 3:431, in T. A. Larson, "Idaho's Role in America's Women Suffrage Crusade," *Idaho Yesterdays* 18, no. 1 (March 1974): 12.

39. AP to Lee Meriwether, June 1, 1920, NWPP, in Walton, *Woman's Crusade*, 226–27.

40. AP to Whitmore, Oct 29, 1918 NWPP, in Walton, *Woman's Crusade*, 227.

41. Whitmore to AP, November 4, 1918, NWPP, in Walton, *Woman's Crusade*, 227.

42. Ibid.

43. CCC to Maud Wood Park," November 22, 1918, CCC Papers, SCA.

44. Mrs. Guilford Dudley, "The Negro Vote in the South" (National Woman Suffrage Press, May 1918), M.M. Breckinridge Papers. Box 6, Folder 43, UKSC.

45. Louisiana Woman Suffrage Association, August 3, 1918, Clay Papers, UKSC; Kenneth R. Johnson, "Kate Gordon and the Woman-Suffrage Movement in the South," *The Journal of Southern History* 38, no. 3 (August 1, 1972): 389, doi:10.2307/2206099.

46. Dudley, "Negro Vote."

47. NWP Press Release, January 3, 1919, Reel 92, NWPP, in Ford, *Angels*, 236.

48. Zahniser and Fry, *Paul*, 314–15.

49. Charles E. Neu, "Olympia Brown and the Woman's Suffrage Movement," *The Wisconsin Magazine of History* 43, no. 4 (July 1, 1960): 285.

50. Louise Bryant, "Burning His Majesty's Words," Suffragist, December 21, 1918, 8, in Ford, *Angels*, 234.

51. "Louis Brownlow to CCC," February 15, 1919, CCC Papers, SCA.

52. "Rep. Clement Brumbaugh (OH) to CCC," June 28, 1918, CCC Papers, SCA.

53. "CCC to Majorie Shuler," January 7, 1919, CCC Papers, SCA. "Eyes to the Front," in *The Metropolitan Magazine*.

54. "Vox Populi," *The Woman Citizen*, n.d., n.p., Maud Wood Park Scrap Book, SL.

55. Caroline Reilly to AHS, June 11, 1919, Shaw Papers, SL, in Van Voris, *Catt*, 155.

CHAPTER TWENTY-FIVE

Ratification

The race to ratify the Nineteenth Amendment was on as suffragists planned to win the required thirty-six of the forty-eight states. The West, they calculated, would be the easiest, the Deep South mostly opposed, and the Upper South, questionable. Catt wanted early victories to build momentum and implored several governors of states where ratification seemed likely to call their legislatures into special sessions. She encouraged suffragists in marginal states not to press for ratification rather than risk early defeats.

Illinois, Michigan, and Wisconsin ratified on June 10, 1919, competing to be the first. Illinois voted before the others, but the Wisconsin messenger was the first to present Secretary of State Bainbridge Colby with the certificate of ratification. Six days later, Minnie J. Grinstead, the first woman elected to the Kansas House, proudly introduced a ratification resolution and the legislature passed it unanimously, though one member grumbled, "a pan of hot biscuits or a roasted turkey will go a lot further in influencing men than woman suffrage."[1]

Next came four states in the North and East—New York, Ohio, Pennsylvania, and Massachusetts. Pennsylvania was the first state to ratify that did not already have suffrage at the state level. Anna Howard Shaw died of pneumonia a week later at home just outside Philadelphia, living long enough to see her state approve the amendment, but dying too soon to see it become law of the land. Texas governor William P. Hobby called the legislature into special session. Support in the Texas House was strong, and polls indicated a one-vote majority in the Senate, which disappeared when a pro-suffrage senator died in a gunfight. In late June, the House approved the amendment by a vote of 96–21 and, four days later, the Senate passed it by voice vote, making Texas the first Southern state to ratify. Iowa, Missouri, and Arkansas followed in July.

Several western governors hesitated to call special sessions for fear that their political opponents might take advantage of it. After four months, only Montana and Utah had ratified. At the end of October, Catt and others toured the West to spur enthusiasm with conventions and rallies. In South Dakota, she met two dozen suffragists she had worked with three decades before. In San Francisco, an old acquaintance asked Catt to marry him. California and Colorado ratified before the end of the year.

To no one's surprise, the greatest opposition to ratification was in the South. South Carolina and Mississippi, seven Alabama cities, and more than two hundred counties were majority black. "Giving the ballot to 3,000,000 Negro women of the South," James Calloway of the *Macon Telegraph* wrote, will "bring the Negroes back into politics."[2] Some Southern suffragists countered that the Nineteenth Amendment would not undermine white supremacy. "Every red-blooded Mississippian well knows that there is no more danger of Negro women in this state attempting to vote then there is of Negro men attempting to vote," the *Jackson Daily News* stated. "The Negro is finally and forever out of politics in Mississippi."[3] To make their rejection emphatic, Alabama, Georgia, Maryland, South Carolina, and Virginia each passed a "Proclamation of Defeat." When male Mississippi voters defeated the state suffrage referendum, the Jackson *Clarion-Ledger* rejoiced, "the vile old thing is as dead as its author, the old advocate of social equality and intermarriage of the races, and Mississippi will never be annoyed with it again."[4]

In Kentucky, however, ratification seemed likely. Governor Edwin P. Morrow supported the amendment, and all but one Kentucky congressman had voted for it. Madeline McDowell Breckinridge, president of the Kentucky Equal Rights Association, joined other Kentucky suffragists in lobbying legislators, writing to newspapers, and speaking at suffrage rallies across the state. On January 6, 1920, the Kentucky legislature approved the amendment by a 3–1 margin. When Rhode Island became the twenty-fourth state to ratify, suffragists were two-thirds of the way to victory.

In February, the Virginia legislature voted down ratification, and Maryland defeated it twelve days later. Idaho ratified in mid-February, despite Senator Borah's continued opposition. By the end of the month—after Arizona, New Mexico, and Oklahoma approved—all western states except Washington had ratified. Only three more states were needed.

Suffragists were elated in early June when the Supreme Court determined in *George S. Hawke v. Harvey C. Smith* that the U.S. Constitution— not state constitutions—established the procedure for ratification. This meant that a state referendum on suffrage held after the state's legislature ratified it was unconstitutional. An Ohio law prompted the case, but similar laws were common in the South. On the same day as the *Hawke v. Smith* decision, however, the Delaware House delayed voting on the Nineteenth Amendment, which exasperated Catt who had lobbied there for two months. "We are the Chief Reactionary among Nations," she said.[5]

West Virginia seemed promising, with support from Governor John J. Cornwall, most legislators and many prominent citizens. A 1916 state suffrage referendum revealed that the two panhandle counties supported it, the central portion of the state voted slightly against, and Southern coal counties overwhelmingly opposed it. The West Virginia House approved it easily, but the Senate vote tied until one senator rushed home from a California vacation just in time to break the deadlock on March 10. This made West Virginia the thirty-fourth state. Washington approved two weeks later, delayed by the death of its pro-suffrage governor and the reluctance of his replacement to call a special session, despite heavy lobbying from Washington suffragists. Just one more state was needed.

Two New England states and a slew of Southern states had yet to vote. Suffragists lobbied the Connecticut legislature and held mass meetings across the state. Informal polling indicated a favorable outcome, but Governor Marcus A. Holcomb, supported by a powerful Republican machine, saw no "special emergency" that required a special session.[6] The governor of Vermont, too, said he "did not care to make a decision at once."[7]

April passed with no victories, then May, then June. By July, suffragists were worried. National Woman's Party members wearing white dresses and yellow sashes burst into the Republican National Convention at the Chicago Coliseum holding banners aloft. "REPUBLICANS, WE ARE HERE. WHERE IS THE 36TH STATE?" one said.[8] When the Convention passed a platform plank urging its members to support ratification, suffragists hoisted another banner: "WE DO NOT WANT PLANKS. WE DEMAND THE 36TH."[9]

In Louisiana, Kate Gordon led the campaign for a state amendment, while others there worked for the federal amendment. Both efforts failed in early July. In North Carolina, most major newspapers endorsed suffrage, as did several influential politicians and thirty-three of the forty professors at the University of North Carolina. Governor Thomas W. Bickett gave a tepid endorsement after years of opposition. Suffrage might harm women and roil race relations, he told a joint session of the legislature, but it was inevitable. Yet several prominent North Carolina families formed a States' Rights Rejection League, and the Southern Women's

Rejection League gathered in a Raleigh hotel under the motto "Politics are bad for women and women are bad for politics."[10] Both senators and every representative from majority-black districts had voted against the amendment in Congress. So did several representatives in the Piedmont region where a large textile industry employed many women and children. In mid-August, the Senate delayed ratification until voters could have their say in the next elections. North Carolina was out of the running.

Tennessee

Suffragists held out hope for Tennessee, where women could already vote in presidential and municipal elections. But Governor Albert H. Roberts was in a tight race for reelection and feared a special legislative session might benefit his opponents. The Tennessee Constitution, he also noted, required that a federal amendment must be ratified by a General Assembly elected after it had been submitted. President Wilson telegraphed Governor Roberts, urging him to call a special session, and the chairman of the Democratic National Committee phoned him from the Convention floor in San Francisco. Roberts own attorney general advised him that a special session for ratification would be legal, and even his opponent in the Democratic primary warned that unless he acted, a "Republican state will ratify and rob Tennessee of its chance for glory."[11] Governor Roberts finally relented in late June and called for a special session of the Tennessee General Assembly to meet on August 9—four days after the primary. He itemized 142 issues to be addressed, but everyone knew that the Nineteenth Amendment was the central issue. What came next, Roberts later said, was the "most stubborn fight ever seen in the city."[12]

Catt advised Tennessee suffragists to spread their message early and recruit more than a hundred influential men from all political factions to form a ratification committee in support. They should not try to reason with opponents, who will use "lies, innuendos and near truths which are more damaging than lies," especially "the nigger question," she warned. "We have long since recovered from our previous faith in the action of men based upon a love of justice."[13] In mid-July, Catt headed to Nashville, intending to stay only a few days. She took a room on the third floor of the city's premier hotel, The Hermitage, overlooking the Capitol Building. Finding an irritated governor and quarreling suffrage factions, Catt extended her stay.

Anti-suffrage lobbyists headed to Nashville as well. Josephine Anderson Pearson, the fifty-two-year-old head of the Tennessee State Association

Opposed to Woman Suffrage, was at home in rural Tennessee when she received a telegram from Nashville.

Mrs. Catt arrived. Extra session imminent.
Our forces being notified to rally at once.
Send orders and come immediately.[14]

Pearson rushed to the capital city and took a room on the seventh floor of the Hermitage, staying up all night to compose telegrams to anti-suffragists around the nation. Mrs. James S. Pinckard, head of the Southern Women's League for the Rejection of the Susan B. Anthony Amendment and a grand-niece of secessionist John C. Calhoun, arrived. So did Anne Pleasant, the first lady of Louisiana who described herself as "the daughter of Major Matthew General Ector, C.S.A., who had three horses shot out from under him at the battle of Lookout Mountain."[15] Charlotte Rowe, a popular New York anti-suffragist speaker, arrived from lobbying in North Carolina. Suffrage "cheapens women," she told reporters. She had seen them dance on desks and ride on men's shoulders at the Democratic National Convention. One suffragist, she said, "went so far as to do an Indian war dance in front of the speaker's stand."[16] Everett P. Wheeler, a prominent New York attorney and cofounder of the American Bar Association, joined members of the Tennessee legal establishment and several Vanderbilt University professors to form the anti-suffragist Tennessee Constitutional League.

Nashville newspapers divided. The *Banner*, owned by Edward Stahlman, a German immigrant who had made a fortune in the railroads, opposed suffrage. A voting man "is simply the primitive instinctive man being the head of all affairs save the home," the *Banner* said, though some believed Stahlman feared women voters would shut down the railroad industry's lucrative business transporting alcohol.[17] His own granddaughter who worked at the *Banner* said women there "were tolerated and unwanted."[18] The *Tennessean*, Stahlman's main competitor owned by Luke Lea, a Southern progressive a generation younger than Stahlman, supported suffrage.

Tennessee suffragists tracked down uncommitted legislators by car, train, wagon, and on foot, in the heat and in the rain. Sue Shelton White, a thirty-three-year-old former newspaper reporter, joined two other members of the National Woman's Party to lobby across the state. In mid-July, Catt joined Abby Crawford Milton, president of the Tennessee Equal Suffrage Association, on a speaking tour through eastern Tennessee, though Catt suffered one of her periodic "heart attacks" and headed to Chattanooga to recover at Milton's home.[19]

"Beware Men of the South Heed Not the Song of the Suffrage Siren!" a banner read above the Hermitage mezzanine as both sides turned the hotel into a battleground. "The Anthony Amendment Means Sex War!" touted another. Tennessee needed "Real Men" to vote against the amendment, a pamphlet stated, "the true Defenders of Womanhood, Motherhood, the Family, and the State."[20] "A Vote for Federal Suffrage Is a Vote for Organized Female Nagging Forever," a cartoon stated.[21] The Antis displayed *The Woman's Bible*, Elizabeth Cady Stanton's reinterpretation of Scripture published in 1895, and advertised in Nashville newspapers that Catt "denies the divinity of Christ, or that the Bible is the inspired word of God."[22] One suffragist said that it had already turned twenty-six local ministers against ratification. When Abby Crawford Milton pleaded with Catt to distance herself from *The Woman's Bible*, Catt replied that she had already done so many times. "You have got to deny it again," Milton said.[23] Lobbyists for distilleries, manufacturing, and the railroads took a suite on the eighth floor and offered free liquor to legislators. Catt's greatest fear, she told her friend, was a drunken man "[a]nd so many of them were drunk."[24] One suffragist placed a bottle of liquor under Catt's pillow as a prank, but when Catt discovered it during a nap, she thought it was an attempt to smear her. Catt buried the bottle in her suitcase, drove to the outskirts of town, and hid it in an ivy-covered stone wall.

For weeks, Antis and suffragists milled around the Hermitage in mutual hostility. Southern states suffragists Laura Clay and Kate Gordon refused to make eye contact with their former suffrage allies and appealed to legislators with "Negro phobia and every other caveman's prejudice," Catt wrote.[25] Several Antis jostled House suffrage leader Joe Hanover in the elevator and shouted "Bolshevik" as he walked through the lobby.[26] Governor Roberts assigned Hanover a bodyguard after he received telephone threats and offers of late-night dalliances from women. Representative W. W. Philip challenged a traveling salesman to a fight when he refused to doff his hat to suffragists in the elevator. Mrs. Pinckard threatened to sue after hearing rumors that she was secretly employed by the alcohol industry. Charlotte Rowe hired an attorney to file a defamation suit after two suffragists snubbed her as she claimed her mail in the lobby. "Let us move away from that notorious woman," they said.[27] Suffragists accused the Antis of stealing telegrams, spying through windows and transoms, listening in on telephones, and writing "vulgar, ignorant, insane" letters. "In the short time I spent in Tennessee's capital," Catt wrote, "I have been called more names, been more maligned, more lied about than in the thirty previous years in work for suffrage."[28]

On the eve of the special session, the Antis held a reception for legislators at the Hermitage, handing out red lapel roses as a symbol of opposition. Senator Lon McFarland, still uncommitted on suffrage, strolled about in a white linen suit and Panama hat, bolo tie, and a lapel rose, part red and part yellow. Suffragists paraded through the lobby with legislators they had recruited. "Painful," one Anti said as she watched from the Mezzanine. "Disgusting."[29] Still, suffragists felt confident of victory. The Senate was certain to approve, and they counted a twelve-vote majority in the House, whose powerful speaker, Seth Walker, promised to lead the fight.

At noon on Monday August 9, lobbyists from both sides buttonholed legislators as they entered the assembly, handing out roses and urging on supporters like an "old-fashioned Methodist revival," the *Journal and Tribune* wrote.[30] Governor Roberts predicted a session as "strenuous as American football and as gripping as the Derby Day horse race." "Let's make Tennessee a perfect thirty-six!" Senator Erastus Eugene Patton said to cheering suffragists in the galleries as the battle commenced. Senator H. M. Candler from East Tennessee denounced Catt, the "old woman down here at The Hermitage Hotel," who was "trying to dictate to Tennessee's lawmakers."[31] He said he had heard her tell a New York audience "that she would be glad to see the day, when negro men could marry white women without being socially ostracized."[32] When Candler claimed that he spoke for "the mothers who are at home rocking the cradle and not representing the low neck and high skirt suffragists who know not what it is to go down in the shade of the valley and bring forth children," a suffragist shouted from the gallery, "I've got six children!"[33] The Senate approved the amendment after three hours of debate by a vote of 25 to 4. Lon McFarland, the uncommitted senator who had sported the two-toned rose in his lapel, abstained. When a senator who complained "the ladies don't wear petticoats anymore" left the chamber, several suffragists lifted their skirts just enough to reveal petticoats.[34]

In the midst of the Senate debate, Febb Burn, a forty-six-year-old widow from Niota, a small town in southeastern Tennessee, sat down on her front porch to write a letter to her eldest son Harry, a twenty-four-year-old Republican representative in his first term in the General Assembly. Febb was a college graduate and former schoolteacher who read four newspapers daily and a slew of magazines in-between churning butter, milking cows, and doing other chores on her 400-acre farm. Editorials and cartoons lampooned both sides. One cartoon depicted an older woman, supposedly Catt, sweeping the letters RAT with a broom to catch up to the letters IFICATION. Senator Candler's remarks on women angered Febb Burn. Some of the men who worked her farm were illiterate but could vote. Febb did not call herself a suffragist, but she believed that women ought to vote and clean up government. She rarely talked politics with her legislator son and filled seven pages of her letter with chatty news about the weather, family, and neighbors. But this time she offered some advice at the end.

> *Hurrah and vote for Suffrage and don't keep them in doubt . . . I've been watching to see how you stood, but have not seen anything yet. . . . Don't forget to be a good boy, and help Mrs. Thomas "Catt" with her "Rats." Is she the one that put rat in ratification . . . Ha. No more from mama this time.*
> *With lots of love,*
> *Mama* [35]

Febb's brother posted the letter at the Niota post office. It arrived at Harry Burn's office just before the House began to debate a motion to concur in the Senate's approval of the amendment.

On the eve of the House debate, suffragists were shocked to learn that House Speaker Walker had switched sides for reasons he never explained. He delayed the debate for several days as he chipped away at the dwindling majority. On Monday August 16, after five delegates from Davidson County turned against ratification, Walker believed he had enough votes to defeat it and opened debate. "We've got 'em whipped to a frazzle," he said.[36]

Representative Hanover declared women's disenfranchisement a "relic of barbarism" and said that "women from East, West, North and South are looking for us to give them freedom."[37] Representative Gary Odom from central Tennessee argued that the vote would "pollute women." His nine daughters, eight daughters-in-law, and wife all believed that men should represent women in politics. "What's good enough for them will have to be good enough for the rest of the women," he said.[38] A message arrived from a majority of North Carolina legislators, urging their Tennessee counterparts to join them in rejecting the amendment. Antis laughed and cheered as the news spread through the gallery. Some suffragists wept. After several hours, when Walker cut off the debate and adjourned to vote the next day, suffragists counted their votes—48–48, not enough to pass the amendment. That night, the Antis celebrated their imminent victory, belting out "Keep the Home Fires Burning" in their suite on the eighth floor.[39]

The next morning, members found the Capitol exterior draped in yellow bunting, and the National Woman's Party purple, white, and gold suspended along the crowded gallery. Someone had placed a Golden

Glow coneflower on each legislator's desk, tied a yellow sunflower to the bronzed eagle at the head of the chamber, and set a small replica of the liberty bell on the rostrum, ready for the moment of victory. Suffragists in white dresses with "Votes for Women" sashes and yellow flowers in their broad-brimmed hats mixed with Antis sporting bright-red corsages in their lapels. Lobbyists followed undecided representatives onto the floor until the sergeant-at-arms shooed them away. Representative J. Frank Griffin had rushed back from California to vote for suffrage. R. L. Dowlen left his hospital bed and was helped to his desk as suffragists cheered from the gallery. Harry Burn took his seat three rows from the front, near the center aisle, his mother's letter tucked into a pocket. Suffragists and Antis sat in the galleries with a roll call list and a pencil in hand, ready to tick off the votes as Chief Clerk John Green called out names. Catt waited for the result in her suite at the Hermitage.

At 10:30, Seth Walker whacked his gavel and the debate commenced. Hours later, he announced that the "hour has struck," his voice echoing off the walls of gray Tennessee limestone.[40] The Antis cheered. "The battle has been fought and won," Walker said, calculating there were 47 votes in favor and 49 opposed.[41] Employing a procedural tactic that, if successful, would kill the amendment, Walker moved to table the motion to concur with Senate approval.

Clerk Green began to call the roll. All went as expected until he reached the eighty-ninth name, Banks Turner, a Democrat from northwest Tennessee. Walker had counted Turner as an Anti, but that morning Turner received a personal call from James Cox, the Democratic presidential candidate, who urged him to support suffrage so Democrats could claim credit. "Nay," Turner said, stunning the chamber with his surprise vote.[42] Turner's change of heart meant a tie—and a defeat for the motion to table. As Walker rushed forward to check the tally at the clerk's desk, meeting suffrage leader R. K. Riddick in the aisle, the two nearly started to fight. "I have as much right to be in the aisles as Walker does!" Riddick shouted, following with another comment to those nearby. When Walker pivoted to confront him, other members stepped in to separate them.[43] Clerk Green asked for a second roll call to clear the confusion. As he began the roll call again, Walker sat next to Turner, put his arm around his shoulder, and tried to convince him to table the motion. The Chamber grew silent as Green made his way through the list.

"Banks Turner," Green called.

Silence.

"Banks Turner," a second time.[44]

Nothing.

Green moved on to finish the roll call. It was 48–47 in favor of tabling. As Green was about to announce the final count, Turner pushed off Walker's arm and stood up. "I wish to be recorded as against the motion to table," Turner said.[45] His vote tied the motion and defeated it. The ratification debate was still alive in the House, but just barely. Walker quickly changed tactics. He motioned that the House concur with the Senate ratification, calculating that his forty-eight anti-suffrage votes were enough to defeat the motion.

Clerk Green began the call as the Chamber filled with a palpable tension. Ratification seemed about to fail in yet another state. Green called the seventh name on the list, Harry Burn, who had just voted to table the motion in the previous vote. "Aye," Burn said.[46] There was stunned silence, then the suffragists roared with excitement. It was the vote they needed for success—if Banks Turner also held. Green suspended the roll call until a semblance of order returned. Anti-legislators gathered around Burn, pressuring him to switch before it was too late.

"Banks Turner," Green called.

"Aye!" Turner shouted.[47] A few moments more and the roll call was finished. The vote was 49 to 47. Walker's tactic backfired—the motion to approve the amendment passed. Suffragists shouted for joy as they threw cascades of yellow flowers onto the House floor, a din so loud that Catt heard it in her Hermitage suite. Anti-suffragist Josephine Pearson shouted to Burn that he was "a traitor to manhood's honor."[48] The sergeant at arms searched for Burn in the tumult to have a state trooper escort him out, but Burn sidled into the clerk's office, climbed out the window, and scooted along a narrow ledge two stories above ground, reentering to the rear of the Chamber and quietly left. He later called his mother to tell her that he had cast the deciding vote. "I am glad that he loved me enough to say afterward that my letter had so much influence on him," Febb told the newspapers.[49]

News of the success spread quickly. Franklin Delano Roosevelt, the Democratic candidate for vice president, sent a telegram. "The action of Tennessee assures the greatest step that could possibly be taken for human rights and better American citizenship through the great moral influence of the women of America," he wrote. "True progress will be guaranteed."[50] NAWSA received a cablegram from London: "Heartiest Congratulations from British Suffragists."[51] Many opponents were in disbelief. State suffragist Kate Gordon was bitter that her lobbying against a federal amendment failed. "I am in the position of a woman who has worked for suffrage all her life, and now that it has come about I do not want it."[52]

For Walker, the fight was not over. Before Clerk Green announced the final tally, Walker quickly switched his vote to "yea,"—making the vote 50–46—and motioned to reconsider, which by House rules gave him an exclusive right for three days to call up the motion again—enough time, he hoped, to find a legislator willing to change his vote.[53] The next day, in front of three thousand Antis at the Ryman Auditorium in downtown Nashville, Walker entered the stage to the tune of "Dixie," looking like Andrew Jackson, one newspaper wrote. "Forty-seven names have been signed in the blood of the South to keep this a white man's country and a white man's government," he told the crowd.[54] He promised the amendment would be defeated on reconsideration.

Louisiana First Lady Anne Pleasant traveled to Niota to ask Febb Burn to repudiate the letter to her son. But Febb found the First Lady insulting and "had a hard time to get her out of my home," she told reporters.[55] Febb telegraphed suffrage headquarters in Nashville to make sure there was no misunderstanding. "The letter was authentic," she wrote. "I stand squarely behind suffrage and request my son to stick until the end."[56] Rumors spread that Harry Burn had accepted a bribe to vote for suffrage— some said as much as $10,000. Burn resented the allegations and inserted his explanation into the House Journal the next day. Suffrage was morally and legally right, he wrote, and when Walker's change of tactics meant that his one vote could make the difference, he seized the opportunity. "I know that a mother's advice is always safest for her boy to follow, and that my mother wanted me to vote for ratification."[57]

Walker worked to find a convert while suffragists lobbied to hold the loyalty of their slim majority. Some representatives complained of being "called up every half hour day and night."[58] Senator Fuller, a suffrage supporter from Memphis, felt "badgered" by out-of-state suffragists who lobbied too aggressively. "Attempting to guide the thought of a Southern man in politics is a psychological blunder," he said.[59] Unable to find a convert, Walker declined to hold a vote before his three-day option to reconsider ratification expired on Friday night. The next morning, Riddick prepared to call up the motion to reconsider, confident that his suffrage majority still held. But Walker announced that he had filed an injunction to prevent Governor Roberts from certifying ratification, and that thirty-seven Antis had left the state to prevent a quorum. This "Red Brigade," the newspapers dubbed them, had left in the middle of the night and were biding their time in a hotel in Decatur, Alabama, a last-ditch effort, they claimed, to defend the Tennessee Constitution and preserve states' rights. Some Tennessee newspapers supported them, but others called the Red Brigade "outrageously unlawful" and lamented the damage to the state's reputation.[60] The Virginia *Roanoke Times* called the House the "laughing stock of the country."[61] The *New York Tribune* called them the "bitter-enders."[62] Riddick proceeded without a quorum, and the House voted 49–0 not to reconsider ratification.

For two days, Governor Roberts hesitated to sign the certificate of ratification. But after Tennessee chief justice D. L. Lansden superseded Walker's injunction and Attorney General Frank M. Thompson advised him that the ratification had been lawful, Roberts decided to proceed. At midday on Tuesday August 24, in a private room with no reporters present, he signed the certification of ratification and sent it by registered mail to Secretary of State Bainbridge Colby in Washington, announcing his action one hour *after* the train bearing his letter had left the station. Secretary Colby had followed the turmoil in Tennessee and left word at the State Department to wake him up when the certificate arrived. The solicitor delivered it to Colby's home shortly after 4 A.M., but Colby waited for a "more dignified" hour to proceed.[63] At 8 A.M., still at home, Colby signed it with an ordinary steel pen and issued a proclamation that the Nineteenth Amendment was officially part of the Constitution.

Catt arrived in Washington a few hours later and telephoned Colby. He had signed the certificate, he told her, and invited her to see it. When Catt, Maud Wood Park, and Harriet Taylor Upton met Colby in his office, he gave Catt the pen used to sign it. Alice Paul and a delegation from the National Woman's Party arrived later that day, but Colby kept them waiting while he met with the Spanish ambassador, and they left. Colby refused requests for an official ceremony or a reenactment of signing the proclamation, unwilling, he said, to mediate between quarreling suffrage factions. That night, suffragists rejoiced at Poli's Theater, the largest auditorium in Washington, D.C., just a block from the White House. Suffragists who had battled in Tennessee regaled the crowd with stories, and Colby offered President Wilson's congratulations. The next morning, Catt took the train to New York, where more than four hundred people greeted her as she stepped off the train. Supporters gave her a bouquet of blue delphiniums and yellow chrysanthemums with a ribbon inscribed, "To Mrs. Carrie Chapman Catt from the Enfranchised Women of the United States" as a band played "Hail lady Conquering Hero."[64] New York governor Alfred E. Smith offered the state's official congratulations. For the first time in months, a friend observed, Catt seemed relaxed and happy. Later that day, New York suffragists began their final parade with mounted police, flag bearers, and a band as they escorted Catt and NAWSA leaders up 7th Avenue to celebrations at the Waldorf Astoria Hotel in midtown. "This is a glorious and wonderful day," Catt said that night. "Now that we have the vote let us remember we are no longer petitioners. We are not wards of the nation but free and equal citizens. Let us do our part to keep it a true and triumphant democracy."[65]

Back in Tennessee, Walker had not given up the fight. When the "Red Brigade" returned after ten days, he ordered the sergeant at arms to round up missing representatives, including Harry Burn. The Antis then passed resolutions to reject ratification, to purge the official record of the successful August 21 suffrage vote—which they considered as invalid without a quorum—and to have Governor Roberts notify Washington of these changes. Some suffrage supporters voted against the resolutions, but twenty refused to vote at all. Governor Roberts dutifully sent notice of the Antis resolutions, but Colby ignored them. The federal government had long held that an amendment once ratified became law of the land. Still, Walker persevered. In mid-September he led a group of Antis to Connecticut on a futile mission to convince its legislators to oppose ratification. Connecticut legislators ratified in mid-September anyway.

Suffragists had won. It had been seventy-two years since women first called for the right to vote at the Seneca Falls Convention in 1848. Suffragists had tried nearly 480 times to have state legislatures put suffrage before voters, led 277 campaigns to get state party conventions to include woman suffrage planks, and attempted 47 times to have state constitutional conventions add woman suffrage. At the federal level, suffragists made thirty attempts to have woman suffrage planks adopted at presidential campaigns and pressed for suffrage in each of the past nineteen Congresses.

On September 12, 1920, seven weeks before she would vote for the first time in a national election, Rev. Olympia Brown rose to address her former congregation in Racine, Wisconsin. She was eighty-five-years-old and had fought for women's rights for seven decades. Before the Civil War, she had overcome resistance to women's education at Antioch College in Ohio and the Theological School of St. Lawrence in New York. She had become the first ordained woman minister recognized by a denomination and won acceptance by her congregations in Vermont, Massachusetts, Connecticut, and Wisconsin. After the Civil War, she had organized the Equal Rights Association to work for the rights of black men and women and traversed Kansas with Lucy Stone and Henry Blackwell in the hot summer of 1867, giving more than three hundred speeches as she tried to convince men to support a suffrage referendum. She had formed the New England Suffrage Association alongside Lucy Stone and Julia Ward Howe in 1869, testified before Congress in 1876, and a decade later fought a battle through the courts for the right to vote in city elections in

Wisconsin. At the Congress of Representative Women during the Chicago Fair in 1893, she defended religion as a progressive force in society and founded the Federal Equality Association in 1902 after NAWSA adopted a state strategy. She testified before Congress in 1914, nearly four decades after her first appearance, and burned Wilson's speeches at the gates of the White House alongside Alice Paul's National Woman's Party in 1917. At NAWSA's final meeting in February 1920, she was the guest of honor.

Brown reminded the congregation that she had resigned her pastorate thirty-three years before. It was "a long time and many things have happened," she told them, "but the grandest thing has been the lifting up of the gates and the opening of the doors to the women of America, giving liberty to twenty-seven million women, thus opening to them a new and larger life and a higher ideal. The future opens before them, fraught with great possibilities of noble achievement," she said. "It is worth a lifetime to behold the victory."[66]

Notes

1. Lori Enicks-Kniss, *The Lady from Seward: Minnie Grinstead* (Emporia, KS: Emporia State University, 2014), 22.

2. James Callaway, "The White Woman's Problem," in *Woman Patriot*, June 26, 1920, 8, in Elna C. Green, *Southern Strategies: Southern Women and the Woman Suffrage Question* (Chapel Hill, NC: University of North Carolina Press, 1997), 86–87.

3. *Jackson Daily News*, January 18, 1920, in A. Elizabeth Taylor, "The Woman Suffrage Movement in Mississippi," *Journal of Mississippi History* 30 no. 1 (March 1968): 27.

4. *Clarion Ledger*, February 19, 1920, in Taylor, "The Woman Suffrage Movement in Mississippi," 31.

5. CCC to Mary Gray Peck, March 28, 1920, Catt Papers, Reel 5, in Graham, *New Democracy*, 141.

6. Catherine Cole Mambretti, "The Burden of the Ballot: The Woman's Anti-Suffrage Movement," *American Heritage* 30 (1978): 16.

7. Ibid.

8. Ibid.

9. Ibid.

10. The News and Observer, June 6, 1920, in A. Elizabeth Taylor, "The Woman Suffrage Movement in North Carolina," *The North Carolina Historical Review* 38 no. 2 (April 1961): 184.

11. Mambretti, "Burden," 19–20.

12. A. H. Roberts to J. C. Williams, August 18, 1920, Gov. Albert H. Roberts Papers, Box 20, Folder 7, TSLA, in Robert B. Jones and Mark E. Byrnes, "The

'Bitterest Fight': The Tennessee Gen. Assembly in the 19th Amendment," *The Tennessee Historical Quarterly* 68, no. 3 (2009): 270.

13. CCC to Mrs. John M. Kenny, June 29, 1920, in A. Elizabeth Taylor, *The Woman Suffrage Movement in Tennessee* (New York: Bookman Associates, 1957), 108.

14. Josephine Anderson Pearson, "My Story: Of How and Why I Became an Anti-suffrage Leader," in Wheeler, *Votes for Women*, 236.

15. Carol Lynn Yellin and Janann Sherman, *The Perfect 36: Tennessee Delivers Woman Suffrage*, ed. Ilene Jones-Cornwell (Oak Ridge, TN: Iris Press, 1998), 95.

16. Ibid., 90.

17. "Attitude in Robertson County," *Nashville Banner*, August 21, 1920, 1, in Jane Marcellus, "Southern Myths and the Nineteenth Amendment: The Participation of National Newspaper Publishers in the Final State's Ratification," *Journalism and Mass Communication Quarterly* 87, no. 2 (Summer 2010): 252.

18. Mary Stahlman Douglas, "The Publisher's Granddaughter Remembers Him," in Yellin and Sherman, *Perfect 36*, 122.

19. Debbie Crawford Milton, oral history, August 3, 1983, interview by Marilyn Bell, TSLA, in Carole Stanford Bucy, "'The Thrill of History Making': Suffrage Memories of Abby Crawford Milton," *Tennessee Historical Quarterly* 55, no. 3 (Fall 1996): 231.

20. Peter Lyon, "The Day the Women Got the Vote," *Holiday* 11 (1958): 68.

21. "America When Feminized," Josephine A. Pearson Collection, Tennessee State Library and Archives, Nashville, Tennessee (hereafter referred to as TSLA).

22. Yellin and Sherman, *Perfect 36*, 101.

23. Bucy, "Abby Crawford Milton," 233.

24. Ibid.

25. CCC to Peck, August 15, 1920, Catt Papers, LC, in Van Voris, *Catt*, 160.

26. Mambretti, "Burden," 30.

27. Ibid.

28. Catt, *Woman's Citizen*, September 4, 1920, 364.

29. Lyon, "Vote," 69.

30. *Knoxville Journal and Tribune*, August 9, 1920, in Jones and Byrnes, "Bitterest Fight," 272.

31. Yellin, *Perfect 36*, 100.

32. *Nashville Tennessean*, August 14, 1920, in Taylor, *Woman Suffrage Movement in Tennessee*, 117.

33. Mambretti, "Burden," 30.

34. Yellin and Sherman, *Perfect 36*, 100.

35. Febb Burn to Harry Burn, August 17, 1920, 6, Calvin M. McClung Historical Collection, East Tennessee History Center, Knoxville, Tennessee.

36. *Knoxville Journal and Tribune*, August 17, 1920, in Jones and Byrnes, "Bitterest Fight," 275.

37. *Nashville Banner*, August 16, 1920, in Jones and Byrnes, "Bitterest Fight," 276.

38. Lyon, "The Day," 122.

39. Ibid.

40. Ibid.

41. Ibid., 124.

42. Ibid., 125.

43. Elaine Weiss, *The Woman's Hour: The Great Fight to Win the Vote* (New York: Viking, 2018). For a list of contemporary newspaper coverage of the suffrage debate in the Tennessee legislature, see note 300, p. 376.

44. Lyon, "The Day," 126.

45. Ibid.

46. Yellin and Sherman, *Perfect 36*, 106.

47. Ibid.

48. Judith Newman, "Mother Knew Best," *American History* 45, no. 4 (October 2010): n.p.

49. "Mrs. Burn Tells Story of Son Who Gave Suffrage," *The Nashville Tennessean*, August 23, 1920.

50. F. D. Roosevelt to A.H. Roberts, August 19, 1920, Roberts Papers, in Taylor, *Woman Suffrage Movement in Tennessee*, 124.

51. "British Send Greetings," *NYT (1857–1922)*, August 21, 1920, 3, 97925810, ProQuest Historical Newspapers: *NYT*.

52. Times-Picayune, August 19, 1920, cited in Elna C. Green, "The Rest of the Story: Kate Gordon and the Opposition to the Nineteenth Amendment in the South," *Louisiana History: The Journal of the Louisiana Historical Association* 33, no. 2 (April 1, 1992): 187–88.

53. Yellin and Sherman, *Perfect 36*, 106.

54. "People Protest Suffrage Action," *Nashville Banner*, August 20, 1920, 1–2, in Marcellus, "Southern Myths," 251.

55. "Mrs. Burn Stands by Son and Suffrage," *The Nashville Tennessean*, August 22, 1920, n.p., Harry T. Burn Scrapbook, University of Tennessee Libraries, Special Collections.

56. William Cahn, "The Man Whose Vote Gave Women the Vote," *Look Magazine*, August 25, 1970, 63.

57. "House and Senate Journals of the Extraordinary Session of the Sixty-First General Assembly of the State of Tennessee," 1920, 95, Government Records, TSLA.

58. Shuler, "On the Tennessee Firing Line," 332, in Anastatia Sims, "Powers That Pray and Powers That Prey": Tennessee and the Fight for Woman Suffrage," *Tennessee Historical Quarterly* 50, no. 4 (December 1991): 219.

59. Louise Graham. "Women Are Watchful; Fear Ratification," *NYT (1857–1922)*, August 19, 1920, 2, 98036972, ProQuest Historical Newspapers: *NYT*.

60. *Memphis Commercial Appeal*, August 23, 1920, *Bristol Herald Courier*, August 23, 1920, in Jones and Byrnes, "Bitterest Fight," 283.

61. *Chattanooga News*, September 4, 1920, in Jones and Byrnes, "Bitterest Fight," 287.

62. Ibid.

63. "Colby Proclaims Woman Suffrage," *NYT (1857–1922)*, August 27, 1920, 1, 97948156, ProQuest Historical Newspapers: *NYT*.

64. "Will Welcome Mrs. Catt," *NYT (1857–1922)*, August 25, 1920, 98172121, ProQuest Historical Newspapers: *NYT*.

65. CCC, *Woman's Citizen*, September 4, 1920, 364, in Van Voris, *Catt*, 161–62.

66. Olympia Brown, "The Opening Doors: A Sermon Preached in the Universalist Church," Racine, Wisconsin, September 12, 1920, in Coté, *Brown*, 193.

CHAPTER TWENTY-SIX

Epilogue

More than twenty-six million Americans voted on November 2, 1920, a 44 percent increase since the last presidential election.[1] Charlotte Woodward Pierce, the only known living signer of the 1848 Declaration of Sentiments, was ninety-one years old and too ill to vote. Antoinette Brown Blackwell was eager to cast her ballot. She protested women's subordination with Lucy Stone at Oberlin College in the 1840s, promoted the compatibility of Christianity with women's rights at the Worcester Convention in 1850, became the first ordained woman preacher in a mainstream Protestant church, and bore seven children. When ninety-five-year-old Blackwell entered her local polling station, voters stepped aside to let her go next. Blackwell's eyesight was so poor that a clerk accompanied her into the booth, and when Blackwell's voice rang out from behind the curtain—"I wish to vote the Republican ticket, all things considered, at the present time. It seems to me the wisest plan"—the voters applauded.[2] Forty-eight-year-old Madeline McDowell Breckinridge, who had led the fight for ratification in Kentucky and then attended the International Woman Suffrage Alliance in Geneva, Switzerland, voted for the Democratic ticket with its support for the League of Nations—and died unexpectedly from a stroke three weeks later.

Harry Burn faced a backlash after casting the deciding vote for suffrage in the Tennessee legislature. Abby Crawford Milton, leader of the Tennessee Equal Suffrage League, felt obligated to support him and went to his district to campaign. "Now is no time to think about Republicans and Democrats," she told a crowd at a courthouse in eastern Tennessee. "This boy is just being punished and it's not fair for the women to benefit by his votes to stand by and do nothing."[3] Burn won reelection. His mother Febb voted for him after registering as voter number one in McMinn County on a form that still only recognized "his" right to cast a ballot.[4]

Some early suffrage opponents had changed their minds by 1920. Ben Sheeks, who led the opposition to suffrage in Wyoming in 1869, and tried to repeal it in 1871, said he was "willing to admit that I have learned some things since."[5] President Wilson, who found suffragists repulsive as a young man, declared it "one of the greatest honors of my life that this great event, so stoutly fought for, for so many years, should have occurred during the period of my administration."[6]

Maine voters passed a suffrage referendum in 1920, after the Nineteenth Amendment was already ratified, though 30,462 still voted against it. Florida, South Carolina, Georgia, Louisiana, and North Carolina ratified the amendment between 1969 and 1971, and Mississippi was the last to ratify in 1984.

Some suffragists put the struggle behind them. "I don't want to do anything more," Lucy Burns said, retreating to family life to care for her orphaned niece in Brooklyn. "I think we have done all this for women, and we have sacrificed everything we possessed for them."[7] Burns lost contact with fellow suffragists and never attended their reunions. Louisiana suffragist Jean Gordon felt embittered by her unsuccessful fight against the Nineteenth Amendment in Tennessee so that state suffrage could prevail. It "was months before I could allow myself to even think of the horrible experience," she wrote in 1923. She later joined her sister Kate Gordon to lobby Louisiana politicians to support sterilization laws and disenfranchise the "genetically unfit."[8] Jeannette Rankin left politics for several decades after her unsuccessful campaign for a Montana Senate seat in 1918, but voters returned her to the House in 1940 at the age of sixty. Still an ardent pacifist, Rankin was the only Representative to vote against a declaration of war after Pearl Harbor.

For many, the suffrage struggle was the first step in a long march to reenvision the role of women in all of society, not just in the political process. The problem, attorney Crystal Eastman wrote just a month after women voted in 1920, is "how to arrange the world so that women can be human beings, with a chance to exercise their infinitely varied gifts in infinitely varied ways, instead of being destined by the accident of their sex to one field of activity—housework and child-raising." Or, if they elected to raise children and care for a home, "to have that occupation recognized by the world as work, requiring a definite economic reward and not merely entitling the performer to be dependent on some man."[9] Alva Belmont kept working for women's rights as she moved between her palatial homes in the United States and France. She paid Alice Paul a salary to continue working for women's rights and maintained a house on

Women were finally granted the right to vote on August 26, 1920 after the Nineteenth Amendment was ratified. Technically, the 19th Amendment did not become law (and women could not vote) until Sec. of State Bainbridge signed the a certificate on the 26th. The women's rights movement fought a seventy-year battle with the government to allow women to vote. (Library of Congress)

Capitol Hill for the National Woman's Party on the condition that they never permit a man to head the organization. At her death in 1933, Belmont bequeathed a tenth of her estate to the women's cause and had a well-orchestrated funeral at St. Thomas Church in Manhattan with over a thousand mourners. Alice Paul and English suffragist Christabel Pankhurst were among the pallbearers, and the processional all wore the suffrage colors of purple, white, and gold. Atop her velvet-covered coffin were flowers and a banner with Susan B. Anthony's final words, "Failure Is Impossible." Mourners sang a hymn Belmont had specially written for the occasion with the words,

> "No waiting at the Gates of Paradise,
> No tribunal of petty men to judge."[10]

For a while, Paul was too exhausted by the suffrage struggle to think of another entanglement. She enrolled in law school and, together with Crystal Eastman, drafted the Equal Rights Amendment, first introduced in Congress in 1923. In 1938, she moved to Switzerland to lobby for women at the League of Nations and took in Jewish refugees during World War II. In the 1960s, Paul pressed to have women included in the 1964 Civil Rights Act and watched as a new generation of activists resurrected her Equal Rights Amendment. In January 1977, when she was ninety-two years old and living with her sister in a nursing home, New Jersey and Pennsylvania celebrated "Alice Paul Day," and First Lady Betty Ford called Paul for a brief chat. Paul died six months later.

In parts of the South, literacy tests, poll taxes, and other means suppressed the vote of black women. In Florida, when as many black women as white women registered to vote in October 1920, there was an all-out effort by Democratic women to register white women. Georgia and Mississippi prevented all women from voting in 1920 by not extending the registration period after the Nineteenth Amendment was ratified. Black women continued to struggle against subordination by race and sex. When Anna Julia Cooper, who had been born into slavery, received her PhD in history in 1925 at age sixty-five, she wrote that her "one aim is and always has been to hold a torch for the children of the group too long exploited and too frequently disparaged in its struggling for the light."[11] Restrictions on citizenship and voting rights prevented other groups from voting as well. Native Americans could vote after receiving citizenship in 1924 (and some states delayed that another three decades). Chinese Americans could vote after 1943; Indian Americans after 1946; and Japanese Americans after 1952. The Civil Rights Act of 1965 finally guaranteed full voting rights for black Americans.

In 1923, in a book she wrote about the suffrage struggle, Catt pondered why it had taken seventy-two years to prevail.[12] American history and principles should have made it the first nation to grant suffrage, but by the time it did, twenty-six others had already done so. She attributed the delay to the link between women's suffrage and prohibition. Victory was largely won by the suffragists who did steady, organized political work behind the scenes, the kind of women she led in the many state and national campaigns. It was won "not by the brilliancy," Catt told Vassar graduates in 1938, but by those who were willing "to perform drudgery."[13] Others credited militants led by Alice Paul for the victory. North Carolina's Supreme Court chief justice Walter Clark wrote to congratulate Paul on the innovative tactics of the National Woman's Party that focused national attention on suffrage. "It is certain that, but for you," he told her, "success would have been delayed for many years to come."[14]

As the second generation of suffragists died and the nation was absorbed by Depression and war, it was left to historians to record the struggle. Late in life, Stanton realized that she and her cohorts "will probably be under the sod" before women got the vote. She felt it was "enough for us to know that our daughters to the third and fourth generation will enjoy the fruits of our labors, reap the harvest we have sown, and sing the glad songs of victory in every latitude and longitude, from pole to pole, when we have passed to other spheres of action."[15] After Stanton died, Anthony wrote to a friend that "the world will soon forget her, I suppose, as it has all who have gone before and as it will all who go after. Our names may be mentioned now and then but there will be no feeling of 'Presence.'"[16] Someone once asked Anthony what thanks she received for her efforts to win suffrage, and Anthony replied that her thanks was to retain her own self-respect. "I was never discouraged, because I knew that my cause was just, and I was always in good company."[17]

Doris Stevens, a National Woman's Party official who was arrested several times for protesting at the White House, acknowledged "the long, wearying struggle," but also "compensatory moments of great joy and beauty." Many women resented that they had worked so hard for so long "for so simple a right," she said, but there was no "residue of bitterness." They had "kept their faith in women."[18] Clara Barton died eight years before the Nineteenth Amendment passed, but predicted it would come "sooner or later," and once accomplished, "all will wonder, as we have done, what the question ever was."[19]

Controversies around suffragists lingered. Stanton's attacks on religion continued to offend, and when a publisher reissued her autobiography in 1922, her children removed the chapter on *The Woman's Bible*. Historians rightfully exposed the racism and elitism of Anthony, Stanton, and many other suffrage leaders to highlight the hypocrisy in their call for an extension of human rights. For traditionalists, women's suffrage remained suspect. A Tennessee legislator claimed in the 1930s that suffragists inspired Adolf Hitler and his book *Mein Kampf*. And when Kathrine Switzer faced hostile questions from reporters after she ran the male-only Boston Marathon in 1967, a reporter asked her if she was "a suffragette."[20]

Shortly after ratification, the National Woman's Party commissioned Adelaide Johnson to sculpt a tribute to women's rights. The result was an eight-ton statue of Elizabeth Cady Stanton, Lucretia Mott, and Susan B. Anthony, their bodies only partially carved out of a base of uncut marble, representing the unfinished business of women's rights. Its inscription in gold relief said, "Woman first denied a soul, then called mindless, now declaring herself an entity to be reckoned." At its unveiling in the U.S.

A marble statue of suffragists Susan B. Anthony, Lucretia Mott, and Elizabeth Cady Stanton at the U.S. Capitol. (Library of Congress)

Capitol Rotunda on Anthony's birthday in 1921, politicians mingled with representatives from over seventy women's groups. The next day, Congress had the inscription removed and relocated the statue to the crypt a floor below, where it sat for the next forty years in a service room with brooms, mops and buckets. In 1963, Congress opened the crypt to visitors, and in 1995, prompted by the seventy-fifth anniversary of the Nineteenth Amendment, a bi-partisan coalition pressed to have the statue relocated to the main floor. After raising private funds to move it, the statue was returned to the Rotunda in May 1997 to the cheers of onlookers. Its inscription remains blank.

The suffrage movement was more than just a struggle to win the right to vote. It was a step in a larger, longer struggle against the subordinate status of women. Gaining the right to vote did not simply mean going to the polls or engaging in politics, a Colorado woman wrote in 1908. Its most vital effect was "in teaching us our relationship with the life around us," she said. "The real significance lies in getting in touch with what newspaper people call 'the human interest' of daily life, and finding one's own place in the great scheme of the universe. And to be enfranchised means to make mistakes? Yes, dozens of them. And failures? Yes, scores, and some of the worst of them come in the guise of successes. That's what it means to be alive."[21]

Notes

1. Appendix B "Presidential Elections (1904–1932), in John M. Blum, William S. McFeely, Edmund S. Morgan, et al., eds., *The National Experience: A History of the United States*, Eighth Edition (New York; London: Harcourt Brace Jovanovich College Publishers, 1963), A20.

2. Handwritten note, one page, probably from Agnes Blackwell Jones, Blackwell, SL, in Elizabeth Cazden, *Antoinette Brown Blackwell: A Biography* (Old Westbury, NY: The Feminist Press at CUNY, 1993), 267.

3. Bucy, "Abby Crawford Milton," 234.

4. Judith Newman, "Mother Knew Best," *American History* 45, no. 4 (October 2010): n.p.

5. Sheeks, in Grace Raymond Hebard, *How Woman Suffrage Came to Wyoming*, 10, in Chapman, *Wyoming Suffrage*, 78.

6. *NYT*, August 27, 1920.

7. *Notable American Women* IV, 124–25, in Lunardini, *Equal Suffrage*, 152.

8. Kate Gordon to Laura Clay, March 22, 1923, Clay Papers, in Green, "Kate Gordon," 188.

9. Crystal Eastman, "Now We Can Begin," December 1920, reprinted in Blanche Cooke, ed., *Crystal Eastman on Women and Revolution*, 53–54, in Lunardini, *Equal Suffrage*, 151–52; *NYT*, February 13, 1933, cited in Walton, *A Woman's Crusade*, 248.

10. *Equal Rights*, February 4, 1933, in Janet W. Buell, "Alva Belmont: From Socialite to Feminist," *The Historian* 52, no. 2 (Feb 1990): 241.

11. Anna Julia Cooper, *The Third Step* (Autobiographical). Privately printed, n.p., n.d., cited in Leona C. Gabel, *From Slavery to the Sorbonne and Beyond: The Life and Writings of Anna J. Cooper* (Northampton, MA: Smith College Library, 1982), 91.

12. The United States was the twenty-seventh nation to grant women full suffrage. Others were Australia, Austria, Belgium (municipal), British East Africa, Burma (municipal), Canada, Czechoslovakia, Denmark, Estonia, Finland, Germany, Great Britain, Holland, Hungary, Iceland, Isle of Man, Latvia, Lithuania, Luxembourg, New Zealand, Norway, Poland, Romania (municipal), Rhodesia, Russia, and Sweden.

13. CCC, "'The Inheritance of the Woman Movement' Speech at Vassar College," April 14, 1933, CCC Papers, SCA.

14. Walter Clark to AP, Telegram, June 4, 1919, NWP Papers, in Lunardini, *Equal Suffrage*, 149.

15. "The Ethics of Suffrage," [Written by ECS but delivered by someone else], Sewell, *Congress of Representative Women*, 487–88.

16. SBA to daughter of Joslin Gage, June 16, 1903, in Leila R. Brammer, *Excluded*, xv.

17. "Miss Susan B. Anthony's Views," *Caucasian* of Shreveport LA, February 11, 1900, 56, *SBASB*, 30.

18. Doris Stevens, *Jailed for Freedom: American Women Win the Vote*, ed. Carol O'Hare (Troutdale, OR: New Sage Press, 1995), 343.

19. "Clara Barton for Woman Suffrage," August 20, 1898, Laura Clay Scrapbook 1897–1900, UKSC.

20. 1967 Boston Marathon: The Real Story | Kathrine Switzer—Marathon Woman at https://kathrineswitzer.com/1967-boston-marathon-the-real-story/.

21. Document 28: Ellis Meredith, "What It Means to Be an Enfranchised Woman," *Atlantic Monthly* 102 (August 1908): 196–202, http://womhist.alexanderstreet.com/colosuff/doc28.htm.

Acknowledgments

I am profoundly grateful to the historians and archivists who make writing suffrage history possible by recording and preserving many facets of this century-long struggle. In particular, I thank the archivists and librarians who facilitated my research at the Indiana University Bloomington Library Collections, Louisiana State University Special Collections, Schlesinger Library, Smith College Special Collections, Swarthmore College Friends Historical Library, Tulane University Archives, the University of Kentucky Special Collections, Vassar College Archives and Special Collections Library, Wheaton College Special Collections; and the Aspen Historical Society, Free Library of Philadelphia, Library Museum of Freemasonry (London), McMinn County Living History Museum, Knox County Public Library System Calvin M. McClung Historical Collection, San Francisco Public Library Archives and Manuscript Collections; and the National Archives, Library of Congress Rare Books Room, Women's Rights National Historical Park Collections, Tennessee State Library and Archives, and East Tennessee Library and Archives. I am also grateful to several groups at the University of Scranton who made this research possible: the librarians who provided expertise in finding elusive material; administrative assistants Jennifer Kretsch and Jane Wesloski and the many work-study students in the Department of History who cooperated with good cheer; and the University of Scranton Faculty Research Committee for its generous support in the past decade.

A comprehensive project such as this is humbling, and I thank the readers and editors who helped refine the manuscript, especially William Houser, Gail Sutton, Len Gougeon, Isabel Faix, Elizabeth Polishan, and Julia Frakes. All errors are of course my own. I am grateful to Suzy Evans at the Dykstra Agency and Hilary Claggett, Tessa Somberg, and Eswari Maruthu at ABC-CLIO for their assistance in bringing this work before the public.

Selected Bibliography

The women's suffrage movement in the United States has a rich history that continues to deepen as scholars produce new works. This study focuses primarily on national leadership, but much of the suffrage struggle took place at the state and local levels. Recent studies highlight how these movements interacted with national leadership in sometimes contentious and other times cooperative relations. They also reveal how the challenges suffragists faced varied widely even within states.

Suffragists themselves left an extensive record, some compiled during the struggle for the vote and others as memoirs after the Nineteenth Amendment was ratified. They serve as foundational primary resources, though they also reflect the inherent bias that accompanies such works. They include *History of Woman Suffrage* (6 vols.) ed. Susan B. Anthony, Matilda Joslyn Gage, and Ida Husted Harper, Reprint Edition (New York: Source Book Press, 1970); Ida Husted Harper, *Life and Work of Susan B. Anthony* (3 vols.) (Salem, MA: Ayer Company Publisher, 1983). More recently, a meticulously edited compilation of communications involving Stanton and Anthony is provided in *The Selected Papers of Elizabeth Cady Stanton and Susan B. Anthony* (6 vols.) ed. Ann D. Gordon, et al. (New Brunswick, NJ; London: Rutgers University Press, 1997–2013). Several memoirs published by suffragists give their version of history, including Carry Chapman Catt, *Woman Suffrage and Politics; The Inner Story of the Suffrage Movement*, Reprint Edition (Seattle: University of Washington Press, 1969); Inez Haynes Irwin, *The Story of the Woman's Party* (New York: Harcourt, Brace and Company, 1921); Maud Wood Park, *Front Door Lobby* (Boston: Beacon Press, 1960); The National American Woman Suffrage Association, *Victory: How Women Won It, a Centennial Symposium, 1840–1940* (New York: H. W. Wilson Company, 1940); Doris Stevens, *Jailed For Freedom* (New York: Schocken Books, 1976).

Women's historians in the mid-to-late twentieth century began to provide a metanarrative. These include Eleanor Flexner's pioneering work, *Century of Struggle: The Woman's Rights Movement in the United States*, Revised Edition (Cambridge, MA: Belknap, 1959); Aileen S. Kraditor, *The Ideas of the Woman Suffrage Movement, 1890–1920* (New York: W. W. Norton, 1965); Anne F. Scott and Andrew W Scott, *One Half the People: The Fight for Woman Suffrage* (New York: J. B. Lippincott, 1975). More recent studies include Corinne M. McConnaughey, *The Woman Suffrage Movement in America: A Reassessment* (Cambridge: Cambridge University Press, 2013), and the many books and articles by Ellen Carol DuBois that provide foundational understanding of the suffrage movement. This selected bibliography contains only some of the many works consulted and cited in the writing of this book.

For Lucretia Mott, see Carol Faulkner, *Lucretia Mott's Heresy* (Philadelphia: University of Pennsylvania Press, 2011); Dorothy Sterling, *Lucretia Mott*, Third edition (New York: The Feminist Press at CUNY, 1999); Jennifer Fisher Bryant, *Lucretia Mott: A Guiding Light* (Grand Rapids, MI: Eerdmans Pub. Co., 1995); Margaret Hope Bacon, *Valiant Friend: The Life of Lucretia Mott* (New York: Walker & Co., 1980); Beverly Wilson Palmer, ed., *Selected Letters of Lucretia Coffin Mott*, Annotated Edition (Urbana: University of Illinois Press, 2002).

For Elizabeth Cady Stanton, see: Elisabeth Griffith, *In Her Own Right: The Life of Elizabeth Cady Stanton* (New York; Oxford: Oxford University Press, 1984); Lois W Banner, *Elizabeth Cady Stanton, A Radical for Woman's Rights* (Boston: Little, Brown, 1980); Lori Ginzberg, *Elizabeth Cady Stanton: An American Life* (New York; London: Hill and Wang, 2009); Geoffrey C. Ward and Kenneth Burns, *Not for Ourselves Alone: The Story of Elizabeth Cady Stanton and Susan B. Anthony*, First Edition (New York: Knopf, 1999); Ellen DuBois, *Elizabeth Cady Stanton, Feminist as Thinker*, ed. Ellen Carol DuBois and Richard Cándida Smith (New York: New York University Press, 2007); Ellen Carol DuBois and Gerda Lerner, eds., *The Elizabeth Cady Stanton-Susan B. Anthony Reader: Correspondence, Writings, Speeches*, Revised Edition (Boston: Northeastern University Press, 1992); Theodore Stanton and Harriot Stanton Blatch, *Elizabeth Cady Stanton: As Revealed in Her Letters, Diary and Reminiscences*, originally published by Harper and Brothers Publishers, New York and London: 1922, (n.p.: Forgotten Books, 2012); Elizabeth Cady Stanton, *Eighty Years and More: Reminiscences 1815–1897* (Boston: Northeastern University Press, 1993).

For Lucy Stone, see Sally G. McMillan, *Lucy Stone: And on Apologetic Life* (Oxford; New York: Oxford University Press, 2015); Joelle Million, *Woman's Voice, Woman's Place: Lucy Stone and the Birth of the Woman's Rights*

Movement (Westport, CT; London: Praeger, 2003); Andrea Moore Kerr, *Lucy Stone: Speaking Out for Equality* (New Brunswick, NJ: Rutgers University Press, 1992); Elinor Rice Hays, *Morning Star: A Biography of Lucy Stone, 1818–1893* (New York: Harcourt, Brace and World, 1961).

For Sojourner Truth and other black women's rights reformers, see Sojourner Truth, *Narrative of Sojourner Truth* (New York; Oxford: Oxford University Press, 1991); Nell Irvin Painter, *Sojourner Truth: A Life, A Symbol* (New York; London: W. W. Norton & Company, 1996); and D. Gordon, ed., *African-American Women and the Vote, 1837–1965* (Amherst: University of Massachusetts Press, 1997); Anna Julia Cooper, *A Voice from the South* (New York; Oxford: Oxford University Press, 1988); Jacqueline Bernard, *Journey toward Freedom: The Story of Sojourner Truth* (New York: W. DW. Norton & Company, 1967); Jane Rhodes, *Mary Ann Shadd Cary: The Black Press and Protest in the Nineteenth Century,* (Bloomington: Indiana University Press, 1998); Jane, Rhodes, *Mary Ann Shadd Cary: The Black Press and Protest in the Nineteenth Century* (Bloomington; Indianapolis: Indiana University Press, 1998); Paula Giddings, *When and Where I Enter: The Impact of Black Women on Race and Sex in America* (New York: William Morrow and Company, 1984).

For Susan B. Anthony, see Kathleen Barry, *Susan B. Anthony: A Biography of a Singular Feminist* (New York; London: New York University Press, 1988); Lynn Sherr, *Failure Is Impossible: Susan B. Anthony in Her Own Words* (n.p.: Random House, 1995); Rheta Childe Dorr, *Susan B. Anthony: The Woman Who Changed the Mind of a Nation* (New York: AMS Press, 1928; reprint 1970); Alma Lutz, *Susan B. Anthony: Rebel, Crusader, Humanitarian* (Boston: Beacon Press, 1959).

For antebellum women's rights, see Sally M. McMillen, *Seneca Falls and the Origins of the Women's Rights Movement* (New York: Oxford University Press, 2008); Judith Wellman, *The Road to Seneca Falls: Elizabeth Cady Stanton and the First Woman's Rights Convention* (Urbana; Chicago: University of Illinois Press, 2004); Katherine Kish Sklar, *Women's Rights Emerges within the Antislavery Movement, A Brief History with Documents* (Boston: Bedford/Saint Martins, 2000); Ellen Carol DuBois, *Feminism and Suffrage: The Emergence of an Independent Women's Movement in America, 1848–1869* (Ithaca, NY: Cornell University Press, 1978); Yuri Suhl, *Ernestine L. Rose and the Battle for Human Rights* (New York: Reynal & Co., 1959; Elaine Showalter, *The Civil Wars of Julia Ward Howe: A Biography* (New York: Simon and Schuster, 2016); Sherry H. Penney and James D. Livingston, *A Very Dangerous Woman: Martha Wright and Women's Rights* (Amherst; Boston: University of Massachusetts Press, 2004); Janet Zollinger Giele, *Two Paths to Women's Equality: Temperance, Suffrage, and the Origins of Modern*

Feminism (New York: Twayne Publishers, 1995); Ira V. Brown, *Mary Grew: Abolitionist and Feminist, 1813–1896* (Selingsgrove, PA: Susquehanna University Press, 1991).

For women during the Civil War, see Laura E. Free, *Suffrage Reconstructed: Gender, Race, and Voting Rights in the Civil War Era* (Ithaca, NY; London: Cornell University Press, 2015); Judith Ann Giesberg, *Civil War Sisterhood: The U.S. Sanitary Commission and Women's Politics in Transition* (Boston: Northeastern University Press, 2000); Nina Silber, *Daughters of the Union: Northern Women Fight the Civil War* (Cambridge, MA; London: Harvard University Press, 2005); Wendy Hamand Venet, *Neither Ballots nor Bullets: Women Abolitionists and the Civil War* (Charlottesville, VA; London: University Press of Virginia, 1991); Elizabeth D. Leonard, *Yankee Women: Gender Battles in the Civil War* (New York; London: W. W. Norton & Company, 1994); *Proceedings of the Meeting of the Loyal Women of the Republic Held in New York, May 14, 1863,* (New York: Phair & Co, 1863); Charlotte Fortin Grimke, *The Journals of Charlotte Fortin Grimke,* Brenda Stevenson, Editor (New York; Oxford: Oxford University Press, 1988); Mary Elizabeth Massey, *Women in the Civil War* (Lincoln: University of Nebraska Press, 1966); Sharon M. Harris, *Dr. Mary Walker: An American Radical, 1832 to 1919* (New Brunswick, NJ; London: Rutgers University Press, 2009).

For the international connections in the women's rights movement, see Bonnie Anderson, *Joyous Greetings: The First International Women's Movement, 1830–1860* (New York: Oxford University Press, 2000); Allison Sneider, *Suffragists in an Imperial Age: US Expansion and the Woman Question, 1870–1929* (New York: Oxford University Press, 2008); Patricia Greenwood Harrison, *Connecting Links: The British and American Woman Suffrage Movements, 1900–1914* (Westport, CT: Greenwood, 2000); Laila J. Rupp, *Worlds of Women: The Making of an International Women's Movement* (Princeton, NJ: Princeton University Press, 1997).

For studies of Victoria Woodhull, see Lois Beachy Underhill, *The Woman Who Ran for President: The Many Lives of Victoria Woodhull* (New York: Penguin Books, 1995); Barbara Goldsmith, *Other Powers: The Age of Suffrage, Spiritualism, and the Scandalous Victoria Woodhull* (New York: Alfred A. Knopf, 1998); Amanda Frisken, *Victoria Woodhull's Sexual Revolution: Political Theater in the Popular Press in Nineteenth-Century America* (Philadelphia: University of Pennsylvania Press, 2004); Helen Lefkowitz Horwitz, *Rereading Sex: Battles over Sexual Knowledge and Suppression in Nineteenth-Century America* (New York: Random House, 2003).

For suffrage in the late nineteenth century, see N. E. H. Hull, *The Woman Who Dared to Vote: The Trial of Susan B. Anthony* (Lawrence: University

Press of Kansas, 2012); Lisa Tetraut, *The Myth of Seneca Falls: Memory and the Woman's Suffrage Movement, 1848–1898* (Chapel Hill: University of North Carolina Press, 2014); Beverly Zink-Sawyer, *From Preachers to Suffragists: Woman's Rights and Religious Conviction in the Lives of Three 19th-Century American Clergywomen* (Louisville; London: Westminster John Knox Press, 2003); Faye E. Dudden, *Fighting Chance: The Struggle over Woman Suffrage and Black Suffrage in Reconstruction of America* (Oxford; New York: Oxford University Press, 2011); Karen J. Blair, *The Club Woman as Feminist: True Womanhood Redefined, 1868–1914* (New York: Holmes and Meier Publishers, 1980); Barbara A. White, *The Beecher Sisters* (New Haven, CT; London: Yale University Press, 2003); Dana Greene, ed., *Suffrage and Religious Principle: Speeches and Writings of Olympia Brown* (Metuchen, NJ; London: The Scarecrow Press, 1983); Jean H. Baker, *Sisters: The Lives of America's Suffragists* (New York: Hill and Wang, 2005); Charlotte Cote, *Olympia Brown: The Battle for Equality* (n.p.: Mother Courage Press, 1988; Elizabeth Cazden, *Antoinette Brown Blackwell: A Biography* (Old Westbury: The Feminist Press, 1983); Marlene Deahl Merril, ed. *Growing Up in Boston's Gilded Age: The Journal of Alice Stone Blackwell, 1872–1874* (New Haven, CT; London: Yale University Press, 1990); Martha M. Solomon, *A Voice of Their Own: The Woman Suffrage Press, 1840–1910* (Tuscaloosa, AL; London: The University of Alabama Press, 1991); Roger Streitmatter, *Voices of Revolution: The Dissident Press in America* (New York: Columbia University Press, 2001); Lana F. Rakow and Chris Kramarae, eds., *The Revolution in Words: Righting Women, 1868–1871* (New York, London: Routledge, 1990).

For works on race and suffrage, see Martha S. Jones, *All Bound Up Together: The Woman Question in African-American Public Culture, 1830–1900* (Chapel Hill: University of North Carolina Press, 2007); Rosalyn Terborg-Penn, *African-American Women in the Struggle for the Vote, 1850–1920* (Bloomington; Indianapolis: Indiana University Press, 1998); Alison M. Parker, *Articulating Rights: Nineteenth-Century American Women on Race, Reform, and the State* (DeKalb, IL: Northern Illinois University Press, 2010); Louise Michele Newman, *White Women's Rights: The Racial Origins of Feminism in the United States* (Oxford; New York: Oxford University Press, 1999); Angela Y. Davis, *Women, Race & Class* (New York: Vintage Books, 1981).

On suffrage opponents, see Susan E. Marshall, *Splintered Sisterhood: Gender and Class in the Campaign against Woman Suffrage* (Madison: University of Wisconsin Press, 1997); Jane Jerome Camhi, *Women against Women: American Anti-Suffragist Them, 1880–1920* (Brooklyn, NY: Carlson Publishing, 1994).

For insights into how suffrage varied by region and within regions, see Elna C. Greene, *Southern Strategies: Southern Women and the Woman Suffrage Question* (Chapel Hill: University of North Carolina Press, 1997); Marjorie Spruill Wheeler, *New Women of the New South: The Leaders of the Woman Suffrage Movement in the Southern States* (New York: Oxford University Press, 1993); Sara Egge, *Woman Suffrage and Citizenship in the Midwest, 1870–1920* (Iowa City: University of Iowa Press, 2018); Rebecca J. Mead, *How the Vote Was Won: Woman Suffrage in the Western United States, 1868–1914* (New York: New York University Press, 2004); Beverly Beeton, *Women Vote in the West: The Woman Suffrage Movement, 1869–1896* (New York: Garland Press, 1986). The many commendable histories of suffrage at the state and local levels are too numerous to list here.

For the final wave of suffragists, see Ellen Carol DuBois, *Harriet Stanton Blatch and the Winning of Woman Suffrage* (New Haven, CT: Yale University Press, 1997); Tricia Franzen, *Anna Howard Shaw: The Work of Woman Suffrage* (Urbana: University of Illinois press, 2014); J. D. Zahniser and Amelia Fry, *Alice Paul: Claiming Power* (New York: Oxford University Press, 2014); Bernadette Cahill, *Alice Paul, the National Woman's Party and the Vote: The First Civil Rights Struggle of the 20th Century* (Jefferson, GA: McFarland and Company, 2015); Christine A. Lunardini, *From Equal Suffrage to Equal Rights: Alice Paul and to the National Woman's Party, 1910–1928* (San Jose, CA; New York: Excel, 1986, 2000); Mary Walton, *A Woman's Crusade: Alice Paul and the Battle for the Ballot* (New York: Palgrave MacMillan, 2010); Katherine H. Adams and Michael L. Keene, *Alice Paul and the American Suffrage Campaign* (Urbana: University of Illinois Press, 2008); Jacqueline Van Voris, *Carrie Chapman Catt: A Public Life* (New York: Feminist Press of the City University of New York, 1987); Robert Booth Fowler, *Carrie Catt: Feminist Politician* (Boston: Northeastern University Press, 1986); Louise W. Knight, *Citizen: Jane Addams and the Struggle for Democracy* (Chicago: University of Chicago Press, 2006); Linda G. Ford, *Iron Jawed Angels: The Suffrage Militancy of the National Woman's Party, 1912–1920* (Lanham, MD; London: University Press of America, 1991); Linda J. Lumsden, *Inez: The Life and Times of Inez Milholland* (Bloomington; Indianapolis: Indiana University Press, 2004); James J. Lopach and Jean A. Luckowski, *Jeannette Rankin: A Political Woman* (Boulder: University Press of Colorado, 2005); Nancy F. Cott, *The Grounding of Modern Feminism* (New Haven, CT; London: Yale University Press, 1987).

Index

Page numbers in *italics* indicate photos.

About the Author

Susan L. Poulson is a professor of U.S. history at the University of Scranton, Scranton, Pennsylvania, where she teaches courses in women's history and twentieth-century U.S. history. She is coeditor of *Challenged by Coeducation: Women's Colleges since the 1960s* and *Going Coed: Women's Experiences in Formerly Men's Colleges, 1950–2000* as well as author of several chapters and scholarly articles.